CHILD CARE
AIDE SKILLS

CAREERS IN HOME ECONOMICS

Preparing for a Home Economics Career
Jacoby

Child Care Aide Skills
Conger · Rose

Children: Their Growth and Development
Terry · Sorrentino · Flatter

Child Nutrition and Health
Hutchins

Food Safety and Sanitation
Border

ABOUT THE AUTHORS

Flora Stabler Conger is child development instructor and head of the Child Development Education Center at Okaloosa-Walton Junior College in Florida, where she currently serves as chairperson of the home economics department. After receiving a degree in home economics education from Drexel University, she joined the New York State Extension Service. This experience stimulated her interest in the origins of social-emotional behaviors and gave direction to her graduate work at the University of North Carolina, Greensboro, where she earned a master of science degree in home economics with a major in child development. Then she applied her learnings about young children as executive director at Sheltering Arms Association of Day Care Centers in Atlanta, Georgia. Six years later she joined the Atlanta Public Schools as child development coordinator in the Vocational Education Division. Flora Stabler Conger wrote the first draft of the day care standards and developed the first short term course known as "Basic One" for day care workers in Georgia.

Irene B. Rose is the instructional supervisor of the Child Development and Food Service Programs at Atlanta Area Technical School in Georgia. She received her bachelor of science degree in home economics education at the University of Wisconsin and masters degree in education at the University of Georgia at Athens. Irene Rose has participated in the development of occupational home economics programs in child development, homemaker services, and clothing alteration in Ohio. As a member of the National Advisory Committee to the American Home Economics Association, she has worked on the development of competency-based training modules for home economics related occupations. In addition, she has served as consultant on the design of the child care laboratory building at Atlanta Area Tech. Ms. Rose is currently a member of the board of directors of the Council for Children and of the Sheltering Arms Day Care Association in Atlanta.

CHILD CARE AIDE SKILLS

FLORA STABLER CONGER
Okaloosa-Walton Junior College
Niceville, Florida

IRENE B. ROSE
Atlanta Area Technical School
Atlanta, Georgia

ELIZABETH SIMPSON
CONSULTING EDITOR
University of Wisconsin
Madison, Wisconsin

Gregg Division
McGraw-Hill Book Company

New York St. Louis Dallas San Francisco Auckland Bogotá
Düsseldorf Johannesburg London Madrid Mexico Montreal New Delhi
Panama Paris São Paulo Singapore Sydney Tokyo Toronto

Library of Congress Cataloging in Publication Data

Conger, Flora Stabler.
   Child care aide skills.

   Includes index.
   1. Day care centers.   2. Child development.
3. Children—Care and hygiene.   I. Rose,
Irene B., joint author.   II. Simpson, Elizabeth
Jane, (date)   III. Title.
HV851.C67   362.7'1   78-13217
ISBN 0-07-012420-5

Child Care Aide Skills

   3 4 5 6 7 8 9 0 VHVH   8 3 2 1 0

The editors for this book were Gail Smith and Claire Hardiman, the designer was Eileen Thaxton, the art supervisor was George T. Resch, photo editor Gina Jackson, and the production supervisor was Regina R. Malone. It was set in Times Roman by Waldman Graphics, Inc. Cover photograph: Mimi Cotter; photograph on page 1, Bart Fleet; page 45, Mimi Cotter; page 79, Jesse Alexander/Nancy Palmer Photo Agency; page 283, Jane Hamilton-Merritt; page 301, Jane Hamilton-Merritt.
Printed and bound by Von Hoffman Press, Inc.

CONTENTS

PREFACE

Child Care Aide Skills is a textbook that focuses on the skills essential to people involved in the fascinating world of child caregiving. It is a "how to" book emphasizing ways child care aides can perform their tasks with competence. *Child Care Aide Skills* is written specifically for home economics students—high school or adult classes—who are seeking employment or are already employed in child care. Of course, any one who interacts with children should find the recommended guidelines and techniques useful, including parents, teachers, and volunteers in community groups such as Scouts, 4H clubs, or Sunday school.

Child caregivers are important to our society for they teach today's children, who become tomorrow's adults. The need for competent child caregivers is not new. Historically mothers have performed this function in the home, and many still do. However, in more and more families parents work outside the home and use child care services for their children. In the U.S., record-breaking numbers of children are being served in child care centers. Employment opportunities increase as more parents seek competent child caregivers.

Written to be easily read, *Child Care Aide Skills* is divided into five parts. Part One gives an overview of child care services, roles of child care aides, and program activities to benefit the whole child. Parts Two, Three, and Four focus on skills needed with different age groups: Part Two with infants and toddlers; Part Three with children three and four years of age; and Part Four with school-aged children up to eight years of age. Part Five highlights interaction skills with staff and parents and professional and personal growth of the child care aide.

Content of the book is organized around the practical everyday tasks that are performed by trained child care aides. These tasks are generally typical in any given program provided for children, whether it be a public or private kindergarten, play school, nursery school, or day care center serving children from infancy through the primary grades. The following skills are described for each major task area:

1. Understanding the value of learnings related to the task
2. Preparing and planning for activities
3. Performing the task—carrying out the planning
4. Cleaning up, putting away, and evaluating the task

When these skills have been achieved, all child caregiving personnel—whether they are called child care aides, child care assistants, child development associates, paraprofessionals, or child care workers—are considered competent.

Certain assumptions have been made regarding performance of personnel in centers providing child care services. These assumptions are:

1. Teachers carry the responsibility for planning the children's program and evaluating their growth and development.
2. Aides implement teacher planning and extend the professional effectiveness of the teacher. Aides assist in planning under direction of the teacher as their competency increases.
3. Competence of child care aides is gained by direct experience with children. Therefore it is desirable that a laboratory setting be available as well as field trips and assignments involving child care centers in the community.

Each chapter in the book is headed with four or five major behavioral objectives, which are stated simply and directly. The student should be able, after studying the chapter, to perform the objectives. A summary at the end of each chapter makes it easy for the student to review the chapter content. Each of the student activities is designed to help students review and test themselves on what they have read and learned. A unique feature for chapters focusing on specific skills is a series of situations called "WHIF'S" (what if?). These are designed to be thought-provoking, to stimulate group discussion, and to encourage application of principles in real-life situations. Each "WHIF" may have several correct answers, depending upon the situation. Students are encouraged to discuss their choices and rationale for their answers. The Projects, Decisions, and Issues section urges students to be actively involved in learning beyond the textbook. The more highly motivated students will find these activities challenging and real as they use the community and other resources to extend their learnings about young children and services available to them.

We believe that training makes a positive difference in the performance of a child care aide, particularly when the training is focused on achieving the competencies related to each task. Indeed, we believe that the level of competency at which tasks are performed makes a significant difference between minimal and optimum growth and development of children. We trust that this textbook will serve as a tool to increase the level of child caregiving for young children in our nation.

Flora Stabler Conger
Irene B. Rose

PART
ONE

PEOPLE, PLACES, AND PROGRAMS

Chapter 1 reviews what child care is and tells what child care workers and child care aides do. It describes the kind of people who are best suited for child care assignments. The importance of child care—to the children themselves as well as their families—is discussed. The types of duties that child care aides have to perform are listed. Finally, Chapter 1 explains the importance of the child care team.

Chapter 2 tells about the different kinds of child care and the settings in which child care aides work, including day care centers, Head Start programs, and kindergartens. Although child care centers are different in terms of their services, staffs, locations, and other things, the children and aides in any child care center should have fun learning together.

Chapter 3 looks at the qualities of a good child care program. It explains the importance of a well-trained staff, a good setting for learning, and carefully planned programs. For instance, you will learn that play is not a waste of time but a way in which children learn. You will see that toys help children to master many skills.

Together, these first three chapters will help you decide whether you want to be a child care aide. If you do, they will tell you how you can become a good one.

1 | THE CHILD CARE PROFESSION AND YOU

After you have studied Chapter 1, you should be able to:

1. Identify three ways in which child care training will help you
2. Define basic child care terms
3. With regard to child care occupations, give examples of:
   a. The importance of child care aides
   b. Things child care aides do
   c. Ways child care staff work together
   d. Job opportunities
4. State four personal traits a good child care aide must have
5. Point out advantages and disadvantages of being a child care aide

PERSONAL BENEFITS

Why does child care training help you become a winner? Because as you learn about young children, you learn about yourself. The children you teach will remind you of your own childhood. During your training, you will notice feelings you have not had before. You will begin to understand the feelings of others, and you may become more open-minded and patient about their behavior. You can find satisfaction in helping children to succeed in small tasks. You will enjoy special moments with them. And besides these kinds of personal growth, when you finish your program, you will know how to work with children.

BENEFITS IN OTHER CAREERS

After you have worked with children for awhile, you may decide that you do not want to make a career of child care. In that case, you will still be a winner, because you will know what you do *not* want to do. And you will have been able to make your decision in a fairly short time.

Even if you choose another career, you still can't lose. After working with children, you will find that you get along better with your *peers* (persons of the same age) and coworkers. Child care experience will make you more open-minded and more aware of how adults get along with each other. Good human relations on the job go a long way toward job success.

Suppose you decide to get married and start a family rather than get a job. The skills you must learn to get a job in child care occupations will also help you in your own family life. If you know how people—especially chil-

Figure 1-1. Child care is more than just "taking care of" children. Good child care provides children with lots of nurturing. (Michael Weisbrot)

CHILD CARE

Child care means to provide care for a child or children. To stress the idea of giving of oneself, we also speak of *child caregiving*. For example, you may put the children's needs before your own and encourage them to try new experiences. When you do this, you are giving of yourself. A person who provides this kind of care may be called a *child caregiver*.

Nurturing involves close contact and emotional warmth while caring for children. It is an important part of child caregiving. Younger children especially need nurturing, most of all during play, feeding, toileting, and rest periods. At times, nurturing may involve little more than cuddling a child, providing a lap to sit on, or offering a hand to hold. These are important to young children who are away from familiar people and things. An easy way to understand nurturing is to remember that it is more than just "taking care of" children; it is truly *caring for them*.

CHILD CARE WORKERS

A *child care worker* is a person who has a job relating to children. The term is also a title or label for such a person.

Child care workers do many things and have different occupations, assignments, and skills. For example, teachers, social workers, child caregivers, child care aides, administrators, counselors, and nurses and other medical workers are child care workers when they work with or for children. Their individual titles describe their special assignments and the organizations to which they belong. A *teacher* may be the lead teacher in a child care center; an *administrator* may be the director of a children's home; and a *social worker* may be a worker in a child welfare agency.

CHILD CARE AIDES

A *child care aide* is a child care worker who helps someone else provide child care. A good child care aide really likes children and enjoys both giving them care and helping them learn as they grow and develop. To do the job right, child care aides are trained to be responsible

dren—get along, it will help you both on the job and in your home. What better way to apply child care skills than as a parent? In fact, human relations are as important in the family as on the job, perhaps even more so.

It should be clear now that you will benefit from child care training in the following ways:

- *Personal growth:* In learning about children, you will learn about yourself.
- *Child care job skills:* You will learn how to care for children.
- *Improved human relations:* Whatever career you choose, you will be able to get along better with others.

CHILD CARE TERMS

Before you look at how child care programs help children and their families, you need to understand the following basic terms:

4

for the daily activities of children and to carry out successfully someone else's plans for the children's programs.

Some other titles for child care aides—all of whom help the person in charge—are *teacher's aides, paraprofessionals,* and *recreation leaders.* In this book, the term *child care aide* refers to the role of aiding or helping someone else. Anyone who assists in child caregiving is a child care aide, regardless of the job title used.

CHILD CARE SERVICES

The term *child care services* refers to the many kinds of services provided in various child care settings and programs. If child care is given for a fee to children who are not related to the people offering the care, then child care services are being performed.

CHILD CARE CENTERS

A *child care center* is a place where a group of children are cared for. The number of children who are needed to make up a child care center is decided by state regulations and varies from state to state.

CHILD CARE STAFF

A *child care staff* is made up of everyone who is employed to carry out a child care service. As a child care aide, you will be part of a child care staff. Sometimes this staff is called a *child care team,* because the staff members work together as a team to provide child care services.

CHILD CARE OCCUPATIONS

All the jobs that relate to children and to child care services are included in the term *child care occupations.* We will now look closely at children's needs and how child care occupations meet those needs.

CHILD CARE OCCUPATIONS

This section discusses the following key ideas about child care occupations:

- The importance of child care aides to children and their families
- The tasks that child care aides are given
- The ways that child care staff members work together
- Job opportunities in child care occupations

IMPORTANCE OF CHILD CARE AIDES

You are learning how to become a child care aide. The things you will learn and how you apply them with children are very important. What children learn from you may stay with them for the rest of their lives. The following poem by Walt Whitman expresses this thought:[1]

There Was a Child Went Forth

There was a child went forth every day,
and the first object he look'd upon and received
  with wonder
or pity or love or dread that object he became,
And that object became part of him for the day
Or a certain part of the day . . .
Or for many a year or stretching cycles of years.

Child Care Aides and Children. As a child care aide, you will be important to children because you will help meet their needs. Let's consider what these needs are.

Children Need Good Models. What you say and do as a child care aide is important to young children. You are a *significant other,* an important person in the life of a child. Children follow the examples set for them by significant others. Your example is important to children, and you should work hard to be a good model, which means to set a good example.

Children Need Stimulating Experiences. Stimulating experiences are those that help children become aware of, curious about, and responsive to learning. A child adds the experiences of each day to those of previous days. When these experiences are stimulating, children are interested and curious. They want to know about new things, actions, people, and ideas. From curious and confident children, you may have heard such comments as: "The

[1] Walt Whitman, *Leaves of Grass,* Malcolm Cowley (ed.), Viking, New York, 1967, p. 138.

Figure 1-2. As a child care aide, you are just as important to the family as you are to the child. (Michael Weisbrot)

brushes are big, fat ones today''; "Look at the new buttons on Raggedy Ann''; "What makes this clock tick?'' "Will my boat float or sink? I think I'll put it in some water and see.'' Child care aides play an important part in providing stimulating experiences for children.

Children Need to Feel Good about Themselves. When early experiences are mostly good ones, children grow into mature adults. "Watch me jump over this puddle,'' they brag; or "I can get the flannel board for you. I know where it is.'' Properly guided, children will learn when to ask for help from adults and when to do things for themselves: "Please help me with this loop. I can do the first part by myself.'' The way in which you help young children to gain a good self-concept, or a good mental picture of themselves, is important.

Children Need to Be Protected. As a child care aide, you must put safety first when working with children. You can help them to become aware of dangers, you can teach them safe practices: "My teacher says that the first thing to do when getting into a car is to fasten the seat belt.'' Your guidance and example in safety matters is important to children.

In summary, children need

· Good models
· Stimulating experiences
· To feel good about themselves
· To be protected

You need

· To set an example as a significant other

· To help good experiences happen
· To help each child gain a good self-concept
· To put safety first

Child Care Aides and Children's Families. As a child care aide, you will touch the lives of children *and* their families. In working on the child care team, you will be important to the families of the children you work with. In order to see the importance of child care aides to families, let's look at why a family might need child care services.

A family might need child care services for several reasons. Some families have many needs, and they may require different kinds of help. The usual reasons for needing child care services are listed below:

1. *To solve a family problem:* Child care services make it possible for families to solve their own problems. Often a child is placed in a child care center because the family has a problem, and good child care can free the family to work it out. For example, by putting a child in a child care center, parents can work extra hours and pay off the family bills.

2. *To care for children while parents work:* Each year more mothers decide to get jobs, and more single parents must raise their children alone. As a result, more child care services are needed each year.

3. *To get help with parenting skills:* Some families have weak *parenting skills;* that is, they need help in guiding their children's growth and development. Such families find child care services helpful. As a child care aide, you will teach by example. Parents will watch what you do and will learn from the methods you use.

The following examples show how important a child care aide can be in helping families who have problems with parenting skills:

Parents Who Overprotect. Some children are overprotected by their parents, who consider other children to be too rough. But if they do not meet other children, little ones can become afraid to speak or play with anyone outside their families. Child care aides can guide and support such children by helping them to meet and play with peers in the child care center. When children are successful at this activity in the center, the parents may realize that their children are able to relate to others without any trouble.

Parents Who Don't Discipline. Because their parents have weak parenting skills, some children may tell their parents what to do, rather than the other way around. The parents then complain: "Johnny doesn't obey." Trained child care aides can show parents how to guide young children. By watching the child care aides, parents can learn to guide their young children better.

Parents Who Expect Too Much. Parents may lose their tempers with a young child's questioning. They may expect the child to be seen but not heard. If so, they are expecting too much of their young child. By watching child care aides taking the time to listen and respond to children's questions, parents may learn to be more patient and helpful at home.

Child care aides can help parents to improve in these situations because children learn to act in ways that show how they live, whether in the home or the child care center, whether in good or bad settings. The following poem, by Dorothy Nolte, illustrates this point:[2]

[2]S. H. Leeper, R. J. Dales, D. S. Skipper, and R. L. Witherspoon, *Good Schools for Young Children,* Publishers, 1968, frontispiece.

Children Learn What They Live

If a child lives with criticism,
  He learns to condemn.
If a child lives with hostility,
  He learns to fight.
If a child lives with ridicule,
  He learns to be shy.
If a child lives with jealousy,
  He learns to feel guilty.
If a child lives with tolerance,
  He learns to be patient.
If a child lives with encouragement,
  He learns confidence.
If a child lives with praise,
  He learns to appreciate.
If a child lives with fairness,
  He learns justice.
If a child lives with security,
  He learns to have faith.
If a child lives with approval,
  He learns to like himself.
If a child lives with acceptance and friendship,
  He learns to find love in the world.

Children play a part in what happens with their families. Child care workers and parents work together to provide healthy childhood experiences. It is very important that you recognize family values and the wishes of parents in terms of their goals for their children. The child caregiver's job is to assist parents—not to compete with them or to take over the parents' right to decide on the values they want to pass along to their children.

PLACES WHERE CHILD CARE AIDES WORK

Child care aides may work in many different places or settings. The most common settings for child care occupations are child care centers and schools. Other places where child care aides can find jobs are churches, hospitals, recreation areas (such as playgrounds and parks), department stores, libraries, resorts (beaches, ski lodges, campgrounds), and transportation areas (bus and train stations and airports).

Child care aides may also work in homes that provide day care or in parent-teacher cooperatives. Aides can also work in private homes or

Figure 1-3. Child care aides work in playgrounds and parks as well as hospitals and day care centers. (Betty Terhune)

in public settings, or at children's parties where they serve food, make up games, and supervise the children's activities.

TASKS THAT CHILD CARE AIDES ARE GIVEN

The tasks of child care aides may be divided into two groups: direct child care and supportive child care.

Direct Child Care Tasks. Whenever child care aides work directly with children, they are doing *direct child care tasks*. Depending on the age of the children and the setting, these aides usually supervise such things as children's rest, health, safety, and self-help skills. Aides also carry out planned programs to teach children art, language, music, science, mathematics, and social subjects as direct child care tasks. They help children to develop physical skills, such as running, climbing, and jumping. Each of these program areas is discussed in more detail in following chapters.

Supportive Child Care Tasks. Jobs that help

produce a safe and stimulating environment for children are called *supportive child care tasks*. These are "behind the scenes" jobs that help make a child care program run smoothly. They include such things as cooking meals, mixing paints, preparing bulletin boards, and keeping records about the children.

Usually, child care aides do both direct and indirect child care tasks. Often a child care aide is in an *entry-level position*, a position for inexperienced beginners. After gaining some experience, trained child care aides are usually considered for the more advanced jobs that may open up.

WAYS THAT CHILD CARE STAFF WORKS TOGETHER

A useful child care staff works together as a team. This *child care team* is often made up of a director, a teacher, and a child care aide. Members of the team work together to plan and carry out the child care tasks and program activities. As a child care aide, you will work *with* other team members, not *for* them.

The term *staff role* is used to describe the

duties of a child care worker and the relationship of one staff member to another. Within a child care setting, the *levels of employment* identify the relationships among staff positions. In recent years, the terms *career ladder* and *career lattice* have been used to describe these relationships.

A *career ladder* places jobs in steps that look like the rungs of a ladder. In Table 1-1, which shows a child care career ladder, you'll see that there are several titles for the entry-level or *Level-I* child care worker. The entry-level person carries out someone else's plans under the guidance of a teacher or assistant. A child care aide serves at this beginning level on the career ladder.

The next staff level indicated in Table 1-1 is that of an assistant or *Level-II* child care

Table 1-1 CAREER LADDER AND CHILD CARE WORKERS

Child care worker level	Child care career level	Titles	General duties	Minimum qualifications
IV	Professional Management	Child Care Center Director Executive Director Assistant Director	Administers program	Bachelor's degree, master's preferred, plus experience and certification in child development or early childhood education.
III	Supervisory	Child Development Director Lead Teacher Professional, Certified Teacher Kindergarten Teacher Teacher, Child Development or Early Childhood Education (sometimes called lead teacher)	Plans work schedules. Supervises other personnel. May work directly with children. Teacher supervises assistant or aide. Educational director supervises teachers.	Bachelor's degree, certification and experience. Bachelor's degree plus experience in child development or early childhood education.
II	Assistant	Child Day Care Asst. Teacher, Day Care Center Child Care Leader Family Day Care Mother Teacher, Nursery School Level II Child Care Worker	Plans and carries out activities for a group of children, with supervision from child development supervisor or teacher.	Vocational-technical certificate or associate degree in child development, preferably in a cooperative program.
I	Entry	Trainee Student in Training Child Care Aide Aide Day Care Aide Child Development Aide Level I Child Care Worker	Carries out someone else's plan. Works with children under supervision, carries out direct and supportive child care tasks.	Child care aide training with on-the-job experience.

Source: Adapted from *Career Ladders and Lattices in Home Economics and Related Areas: Possibilities for Upgrading Household Employment,* American Home Economics Association, 2010 Massachusetts Ave., N.W., Washington, D.C., 20036.

worker. This professional has developed many *competencies* (abilities) and is assigned more responsibility than Level-I child care workers. Assistants have usually received more training than is available in high school. Level-II child care workers plan and carry out their own programs for young children under the guidance of a supervisor.

The supervisory or teacher level requires at least a college degree. Personnel at this level are responsible for other people's work. A teacher supervises assistants or aides.

The last level is *professional management*. Child care workers at this level must have the most experience and training and are responsible for all the center's operations.

In this discussion of staff roles, the word *supervision* has been used several times. It will be helpful to think of it as two words: "super vision." That is, supervision is the ability to see what *is* and what *is not* going on during an activity. The task of a supervisor is to help others carry out their assignments. Supervision is not a matter of catching people doing something wrong. A supervisor must be able to recognize good performance, suggest ways to improve it, and discuss any areas that give staff members trouble.

Child care aides are also supervisors because they supervise children's activities. (And if you have ever watched a group of active young children, you understand why you need "super vision.") By watching children carefully, by reminding them of the center's rules, and by helping them to learn or see that safety comes first, child care aides are supervising. As a child care aide, you need to be expert in "super vision." Simply being there is not enough. You need to pay careful attention to children the entire time you are on duty.

JOB OPPORTUNITIES IN CHILD CARE OCCUPATIONS

Even the best training can lead to frustration if, after you learn about child care, you can't get a job. Fortunately, there are more and more job openings in child care. Every year, more parents, business leaders, and government officials see the value of child care services and help to create jobs in the field. As a result, well-trained, dedicated child care aides can find work almost anywhere in the United States. But most jobs are in or near large cities, and the first job may not be exactly what you want.

After being trained and gaining on-the-job experience, child care aides can move *up* into *different* jobs. Or they may move *across* to a *special area* within the child care field. Movement upward takes place in the form of a career ladder, as described earlier. Look at Table 1-1 again. The first column on the left is a good example of a career ladder that might be found within a large child care center. Notice that child care aides start at the level called "Entry" and may be promoted to "Assistant," "Supervisory," and finally to "Professional Management." This upward movement requires (1) work experience; (2) additional training, such as a college degree; and (3) other special study, as stated under the heading "Minimum Qualifications."

In the *career lattice* concept, a child care aide who prefers to work directly with children may decide to work with a certain age group, such as infants rather than school-aged children. Thus, the child care aide would move *across* from one specialty to another while staying on the same level. Table 1-2 gives examples of a career lattice for child care occupations. The career-lattice approach also allows the child care aide to branch out into different fields and work in various settings. These might include the children's department of a clothing store or a recreation center at a resort.

Whether you want to move up or over in child care work, a good child care aide must develop *competence* in caregiving. Competence is the knowledge and skills necessary to accomplish tasks under given conditions and in a given way. In short, it is the ability to do the right thing at the right place at the right time.

THE CHILD DEVELOPMENT ASSOCIATE PROGRAM

The Child Development Associate program, often referred to as the CDA program, is a nationwide one. It recognizes competence in child

Table 1-2 CAREER LATTICE AND CHILD CARE WORKERS

Existing roles		New roles	
Child care aide working with infants in a child care center	Home visitor in infant stimulation program	Nurse's aide in pediatric ward	Governess
Child care aide working with school aged children in a child care center	Recreation leader in a community center	Teacher's aide in public school system	Recreation leader at resort Summer camp counselor
Child care aide in child care center	Salesperson in a children's clothing store	Designer of children's clothes	Entertainer at children's parties, storyteller at children's library
Cook in child care center	Caterer for children's parties	Nutrition aide in home visiting program	
Custodian in child care center	Equipment repair business	Manufacturer of children's toys	
Child care aide in child care center	Teacher's aide in kindergarten	Aide to children's librarian	
Bus driver in child care center	Bus driver for public school	Tour guide for program at children's museum or zoo	

care workers. A Child Development Associate (CDA) credential is awarded to child caregivers after they have made application to be evaluated, completed a careful assessment procedure, and demonstrated competence in the following areas:[3]

1. Setting up a safe and healthy learning environment
2. Advancing physical and intellectual competence
3. Building positive self-concept and individual strength
4. Organizing and sustaining the positive functioning of children and adults in a group in a learning environment

5. Bringing about optimal coordination of home and center child-rearing practices and expectations
6. Carrying out supplementary responsibilities related to the children's programs

PERSONAL CHARACTERISTICS OF CHILD CARE AIDES

Good child care aides have the following traits: the ability to get along with people, good health, dependability, a professional attitude, and knowledge about child care programs.

ABILITY TO GET ALONG WITH PEOPLE

As a child care aide, you must be able to work with children *and* adults. You will have to deal with adult staff members during planning meet-

[3]The CDA Program, U.S. Department of Health, Education, and Welfare, Office of Human Development, publication no. (HD)75-1065, Washington, D.C.

ings and while working with them as part of the child care team. Cooperation among the staff members helps build a successful child care program. Other adults with whom you may have contact are parents, maintenance workers, and visitors.

GOOD HEALTH

Although child caregiving can be fun and rewarding, it is also challenging and hard work. Therefore, you must stay healthy: eat properly, get enough rest, and exercise regularly. You may be on duty for 8 hours or more during a child care day. Sometimes you may need to carry equipment or lift a child. And when you are absent because of illness, the program suffers. The children tend to feel less secure with a substitute caregiver.

Good health also means good mental health. You need to remain calm in emergencies and you must use common sense to solve problems. Often you will have to put the children's needs before your own, so you must be patient and understanding. In addition, your performance as a child care aide will be judged; therefore, you must be ready to accept criticism as well as praise for your efforts.

DEPENDABILITY

A good child care aide is ready for work on time, carries out assignments as instructed, and follows the rules of the center. Although everyone gets upset at times, a child care aide must be fair and even-tempered, even when the children may not be. What you do and say in certain situations will often be copied by the children.

You also must be dependable about finishing your job after the children have left for the day. Other staff members should not have to finish your chores, such as storing equipment, tidying the art area, and locking the windows.

PROFESSIONAL ATTITUDE

A professional attitude makes the difference between an average child care aide and a good one. Since child care is your job—your profes-

sion and maybe your career—you must take your work seriously. You must also keep to yourself any information that you may have about the children or their parents. You must not discuss the children or their families with anyone except other staff members. Even the most innocent-sounding story from a child may indicate a more serious problem. For instance, if a child tells you that the lights were off all night in his or her house, it is possible that the electric bill was not paid. Tell this story to your supervisor, not to your family or friends.

KNOWLEDGE ABOUT CHILD CARE PROGRAMS

Good child care aides must know about child care programs and what their employers expect. They must also understand how children grow and develop. The following list gives examples of some things child care aides need to know about:[4]

1. Total operation of the child care center's program, including its facilities, policies, and daily routines
2. Employer expectations of a child care worker
3. Basic child development—physical, social, emotional, and intellectual
4. Children's interest in sex, including how to handle it
5. Individual differences in the developmental patterns of children
6. The importance of play for children
7. Ways to care for the needs of several children at one time
8. Basic emotional and personality needs of all people
9. Symptoms of serious behavior problems
10. Role of tension outlets for children
11. Importance of group behavior in social development
12. Extent of adult models' influence on children's attitudes and behavior

[4]Adapted from Judy LeMaster, "Job and Task Analysis: Child Care Aide," *Illinois Teacher,* vol. 15, no. 4, March–April 1974.

As important as it is for child care aides to understand children's growth and development, the *personal* qualities—such as cooperation, good health, dependability, and a professional attitude—are just as important. In fact, if you have these personal qualities along with some basic child care skills, many employers will teach further skills on the job.

ADVANTAGES AND DISADVANTAGES OF BEING A CHILD CARE AIDE

As with all careers, there are both advantages and disadvantages to being a child care aide. Of course, whether something is an "advantage" or a "disadvantage" depends on your personal views and preferences. The following items must be considered as you examine your feelings and interests in becoming a child care aide.

REASONS FOR BECOMING A CHILD CARE AIDE

Let's consider first some benefits of working with young children.

1. *The desire to help others is satisfied.* A good child care aide lives by the golden rule: "Do unto others as you would have them do unto you." Helping children succeed after they have failed (perhaps many times) is a priceless experience—both for the children and for you. It is what child caring is all about. You can understand the value of this when you consider that the results of such events last a lifetime. You may be caring for a future President of the United States or for a child who may become a member of Congress. Such leaders have come from all sorts of backgrounds, including families who needed help in giving care to their children.

   Child care aides are in contact with different family lifestyles and cultures. They learn to understand that people may be *different* without being bad or wrong.

2. *Children are fun.* You will often find that children are amusing. But remember to laugh *with* them, not *at* them. Even young children can tell the difference.

Figure 1-4. One of the greatest benefits of being a child care aide is that the desire to help others is satisfied. (Bart Fleet)

3. *Child care aides can learn as much from their experience as they wish.* The supervisor can help you to find better ways to work with a child who concerns you or to manage a routine more effectively.

4. *Child care settings are informal.* As a result, casual clothes are usually worn. This not only saves you money but allows you to move about freely as you give care to active children. Child care tasks are flexible and challenging. The weather, equipment breakdowns, or children's discoveries and feelings all result in flexibility and challenges for you.

5. *The children love and appreciate you.* There is nothing nicer to hear than: "Where were you yesterday? We missed you." You are an important part of the children's world. Knowing this, it's a pleasure to be on the job on time every day. The children help you to put your best foot forward as you provide a good example.

REASONS AGAINST BECOMING A CHILD CARE AIDE

Following are some reasons why you may *not* want to become a child care aide. Consider them as carefully as you did the reasons *for* becoming an aide.

1. *Child care jobs are not regarded highly in our society.* Even your family or friends may question your desire to be a child care aide.

2. *Child care aides are not highly paid.* Especially at first, aides do not make much money compared with workers in other jobs that require a similar amount of training.

3. *Your hours may be long or irregular.* Most child care centers open at 7 a.m. and close at 6 p.m. Schedules are worked out so that child care aides cover these long hours. Your schedule may affect your personal life in areas such as shopping, dating, or dealing with your family. You will have to try to make friends outside your work, because many staff members are busy with their own families after work hours.

4. *A child care center may be located in an old building.* The center may need repairs and may be poorly heated or air-conditioned. Moreover, the center may be crowded and noisy. Staff members are expected to perform some housekeeping tasks, such as cleaning up spilled milk or washing paintbrushes. The smaller the staff, the more you may have to help with housekeeping.

CHAPTER SUMMARY

1. *Child care,* sometimes called child caregiving, means to provide care in a nurturing way.

2. Child care aides are child care workers who help someone else provide child care.

3. Training helps child care aides become effective child caregivers. In addition, child care training will help make you a better person because, as you learn more about children and how to give them care, you will learn more about yourself and other adults.

4. Many children and families need child care services. As a result, there are many job openings in different locations. Within most of these settings, child care aides work as part of a team with other staff members, all of whom have different roles and duties.

5. As child care aides advance in the child development field, they either move *up* to other positions or *over* to special activities, depending upon their training, experience, and performance (competence). Tables 1-1 and 1-2 review the ways in which child care aides can move up or across into different child care roles.

6. Child care work has both good and bad aspects; therefore people who want to be child care aides must have certain traits which indicate that they are suited for this kind of work. This chapter will help you decide whether professional child caregiving should be part of your future.

• WHAT NEW TERMS HAVE YOU LEARNED?

Several new words and ideas were presented in this chapter. To see whether you understand them, match the letter of each term below with the numbered phrases under ''Definitions.''

Terms
a. Child care aide
b. Child care worker
c. Significant other
d. Competence
e. Supportive child care tasks
f. Staff role
g. Professional management
h. Child caregiving

Definitions
1. Knowledge and skills necessary to complete a task successfully
2. Director of child care center
3. A person who has a job relating to children
4. Assistant who is responsible for a group of children under the direction of a lead teacher
5. Nurturing children while caring for them
6. Behind-the-scenes tasks such as preparing food, mixing paint, and keeping records
7. An important person in a child's life

8. The assignment each staff member carries out

● STUDENT ACTIVITIES

1. Identify three ways in which child care training will benefit you personally.

2. List the key points about child care occupations mentioned in the chapter and give examples of each.

3. State four essential personal traits of a good child care aide.

4. List at least two advantages and two disadvantages of being a child care aide.

2 | DIFFERENT KINDS OF CHILD CARE

After you have studied Chapter 2, you should be able to:

1. List three items in the different environments of child care services that affect the children's program or the staff's assignments
2. Identify five key ideas about child care centers
3. Name three enrichment programs that may employ child care aides
4. Explain the purpose of compensatory education programs and identify three that employ child care aides

Child care services differ in both their settings and the services they offer. The *sponsorship,* or the people or organization responsible for the service, also affects the services given.

At various times, child care services may be offered in homes or in centers. Services may stress the total care of children or offer only social or educational enrichment. Child care may be organized as a social service or as a private business. In this chapter you will look at the different kinds of child care services and at the settings in which they are given.

CHILD CARE ENVIRONMENTS

Child care services are offered in many settings. The word *environment* means the setting or the surroundings in which child care takes place. The following items in the environment affect the child care program and the staff's assignments.

THE BUILDING

Child care services are located in all sorts of buildings: schools, remodeled homes, stores, churches, and even warehouses. A modern, attractive building is certainly a big help, but it does not, in itself, ensure good-quality child care.

THE EQUIPMENT

The amount and type of equipment also affects the environment. The equipment in some child care centers is very limited or in poor shape. As part of your training as a child care aide, you will learn how to use and handle problems with equipment.

Figure 2-1. Child care services are offered in many different settings: homes, schools, and churches; in the country; and in the city. (Michael Weisbrot; Betty Terhune)

TRANSPORTATION

The duties of child care aides are affected by the way in which the children are taken to and from the child care center. If buses or cars are used, someone on the child care staff must watch over the loading and unloading of the children.

THE WEATHER

The usual weather conditions of an area affect the children's program. For example, in warm, sunny climates, workers can plan more outdoor activities. In a snowy or rainy area, part of the day is spent helping children to put on and take off snowsuits, raincoats, and boots.

Child care services vary from community to community, from program to program, and even from center to center. For example, a small child care center in a remodeled home may offer special care for handicapped children, while another center in a similar setting may offer child care for children who do not have such handicaps.

CHILD CARE CENTERS

When child care services are offered to a group of children in one location, the setting is called a *child care center*. Key ideas about child care centers include kinds of child care offered, types of centers, staffing patterns, licensing, and family day care.

DAY CARE CENTERS

Day care centers are child care centers. State regulations define what a day care center is. These regulations may vary slightly from state to state. However, they usually say that the care is offered in the daytime, that the children live with their parents, and that a fee is charged for services provided regularly. For example, the state of Georgia defines a day care center this way:

> "Day care center" shall mean: any place operated by a person, society, agency, corporation, or institution or any other group wherein are received for pay seven or more children under 18 years of age for group care, without transfer of custody, for less than twenty-four hours per day.

Day care centers are open long hours. Usually they open around 7 a.m. in the morning and close around 6 p.m. in the evening. In a good day care center, you will find sensitive caregivers, supervised routines, and an enriched program.

KINDS OF CHILD CARE OFFERED IN CHILD CARE CENTERS

There are basically three kinds of child care centers: (1) *comprehensive care,* (2) *developmental care,* and (3) *custodial care.*

Comprehensive Child Care Centers. Child care centers offering *comprehensive care* provide a safe environment, enriched child care programs, and health and social service to children and their families. *Comprehensive child care centers* usually serve a large number of children and have a *governing board* made up of professional, business, and community leaders. This board sets the guidelines for the center's operation.

The many services offered by comprehensive child care centers may include:

1. Safe, nurturing child care for the time when the child is in the center each day
2. An enrichment program as a part of the daily activities
3. A professional staff
4. A *parent-involvement* program (a program in which parents participate in child care activities)
5. Social services for the families served

6. Health services or referrals to health agencies when needed
7. A sliding scale of fees, which varies according to family financial situations.
8. Research or experimental programs
9. Family day care, sometimes as part of the center's program
10. Transportation

Not all of these services are available in every comprehensive center. This type of center is considered a family service because it helps not only the children who are enrolled but also their families.

Developmental Child Care Centers. In child care centers that offer *developmental care,* the program includes activities to help children develop socially, emotionally, physically, and intellectually. In addition, they usually provide a safe and enriched environment. Many day care centers are developmental centers because they provide stimulating programs that help strengthen children's abilities.

Figure 2-2. Developmental child care programs offer activities to help children develop intellectually. (Michael Weisbrot)

Custodial Child Care Centers. Child care centers that offer *custodial care* meet only the lowest requirements of *child care licensing* (government regulations). When only custodial care is provided, children are safe, but they do not get the stimulation of interesting things to do.

TYPES OF CHILD CARE CENTERS

Child care centers are often grouped according to sponsorship and services offered. The location and the size of the center may also be noted.

Proprietary Child Care Centers. Child care centers that operate to make a profit are called *proprietary child care centers,* or profit child care centers. These centers are private businesses. They provide a service to parents in return for money (usually called *parent fees*).

Small Proprietary Child Care Centers. Most small private child care centers serve fewer than 30 children and are found in residential areas, where they provide care for children who live nearby. Such centers may be very good for children, because the small number served makes it possible to offer special attention. In such a setting the center is like a large family. Staff members know each other and the children well.

Sometimes this kind of center may not provide high-quality care. If parent fees do not raise enough money, the owner (often called a *day care operator*) may try to do too many things without help. If so, the children do not receive the best care.

Large Proprietary Child Care Centers. Child care centers that have more than 30 children and operate as private businesses are considered large proprietary child care centers. They may be owned by private individuals or may be sponsored by some community organization. In both cases the center is operated for profit as well as to provide service.

Some large proprietary child care centers are run by their owners. These have usually operated for many years and were once small proprietary centers.

Another kind of center is owned by a group of people who pay to set it up but who hire someone else to run it. Such centers often are part of a *franchise* (that is, part of a chain of child care centers, much as there are department store or supermarket chains). The centers are located in different cities or parts of cities, and they all have the same name, the same kinds of buildings and equipment, and the same staffing pattern. Usually, a business manager handles money matters while a child development person supervises the staff and the center's programs.

Sometimes on-the-job training is offered to employees.

Nonproprietary Child Care Centers. Nonproprietary child care centers are usually called *nonprofit child care centers.* They are sponsored by community organizations, social agencies, or schools that take responsibility for, and in many cases provide the money for, a center's operation. At nonprofit centers, parents are charged fees on the basis of their ability to pay. If more money is needed to run the center, it comes from the community (from the United Fund, for example). Sometimes the money comes from state and federal government grants or from private foundations. Neighborhood groups may join together as a nonprofit organization in order to sponsor a child care center.

State laws require nonprofit centers to have a *governing board* (usually made up of professional, business, and community leaders) to define policies and to hire a director who runs the program as defined by the governing board.

Other Kinds of Child Care Centers. Besides full-time programs, some child care centers offer services on a part-time, hourly basis. If care is needed day and night, children may receive it 24 hours per day in *children's homes.* Child care services that are *home based*—either in the child's own home or in another family's home—are not considered child care centers.

Hourly Child Care. Child care centers located on college campuses and military bases or in shopping centers, bowling alleys, hotels, and family day care homes provide *hourly care* for children. These centers are planned so that children are safely supervised and supplied with playthings. This type of hourly service is often called *drop-in service*. Activities are planned to benefit children as they come and go at different times.

Hourly care (paid for by the hour) is offered by some child care centers during the night or in the early morning for parents who work very late or very early. Sometimes, industry provides hourly care for employees who need child care services at unusual hours.

Twenty-four-Hour Child Care. Sometimes there is a need for child care round the clock. A child who has a medical problem may need to be hospitalized for several weeks. A child who is abused, neglected, or abandoned may need 24-hour care in a children's home, an emergency shelter, a juvenile home, or a foster home. A child who has a severe handicap may need to live in an institution for a period of time.

LICENSING CHILD CARE CENTERS

A *license* is a document provided by state governments that gives a child care center legal permission to operate.

Although regulations are not the same in all states, their purpose is the same—to ensure the safety of the children. The building must pass an inspection by the fire and health departments; it must have good lighting, sanitation, and toileting facilities, as well as fire exits. The type of heating used and the way food is prepared are also considered before a center is given a license. When a center applies for a license, it must make known its program and staff assignments.

Licenses are usually granted for 1 year. During this period, inspectors will visit a center regularly to make sure that requirements are being met. When the year is up, the center is inspected again before its license is renewed.

Most states require centers to display their license, their policies, a complete description of their program, the ages of the children served, and the hours and days they are open. This information must be displayed in some part of the center that is open to the public, so that visitors can see at once what standards the center meets and what services it offers.

Most child care licensing focuses on *minimum requirements;* that is, the rules by which

centers operate are the very least needed to ensure the safety and well-being of the children. However, most center owners and operators want to provide the best care possible, so they try to reach *desirable standards* by providing an enriched program that will benefit children.

FAMILY DAY CARE

Child care that is provided for less than 24 hours, in private homes, for a few children who are not related to the caregiver is called *family day care*. The largest number of children that may be enrolled in a family day care home is usually given in state licensing regulations.

Family day care is one of the oldest forms of child care. For many years the nurturing person, or the caregiver who provides family day care, has been called a *family day care mother*. Perhaps in the future more men will provide family day care and be called family day care fathers.

Family day care is usually arranged by a parent with a neighbor or a friend. The hours, service, and fee are agreed upon by the parent and the caregiver. This informal method of child care is used all over the country.

Some family day care homes are nonprofit organizations. They are part of a social agency, much as some comprehensive centers are. The people who provide this kind of family day care service are paid a salary as staff members of the agency. In addition, the agency may have a list of other licensed day care homes for parents who need child care service.

Many family day care homes offer outstanding opportunities for children to learn and grow. Studies of family day care show that it can offer excellent child care services. Some of the advantages of family day care are:[1]

1. An atmosphere that is like a large family
2. A wider variety of age groups, so that brothers and sisters of the same family can be cared for in one setting

[1]June Solnit Sale, "Family Day Care: A Valuable Alternative," in Jan McCarthy and Charles R. May (eds.), *Providing the Best for Young Children*, NAEYC Bulletin, 1974, p. 31.

Table 2-1 STAFF POSITIONS IN CHILD CARE SERVICES

	Director (Administrator)	Director (education)	Social worker	Parent coordinator	Lead teacher	Teacher	Assistant—Level II	Aide—Level I	Home visitor	Cook	Housekeeper	Janitor	Driver	Licensing worker—evaluates center	Babysitter
Child care centers															
Comprehensive centers	U	U	U	U	U	U	U	U	U	U	U	U	U	U	
Developmental centers	U	S	S	S	S	U	S	U		U	U	U	S	U	
Custodial centers							U	S		U	S	S	S	U	
24-hour care															
Children's Hospitals	U	S	U	S		U	S	S		U	U	U	S	S	
Children's homes	U	S	U			S	U	U		U	U	U	U	S	
Juvenile homes	U		U				U	S		U	U	U			
Foster homes	U	U*					U							U	
Other child care services*															
Family day care	S*						U	S		S*			S*	S	S
Hourly care	S*						U	S		S*	S*	S*	S*		U
Weekend care							U	S		S*	S*	S*	S*		U
Enrichment programs															
Play schools	S*	S*					U	S	S	S	S	S	S		

3. Lower costs than group child care centers
4. Hours that can easily be arranged to fit parents' work schedules
5. Care of the slightly ill child (upper respiratory illness)

STAFFING PATTERNS OF CHILD CARE CENTERS

The term *staffing pattern* refers to the organization that a child care center uses to group staff members and their responsibilities. Just as programs and settings differ from one center to another, so do the staffing pattern, individual responsibilities of staff members, salaries, and fringe benefits. Large, well-organized centers may have more regulations about personnel policies, salary scales, and specific job duties than do small, home-type centers.

You may decide you would like to work in a small center, where the staff is like a large family. Or perhaps you would prefer to belong to the staff of a large center that serves many children. Whatever you decide, good jobs can certainly be found in centers both large and small.

Table 2-1 STAFF POSITIONS IN CHILD CARE SERVICES (Continued)

	Director (Administrator)	Director (education)	Social worker	Parent coordinator	Lead teacher	Teacher	Assistant—Level II	Aide—Level I	Home visitor	Cook	Housekeeper	Janitor	Driver	Licensing worker—evaluates center	Babysitter
Day camps*	U	S				S	U	S		U	U		S		
Home visitor*						S	U	S	U						
Educational television*		S							U						
Nursery schools*	S	U		S	S*	U	S	U		S	U	U	S	S	
Kindergartens*	S	U		S	S*	U	S	U		S	U	U	S	S	
Parent cooperatives	S	S	S		U		S			S	S	U	S		
Laboratory schools	S	U		S	U	S	S	U	S	U	U	U	S	S	
Compensatory educational programs Parent-child centers	U	U	U	U	U	U	S	U	U	U	U	U	U	S	S
Head Start programs	U	U	U	U	S	U	S	U	U	U	U	U	U	S	S
Follow-Through programs	U	U	U	U	U	U	S	U	U	U	U	U	U	S	S
Special needs programs*	U	S	U	S	S	U	S	U	S	U	U	U	S	S	

U = Usually   S = Sometimes
* May be part of service given by child care center or agency

Table 2-1 shows the staff positions usually found in the different types of child care centers and programs. Most of the programs mentioned in this chapter have child care aide positions.

ENRICHMENT PROGRAMS

When child caregivers use the term *program,* they are talking about activities and experiences that are planned for children. Child development programs that supplement home experiences are called *enrichment programs.*

SOCIAL ENRICHMENT PROGRAMS

Social enrichment programs are designed to help children learn how to get along with others.

Playschools give preschool children the chance to play in groups. They are often organized by parents, who take turns supervising children's play. Churches, community centers, recreation departments, and child care centers may also provide playschool groups at certain times during the week, usually in the morning.

As a rule, *day camp* is scheduled during the

summer in week-long sessions. Day camp programs generally focus on children's physical skills as well as social and emotional development.

EDUCATIONAL ENRICHMENT PROGRAMS

Educational enrichment programs are directed toward children's intellectual development. They are designed to make the best use of those times when children are ready to learn.

Home-Based Enrichment Programs. *Home-based enrichment programs* focus on children's learning activities within the home and family; they usually encourage parents to teach their own children. In some communities, child care aides are known as *home visitors*. They visit homes to show parents how they can teach their children.

It is not the purpose of a home visit to *tell* parents how to raise their children. Instead, home visitors are often neighbors, as well as educational aides, and they work *with* parents in helping children learn and grow. Home visiting is very often an important part of the

social service of a comprehensive child care program.

In some parts of the country, *educational television programs* are used with young children. Along with home visits, these help parents get involved with their children's learning.

Center-based Enrichment Programs. *Center-based enrichment programs* focus on children's learning in group settings. The following programs offer educational enrichment in settings like public buildings, private centers, and churches.

Nursery School. Nursery school offers half-day programs of educational enrichment for children 2 to 4 years old. While the programs vary, most of them consider play an important tool for learning. Some nursery schools stress intellectual development. Others may emphasize social development. In a large community, parents can choose from many different kinds of nursery schools.

Kindergarten. Like nursery school, kindergarten focuses mainly on educational enrichment. Although 4-year-olds may be enrolled, *kindergarteners* are usually 5-year-old children.

Parent Cooperatives. Sometimes parents may form a group and help run a program for their children. This is called a *parent cooperative*. Such parents usually hire a teacher to plan and run the children's program. Sometimes a qualified parent acts as "head teacher" and is paid a salary. An advisory group of parents works closely with the teacher, and all the parents in the program take turns helping. Regular training meetings are held to help parents become more skilled in teaching their children.

Laboratory Schools. Laboratory schools are usually connected with child care training programs at high schools, vocational-technical schools, junior colleges, and universities. The main purpose of laboratory schools is to teach students how to work with young children. Students first watch a professional teacher plan and guide the children's learning. Then they have supervised experiences with the children, who are enrolled in a nursery school or other program that takes place at the laboratory school. The students are able to see how young children behave, and they also have the chance to test their own skills in working with young children.

Figure 2-3. In a family day care house, a qualified parent acts as "teacher," is paid a salary, and runs the child care program in his or her home. (Michael Weisbrot)

COMPENSATORY EDUCATIONAL PROGRAMS

It has become clear that children who have been troubled at home have a hard time at school. Recently, private foundations, educational groups, and government agencies have shown concern about this. As a result, they have given money for programs to help children make up, or *compensate* for, the experiences they missed in their early years. Such programs are called *compensatory educational programs*. Their purpose is to add to children's experiences through information and activities that will help them learn in school. Nearly all compensatory educational programs employ child care aides, and child care teamwork is stressed.

The following compensatory programs are designed for children of different ages. Although the purpose of each program is to add to children's experiences, the teaching methods, subjects taught, and staffing patterns may change from one program to another.

PARENT-CHILD CENTERS

Infants, toddlers, and parents of low-income families take part in a parent education program at a *parent-child center*. These programs include activities at the center as well as home visits. Their main goal is to help parents become skillful in stimulating their children's learning activities.

HEAD START PROGRAMS

Head Start is an educational program for prekindergarten low-income children. It aims to prepare children for school and learning. Parents are involved with the program, which is designed to help children from disadvantaged families "catch up." The program provides learning experiences that are not available in the home. Health and social services are also part of the Head Start program.

FOLLOW-THROUGH

Follow-Through, a federally supported program, provides compensatory programs for

Figure 2-4. Child care centers for handicapped children give them special care and attention. (Sam Teicher, School for the Deaf)

children in kindergarten and grades 1, 2, and 3. In Follow-Through classrooms, teachers and aides work as teams providing both group experiences and individual help for children. In addition, health and social services, home visiting, and parent involvement programs are important parts of Follow-Through.

CHILDREN WITH SPECIAL NEEDS

Child care centers for children with special needs have been started within the past few years. Often these programs are comprehensive, not only developmental. They provide help for children who are emotionally, physically, or intellectually handicapped and their parents.

Day care programs are planned by a trained staff to meet the unusual needs of these children, and child care aides play a part in this. Centers for handicapped children can accomplish three important things: (1) They give parents a rest from the need to provide constant care for a handicapped child; (2) they teach parents how to work with their own children; and (3) they assist the children by giving them extra help and attention.

CHAPTER SUMMARY

1. *Child care services* refers to the many kinds of child care that can be provided in various environments.
2. When child care services are offered to a group of children in one location, the setting is called a *child care center.*
3. Child care centers may be grouped according to the kinds of child care they provide—comprehensive, developmental, or custodial.
4. When a child care center is owned by one person or by a group and is run as a business, it is called a *profit* or *proprietary center. Nonproprietary centers,* sometimes called *board-sponsored* or *nonprofit centers,* are sponsored by community groups, social agencies, and government grants.
5. Staffing patterns are designed to meet the needs of individual centers.
6. Child care centers are licensed in order to protect the children and ensure that they get at least the minimum standards of child care.
7. *Enrichment programs* add to children's home experiences by providing social and educational experiences.
8. *Compensatory programs* are designed to help children make up for experiences that were missing in their early years at home.

• WHAT NEW TERMS HAVE YOU LEARNED?

Several new words and ideas were presented in this chapter. To see whether you understand them, match the letter of each term below with the numbered phrases under "Definitions."

Terms

a. Play school
b. Sponsorship
c. Comprehensive care
d. Developmental care
e. Custodial care
f. Franchise center
g. Nursery school
h. Environment
i. Proprietary center
j. Parent fees
k. Family day care
l. 24-hour care
m. Hourly care
n. Compensatory education programs
o. Parent involvement

Definitions

1. The physical setting in which child care service is offered
2. Mothers and fathers participating in child care activities
3. A combination of services such as health care, an enriched program, and social services
4. Child care which provides only for children's physical safety
5. The money paid by parents for child care
6. Short-term care provided on college campuses, in shopping centers, or on military bases
7. Programs designed to help children to catch up on experiences lacking in the early years
8. A center owned privately and operated for profit
9. A chain of centers owned and operated by a corporation
10. Social enrichment program
11. Child care provided in a home
12. Care provided in foster homes and children's homes
13. Child care center program which includes program activities focusing on all aspects of a child's development
14. A group program for 3- and 4-year-olds which supplements home care and focuses on children's educational development
15. A person, persons, or organization that provides guidelines and money for the operation of a center

• STUDENT ACTIVITIES

1. Make a list of at least three items in the environments of different child care services that affect the child care programs and staff assignments.

2. Compare a developmental child care center, a comprehensive child care center, and a custodial child care center.
3. Describe a proprietary day care center *or* a nonproprietary day care center.
4. Define hourly care and tell how it helps families.
5. When is 24-hour child care used?
6. Using Table 2-1, select a child care center or program and list the staff positions usually found there.
7. Using Table 2-1 or text, name three enrichment programs that may employ child care aides.
8. Explain the purpose of compensatory education programs and identify three that employ child care aides.

• PROJECTS, DECISIONS, ISSUES

1. Identify the licensing agency for child care services in your community and get a copy of the local child care licensing standards.
2. Using a set of licensing standards from your state agency, report on information given in the standards regarding indoor and outdoor space, food requirements, and child-staff ratio.
3. Name five different child care centers in your community. Visit one and find out whether the program offered is a custodial, comprehensive, developmental, or an enrichment program.
4. Select a center in your community in which you would like to work. Make arrangements with the person in charge (your teacher may need to help make the arrangements) and volunteer to work in this center for a whole day—from opening to closing. Evaluate your career goals after this experience.
5. Interview a family child care mother. What arrangements does the home setting offer children? Is the home licensed? What are the children doing? How many children are there and what are their ages?

• WHIFS (WHAT WOULD YOU DO *IF* . . .)

1. A friend asks you to recommend a day care center for his 4-year-old daughter. What would you do?
   a. Name one that you know
   b. Check the yellow pages for day care centers
   c. Tell him about licensing standards
   d. Discourage him from using day care
   e. Other responses

2. You have a 9-month-old baby and a job offer to go to work the next day on the swing shift (3 p.m.–11 p.m.). What would you do?
   a. Refuse the job
   b. Ask a high school student to baby-sit
   c. Find a qualified family day care home
   d. Find a day care center that has a low fee and provides transportation
   e. Other responses

3. Your nephew (3 years old) lives far away from other children and his mother wants to use a child care service so that he can have some playmates. What would you do?
   a. Look at newspaper ads for family child care homes
   b. Check local churches for nursery or playschools
   c. Buy him a coloring book and have him stay home
   d. Call the day care licensing office for advice
   e. Other responses

4. You visited a child care center and counted 25 children (5 of whom were babies) and only one child caregiver, who was watching television. What would you do?
   a. Notify your local licensing office
   b. Tell your friends not to send their children to that center
   c. Use the center anyway because it charges a small fee
   d. Write a letter to the editor of the local paper
   e. Other responses

3 | CHILDREN DO ALL KINDS OF THINGS

After you have studied Chapter 3, you should be able to:

1. Describe three basic qualities of a good program for young children
2. Identify three items which show that the program is planned
3. Summarize three characteristics of the physical setting and play equipment that affect the learning environment
4. Name two main steps in the program planning process and state three reasons why program goals are important

QUALITIES OF A GOOD PROGRAM

The experiences and activities provided for young children in child care services are called *programs*. In developing good programs for young children, you must keep two broad areas in mind: (1) the essential qualities of a good program and (2) the ongoing process of program planning.

Resources, such as equipment, space, staff, and time, affect programs for young children. Good resources, if used well, result in good programs. Poor resources, regardless of how well they are used, make it harder to provide good programs.

You need to know the qualities of a good program because, as part of a child care team, you will help plan programs for young children. In a good program, the staff is qualified, there is careful planning, and the environment is good for learning.

A WELL-QUALIFIED STAFF

Qualified child caregivers must nurture and guide children, handle unexpected situations, and use resources well. A qualified staff brings the following things to the child care setting:

Positive Adult-Child Interaction. Feelings and communication among children and adults make a difference in children's experiences.

Relaxed Atmosphere. Children are nurtured in a good program. Adults and children enjoy each other. They listen and talk together. Children trust child caregivers who follow through on promises.

Children thrive on cooperative effort among staff members. Everyone makes a contribution. One child may get along better with the child care aide than with the teacher. Both the aide and the teacher are glad when a child seeks out an adult, no matter who it is.

When planning is done together, the adults work better for the children and their families. Parents' ideas and values are respected and considered. Parents are welcome to visit and to help in the child care center. Sometimes they come to the center and bring a treat or play a musical instrument.

Clear and Consistent Guidance. Child care aides should generally act the same way toward children most of the time; this helps children know what to expect. When *limits* (rules) are explained clearly and are enforced, children usually behave as their teachers want them to.

It is wise to notice and encourage good behavior. When child caregivers learn how children respond, they focus on what they *want* the children to do rather than on what they do *not want* them to do. The results of poor behavior (behavior that needs improvement or change) are known to the children, and rules are enforced. The children know the limits and can count on them to be applied consistently.

Of all the resources available to children in a child care program, the people who work with them are the most important. Whether they are called child care workers, teachers, or child care aides, those who work with children make the difference between a good or bad experience for the children.

CAREFUL PLANNING

Good planning in child care services is based on three things: (1) each child is seen as an individual as well as part of the group, (2) play is seen as a learning tool, and (3) a relaxed, orderly schedule is provided. Qualified staff members influence what is planned and how resources are used.

CONSIDERING THE CHILDREN

In a good program, each child's growth and development are encouraged. This is done by seeing how children grow and develop and then matching children's needs, abilities, and interests with the right setting and program. This process is illustrated in Figure 3-1.

Children's Growth and Development. The following important facts about children's growth and development are used in planning good programs for young children:

1. Each child is different from all other children in some way.
2. Children cannot reach their highest level of development unless they receive good care.
3. All normal children grow from one stage to another, but no two children go through a stage in exactly the same way or at exactly the same time.
4. Children do not always grow at a steady

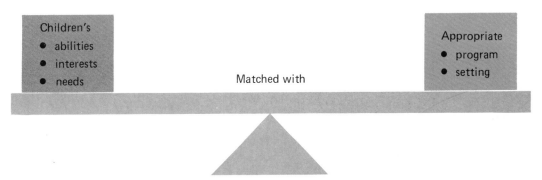

Figure 3-1. A good child care program matches children's abilities, interests, and needs with the right setting and program. (J. McV. Hunt, *Intelligence and Experiences*, Ronald, New York, 1961, p. 268.)

Figure 3-2. A good child care program emphasizes social development. Children learn to play and get along with each other. (Bart Fleet)

rate, nor is their growth always a smooth process. Sometimes they are difficult to handle for a time. At other periods, they are easy to manage and anxious to please.

5. Children develop in four different ways—physically, emotionally, socially, and intellectually.

   a. *Physical development*. Children's use and development of their bodies is called *physical development*. The use of large and small muscles and the development of good health and safety habits are stressed in a good program. Caregivers should not judge children's behavior on only part of their development. Some 4-year-olds may be as tall as 6-year-olds, for example, but this only means that their physical development is advanced. It does not mean that the taller children should or will behave as 6-year-olds do.

   b. *Emotional development*. This refers to children's feelings and emotions. When most of children's experiences are successful, they feel good about themselves. Chances to try things out, to make mistakes, and to learn from them help children to learn about and handle their emotions.

   c. *Social development*. How children get along with others is called *social development*. In a good program, children enjoy each other and have fun. Friendships come and go as young children play together and practice the give-and-take of social development.

   d. *Intellectual development*. This refers to mental growth, or how children use their minds. Thinking, problem solving, and using language are signs of intellectual development. It is encouraged by activities that are new enough to be interesting but familiar enough to build the child's self-confidence.

Children's Experiences. The number and kind of experiences that children have had are considered when a program is planned. Some experiences are more important than others. How an experience affects a child and how the child *copes with* (handles) the experience determine the importance of *that* experience for *that* child.

Children do not cope with situations in the same way as adults; they are not experienced in coping. As a child caregiver, remember that what seems to be a small problem to you may be a very large one for young children. And problems that seem large to you may seem unimportant to the children.

Children's Age Groups. Caregivers try to learn as much as they can about the behavior typical of the age group with which they are working. Younger children have had less experience; therefore, they need more help from adults. Planned experiences should match the abilities of the children in a given age group.

The staff considers the make-up of the group of children when a program is planned. Just as no two children are alike, neither are two groups. For example, last year's 3-year-old children may have been quiet, while this year's 3-year-olds are talkative.

In most centers, children are grouped by age. However, in small centers where the staff is not large enough for many age groups, children of different ages may be put together.

Children's Home Life. Knowing about the children's home life will help caregivers plan a program. Children's home life has a lot to do with their behavior. Do they get too much or too little attention from their parents? Do they have the chance to play with other children? Is their family large or small? Are they living with both parents or only one? Do family members speak another language at home? How many times has a child's family moved during the child's lifetime? What kind of neighborhood does the family live in? Is their house small or large? Are the children healthy? Caregivers must ask themselves such questions when planning the child care program.

Children's Values. The events that *children* think are important should be considered in program planning. The values of adults and the values of young children are different. Adults are likely to measure success and accomplishment by such things as money earned, honors won, and grades received. This is not the case for young children. Here are some things that young children value:

1. *The feeling of belonging.* Children want to feel safe and secure, to have a part in the peer group, and to know that their part counts. "Mary is good at finishing puzzles and putting them back on the shelf." "Jimmy knows how to tuck the dolls into bed at clean-up time."

2. *Spur-of-the-moment laughter.* Laughter is a sign of shared happiness. When awkward moments are eased with laughter, it reassures children and builds good fellowship. "Mrs. Smith laughed when she got all wet as the sprinkler came on. We laughed too."

3. *Learning at one's own pace.* Children are most comfortable with new experiences that they can understand.

4. *Having accomplishments noticed.* "I can tie my shoes." "Look! I can hop on one foot." "I did it; I unzipped my jacket all by myself." The praise that comes with success is encouraging.

5. *Special occasions.* "Our dog had puppies on the kitchen floor!" "An owl was on my windowsill this morning." "My Grandie comes this afternoon. It's my 4-year-old birthday."

6. *Time to discover.* Children need time to look and feel, to wonder and dream.

7. *Reassurance.* Children want to feel loved and wanted *all* the time, especially when they make mistakes and are not sure of your reaction. "Jonathan, get the sponge and wipe up the milk that is spilled. Everyone spills things sometimes."

8. *Help in handling mistakes.* Children need to know what went wrong and how to avoid making the same mistake again.

9. *Help in getting along with peers.* "I want to play with the big airplane," pouts Stephen. His teacher suggests that he build a hangar out of blocks for the airplane. Later, Maria asks Stephen if she can put the big airplane in his hangar, and two children have experienced friendship.

10. *Adults who live life fully.* Children enjoy adults who *do* what they *say* and who love to learn.

PLAY AS A LEARNING TOOL

Learning tools are ways to learn, and children learn through play. Dr. Jerome Bruner has said, "Play allows practice for the problem-solving and creativity that come later."[1] The value of play as a tool for learning is recognized in a good child care program. Play lets children learn, grow, understand, and practice handling problems. Table 3-1 will help you understand the many ways that children grow and develop through play.

A Relaxed, Orderly Schedule. Children who are enrolled in a child care center are often hurried in the process of getting up, getting ready, and being brought to the center. This hurrying can strain relationships between parents and children.

A good program is relaxed, and the day's schedule is basically the same each day. Yet it is flexible enough to take advantage of special events and unplanned teaching moments. Children will know what will come next when they learn the pattern of the daily schedule (see Tables 3-2 and 3-3).

[1]Jerome S. Bruner, "Play Is Serious Business," *Psychology Today,* January 1975, p. 81.

Table 3-1 CHILDREN GROW AND DEVELOP THROUGH PLAY*

Recognize developmental needs	Watch for interests	Provide Equipment or Activities for—*		
		Toddlers	Preschool children	School-aged children
To use sense of sight	Looking at pictures	Nursery rhymes with large pictures	Collection of pictures	Prints of famous paintings
	Noticing colors	Spool board	Colored cloth or painted spools	Watercolors Puzzles
To develop visual discrimination	Matching shapes	Pots and pans	Jigsaw puzzles Classifying games	Birdhouse building, etc. Sewing (doll clothes)
	Reading		Stories of animals and children	Books of adventure, fiction
To use sense of hearing	Making noise	Rattle Stiff paper Bells	Humming Singing	Group singing Whistling
To develop auditory discrimination	Using rhythm	Pot lids to rattle	Rhythm instrument Record player, records	Musical instruments Record player, records Square dancing Children's concerts Music on radio/ TV
	Enjoying harmony			
To develop sense of balance	Climbing	Steps Small slide	Jungle gym Slide	Tree climbing
	Riding	Rockinghorse	Seesaw Tricycle	Scooter Bicycle Skates
	Dancing			Square dancing
To use sense of touch To develop tactile discrimination	Feeling	Cuddly toy Rag doll	Clay Fingerpaint Materials of different texture	Clay Fingerpaint Handicrafts

*Many toys and activities suggested for a younger age group will still be suitable for an older age group.

Table 3-1 CHILDREN GROW AND DEVELOP THROUGH PLAY* (Continued)

Recognize developmental needs	Watch for interests	Provide Equipment or Activities for—*		
		Toddlers	Preschool children	School-aged children
To achieve finger control through use of small muscles	Taking toys apart or putting them together	Nest of cans or boxes Pegs, pegboard Coupled train cars	Clothespins on pan Simple puzzles String macaroni Shoes and shoe strings	Weaving set Marionettes Writing Drawing
To use large arm muscles	Throwing	Stuffed animal Large rubber ball	Bean-bag games Ball throwing Ring toss	Darts Softball Basketball or volleyball Archery set
	Building	Large blocks	Interlocking blocks, trains, or trucks	Tool set, boards, nails, hammer
	Pounding	Clay dough		Punching bag Hammer, nails, wood
	Digging	Sandbox, shovel spoon	Sandbox, shovel	Garden tools
	Lifting Jumping Running Skipping		Hollow blocks Large boxes Kite	Equipment Hopscotch Volleyball Jumping rope
To develop creative ability	Creating	Sand Water	Crayons, plain paper Clay Puppets Blocks	Fingerpaint Paper, watercolors Marionettes Soap carving
To use and develop imagination	Making believe		Playhouse Cans, boxes for playing store Costumes Doll clothes	Dolls, doll house Housekeeping toys Magic set
To acquire skills	Gaining know-how	Any toy that helps child coordinate mind and body	Storytelling Play with other children Discovery of space, nature, use of body	Games, such as dominoes Sewing kit Camera and developing set Crafts (metal, glass, leather) Chemistry set

Table 3-2 SAMPLE DAILY SCHEDULE FOR ALL-DAY CHILD CARE PROGRAM IN CHILD CARE CENTERS

Time	Activity	Children	Staff
7:00 a.m.	Center opens—play equipment and free choice activities require little supervision.	Children arrive at various times; assemble in one group.	Skeleton staff (one or two on duty). Other staff arrive at various times.
8:00 a.m.	Breakfast served in some centers.	Breakfast, if served.	Staff arriving.
8:30 a.m.	Indoor activities in assigned groups (in summer, outdoor activities at this time). Free choice of activities.	Most children have arrived. Children in groups, usually by ages. Children choose activities from equipment and experiences available.	Staff available for each group. Staff supervise children's activities.
9:30 a.m.	Clean-up and transition.	Children put things away, use bathroom, then go to next activity (group activity).	Teachers teach children to clean and put things away by themselves. Assist with toileting and transition.
9:45 a.m.	Group time. Music activities.	Children participate in group musical activities.	Teachers lead group time.
10:00 a.m.	Snack.	Children help get it ready (set table and put snack on table).	Teacher gets snack ready during group time. Teachers sit at table with children.
10:15 a.m.	Outdoor learning.	Children go outdoors.	Teachers outdoors too.
11:00 a.m.	Transition (change) from outdoors to indoors.	Children help put equipment away, use bathroom.	Teachers supervise transition activities.
11:15 a.m.	Group time. Language arts.	Children participate in story time, poetry, listening, finger play.	Teachers lead group time.
11:30 a.m.	Lunch.	Children eat and help clean up.	Teachers eat and supervise lunch experience.

Table 3-2 SAMPLE DAILY SCHEDULE FOR ALL-DAY CHILD CARE PROGRAM IN CHILD CARE CENTERS (Continued)

Time	Activity	Children	Staff
12 p.m.	Bathroom. Get ready for nap.	Take off shoes, help with cots, get comfortable.	Follow naptime routine, set stage for rest.
1:30 p.m.	Nap—go to sleep. Transition. Get up—bathroom.	Children get up at various times, use bathroom, dress, help put cots away.	Teacher supervises nap and dressing procedure, puts cots away.
2:30 p.m.	Snack.	Eat snack.	Teachers prepare and eat snack with children.
3:00 p.m.	Outdoors if weather permits.	Children outdoors.	Teachers outdoors.
4:00 p.m.	Indoors—transition.	Children put outdoor equipment away, use bathroom, get ready to go home.	Teacher supervises.
4:00 to 6:00 p.m.	Free choice. Going home.	Children go home at various times.	Skeleton staff after most children have gone home.

Table 3-3 SAMPLE DAILY SCHEDULE FOR PART-DAY CHILD CARE PROGRAM

Time	Activity	Children	Staff
8:30 a.m.	Children arrive.	Children usually arrive about the same time and go to assigned groups.	Teachers greet children in their groups.
	Free choice of activities.	Children choose activities from prearranged supplies and equipment.	Teachers have prepared room with different projects.
9:30 a.m.	Transition.	Children clean up, use bathroom, come to group time.	Teachers supervise help children learn how to clean up and use bathroom by themselves.
9:45 a.m.	Group time—language arts and music.	Children participate in group time.	Teacher leads.

Table 3-3 SAMPLE DAILY SCHEDULE FOR PART-DAY CHILD CARE PROGRAM (Continued)

Time	Activity	Children	Staff
10:00 a.m.	Snack.	Children eat snack, help get ready, and clean up.	Teachers supervise and eat with children.
10:15 a.m.	Outdoors.	Children outdoors.	Teachers outdoors.
10:55 a.m.	Transition indoors.	Children put toys away, use bathroom.	Teachers supervise.
11:10 a.m.	Rest.	Children rest (mats).	Teachers supervise.
11:25 a.m.	Get ready to go home.	Children get ready to leave.	Teachers supervise.
11:30 a.m.	Dismissal.	Children get art work and wraps, put on wraps. Children go home.	Teachers supervise.

Balance between active and quiet periods keeps children from getting too tired or too excited. When the program is divided into large blocks of time (about 1 hour long), children are able to get involved in what they are doing. Activities that need lots of preparation and clean-up time are scheduled when children and staff are fresh, usually in the morning.

Transition Periods. *Transition periods* are times spent in changing activities, such as cleaning up, using the bathroom, and getting ready to go outside. When children have a pattern that they know, these times go smoothly and need little supervision.

Routines. Toileting, nap time, and snack and meal time also follow a regular pattern, or *routine*. The framework is basically the same from day to day. The children come to the same room in the same building, use the same equipment, and live with the same child caregivers daily. These things are regular, and the children come to expect them.

AVAILABLE LEARNING ENVIRONMENT

The environment gives the children many chances to learn. The physical setting affects the learning environment. Children have good experiences in an orderly, inviting setting that includes good equipment and enough materials.

The Physical Setting. Space can be organized, kept in order, and defined in terms of activity areas. These are ways of creating an environment for learning. Child caregivers know how to use the physical setting to help children learn.

The size and shape of the playing space influence children's decisions and plans. For example, a long, narrow room where sounds bounce off the walls causes children and teachers to raise their voices so as to be heard. When everyone talks a little louder, it is impossible to have a relaxed setting. Communication becomes difficult as the room gets more noisy, and words are not heard clearly.

If the quality and amount of indoor space is limited, outdoor space is used for some activities. For example, musical instruments may be used outdoors, as children march in and out among trees to the beat of the drum. Sometimes a field trip is planned, and the children go to special places like the firehouse, the zoo, a farm, or a grocery store.

Organizing Space. How space is organized and how equipment is used in the space are as

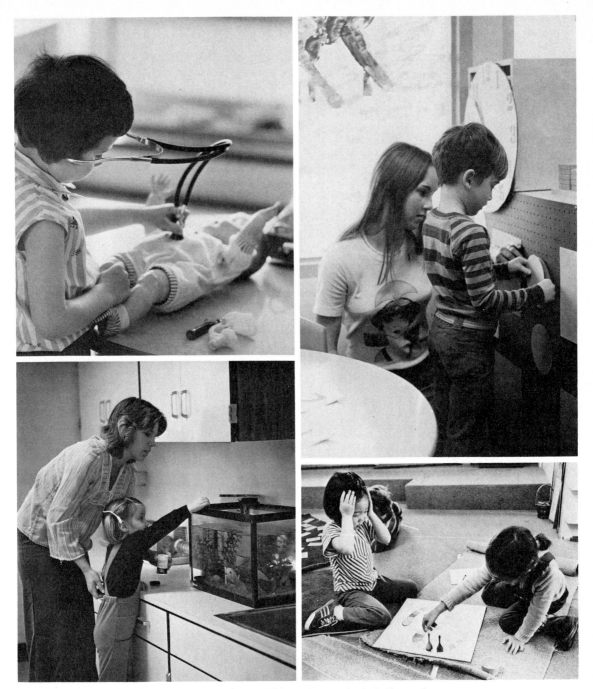

Figure 3-3. Some of the activity areas found in a child care center include the math area, manipulative area, dramatic play area, and science area. (Bart Fleet; Jane Hamilton-Merritt; Rita Freed, Nancy Palmer Agency; Bart Fleet)

Table 3-4 ACTIVITY AREAS (LEARNING CENTERS)

Area	Considerations	Objectives
Art	Preferably near water and natural light (window) May be set up outside when weather permits	To encourage creativity To develop self-confidence To establish good work habits To help children enjoy the experience To encourage interaction among children and between child and teacher
Literature—Language Arts	Arranged so that children can see book covers and make choices Should invite looking and listening Need table and floor space so that children can look at books	To help children understand and use spoken language (to listen and to speak) To develop prereading skills such as recall, visual memory, recognizing likenesses and differences (visual discrimination) To develop prewriting skills such as using tactile letters and shaped blocks To follow directions To express feelings
Block	Away from traffic patterns Rug may lessen noise Enough space so that children do not get in each other's way	To become aware of related sizes, fractions (1 unit, 1/2 unit, double unit, etc.) To build projects with other children To complete a task To develop good work habits, such as putting blocks away when finished To classify sizes, shapes To develop eye-hand coordination To stimulate language To make decisions To solve problems
Music	Musical instruments available for children to try out (some will need close supervision, while others can be explored with little supervision)	To explore sounds and different forms of music To enjoy singing, listening, and moving to music To develop skill in moving to music and singing To develop vocabulary of musical terms To develop auditory discrimination To develop auditory memory
Dramatic play (Housekeeping or doll area)	May incorporate cooking experiences into housekeeping area	To try out how it feels to behave the way family members do To learn to control part of the world, which is so much larger than children To act out and express feelings To practice getting along with peers To internalize roles: "This is what you do in a restaurant."

important as the *amount* of space—perhaps even more so. When space is well organized, comfortable, and useful, children tend to make the most of it. Storage space, equipment, and activities can be located in a way that encourages the children's involvement.

Creating Order. "There is a place for every-thing, and everything is in its place" is a rule that is followed in a good program. Equipment and materials are put on open shelves so that children can see what is available. They can pick out what they want to use and return it to the right place when they are finished. This not only helps the staff keep things in order but also

Table 3-4 ACTIVITY AREAS (LEARNING CENTERS) (Continued)

Area	Considerations	Objectives
Manipulative activities	Open shelves so that children can get table games or manipulative toys, take them to a floor space or a nearby table and put them away when finished	To manipulate objects To improve eye-hand coordination To stimulate language To make decisions To solve problems To stimulate interaction among children To complete a task
Science	Materials for nature study and science grouped together in one part of the room or placed around the room where children can get them easily; arranged ways that make the room attractive	To explore natural world: plants, rocks, seeds, animals To explore physical properties of the world To encourage scientific process To observe To state hypotheses To experiment To record results To evaluate
Math	May be part of table activities or near them; encourages getting, using, and returning things to storage place	To experience use of number concepts (sets, one-to-one relationships, cardinal and ordinal numbers, comparison of numbers, parts-whole, counting) To develop processes, visual perception, auditory perception, classification, seriation, shapes, sounds, and numbers)
Carpentry	Away from quiet area, off carpet, and where it can be supervised easily Storage of tools nearby	To enjoy creating To practice changing practical shapes To manipulate materials To release tension through pounding and sawing To complete a task
Water-sand	Placed where it can be swept or mopped up easily (on porch or patio, or in play yard) Smocks for water play, unless it's warm weather	To observe and handle properties of water and sand To measure To release tensions To interact with other children

helps the children to feel the satisfaction of making choices. A child enjoys following through on a task and "doing it all by myself."

Identifying Activity Areas (Learning Centers). For many years, preschool programs have set aside parts of a room for different activities; thus, there is a block area, a music area, a science area, and so on. These locations, or zones, may be called *activity areas, play areas, centers of interest,* or *learning centers.* Today, learning centers are also used in elementary schools.

Activity areas, as identified in Figure 3-3 and Table 3-4, group all the items that are used together in one place so that they are on hand when needed. For example, the toy animals and trucks that children use with blocks are placed near the block area.

When things that go together are available, children get involved in using materials. They learn as they discover concepts for themselves. For instance, in making a "barn" for animals, John discovers that two unit blocks are the same length as one double-unit block.

Play Equipment. In the child development vocabulary, *toys* are called *play equipment.* They need to be well chosen, and there should be enough toys to encourage group play while meeting the needs of a child playing alone.

While you will not have the responsibility of selecting play equipment as a child care aide, you should recognize the characteristics of good play equipment. Equipment should be:

1. Simple, with parts that cannot come off
2. Attractive and pleasant to touch
3. Durable, well constructed, and in good working order
4. Versatile (can be used in more than one way and can be moved easily)
5. Stimulating enough to encourage children to do things for themselves
6. Easily stored in available space
7. Reasonably priced and of good quality

PROGRAM PLANNING

Everyone on the child care staff helps to plan the program. Staff members, children, and parents are considered part of the center's resources, and they all affect program planning. Of course, the educational director, the teachers, and the assistants are responsible for the actual planning. But child care aides help by sharing their thoughts about the children and the program.

Program planning takes place at staff meetings and during short, unscheduled meetings called *pop* (planning of program) *conferences*. For individual and group planning, special times (called *planning periods*) are scheduled. During these periods, the teacher and aide can be away from the children and can discuss them quietly in private.

Program planning for young children focuses on their experiences in the child care center. Plans are made for ways to teach, schedules, room arrangements, and equipment or resource materials. The planning process involves two main steps: (1) identifying program goals and (2) deciding how best to meet those goals.

IDENTIFYING PROGRAM GOALS

Why are goals important in planning a child care program? Caregivers know that children change their minds quickly and that good teachers act on children's interests and curiosity. They also know that children will stay with an activity longer when they themselves start it than when the teacher begins it. So why plan? Why not let the program just happen and let teachers concentrate on responding to the children? *Program goals* are used to keep the purpose of the program in mind. They show what is to be done, and they are important for these reasons:

1. *Long-term goals* give a direction to the program; they describe the program's purpose over a long period of time, perhaps months or years. For example, when a child care center first opens, only the most needed equipment may be available. With a long-range goal, staff members can select items to be added when more money becomes available.

2. *Short-term goals,* often called *objectives,* help to determine daily or weekly plans. They help the staff to work as a team. For example, after discussing Dan's shyness at a staff meeting, each person who works with Dan can help him to stand up for his own rights. As a result, Dan can overcome his shyness and his fear of other children.

3. If a goal is clearly stated and understood by all involved, each caregiver knows when it is reached. For example, if a goal for the 4-year-old group is to be able to walk the balance beam without stepping off of it, the balance beam is located so that children can use it while the staff watches. If a child is unable to meet the goal, special plans are made for him or her. When all children have been able to walk the beam, the goal has been reached.

4. Identifying short-term goals helps the staff prepare. After a planning session, workers know who is going to supervise various activities within the room. With such plans in mind, when the children arrive, you can give all your attention to them and their needs.

Identifying program goals is the first step in planning a program. In choosing goals, you must decide what is important for children and why it is important.

Not all child care programs have the same goals, for educators do not agree on the best way to help children learn. *Child-centered programs* focus on the children, using resources available. *Curriculum-centered programs* focus on the subjects to be taught and are often based on a specific set of educational methods.

WORKING TOWARD PROGRAM GOALS

Once goals have been established, the child care staff knows where the program is heading. The details of planning (such as what activities are included and when and where) then must be decided.

Program planning involves several things. The children's needs are considered, as is the center's schedule. Activities are chosen to meet the program goals, and teaching assignments are identified. Then the needed equipment, materials, and supplies are made available.

Children's Needs. As mentioned earlier, program goals should meet children's needs. Long-term goals focus on meeting the overall needs of groups of children. Short-term goals are more specific and focus on individual children within a specific group for a defined period of time.

Qualified child caregivers know that children's needs can be seen in their behavior. Therefore, in making plans, they consider the needs of individual children as well as the group's needs.

Teaching Strategies. When staff assignments are made, *teaching strategies* (the methods used in teaching) are decided. Plans to involve parents are discussed, so that children may continue their learning experiences at home.

Teaching strategies influence what methods will be used in children's programs. In some centers, teachers decide what will be in the program, while the children carry it out. In other centers, children choose from what is available. Child caregivers should provide a stimulating environment so that children can select or start their own learning experiences.

Children's *learning styles,* or the way they learn best, are different. Some children like the teacher to direct the instruction, while others like the freedom of choosing and making decisions. Table 3-5 shows the various teaching strategies and the choices available to children.

Table 3-5 TEACHING STRATEGIES IN CHILD CARE PROGRAMS

Child free play	Child free choice	Child chooses/ Teacher plans	Teacher plans and directs	Teacher directs
Child chooses what to do; no preparation or planned activity provided by the teacher.	Child chooses from pre-planned activities, equipment, and materials provided by teacher.	Children free to choose activities; preparation based on teacher's observation of individual children.	Preparation based on observation of individual children; children respond in small groups or as total group to teacher's direction.	Teacher directs whatever children do (may be based on educational goals). Activities are highly structured and tightly scheduled. Activities may include total group activities or individual activities assigned by teacher.

CHAPTER SUMMARY

1. A good child care program should:
   a. Have a well-qualified staff
   b. Plan for individual and group needs
   c. Match children's abilities with the activities offered
   d. Provide enough time, space, equipment, and materials
   e. Keep the environment orderly
   f. Prepare equipment and materials ahead of time
   g. Encourage children to start projects themselves and allow them to grow at their own rate

2. The most important resource in a child care program is a qualified staff of caregivers.

3. Program planning includes establishing program goals, outlining a routine, planning and preparing for activities, deciding on teaching strategies, making staff assignments, and coordinating efforts between the children's homes and the center.

4. Program planning helps a teaching staff meet both long- and short-term goals. It makes the best use of the center's resources because activities are prepared in advance, so that teachers, assistants, and aides can focus on the children.

5. Program goals vary. Some are child-centered and others are curriculum-centered.

6. Teachers have different ideas about the best way for children to learn. *Teaching strategies* are the methods or ways of teaching, and they affect which kinds of activities a program will include.

7. Children's needs should determine short-term program goals and should be considered in establishing long-term goals. Through training, child caregivers come to understand how children grow, how their experiences affect their behavior, and what is important to them.

• WHAT NEW TERMS HAVE YOU LEARNED?

Several new words and ideas were presented in this chapter. To see whether you understand them, match the letter of each term below with the numbered phrases under "Definitions."

Terms

a. Teaching strategies
b. Programs
c. Activity area
d. Objectives
e. Resources
f. Pop conferences
g. Qualified staff
h. Transition periods
i. Curriculum-centered program
j. Child-centered program
k. Limits
l. A child's learning style

Definitions

1. Program built around children's needs and interests, using resources available
2. Location in the room used for special activity such as art
3. Methods teachers use to help children learn
4. Staff, facilities, and money
5. Change-of-activity times
6. The most important resources in a child care program
7. Another word for *curriculum*
8. Short-term goals are sometimes called _____
9. The way a child learns
10. Short, unscheduled times for planning
11. All children do as teacher plans and says
12. Rules of the child care center

• PROJECTS, DECISIONS, ISSUES

1. Visit a day care center. Make a report to class of the daily schedule used in the day care program, the ages of the groups of children, and the activities used during the time blocks identified on the schedule.

2. Visit a child care center or children's laboratory and make a sketch of the placement of the equipment and materials. Identify activity areas or, if such an arrangement is not evident, arrange the room into effective activity areas (on paper).

3. Using descriptions selected from a catalog or provided by the teacher, evaluate three or more pieces of play equipment according to the qualities of good play equipment mentioned in this chapter.
4. Visit an early childhood education program and a child development program, then point out likenesses and differences between the two.
5. Check yourself:
   a. Do you share ideas with the staff?
   b. Do you respect children's play?
   c. Do you know the program goals of your child care center?
   d. Do you recognize qualities of good play equipment?
   e. Do you know program terms?
   f. Do you share information with the staff?

• WHIFS (WHAT WOULD YOU DO IF . . .)

1. Two-year-old Jason likes you better than any other staff members. What would you do?
   a. Bring him candy
   b. Nurture him
   c. Avoid him because you're not his teacher
   d. Guide him as you do the other children
   e. Tell all your friends
   f. Report his behavior at staff meeting
   g. Other solutions

2. Brian's father asks you if he can come to visit and play his harmonica for the children. What would you do?
   a. Tell him to come and make a date for his visit
   b. Thank him for offering
   c. Change the subject in a hurry
   d. Report his desire to your supervising teacher
   e. Tell him not to come, it's against center policy
   f. Ask him what songs he can play on the harmonica
   g. Other ideas

3. Your supervising teacher comments that Esther does not know her colors, but you have heard her name them correctly as she was stringing beads. What would you do?
   a. Watch and listen to Esther more closely
   b. Promptly tell your teacher that she's wrong
   c. Keep quiet and let the teacher find out for herself
   d. Tell your supervising teacher what you have heard Esther say
   e. Other ideas

4. The paths between the activity areas are not clearly defined and you have an idea regarding how to arrange them to allow easier movement between the activity areas. What would you do?
   a. Shove the furniture around when you get a chance
   b. Talk it over with your supervising teacher
   c. Complain about the room arrangement
   d. Tell a friend about your ideas
   e. Other ideas

5. Someone tells you that early childhood education is not the same as child development. What would you do?
   a. Disagree in no uncertain terms
   b. Agree pleasantly
   c. Tell the person you don't know
   d. Look up references
   e. Other ideas

• STUDENT ACTIVITIES

1. List three qualities of a good program for young children.
2. What conditions does a well-qualified staff provide in a child care setting?
3. Name four ways children grow and develop through play.
4. Describe three characteristics of good play equipment.
5. Identify three reasons for establishing program goals.
6. What items show that a child care center's program is planned?
7. Name three characteristics of the physical setting that affect the learning environment.
8. What two steps does a qualified staff take when planning a child care program?

PART TWO

CHILD CARE AIDES CARE FOR INFANTS AND TODDLERS

VERY YOUNG CHILDREN

Very young children are known as *infants* and *toddlers*. In this text, children are considered *infants* or *babies* up to 12 months of age. Infants differ in their physical characteristics and behavior. Most infants are not able to walk without help during the first year, a period usually called *infancy*.

When infants are able to walk without support (usually in the second year of life), they become *toddlers*. Children are called toddlers from the time they begin to walk alone until their movements are coordinated and sure enough so that they can walk without thinking about controlling their bodies (this usually occurs by the beginning of the third year).

Infants and toddlers each have special needs. Caregiving for infants is discussed in Chapter 4, and caregiving for toddlers is covered in Chapter 5.

NEEDS OF INFANTS AND TODDLERS

Infants and toddlers have many of the same needs. They need nurturing care, along with a responsive, healthy, and safe environment.

NURTURING CARE

Infants and toddlers require nurturing care as they are fed, dressed, and diapered or toileted. Infants are unable to do these things for themselves, and toddlers are just learning how to do them. In both cases, caregivers must help children with all or most of these routines.

You can easily see that it is important for caregivers to help with these routines in order to keep young children clean, comfortable, and well fed. But the *nurturing way* in which caregivers do this is just as important. In order to stimulate growth and learning, caregivers must use these daily routines as opportunities to love, cuddle, touch, talk to, and teach infants and toddlers.

Infants and toddlers must receive *consistent care*; that is, they should receive the same kind of care most of the time. In this way, they *build an attachment,* or close relationship, with another person. This is like building an "emotional bridge." Very young children are usually able to build attachments with a main caregiver and another caregiver if both these people respond to the infant's needs in similar ways.

Parents are usually the main or *primary* caregivers for infants and toddlers. When work causes parents to be away from their children during most of the time their children are awake, childcare workers serve as the primary caregivers for these children. Parents and caregivers need to work together to make sure that nurturing routines follow the same basic pattern every day and that these routines are the same in the center as they are in the home. When infants and toddlers are made to feel loved and cared for, they are able to build attachments. As a result, they learn to trust the people around them.

Changes between caregivers should be made smoothly. Infants and toddlers should be brought to the center early enough so that the parents can stay until children and caregivers are settled into the day's routine. The daily *transition,* or change, from one staff person to another is important. The center's schedule and staff assignments should be the same every day, so that infants and toddlers will receive consistent care. Staff members who relieve each other should allow enough time to compare notes on the children's day.

Since consistent care is so important in the lives of infants and toddlers, parents and caregivers must work together as a team. Parents and caregivers can work as a team by doing the following things:

What Parents Can Do

Have the infant or toddler immunized.

Fill out family history forms honestly.

What Caregivers Can Do

Call parents by name and make them feel welcome.

If a child is brought to the center in the parent's arms, you, the

What Parents Can Do

Arrive at the center early enough to allow transition time for consistent care.

Report to the caregivers anything that will make a difference in the infant's or toddler's day (patterns of eating, sleeping, or bowel movements).

Bring enough food and clothing each day.

Keep the center up to date about home and business phones and addresses.

Provide written permission when medicine is to be given.

Pick up the infant or toddler in time to find out about the day (feeding, sleep, activities, etc.).

Talk about the home activities of the infant or toddler.

Ask questions and be willing to learn.

Parents should remember that they are teachers, too.

What Caregivers Can Do

caregiver, should receive the child in your arms.

Speak slowly and calmly, in a friendly voice.

Make the child feel welcome by using body contact. Tell the parent to ''Have a nice day,'' and then quickly involve the child in an activity.

Enjoy yourself while you work with toddlers or infants and show it by the way you act.

Keep clear, honest records of the child's day (feeding, bowel movements, giving of medicine, etc.) and report this information to the parents.

Follow established routines regarding medication (written permission is usually required).

Have daily pop conferences. Schedule private conferences from time to time.

Encourage parents to talk by asking questions. (''Tell me where you feed Arthur at home. Does he use a high chair, or do you hold him?'')

Make suggestions to parents who have questions or problems. (''Don had a short nap today. He'll probably be ready for an early bedtime tonight.'')

Be a professional who respects parents' privacy.

A RESPONSIVE ENVIRONMENT

In Chapter 3, you learned that a good child care program should provide a *good match* between the environment and a child's growth stage. In this respect, infants and toddlers are like all children. They will develop in a healthy, normal way if the amount and kind of stimulation in their environment is suited to their rates of development.

In Chapters 4 and 5, you will learn specific ways in which the environment can stimulate infants and toddlers.

A HEALTHY, SAFE ENVIRONMENT

Good nourishment, protection from disease, and a setting that helps avoid accidents make up a healthy, safe environment in which to provide care for infants and toddlers.

Protection from Disease. Very young children can become sick very quickly. Centers that provide care for infants and toddlers must be sure to prevent diseases such as colds or flu, which are caught by being in close contact with someone who has them. The following health precautions should be taken with infants and toddlers:

1. You can protect infants and toddlers from exposure to diseases by limiting the number of people caring for them, by avoiding overcrowded areas, by carefully cleaning and disinfecting the equipment used by infants and toddlers, by removing dirty diapers and bedding promptly, and by making sure that food and play areas are clean.

2. Disease should be kept from spreading by keeping individual children's equipment separate, requiring all caregivers and children to have necessary immunizations (shots), and keeping sick infants and toddlers in *isolation* or apart from the group.

3. Caregivers should wash their hands immediately after diapering an infant and before handling food.

Some of these precautions are repeated in more than one chapter in this text because they are so important in any child care program. Caregivers must always be alert about health dangers and must practice good health care habits themselves.

Protection from Accidents. An *accident-proof environment* is a safe environment. Besides the general safety measures mentioned in Chapter 10, which should be part of any child care program, infants and toddlers have some special safety needs.

1. Toddlers and infants should never be left unsupervised without a protective barrier between them and dangerous places—as near water or a surface high off the floor or near stairs, heaters, and traffic ways. Supervision should be provided *at all times* outdoors. Caregivers must get rid of dangers such as barriers and shrubs, sharp objects, insects, bug killers, and fertilizer.

2. In order to handle emergencies, special plans must be made and all caregivers should know them. They should know several ways of removing infants and toddlers from the center in an emergency.

3. Paint used on cribs, playpens, and any equipment for infants and toddlers should be lead-free (nontoxic).

4. The bars on cribs and playpens should be spaced closely enough so that infants and toddlers cannot get their heads caught between them. Crib sides should always be locked in place.

5. Plastic bags, mattress and pillow covers, and any bits of plastic should be kept out of reach, as they can smother or strangle very young children.

6. Small or sharp parts should be removed from toys, and small objects should be kept out of infants' and toddlers' reach.

7. The cooking area should be separate from the child care area. Infants and toddlers should not enter the cooking area.

8. Water temperature should always be checked; it should be lukewarm for bathing infants and toddlers.

9. Clothing for infants and toddlers should be comfortable and should be designed so that it cannot strangle or trip a child.

GROUP CARE

Recent studies have shown that very young children can receive quality care in the group setting of a child care center. However, the center must provide a stimulating environment and enough trained caregivers so that children can build attachments as they receive nurturing care. Many parents now need infant and toddler care services, and the need is growing steadily. Thus, the demand for qualified infant and toddler caregivers will continue to grow.

Even though all their physical needs are met, infants and toddlers may suffer from inadequate care. Infants who are not receiving enough tender, loving care may respond in a physical way—they may suffer from skin rashes, vomiting, diarrhea, constipation, wheezing, body rocking, and failure to grow normally in height and weight. In toddlers, slow progress in speech growth or other areas of development may be the signal that their environment and the people in it are not meeting their needs.

When young children are not receiving enough stimulation from their environment, they may lose interest in their surroundings. And when the environment is too stimulating and has too many changes in routine, the children may become overactive.

4 | INFANTS:
THE DEPENDENT ONES

After you have studied Chapter 4, you should be able to:

1. Point out at least three special needs of infants
2. Name two main parts of a good infant program in a child care center
3. Tell what infants are like at different ages and what caregivers do to provide good infant care for them at these ages
4. Describe the process of diapering an infant, feeding an infant, bathing an infant, and taking an infant's temperature; demonstrate if possible

SPECIAL NEEDS OF INFANTS

Infants, as you know, are very young children—children in their first year of life. They are small and helpless, and they must depend on adults to care for and protect them.

During the period of infancy, growth and development occur at a rapid rate, bringing many changes in appearance and behavior. During infancy, we plant the roots for a child's later growth. Every bit of care babies receive affects the way they will grow and develop.

PHYSICAL CARE

Very young children must build attachments with their caregivers if they are to develop normally. For infants, it is far easier to build this kind of "emotional bridge" with one person than with several people. But an infant can usually build attachments with more than one person when each caregiver responds to the infant's needs in similar ways. When too many people care for a child in different ways, he or she becomes confused.

In very early infancy, babies have not learned to recognize one particular caregiver. Usually, by 6 months of age, they are familiar with the way caregivers care for them. They learn to anticipate things by the order in which they usually happen. It is very important to care for infants in the same way each time.

Physical Care. Caregivers provide for an infant's physical needs—feeding, cleanliness, rest, and so on.

Feeding. Infants should be fed enough nutritious food, but they should never be overfed. Feeding should not become the only answer to an infant's crying. Infants cry for many reasons, and hunger is only one of them. The feeding guidelines given by an infant's doctor should be followed, and the feeding pattern should be fairly regular. Solid foods and drinking from a cup should be allowed when the infant shows signs of being ready for them, such as appearing hungry after having the bottle or wanting to hold the bottle. Some infants refuse to take their food or spit it up after feeding. Others may eat everything given to them, as well as things they find. Extremes in eating are signs that infants are not being given the care they need.

Rest. As infants grow, they need less sleep. Individual infants have different needs for rest. Therefore decisions about the timing and length of rest periods should be made individually for each infant. As with eating, extremes of sleep in either direction are signs that care is inadequate. When they are very young, infants' natural rhythms and comfort help them to sleep. As they become more alert and respond more easily to the environment, they need quieter surroundings in order to rest.

Cleanliness. Infants should be kept clean and fresh, not only for their health but also for their comfort. Infants and their surroundings should be kept clean and sweet-smelling. If the infants' room in a child care center has a strong, unpleasant odor of urine and body wastes, it is not clean and is unpleasant both for the infants and for the caregivers who work with them.

Infants' bedding and cribs must be kept clean and dry. Floors and all equipment used by infants should be cleaned and disinfected daily. When they are vacant, infants' rooms should be aired by opening windows and doors.

A RESPONSIVE ENVIRONMENT

As you know, a responsive environment is made up of people and things that respond to infants. Responsive caregivers and/or objects that move or make noises help to make up a responsive environment. Infants' environments should match their levels of growth. Figure 4-1 shows you a responsive environment.

Much of the stimulation in an infant's environment must come from the caregivers. Nurturing routines offer opportunities to stimulate and teach infants. During routine activities, caregivers touch, cuddle, smile at, and talk to infants. In doing this, they encourage infants to communicate.

FREEDOM AND PROTECTION

Infants are always growing, so they need to be able to move freely. A good environment allows them to move freely while protecting them from harm at the same time.

EXPERIENCING THE ADULT WORLD

Infants need to meet other adults or older children and to become aware of the larger world. A stimulating environment lets infants experience and interact with people and things not directly involved in their nurturing routines.

Figure 4-1. Infants need an environment that is just stimulating enough without being overwhelming. (Michael Weisbrot)

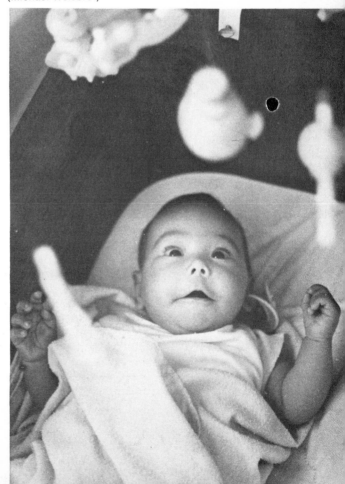

A GOOD INFANT PROGRAM

The two main parts of a good infant care program are (1) a carefully planned schedule for each infant in a healthy, safe, stimulating environment and (2) enough well-qualified infant caregivers.

A CAREFULLY PLANNED SCHEDULE

When infants are involved, *scheduling* means managing the whole day. Routine activities cannot be scheduled for infants in the same way as for older children. A schedule for infants should fill the following needs:

1. There should be an individual schedule for each infant.
2. As infants grow, they need a changing schedule of sleep, more play time, and a different feeding schedule.
3. Daily routines should be planned for individual infants, not groups. Not all babies will follow the same routines.
4. There should be opportunities for rest, eating, and play outside the crib (including time outdoors when the weather is nice) on a regular but flexible basis.
5. As much as possible, individual infants' routines at the center should fit into parents' scheduled time with their infants.
6. Individual attention (or special nurturing) and play with the same significant other should be provided each day.
7. There should be a balance between routines and variety within each day's framework.

WELL-QUALIFIED INFANT CAREGIVERS

Infant caregivers perform the same general duties each day. Most of these duties are concerned with physical care. Infant caregivers make decisions about how and when to feed, dress, or diaper infants. They decide what the temperature of the infants' room should be and how much clothing or cover to use. They choose the positions in which an infant is held and how to place the infant in the crib (on the stomach or back, at the head or foot of the crib). When an infant cries, caregivers determine what the reason is and how to respond to the crying. Since infants have no control over what happens to them, the caregivers make decisions about their needs.

Infant caregivers enjoy infants enough to perform the same routines week after week. They are patient, warm, and loving. They are sensitive to small changes in infants' behavior, and they know how best to respond to those changes.

OVERVIEW OF WHAT AN INFANT CAREGIVER DOES

During the first year of life, babies depend on caregivers to take care of them. Based on each baby's needs, the care is individualized and personalized. Most care focuses on physical needs. However, infant caregivers understand that babies have social, emotional, and intellectual needs besides physical ones. Therefore they plan ways to meet these needs, often making them part of the physical care.

Effective caregiving is based on sensitive and accurate observing. By watching carefully, caregivers see changes in babies' behavior when they occur. Some changes will relate to immediate needs. For example, the baby may wake up and cry. Past experience tells the caregiver that the baby is hungry. Changes in temperature, behavior, or appearance may indicate illness or the need for special help.

People who care for infants enjoy the thrill of "firsts" such as the first time the baby claps his or her hands together, the first time the baby rolls over, the first tooth, and so on. They watch for new developments and see them as part of the infant's growth during the first 12 months.

SPECIAL TASKS IN AN INFANT PROGRAM

There are many ways in which caregivers can make the infant's day at a child care center a stimulating learning experience.

Figure 4-2. This is one of the correct methods of carrying an infant. The child is held securely and the neck and head are given extra support. (Michael Weisbrot)

HANDLING INFANTS

It is as essential to handle infants as it is to feed them. An infant's sense of touch develops very early. The loving and caring that babies need to grow is communicated to them when they are held gently and securely by their caregivers.

As an infant caregiver, you need to understand that body touch, eye contact, and the rhythm of your heartbeat are comforting to infants. When you hold, feed, diaper, dress, cuddle, and talk to the infants in your care, you will become an important person—a *significant other*—in their lives. You help them to build an attachment for you. You help them develop a sense of trust toward you and others.

Figure 4-2 shows how to hold an infant properly—securely and with the infant's neck and head supported.

DIAPERING INFANTS

Chances are that you will be diapering each infant in your care several times each day. Make the experience safe, sanitary, and secure for the infants.

Diaper infants before and after feeding, before they are put to bed, and whenever they seem uncomfortable because they are wet. Infants' sleep should never be disturbed in order to diaper them, nor should they be diapered when they are hungry and crying for their bottle.

In most cases, parents bring a day's supply of diapers to the center each morning. Some centers offer diaper service for an additional fee; usually, a commercial diaper service or disposable diapers are used. Occasionally a center will launder its own diapers. Caregivers need to know what their center's procedure for using diapers is.

Diapers brought by parents should be used only on the baby for whom they are intended—especially when the diapers are nondisposable. A dirty, nondisposable diaper should be rinsed out in the toilet and stored in a marked plastic bag for the parents to pick up at the end of the day.

Most centers have a supply of extra diapers for emergencies. If diapers are laundered in your center, be careful to use mild soap; fold and store diapers neatly after they have been laundered.

Steps in Diapering. When diapering infants, you should:

1. Collect the things you will need: a clean, folded diaper; a clean, soft washcloth; lukewarm water; baby oil or lotion; talcum powder, and a toy for the infant to hold.
2. Wash your hands thoroughly.
3. Gently place the infant in a safe position on a washable surface—some centers use changing tables, while others use the infant's crib.
4. Always use a clean washcloth, towel, and water for each infant.
5. Speak softly to the infant as you remove the diaper pins or plastic strips—put open safety pins in a bar of soap, not in your mouth, on your clothing, or on the changing surface.
6. When changing an infant after a bowel movement, wipe the baby with the clean part of the dirty diaper—the dirty diaper should be put on a surface that can be disinfected, and it should be removed after you have finished. The infant should never be left alone while you remove the dirty diaper.
7. Sponge off the infant's buttocks with a washcloth and lukewarm water that you have tested on the back of your hand or on the inside of your elbow; talk to the infant while you work; separate the folds of skin around the infant's genitals, cleansing and removing any urine, bowel movement, or old powder.
8. Dry the area you have washed, using a gentle patting motion, and apply lotion or oil as directed by the parents.
9. Lift the infant's feet and place the folded diaper underneath the baby's buttocks. Figure 4-3 shows the steps for folding a diaper.
10. When pinning a diaper, place your fingers between the pin and the infant's body so that the pin does not accidentally poke the infant's skin.
11. If a disposable diaper is used, be sure the plastic strips on the sides are not pulled too tightly across the infant's tummy. Diapers should be snug but not tight or binding.
12. Smile at the infant and talk about the sweet, clean smell.
13. Put the infant in a clean crib while you remove all dirty items and disinfect the surface where the diapering took place.
14. Wash your hands; use a nailbrush if your fingernails are long.

BATHING INFANTS

Even though your center's policy may be to ask parents to give infants their daily bath, sometimes an infant may need bathing. You should know how to do it.

FEEDING INFANTS

There are three major changes in feeding during infancy:

1. For the very young infant, feeding is a time of body contact with the caregiver, and milk is the main food.
2. Within the first 6 months, solid foods are introduced as the infant's doctor recommends. The infant is learning to swallow and chew.
3. As infants become toddlers, they sit in high chairs or at feeding tables; now they become involved in feeding themselves.

Young Infants. Before feeding young infants, you should gather the things you will need for feeding. Then wash your hands and follow the parents' directions for formula preparation (warmed or not warmed), diet, amount of food,

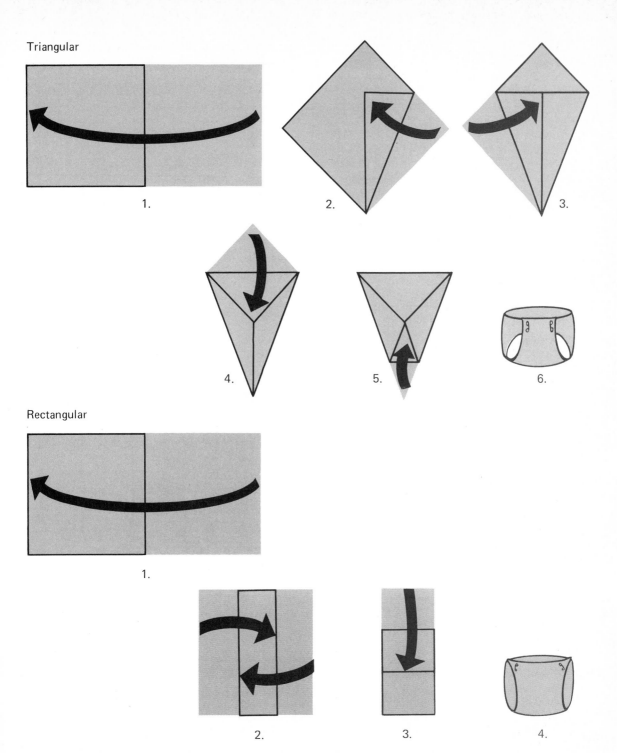

Triangular

Rectangular

Figure 4-3. Follow these steps when folding a diaper in a triangular or rectangular fashion. The triangular method is used most often for baby boys' diapers.

holding position, and schedule. Parents usually bring a daily supply of formula and baby food to the center. Make sure that each container or bottle is marked and kept cool until you are ready to use it.

All feeding equipment must be sterilized (washed in water hot enough to kill all germs) before use. Follow the procedures recommended in child care standards. If you have warmed the infant's formula, check the temperature on the inside of your wrist; it should feel lukewarm, just as bathwater should.

Make sure that the infant is wide awake, comfortable, dry, and hungry. Pick a comfortable chair and sit with the infant cradled in your arms. As in all other routines, it is important to cuddle, talk, and show affection for the infant during feeding. Try holding the infant on your left side, where your heartbeat will be heard.

As you hold the bottle, keep the neck and nipple always filled. Do not urge infants to take more than they want. Never prop the bottle or leave an infant alone to drink it. To burp an infant during feeding, place a diaper on your shoulder and hold the infant in the upright position. Then pat or rub the infant's back until you hear a burp. If you have difficulty in getting an infant to burp, it sometimes helps to lay him or her face down across your knees.

Most infants will spit up a small amount after feeding. This is usual and nothing to worry about. When an infant vomits, the amount will be larger, and the infant will gag or spit it up forcefully.

Caregivers should be calm, patient, and firm with infants during feeding in order to help them develop an eating pattern. If an infant falls asleep before the feeding is finished try burping the child to see whether he or she will wake up. If not, try to resume the feeding a little later on. (Never save an unfinished bottle until the next feeding!)

If an infant should wake and cry after a feeding, try to soothe him or her back to sleep or offer a little water rather than more food. (All water should be boiled before use!) Don't use the bottle as a pacifier if the baby will go to sleep without one. When the baby wakes up, offer the bottle only if you feel that he or she is not taking enough milk from a cup or glass.

It is important to help infants get into a regular, natural routine.

Figure 4-4. Feeding time is nurturing time; caregivers should be calm, patient and loving with infants. (Rohn Engh, Photo Researchers, Inc.)

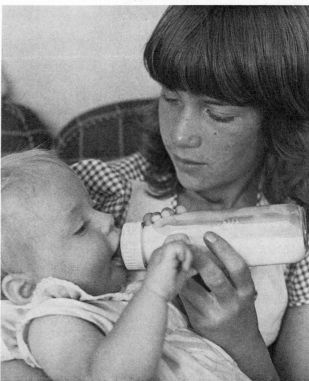

Solid Foods. When giving infants solid foods, hold them on your lap. Babies do not know quite what to do with solid food because they have not learned how to use the tongue and throat muscles to swallow. At the beginning, the food will probably come oozing out of their mouths. If the food on the spoon is placed inside the upper lip, the baby will suck the food to the back of the mouth, thus causing an involuntary swallow. In this way, infants will learn how to use their tongues to move food to the back of their mouths and swallow it. You can help them in this by opening and closing your own mouth so that the infants can imitate you.

In giving infants their first solid food, do it when they are hungry and feeling good—the morning is usually a good time. Offer a familiar food first, and then introduce the new solid food. It should be fully cooked, lukewarm, and soft (semiliquid or mashed). Prepare only small portions, and offer the solid food on a spoon. If cereal is the solid food, it should be thinned with formula or milk.

Always let an infant get used to one new food for a few weeks before you offer another. When you are introducing something new, serve it along with a familiar food you know the infant likes. This provides continuity and ensures that the infant will get enough to eat. If a new food is turned down, try it again at a later time, since the infant simply may not have been feeling well.

Introduce infants to a cup slowly. Offer them a cup at the end of their meal, when they are not so hungry. The *weaning* (or getting away) from the bottle should be slow and easy. You should start by letting infants drink water or juice from a cup, especially after a feeding. Once they show you that they enjoy this, help them to give up the bottle, but do not rush them. When they are 7 or 8 months of age, try seating infants in a high chair or at a feeding table. This gives them a chance to respond to their environment. It also frees you to use both hands for feeding.

ILLNESS

Changes in infants' behavior may mean they are sick. As a caregiver, you should watch for the following signs.[1] A baby may be ill if he or she:

· Is cross though usually happy and playful
· Awakens often and cries though he or she usually sleeps well
· Becomes sleepy and loses interest though is usually playful and active
· Has hot, dry skin with little color or has a fever
· Has a stiff neck
· Pulls at one or both ears
· Vomits (but all babies spit up at times)
· Has bowel movements that are loose and watery, change color, increase in number, or are very hard
· Coughs, is hoarse, or has a runny nose
· Cries as though in pain
· Breaks out in a rash
· Twitches in the arms, legs, or face

A pained cry may be only a delayed burp. If a rash appears, it may indicate an allergy or a disease.

Taking Rectal Temperature. If you suspect that an infant is ill, the first thing to do is to take the *rectal temperature*, which is the temperature in the rectum rather than the mouth. Look at the thermometer and shake the mercury until it is below normal. Dip the bulb of an infant's thermometer in petroleum jelly or cold cream. Place the infant on his or her stomach across your knee or on his or her back on your lap, holding the feet as you would in diapering. In either of these positions, the infant will not be able to squirm out of your grasp.

When the infant is in position, push the thermometer very gently into the rectal opening, letting the thermometer find its own direction. If you hold the thermometer stiffly, it may poke or hurt the infant. Lay the palm of your hand across the infant's buttocks and hold the thermometer lightly between two fingers so that you can control it. Figure 4-5 shows you the posi-

[1]U.S. Department of Health, Education, and Welfare, *Infant Care*, Children's Bureau, Publication No. 8, 1963, p. 72.

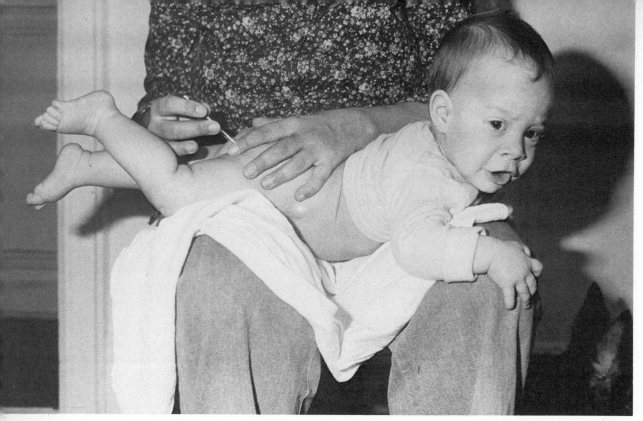

Figure 4-5. This is one correct position for taking rectal temperatures. (Michael Weisbrot)

tion for taking rectal temperatures. A squirming, twisting infant may be hurt if you hold the thermometer too firmly once it is in place.

After 2 minutes, remove the thermometer and turn it between your thumb and index finger until you see the silver band of mercury. After noting the infant's temperature, clean the thermometer by washing and rinsing it twice. Be careful not to use hot water, since this will cause it to break. Dry the thermometer and return it to its assigned place.

Caring for Sick Infants. If an infant's temperature is 101°F [38.3°C] or higher, notify your supervisor. When infants are sick, be strict in following the child care center's procedures. Because infants can become seriously ill so quickly, parents are usually notified at once when a baby shows signs of illness.

Caregivers must try to keep sick infants comfortable until their parents arrive. If the infant has a fever, it is always safe and helpful to offer liquids and to wipe the baby's forehead with a cold cloth. As a caregiver, you probably will want to hold the infant upright and perhaps walk back and forth very slowly, since rhythmic or rocking motion eases pain. The infant will find your motions and the warmth of your body soothing. Whatever you do, do not give the infant any medicine, not even baby aspirin. Your supervising teacher will tell you what to do if an infant becomes ill.

The American Academy of Pediatrics gives the following guidelines with respect to medication for infants and toddlers: "It shall be the responsibility of the director to supervise the administering of medication. Such medication to be adequately labeled, prescribed by a physician, and accompanied by a written request and authorization by parent or guardian to be kept on file."[2]

[2]American Academy of Pediatrics, *Day Care Standards for Children 0–3 Years, 22 Jan., 1970, VI-3*.

INTELLECTUAL STIMULATION
OF INFANTS

It is almost impossible to separate one area of development from another in respect to the activities that stimulate infants' growth. This is especially true with young infants, who are learning so many things at such a rapid rate. Certain kinds of behavior on the part of caregivers stimulate infants' intellectual growth.

Selecting Play Activities. In play, infants make discoveries about themselves and their environment. They learn to use their five senses, their large and small muscles, and their vocal cords. And play lets infants practice what they learn. Infants play by themselves and with their main caregivers; this play is important in their small world. Simple actions such as folding and unfolding the hands or reaching for a bird on a crib mobile are examples of infant play. Infants need quiet times during which they can play with their hands and feet and can make discoveries about their bodies.

Caregivers can help make play a stimulating learning experience for infants. They can respond in the following ways to *infant cues*, or signals given by infants:

At approximately 3 Months

1. When an infant begins to watch movements and seems to follow them with its eyes, caregivers should try placing a simple mobile near the crib for the infant to watch. Caregivers should also keep eye contact with infants when talking to or holding them. Infant caregivers should make their voices and faces expressive. Moving an object from side to side in front of an infant is another way to help visual development.

2. When infants begin to show interest in toys by watching and reaching for them, caregivers should place a few toys within sight and reach. If infants become upset when a toy falls out of reach, caregivers should try to stay nearby to return fallen toys. Tying some toys to the crib is a good way to encourage infants to try to reach fallen toys themselves later on.

3. When an infant is able to hold a toy for even a very short while, caregivers should put the toy (probably a rattle) in the infant's hand, replacing it when it drops. By watching carefully, caregivers will know when an infant tires of this kind of play.

At approximately 6 Months

1. When infants begin to look (even for a moment or two) for a toy that has disappeared from their sight, caregivers should show them how to get back the toys that are tied to the crib. The action should be repeated a few times while talking to the infant.

2. When an infant is able to uncover a toy that is hidden from sight, caregivers can play a hide-and-seek game by putting a toy under the crib blanket. While the infant watches, let her or him find the toy. "I-see-you" and "peek-a-boo" games also help infants to learn how to remember objects that are out of sight.

3. Infants may start to examine and poke toys with their fingers, looking at them very carefully. At this point, caregivers should give infants a few toys at a time to examine.

At approximately 9 Months. At this age, infants will begin to have a favorite toy or to prefer one toy over another. Caregivers should respect infants' preferences by keeping favorite toys nearby. But you should also give other toys to the infants, so that they will not depend on their favorites. Adding a new toy from time to time is a good idea.

At approximately 12 Months. At 1 year, infants may begin to put one object inside of another. Caregivers should provide stacking toys in different sizes, shapes, and colors to stimulate the development of infants' awareness of size and form.

Selecting Toys. Here are some general guidelines to follow when selecting toys for babies. Infants' toys should be:

1. Large enough so that they cannot be swallowed

2. Free of small pieces that can fall off or be removed

3. Clean and in good repair

4. Washable, well constructed, and made of

material that will not splinter or break (wood or metal, for example, rather than plastic or cardboard)

5. Stimulating to the infant's interest and creativity
6. Matched to the infant's stage of development
7. Usable without supervision

Speech Development. Infants must have speech to copy, and they are encouraged to talk by caregivers who talk and listen to them. Infants who have little chance to hear people talk will not develop normal speech.

Between 3 and 6 months, infants will make noises by themselves (gurgling, cooing) in response to hearing similar sounds from others. Caregivers should smile and talk to infants, encouraging their noises. In responding to babies, use a calm, gentle manner, since too strong a response will overwhelm them. When infants begin to show that they are able to tell where a sound is coming from, try calling them without being in their sight. Substitute words for immediate action, such as "I'm coming to fix your diaper. I'll be there soon."

At 6 months, infants will begin to make recognizable sounds. Talk back to them, making sentences out of the sounds they use. For example the baby may make the sound *ba*. Respond by saying, "You want your bottle." As infants begin to say words (*dada, mamma*), caregivers should encourage their efforts by responding with sentences that use those words.

Between 9 and 12 months, most infants begin to understand the simple words caregivers use. Caregivers should make a game of this, repeating the phrase the infant understands, watching the infant react to it, and encouraging responses. Infants of a year will have a vocabulary of about four words that they can understand *and* say. They can understand a larger number of words when spoken by the caregiver. Caregivers should talk to infants in short, descriptive sentences, and they should use eye contact to stimulate language development.

PHYSICAL DEVELOPMENT OF INFANTS

Infants need encouragement and freedom in order to develop their small and large muscles. Caregivers can provide for these needs in the following ways.

From 3 to 6 Months. Between 3 and 6 months, infants progress from a stage of undirected movements, such as kicking and waving arms, to the point where they are able to roll from their stomachs to their backs and back again. Caregivers should allow infants to be free of clothing and covers so that they can kick and wave. When infants are able to raise their heads as they lie on their stomachs, try putting them in different positions in the crib. But be careful not to block their view of things. This will encourage infants to raise their heads and look around.

When infants begin to roll from stomach to back, encourage them by placing them on firm surfaces that will assist their rolling activities. As always, do not leave infants unattended when they are out of their cribs.

As infants become able to sit up straight when supported and later to sit alone, caregivers should respond by holding infants in their laps, next to them, or on the floor in a sitting position. As infants become able to sit without

Figure 4-6. As a caregiver, you should smile and talk to infants. Encourage them to make sounds and talk back. (Mimi Cotter)

support for their heads, caregivers should encourage them by pulling them gently to a sitting position for a short period.

From 6 Months to 1 Year. In the second half of their first year, infants are able to sit up, either alone or with help, and finally they are able to pull themselves up by holding onto the side of the crib or playpen. Infants who do this are sometimes referred to as *pull-ups*.

The world looks quite different to infants from this point of view. It is important that they have the chance to see different objects in different places from their new viewpoint. They also need to move around in protected places, both indoors and outdoors. These areas should have things infants can use to pull up—crib or playpen bars, railings, or furniture. In this way they will become curious and gain confidence. Infants gain confidence when *they* can make a difference in their environment.

Then infants begin to crawl—first on their stomachs, then up on their knees and rocking back and forth, and finally on all fours. Provide a safe, quiet environment for infants, and encourage crawling by dressing them in comfortable clothing that allows movement. Caregivers can further stimulate crawling by talking to crawling infants, calling to them and encouraging them to come to the caregiver.

SOCIAL AND EMOTIONAL DEVELOPMENT OF INFANTS

A stimulating environment and nurturing care will help infants to grow socially and emotionally. The interaction between infants and their caregivers provides the basis for their emotional and social development through childhood and into adult life.

Guidance. The attachment between an infant and a caregiver helps the infant to learn what is acceptable behavior and what is not. Infants communicate by crying, and caregivers should respond to their cries quickly. Caregivers learn to know infants and are able to understand the meaning of their cries. You will not spoil an infant by answering cries. Instead the baby will cry much less than those whose cries are often

Figure 4-7. Learn to recognize the symptoms of various infant problems and behaviors so that you can handle them effectively. (Joan Menschenfreund)

ignored. As infants learn to identify the voice of their caregivers, a call from the caregiver may answer their cry.

CONCERNS FOR INFANTS IN GROUP CARE

Certain behaviors are common to infancy. In addition, some problems are characteristic of infants in groups. Recognizing the following behaviors and problems, as well as their possible causes, is a first step in handling them effectively:

1. Thumbsucking is a natural pacifier for infants, and they use it most often when they are upset or tired. Don't call attention to it

or make it a problem. The use of pacifiers may be encouraged by some physicians; however, because it is unsanitary, it is discouraged in group care of infants.

2. *Diarrhea* (frequent, loose bowel movements) is of great concern. First, it can lead to a loss of water and an imbalance of salt in the infant's body; second, it may be infectious.

   Infant caregivers should take extreme precautions to minimize any risk that the diarrhea will spread to other babies.

   Give infants as much fluid as they will take, and call their parents to alert them and perhaps get some ideas about the cause.

   Parents are advised not to bring infants to the center if diarrhea is evident the next morning.

3. *Constipation* (lack of bowel movement) is seldom serious in infants; in fact, not all infants have daily bowel movements. All infants strain to eliminate during the first few months. Hard, dry bowel movements can usually be controlled by increasing the infants' fluid intake or by changing their diets.

4. Teething by itself does not usually account for actual illness, but it may make infants very uncomfortable. You can help by giving a baby toast or a teething ring to ease sore gums and by being extra patient with infants during the teething period.

5. *Diaper rash* (chafing in the diapered area) is often observed by infant caregivers. Acid from the urine may burn the soft tissue of the baby's buttocks, causing the chafing. Caregivers should work together with parents to clear up the rash. An effort is made to keep the baby dry and comfortable by gently changing the diaper. A soothing lotion or medicated powder may ease the problem.

6. Babies depend on adults for their total care; therefore parents who neglect infants are, in fact, abusing them. Caregivers should report signs of major neglect or abuse of infants to the supervising teacher.

WORKING WITH PARENTS

Guidelines for cooperation between caregivers and parents appear in the introduction to Part II. These should be followed carefully in an infant care program.

CHAPTER SUMMARY

1. The term *infancy* refers to the first 12 months in a child's life. An *infant*, or baby, is therefore any child under a year old. Infants require special care for many reasons.

2. Infants are small and helpless. They must depend on adults to care for and protect them. Infants grow and develop very rapidly in all areas—physical, intellectual, emotional, and social. As they grow and develop, their behavior naturally changes along with their bodies. As infants' strengths and abilities increase, their interests, responses, and understanding change.

3. Because babies have such special needs, the quality and regularity of the care they receive is very important, whether they receive that care at home or in a child care center.

4. A center that provides care for infants must plan special programs and must take measures to ensure the infants' safety, comfort, and health.

5. A child care center for infants must have good communication with the parents of each infant so that special needs and problems can be handled effectively.

● WHAT NEW TERMS HAVE YOU LEARNED?

Several new words and ideas were presented in this chapter. To see whether you understand them, match the letter of each term below with the numbered phrases under "Definitions."

Terms

a. Infants
b. Infant cues
c. Rectal temperature
d. Diarrhea
e. Diaper rash

f. Weaning
g. Infant cries
h. Isolation
i. Pull-ups
j. A good match

Definitions

1. Chafing in the diaper area
2. Frequent, loose bowel movements
3. The way infants communicate
4. Getting children away from the bottle
5. Determining baby's temperature by using rectal thermometer
6. Children in the first year of life
7. The signals babies give to caregivers
8. Keeping a baby away from other infants
9. Infant's environment matches level of growth
10. Infants who pull up in crib

• PROJECTS, DECISIONS, ISSUES

1. Indicate whether you *agree* or *disagree* with the following statements; comment on your answers.
   a. Whatever you do to make a baby feel more comfortable is a good idea.
   b. A child care worker knows a baby better than the pediatrician and should be the one to determine the infant's schedule.
   c. Nurturing is as important to an infant as food and rest.
   d. Infants are learning so much that they need protection from being overstimulated.
   e. The way to feed and hold babies differs with the baby, the caregiver, and the setting.

2. Visit a child care center that cares for five or more infants. Try to observe the caregivers for 2 hours or more. Describe the characteristics of the infants, the personal qualities of the caregiver that you see, and the decisions the caregiver makes in working with infants. Report your observations to the class.

3. Choose one of the following and demon-strate to your classmates the proper procedure to use in:
   a. Taking an infant's temperature.
   b. Caring for an infant who has a fever
   c. Bathing and/or changing clothing
   d. Folding a diaper
   e. Feeding an infant
   f. Holding an infant

• WHIFS (WHAT WOULD YOU DO *IF* . . .)

1. An infant stops crying immediately after being picked up. What would you do?
   a. Keep on holding the infant so that there would be no more crying
   b. Put infant down because crying was for attention
   c. Report to your supervisor that the baby is ill
   d. Take the baby's temperature orally
   e. Make baby comfortable by changing diaper
   f. Burp and feed the baby
   g. Spank and put infant to bed
   h. Other responses

2. You are given responsibility for intellectually stimulating Susan, who is 3 months old. What would you do?
   a. Talk to her
   b. Read her the story of the Three Bears
   c. Sing a lullaby
   d. Smile at her
   e. Cuddle her close to you
   f. Sit her in a chair and show her pictures of alphabet letters
   g. Other responses

3. You discover when changing a diaper that Jonathan has diarrhea. What would you do?
   a. Wash his buttocks and put on a clean diaper
   b. Call your supervising teacher
   c. Call his parents
   d. Isolate him from the other infants
   e. Give him some water
   f. Say nothing; most infants have diarrhea
   g. Other responses

4. Your supervising teacher tells you that James, who is 9 months old, is beginning to crawl, and that you are to encourage his physical development. What would you do?
   a. Exercise his legs in his crib
   b. Hold him up so that he can walk
   c. Put him on a protected carpet area
   d. Hand him a toy so he will stay in one place
   e. Call to him and encourage him to crawl toward you to get a toy you have in your hand
   f. Other responses

• STUDENT ACTIVITIES

1. Name at least three special needs of infants and give examples of each.
2. What are the two main parts of a good infant care program in a child care center?
3. List four points to keep in mind when planning infant schedules.
4. What play activities would you choose for infants at 3 months? 6 months? 12 months?
5. Why is it important to talk to infants?
6. Name four guidelines to use when selecting toys for infants.
7. Tell how caregivers can help infants develop the small and large muscles.
8. Name three reasons why babies cry.
9. Cite four concerns of caregivers for infants in groups.
10. Describe three qualities of a good program for infants.
11. Describe the conditions provided by a well-qualified staff in a child care setting.
12. Name four ways children grow and develop through play.
13. Describe three characteristics of good play equipment.
14. Identify three reasons for establishing program goals.
15. Name several items indicating that a child care center's program is planned.
16. Name three characteristics regarding the physical setting that affect the learning environment.
17. Check yourself. Do you like infants because:
    a. They are so little and need someone to care for them
    b. They smell so good when they have just been diapered
    c. I know how important the first year of a child's life is
    d. I am sensitive to their cues
    e. My decisions affect the rest of their lives
    f. Other reasons

Or do you dislike infants because
    g. They cry a lot
    h. They smell when they have messy diapers
    i. You can never leave them unsupervised
    j. They are boring because they sleep a lot
    k. They cannot talk to you
    l. Other reasons

5 TODDLERS: THE "INTO-EVERYTHING" ONES

After you have studied Chapter 5, you should be able to:

1. Point out the special needs of toddlers
2. List three qualities of a good toddler program in a child care center
3. Describe four or more desirable personal traits of toddler caregivers
4. Summarize and demonstrate where possible how toddlers should be cared for by caregivers in a child care center

CHARACTERISTICS OF TODDLERS

Toddlers are young children who are just beginning to take their first steps. Between the ages of 1 and 3—during *toddlerhood*—they literally *toddle* from place to place.

Most toddlers are in diapers and walk with what is called a *diaper gait*; that is, they walk with their legs far apart for comfort and balance. Their steps are uneven and unsure, and they often fall. Most toddlers do not stiffen their bodies when they fall. Since they are short, they do not fall very far. Therefore, toddlers usually do not hurt themselves when they take a tumble. Young toddlers use their hands for balance, holding their arms high and stretched out. Older toddlers, whose steps are more even, will begin to use their hands and arms for carrying things.

Because the ability to walk without help—or *independent mobility*—is new to toddlers, they have a feeling of independence. In addition, they often test the rules or limits set down by their caregivers. The different aspects of their development are more easily identified as toddlers grow. Their physical development centers around muscle control and growth. Their language and problem-solving skills are signs of intellectual development, and their increased attachment to their caregivers shows emotional development. Toddlers learn to play with other children as a part of their social development.

SPECIAL NEEDS OF TODDLERS

Toddlers have certain needs that are special to their age group.

Figure 5-1. Young toddlers often walk with their legs spread far apart and their arms outstretched for better balance. (Michael Weisbrot)

SEPARATION ANXIETY

The fear and insecurity that result from separation are called *separation anxiety*. This feeling is at its highest point during toddlerhood. Toddlers have not learned to anticipate future events, so they are not able to understand that separation from the caregiver is only temporary. As a result, toddlers often become upset when they are separated from the person to whom they have become attached. Most toddlers have difficulty in coping with changes in their caregivers, routines, and environment.

BEHAVIOR

Toddlers often have problems because their behavior is different from that expected by adults. Toddlers, therefore, need adults who know what kind of behavior can be expected.

LANGUAGE

During the toddler years, children begin to talk.

In order to do this, they need models to copy. Therefore, people must talk to and listen to toddlers if language is to develop.

SELF-SUFFICIENCY

When toddlers learn to do things for themselves, they are becoming self-sufficient and are developing *self-help skills* and *autonomy*. This learning process can sometimes be slow for toddlers. Their efforts can be clumsy and unsuccessful. Toddlers are eager to do things for themselves, however, and they need adults who are patient and encouraging.

EXPLORING IN SAFETY

Toddlers are explorers who get into everything. This exploration is an important part of their development. But toddlers are not aware of danger, and they do not understand what belongs to them and what belongs to someone else. It is important that toddlers have an environment that is safe *for* them and *from* them. They must be protected from danger, and things that they can damage or break should be kept out of their reach.

A GOOD TODDLER PROGRAM

The qualities of a good toddler care program are basically the same as those needed in all child care programs. First of all, a toddler program should include play activities and language experiences that promote learning and offer a good match with the toddler's growth stage. The environment should provide *stimulation*, so as to help toddlers develop good self-concepts. Finally, nurturing care should be given.

In addition to the personal qualities needed by all child caregivers, patience and alertness are most important in people who work with toddlers. Active toddlers are always testing rules and limits. Accidents occur more often during this period than during any other stage of childhood. Thus, toddler caregivers must be alert and quick to act.

ASSISTING WITH A TODDLER PROGRAM

Before studying specific ways to take care of toddlers, let's look at an overview of toddler development and at how caregivers can respond to toddlers' growth.

DAILY ROUTINES OF TODDLERS

Daily routines and play activities can help toddlers to learn when caregivers understand how to encourage and stimulate learning.

Most of a toddler's day is made up of routines. Toddlers want to learn self-sufficiency, and caregivers can help them do this. One way they can help is by keeping routines as free as possible from time limits and adult rules.

Feeding. Feeding is an important experience for toddlers because they are learning to feed themselves. This can be a messy business, but caregivers can make it pleasant for toddlers by doing the following things:

1. Making sure that the activity period before the meal is a quiet one—an excited or overtired toddler is not a good eater
2. Encouraging toddlers to use the bathroom and always to wash their hands before the meal
3. Making sure that mealtimes—and the dining area—are calm and quiet, so that the toddlers can enjoy the food and feeding themselves
4. Acting calmly and not being concerned about table manners
5. Using good table manners so that toddlers can learn from watching caregivers
6. Understanding that toddlers need to touch food and eat it with their hands
7. Making certain that eating utensils are safe and the right size for toddlers
8. Making sure that drinking cups are the right size for toddlers to hold and are not more than half full, which will prevent some of the spills
9. Using tables and chairs that are a comfortable size for toddlers
10. Giving toddlers small portions of food
11. Offering both new and familiar foods at meals to toddlers
12. Serving foods in an attractive way, offering a variety of foods with different colors, textures, and flavors
13. Giving help when it's needed

Toileting. Toilet "training" is an unfortunate term because it implies that a toddler is "trained." Actually, toileting is the process of helping toddlers and young children to develop control of *urination* and bowel movements (the passage of *feces*). It is a gradual process and may take a long time. Toddlers have to control their rectal and bladder muscles before they can use the toilet in an acceptable way.

There are three basic steps in toilet training: (1) *bowel control*, (2) *bladder control* during waking periods, and (3) control of the bladder during sleep. Caregivers are mostly involved with helping toddlers to achieve bowel and bladder control during waking periods.

Since toddlers naturally want to be self-sufficient, they are usually interested in learning control. They are generally ready to begin between 18 and 30 months of age. Caregivers can help, first with bowel control and later with bladder control. With bowel control, caregivers can encourage toddlers by:

1. Watching for signs that toddlers are ready to learn control (when the periods between wetting are longer and the toddler shows interest in the toilet habits of other children and in using the bathroom).

2. Putting training pants on toddlers during the day. (The change will remind toddlers to stay dry.)

3. Making sure parents are dressing toddlers in easy-to-manage clothing that allows them to use self-help skills.

4. Recognizing individual toddlers' signs that they are about to have a bowel movement and placing them on the potty chair at that time.

5. Understanding that there may be no results at first, while the toddlers become familiar with the bathroom and the potty chair.

6. Making sure that toddlers are seated comfortably and securely on potty chairs or toilet seats that are steady. (Toddlers need to have support for their feet and arms so that they can balance themselves.)

7. Acting in a pleasant, calm, unhurried way during toileting. (Anger, disgust, or scolding will upset toddlers.)

8. Helping toddlers to remove clothing as needed, but encouraging them to "do it for themselves," even though it may take longer.

9. Praising toddlers when they are successful, understanding their pride in their success, and inviting them to flush the toilet themselves. (Otherwise, the caregiver will do it after they have left the bathroom.)

10. Encouraging toddlers, but not pushing them. (Praising success too much or scolding failure can make toddlers feel pressured.)

11. Never leaving toddlers on potty chairs or toilet seats longer than 5 minutes.

Not all toddlers will have a bowel movement every day or at a regular time. Parents will give caregivers information about their toddler's bowel habits. In turn, caregivers will record any bowel movements the toddler has (what time it took place, if the movement was hard or soft, if the toddler "strained," and so forth).

Toddlers usually begin to be interested in learning bladder control at about 18 months of age. Caregivers can help them in this by following the same guidelines used in bowel control. Toddlers will learn to control their bladders during the hours they are awake. Nighttime control takes longer, and parents usually supervise this part of toilet training. But caregivers should remember that naptime control is like nighttime control. Diapers during naptime are probably a good idea.

At first, a little boy is likely to sit down to urinate. The caregiver should help him aim his penis into the toilet. Fathers should be encouraged to show their sons how to urinate in a standing position. Caregivers can help by letting boy toddlers watch older boys at the center urinating in this manner. Little girls may want to stand too, but they will quickly learn that this doesn't work for girls. They too need encouragement and will be helped by watching other girls who are somewhat older.

Caregivers need to understand that excitement, hard play, illness, or change in routine can make toddlers "forget" their bladder control. They may have accidents every once in a while.

Nap time. Toddlers normally need only an afternoon nap. Lunch is usually scheduled early in the day and is followed by the afternoon nap. This helps toddlers to get enough rest *and* be ready for an early bedtime. Caregivers need to do the following things when supervising toddlers' nap time:

1. Make sure a quiet activity is scheduled right before nap time.

2. Make sure that the room is darkened and quiet. Soft music may encourage relaxation.

3. Provide a bed and blanket for each toddler.

4. Help toddlers take off shoes and tight-fitting clothing.
5. See that each toddler is settled, giving personal attention where needed. Sometimes a back rub helps to settle a child.
6. Work in a calm, organized way.
7. Supervise toddlers all during their nap.

Dressing and Bathing. As with infants, bathing toddlers at a child care center is done only as needed, not as a daily routine. The same safety procedures apply to both groups. However, toddlers should be encouraged to wash and then dress themselves, under careful supervision. Caregivers should praise and encourage self-help in washing and dressing, but they must be ready to help toddlers as needed. Caregivers should help toddlers to enjoy the routine of washing hands. They should make toddlers feel that self-help in dressing is an accomplishment by praising the toddlers' efforts.

PLAY AND PLAY ACTIVITIES OF TODDLERS

There is a change in the way toddlers play as they develop. At first, babies play with their own bodies. They watch and move their hands, fingers, feet and toes.

By the time they become toddlers, they are able to play with their caregivers. They enjoy smiling and making sounds, action songs and games, handling large objects, and scribbling with a crayon. They watch caregivers turn the pages of a book and then learn to do it themselves.

Toddlers also enjoy playing by themselves with their own toys. This is called *solitary play*. At this point, toddlers are not ready to share toys, because they do not understand the ideas of owning, lending, and sharing. They do not understand that when another child borrows a toy, it is not being taken away forever.

Toddlers play alongside or near other children, but not with them. This is known as *parallel play*. They do not play together in *cooperative play*, as older children do.

Selecting Play Activities. Caregivers can help toddlers to enjoy and learn from play by using the following guidelines:

Figure 5-2. All toddlers go through a stage during which they prefer to play by themselves with their own toys (left). This is called solitary play. (Rita Freed, Nancy Palmer Photo Agency) Sometimes, they prefer to play alongside but not with other children (right). This is called parallel play. (Etienne Marcel)

1. Select toys and activities that match the toddler's age and abilities. Choose safe items to be pushed, pulled, stacked, and handled.

2. Select varied and interesting activities and toys that need few or no rules and lead to success or variety in use. Examples are dough, clay, cloth dolls, balls, and puzzles with a few large pieces.

3. Remember that toddlers have a short *attention span*. That is, they do not spend a lot of time with a toy or activity; they quickly lose interest.

4. Encourage toddlers' play and self-help efforts with praise and pleasure.

5. Give help only when it is needed, encouraging toddlers to try it alone first.

6. Supervise climbing or any other possible dangerous activity closely, but offer help only when necessary.

7. Offer a selection of toys that are alike in shape, use, and color when supervising a group of toddlers. (Toddlers usually want what someone else has, so it is a good idea to provide at least two of the same kind of toy for the group.)

Selecting Toys. How do caregivers know what kinds of toys are best for toddlers? To begin with, toddlers' play equipment should have all the qualities of good toys that were listed in Chapter 3. The kinds of toys that provide good learning experiences for toddlers do have special characteristics, but often, they are not toys at all. Instead, objects found around the home or the center—such as cardboard boxes, plastic bowls, pots and pans, or toys that can be made easily from everyday materials—are good for toddlers. The following list gives some good ideas.

1. *Stacking and/or nesting toys.* Collect cartons, cans, boxes (and so on) that will fit inside each other. Cover them with vinyl self-adhesive paper or paint them with lead-free paint.

2. *Drop containers.* Choose boxes, cartons, and plastic jars without tops or with a slit in the top. Drop small objects through the slit. These may be painted with lead-free paint or covered with vinyl self-adhesive paper.

3. *Pull toys.* Pull toys may be made by attaching a rope or string to almost anything: spools, toilet-paper rolls, plastic bottles, bells, egg cartons, wooden blocks.

4. *Clothespins and can.* Paint a can with lead-free paint (be sure the top rim is smooth). Paint clothespins to be hung over the edge.

5. *Texture book.* Cut pieces of fabric-backed wallpaper or heavy, plastic-coated fabric twice as large as you want the book to be. Stack two pieces, one on top of the other, and sew them through the center. On each page, sew or glue materials of different textures and shapes: corduroy, velvet, leather, fur, sponge, cardboard with ridges, oilcloth, satin, and terry cloth.

6. *Blocks.* Make large blocks by stuffing shoe boxes or milk cartons with newspaper. Tape covers in place and cover them with vinyl self-adhesive paper.

7. *Water table.* Saw a truck tire in half and fill it with water for children to play in. Other containers, such as plastic tubs, also work well.

8. *One-piece puzzles.* Make simple puzzles out of pieces of cardboard by cutting out one shape, either from the edge of the puzzle or from its center.

9. Use of large and small muscles. Items that encourage use of large muscles for climbing, crawling, jumping, such as ladders, barrels, hoops. Items that call for manipulation of small muscles in eye-hand coordination, such as boxes, pegs, and puzzles.

10. Using large muscles—climbing or pedaling a tricycle.

11. Using small muscles—putting pegs into holes, putting rings on pegs, putting two pieces of a puzzle together.

12. Differences in sounds—ringing, banging, talking, singing.

13. Relating names to objects, movements, sounds, feeling, and colors.

You will learn specific ways to help toddlers use their play equipment later in this chapter, when intellectual, physical, emotional, and social development are discussed.

Whether a particular toy is bought in the

store, found, or made by the caregiver, it should allow toddlers to experience some of the following:

1. Differences in sizes and shapes of objects.
2. Differences in the structure of objects. (Boxes and bottles are empty, while blocks are solid and can be put into boxes or stacked on top of each other.)
3. Differences in movements—dropping, rolling, sliding, throwing.
4. Cause and effect. (A pull toy moves when the toddler pulls the string, but a block makes a noise when the toddler hits it with another block.)
5. Recognizing things in pictures.
6. Differences in textures and temperatures— soft and warm, hard and cold.
7. Expressing affection. (A doll or a stuffed animal can be related to affection between people.)
8. Ownership—first for those things that belong to the toddler, and later for things that are not his or hers.
9. Dramatic play—toys that allow toddlers to imitate the actions of adults, such as sweeping the floor or feeding a teddy bear.

INTELLECTUAL DEVELOPMENT OF TODDLERS

It is difficult to identify specific areas of development in the behavior of infants. Just so, it is also difficult to say exactly whether toddlers' behavior shows physical, social, emotional, or intellectual development. Stimulating experiences help toddlers develop in several areas at the same time.

Caregivers can stimulate toddlers' intellectual or *cognitive development* by using the following guidelines. However, these guidelines may also apply to toddlers' physical, social, and emotional development.

Caregivers can:

1. Give toddlers individual attention and let them know there is one special person providing most of their care.

2. Give toddlers affection when they need it, remembering that toddlers still need nurturing care.
3. Encourage toddlers to explore by providing a safe environment and letting them have the freedom in which to discover it.
4. Provide variety in the physical environment by rearranging the furniture a little; by introducing new, stimulating toys; and by including different colors, textures, shapes, and sounds.
5. Introduce new experiences that are a good match with toddlers' activities.
6. Encourage self-expression in speech, dramatic play, or with musical instruments.
7. Provide variety between active and quiet periods.

Language Development. The caregiver's role is important in stimulating toddlers' speech development. Here are some ways in which to help toddlers to develop language skills.

At first, toddlers know only about three words, and they repeat them whenever they hear them said. Caregivers should use the words that toddlers know in simple sentences. They should name actions and objects during

Figure 5-3. Caregivers should use descriptive words and phrases when talking to children about what they want. (Kenneth Karp)

routine and play activities. As toddlers develop, caregivers can describe actions and objects ("run quickly," "walk slowly," "sing softly," "red ball," "little chair," "hot water").

Toddlers chatter a lot, and their speech sounds are often not understandable. Caregivers must try to understand what toddlers mean by watching their body movements and facial expressions and by listening to them. When toddlers make sounds for words that can be recognized, caregivers should use the words in a sentence that says what the toddler is trying to communicate. For example, a toddler may say, "bye bye," and the caregiver may respond, "Susie wants to go bye bye."

Toddlers often show caregivers what they want by pointing to objects. Caregivers should name the objects and encourage toddlers to say what they want, rather than simply responding to the pointing.

At about 18 months, toddlers are usually able to name a few familiar objects seen in pictures. By this time, toddlers will usually know about ten words, and they will begin to understand simple directions. Caregivers should listen and respond to toddlers' speech, and they should read and talk to toddlers to increase their vocabulary. Caregivers should try giving toddlers simple directions to follow ("Go get your ball") and should repeat toddlers' actions ("You got your ball. You listened and did what I told you.")

As toddlers develop language skills, they begin to put two or three words together, and their vocabularies grow to between 20 and 50 words. At this point, caregivers should not correct toddlers' grammar. However, they should use correct grammar themselves and should provide a good example. Caregivers should continue reading, listening, and talking to toddlers. As toddlers' language skills increase, caregivers should use more descriptive words and phrases, ask toddlers questions, and listen carefully to their answers.

PHYSICAL DEVELOPMENT OF TODDLERS

Most of the toddler's physical development centers on muscle control and growth. As the large muscles of the arms, legs, back and neck develop, toddlers achieve *gross motor skills* (they are able to control their large muscles), and their movements become more even. As the small muscles in the hands, fingers, toes, and eyes develop, toddlers achieve *small-muscle control*. They are better able to feed themselves, to drink from a cup, to turn the pages of a book, and to tiptoe.

Caregivers can help toddlers develop motor skills by providing a safe, protected space and careful supervision in a setting that stimulates movement. They can encourage walking and climbing and provide a large, lightweight ball to roll. Caregivers give help with words: "Roll the ball to me."

As their large muscles grow stronger and become more coordinated, toddlers learn to seat themselves in chairs, to move from a standing position to a squatting position and back again, and to run without falling. Caregivers should encourage these accomplishments with praise and recognition. In joining toddlers' activities, caregivers should say things like "Let's run to the corner together"; "Now we'll climb the stairs. I'll hold your hand."

As toddlers' fine motor skills develop, caregivers will notice that they enjoy certain *manipulative* (handling) activities. Such activities require *eye-hand coordination*, or the ability to use eyes and hands together. Caregivers should provide objects that stimulate toddlers to use their small muscles. Boxes with lids and containers with covers will interest toddlers who have just discovered how to take covers off things. Having them scribble on large sheets of paper with a crayon is another way to stimulate eye-hand coordination.

Toddlers who at first can only scribble with a crayon, will learn to make long strokes and, later, circular strokes. Toddlers who are able to turn the pages of a book only three or four at a time learn to turn them one at a time later. Toddlers begin by stacking only two blocks, but they will learn to make piles of five or six. Caregivers should remember to give toddlers plenty of time to repeat actions involving eye-hand coordination and manipulative skills. This is how toddlers learn.

SOCIAL AND EMOTIONAL DEVELOPMENT OF TODDLERS

Toddlers express many emotions as they have their first taste of independence. They are very curious about the world. They have temper tantrums because they cannot express all their feelings in words. Their frustrations lead to hitting, biting, and other physical actions. Toddlers have a short attention span, and they do not understand rules very well. Therefore, their independence and curiosity can sometimes get them into trouble.

Guidance. Caregivers must guide toddlers toward self-control. Wise caregivers stress rules about safety. If a toddler's action is harmful to other people or to property, then it is stopped.

The way to keep rules to a minimum is to provide an environment in which few rules are needed and safety is stressed (see Table 5-1). For example, if they cover electric outlets, caregivers need not worry about keeping toddlers away from them.

Toddlers may dislike being corrected, but it is the caregivers' responsibility to keep toddlers from harm. Directions and corrections should be clear and simple; threats or angry words are unnecessary and unproductive. Caregivers should stress what they want the toddlers to do—this is better than a long string of "don'ts."

Dependence and Independence. Toddlers still need nurturing care as well as adult warmth and affection. They are strongly attached to their main caregivers and have learned to trust, love, and depend on these significant others in their lives. At the same time, toddlers are eager to test their new independence, to be self-sufficient, and to explore their environment. Thus, toddlers feel two opposite emotions—dependence and independence—often within a short space of time. This can be as confusing and frustrating to their caregivers as it is to the toddlers themselves. Children may act dependent one day and independent the next with respect to a given activity.

Table 5-1 SAFETY FOR TODDLERS

Characteristics of toddlers	Safety hazards	Measures of prevention
Investigates, climbs, opens doors and drawers; is curious, takes things apart, may put objects in mouth; likes to play; moves about constantly; tries to do things alone; imitates; runs and is lightning-fast; is impatient with restraint.	Gates, windows doors	Use safety gates to keep children in safe area. Keep doors leading to stairways, driveways, and storage area securely fastened. Use window guards or open windows from top only. Keep screens locked and nailed. Keep away from windows any pieces of furniture on which child could climb.
	Play areas	Keep extension cords and unprotected electrical outlets out of children's reach. Cover hot radiators. Fence the playground. Provide sturdy toys with no small, removable parts, made of unbreakable material and painted only with lead-free paints. Use tables with blunt corners.

Table 5-1 SAFETY FOR TODDLERS (Continued)

Characteristics of toddlers	Safety hazards	Measures of prevention
Investigates, climbs, opens doors and drawers; is curious, takes things apart, may put objects in mouth; likes to play; moves about constantly; tries to do things alone; imitates; runs and is lightning-fast; is impatient with restraint.	Play areas	Securely anchor all rugs, shelves, and bookcases. Use safety plugs in electrical outlets and do not use extension cords. Keep small objects out of reach of children. Have periodic electrical inspection and fire inspection of entire center.
	Poisons	Keep all cleaning supplies and medicines locked away from children.
	Burns	Provide guards for wall heaters, registers, floor furnaces. Have available fully charged fire extinguishers and train each employee in their use.
	Emergencies	Make arrangements with physician or hospital for emergency treatment. Keep current information on how to contact parents or guardian. Keep up-to-date lists of persons to whom child may be released; personally identify individual before releasing child to his or her custody.
	Housekeeping techniques Sanitary measures	Put things away after use, keeping traffic areas free. Handle laundry and store food in a sanitary way to prevent infection.
		See Chapter 4 for further details.

Source: Adapted from *Caring for Infants in Day Care Centers*, Division of Vocational Education, University of Kentucky, Lexington, Ky.; and *Day Care, Health Services,* U.S. Department of Health, Education, and Welfare, Washington, D.C.

Special Problems of Toddlers. Toddlers have special problems that caregivers must handle:

1. *Temper tantrums* (kicking and screaming) are toddlers' ways of expressing their frustrations. Caregivers should remember that, while toddlers are eager to be independent, they are not always successful. Failure is frustrating, and toddlers who cannot express this in words may express it by throwing a temper tantrum. Caregivers should ignore the noise and the show of a temper tantrum while keeping an eye on toddlers to make sure they are not hurting themselves. After the toddler has had a chance to "cool off," the caregiver should

interest the toddler in an activity at which he or she can be successful. When toddlers can talk, encourage them to express what troubles them. Words are better than temper tantrums and other unacceptable physical acts.

2. Toddlers often bite. If a toddler wants a toy that another child is playing with, biting usually produces results. Toddlers don't realize that biting hurts until they themselves are bitten. Rather than telling another child to bite the toddler back or biting the toddler, caregivers should ask the biter to help take care of the child who has been bitten. The toddler should be shown and told that biting hurts.

3. Toddlers may seem unaware of time, and this can frustrate hurried adults. Caregivers should understand that toddlers have their own timetable. It is based on their interest in what they are doing and on their body rhythms.

4. Toddlers may have difficulty in getting used to clothing. They often prefer to wear nothing at all. Caregivers can help toddlers adjust to wearing clothes by making sure that their clothing is comfortable and is the least needed for health and social acceptability.

5. Toddlers say few words, but they sometimes understand what is being said to them before they can use words to express themselves. Caregivers can help toddlers to use expressive language skills by talking and reading to them, as you learned earlier, and by showing them how to express their feelings in words.

6. Physical aggression is another toddler behavior. Hitting, hair-pulling, spitting, and pushing are the most common aggressive acts, but these are really the result of toddlers' attempts to learn about things (how hair feels, for example). Such acts are also the toddler's way of saying "Get out of my way" or "Leave me alone." Toddlers do not realize that their actions can hurt. Caregivers must help them to understand that other children are people, not objects, and that aggressive actions can hurt. Tell them, "It hurts," when they hit, pull hair, and other hurtful activities.

Figure 5-4. Some aggressive acts are the result of toddlers' attempts to learn about things. They don't realize that their actions can hurt. (Michael Weisbrot)

7. As toddlers grow older, they continue to test rules and sometimes threaten to "run away." Caregivers should not give this threat too much attention. Instead, try to interest the toddler in another activity.

8. Some toddlers bump their heads or rock the crib, apparently without hurting themselves. Caregivers should ask the toddler's parents about this behavior and should follow the advice of the toddler's physician.

9. Young children may masturbate (handle their genitals) when they are tired, concerned, or anxious about something. If you notice that there is a pattern to a toddler's masturbation, ask supervisors to suggest possible causes and ways to handle the situation.

10. Some toddlers have physical handicaps, such as poor hearing or eyesight, or developmental problems, such as speech retardation. When caregivers suspect that a toddler has a physical, emotional, or intellectual problem, they should call it to the attention of their supervisor. The toddler can then be examined by trained personnel. When suggestions are given to help a toddler with this kind of problem, caregivers should work closely with parents and supervisors to give the special care needed.

Working with Parents. Effective communication between caregivers and parents is very important in a toddler care program. Review the guidelines given in the introduction to Part II.

CHAPTER SUMMARY

1. Infants' and toddlers' needs are similar in many ways. The main difference lies in the toddlers' desire for independence. Their behavior can be frustrating to caregivers because often toddlers' abilities are not equal to the things they want to do.
2. Because toddlers can move about on their own, they need a safe environment. The main responsibility of a toddler caregiver is to provide a healthy, safe environment that is still flexible and stimulating enough to encourage exploration and the growth of self-help skills.
3. Toddler caregivers need the same personal characteristics as infant caregivers do, but they may need an extra measure of patience.
4. A number of things should be considered when planning a good program for toddlers. Toddlers are beginning to walk and talk; they are starting to become toilet trained and to feed themselves; they often want independence and yet still depend on one or two significant people. Finally, toddlers are learning to play, and they play to learn.
5. Individual toddlers have special needs. Any good program should take into account the particular needs and stage of development of each child.

• WHAT NEW TERMS HAVE YOU LEARNED?

Several new words and ideas were presented in this chapter. To see whether you understand them, match the letter of each term below with the numbered phrases under "Definitions."

Terms

a. Attention span
b. Toddler
c. Autonomy
d. Solitary play
e. Parallel play
f. Feces
g. Bowel control
h. Toddlerhood
i. Urination
j. Bladder control
k. Independent mobility
l. Diaper gait
m. Stimulation
n. Cognitive development
o. Toddle

Definitions

1. Intellectual development
2. To walk alone
3. Walking with legs far apart
4. Staying dry
5. Voiding
6. Bowel movement
7. Unsure, uneven movement with frequent falls
8. Independence
9. Short concentration time
10. Child who is just beginning to walk
11. Using potty or toilet for bowel movement
12. Playing side by side
13. Playing alone
14. Activities planned for learning
15. Approximately 12 months to 3 years

• PROJECTS, DECISIONS, ISSUES

1. Choose a partner and discuss the following statements; rephrase incorrect statements to make them correct.
   a. Effective toddler caregivers give help only when it is needed.

b. Toddler behavior and adult expectations are often different.
c. Toddlers should dress themselves.
d. Toddlers are usually bathed daily in child care centers.
e. Both solitary and parallel play are characteristic of toddlers play.
f. Toddlers' temper tantrums are normal; a child having such a tantrum should be isolated.
g. Toddlers are messy eaters and should not be allowed to feed themselves.
h. Children who are weaned and toilet-trained are called toddlers.
i. Group care, even if it is well done, is bad for toddlers.

2. Construct one simple toy that a toddler would enjoy, give it to the toddler, and observe and record the toddler's response.

• WHIFS (WHAT WOULD YOU DO *IF* . . .)

1. A toddler wets his pants. What would you do?
   a. Spank him
   b. Change them and put on diapers
   c. Change them and say nothing
   d. Change him and warn him not to let it happen again
   e. Remind yourself of the time
   f. Ignore the situation and let him wear wet pants
   g. Other responses

2. A toddler spills her milk. What would you do?
   a. Clean it up
   b. Scold the toddler
   c. Help her clean it up
   d. Call the maid
   e. Other responses

3. A toddler bites another toddler. What would you do?
   a. Bite the toddler yourself
   b. Have the other toddler bite him back
   c. Treat the wound

d. Tell him that biting hurts
e. Other responses

4. A toddler takes off her clothes and runs around in the nude. What would you do?
   a. Pick her up and take her to the bathroom
   b. Stop her and put her clothes on
   c. Encourage her to come to you
   d. Let her run and be free
   e. Laugh
   f. Tell the other children not to look
   g. Other responses

• STUDENT ACTIVITIES

1. Identify four special needs of toddlers.
2. What are three qualities of a good toddler program in a child care center?
3. Describe four or more personal traits that are desirable in toddler caregivers.
4. Describe two ways in which toddler caregivers can stimulate each of the following: intellectual development, physical development, and social-emotional development.
5. List four experiences that toddlers have with toys.
6. Select a topic under "Social and Emotional Development of Toddlers" in this chapter and write a short report on it.
7. From the following statements select those that describe toddler behavior.
   a. Toddlers have a long attention span.
   b. Toddlers play cooperatively most of the time.
   c. Toddlers are usually bathed daily in child care centers.
   d. Toddlers like toys that stack.
   e. Toddlers can wait their turns very patiently.
   f. Toddlers need nurturing care.
8. Describe two ways in which toddler caregivers can stimulate intellectual development, physical development, and social/emotional development.
9. List four experiences that toddlers have with toys.

PART THREE

CHILD CARE AIDES CARE FOR 3-, 4-, AND 5-YEAR-OLD CHILDREN

Part III contains 15 chapters that deal with specific tasks performed by child care aides for 3-, 4-, and 5-year-old children in child care centers.

Part III is actually divided into two sections. The first section—Chapters 6 through 13—deals with supervising routine activities, guarding children's well-being, and guiding their behavior.

Chapters 6 through 9 focus on supervising daily activities that follow the same basic procedure, including self-help skills, food, rest, and housekeeping. Children quickly learn the procedures for each of these routines. But caregivers can make these activities more meaningful by supervising carefully and building learning experiences into what seems like just a routine procedure.

Child caregivers make the most of routine activities in two ways: (1) by recognizing moments of teaching—moments when young children want to know and do—and (2) by bringing to routine procedures something that helps children extend their understanding, their awareness, or their abilities.

Chapters 10 and 11 focus on guarding children's well-being by providing a safe environment, preventing disease, and teaching children good health habits. Chapter 12 deals with guiding young children's behavior—why they need guidance and what methods teachers and caregivers use to guide children and handle problem behaviors. Chapter 13 focuses on outdoor play, which is made up of routines and program activities.

The second section of Part III deals with carrying out program activities. Planning is a joint effort of child care team members. Child care aides carry out the plans developed under the leadership of the person in charge.

Chapters 14 through 20 provide details about programs in specific subject areas. Although the tasks of each subject area are different and require special knowledge and skills, many principles used in planning and carrying out these activities are the same. Following is an outline of how these subject-area tasks—whether music, science, art, math, or other activities—are generally presented:

1. Preparation
   a. Planning what you want to accomplish during the activity
   b. Obtaining and arranging the materials for the activity
   c. Allowing enough space for the activity
2. Participation
   a. Supervising the activity
   b. Observing childrens' behavior during the activity
   c. Maintaining a safe environment, which includes making sure rules are followed
   d. Integrating (combining) the concepts of one activity with another
3. Follow-up
   a. Cleaning up after the activity is finished
   b. Evaluating children's experiences
   c. Evaluating your performance

6 | SUPERVISING SELF-HELP SKILLS

After you have studied Chapter 6, you should be able to:

1. Name at least four self-help skills young children use daily and give an example of each
2. State four benefits that young children get from developing self-help skills
3. Identify indirect and direct ways a child care aide encourages self-help
4. List at least two self-help opportunities in each of the following routines: eating, using the bathroom, dressing, undressing, housekeeping and assisting with teaching; demonstrate how a child care aide would supervise them

BENEFITS OF SELF-HELP SKILLS FOR CHILDREN

Self-help skills are skills that let children perform tasks related to their own care. The development of self-help skills in young children marks the beginning of self-reliance. Children learn to feed and dress themselves, to use the toilet without help, and even to do some of their own housekeeping. Routine activities at a child care center can provide teaching opportunities. When caregivers take the time and trouble to let children help, children can learn and practice self-help skills.

The development of self-help skills benefits children in the following ways:

1. Builds a good self-concept and *self-esteem* (that is, self-value)
2. Helps children respect other people and accept individual responsibility; helps them become part of a team effort (respecting others and accepting responsibility)
3. Gives children experience in decision-making and problem-solving (coping skills)
4. Gives children more effective time with caregivers, who are freed from routines and have more time to interact with the children

A GOOD SELF-CONCEPT AND SELF-ESTEEM

How do self-help skills build a good self-concept and self-esteem? When children are able to do a task successfully—especially when the task is obvious and immediately useful—they place a high value on themselves.

For example, children who button their own coats not only are protected from the cold while playing outdoors but also take pride in having done this. Children who help wipe off the play tables before snack time see the results of their effort at once and have the satisfaction of getting the table ready.

Caregivers must recognize good efforts. They need to use guidance techniques to encourage self-help successes and to build each child's self-esteem and self-concept.

Since many self-help tasks are difficult and require good motor skills, children feel especially successful when they complete them: ''I did it all by myself'' are words that a caregiver hopes to hear often.

RESPECTING OTHERS

Self-help skills strengthen children's respect for other people in two ways:

1. Children learn to understand individual differences. They accept the fact that each person can do some things well and needs to improve in others. For example, it's easy for Julie to tie her shoes, but this task is difficult for Claude. Appreciating differences and helping each other are benefits of working together on self-help skills. It is likely that a child who has learned the skill of shoe-tying can teach peers better than a caregiver could.

2. When children see the result of using their self-help skills in a team effort, they learn to value the contribution of other members of the team (cooperation). For example, when three children put the blocks on the shelf, they are using their self-help skills as a team. The play area can be changed from wall-to-wall clutter to organized neatness when each child uses the skill of putting things in their right places.

ACCEPTING RESPONSIBILITY

Children will enjoy accepting responsibility when:

1. It is expected at appropriate times and in appropriate amounts. They may, for example, like helping to put the blocks away if the caregiver helps and there are not too many blocks.

Figure 6-1. Children enjoy taking responsibility for doing small tasks, for example, putting their blocks away after playtime. (Kenneth Karp)

2. They are rested and not tired or hurried.

3. They are given credit for the task they have performed.

4. The effort is divided into small, simple tasks.

5. Their good efforts are recognized (*positive reinforcement*).

Positive reinforcement encourages children to repeat their good efforts, and good habits are formed by such repetition.

MAKING DECISIONS AND SOLVING PROBLEMS

The best way to learn how to solve problems is to have problems to solve. The best way to learn decision-making is to have decisions to make. Self-help gives children many opportunities to practice these *coping skills* (finding ways to solve problems). "How can I put these blocks away quickly?" "Which foot does this shoe go on?" "What comes first, the top button or the bottom?" Self-help encourages children to find their own solutions and make their own judgments.

ASSISTING THE CAREGIVER

When children develop the skills they need to take care of themselves, your role as caregiver changes, because the children have taken responsibility for many of their own routines. When children use self-help skills, you have more time to help them discover concepts and meanings for themselves. For example, you may call attention to shadows in the playground and then, later in the day, make a light available so that the children can make shadows indoors. Questions that you raise help the children compare likenesses and differences between the outdoor and indoor shadows.

PROVIDING SELF-HELP OPPORTUNITIES

Caregivers provide children with opportunities for learning self-help skills in indirect as well as direct ways.

INDIRECT ENCOURAGEMENT OF SELF-HELP

The environment can be arranged to encourage self-help skills by organizing space and planning the schedule carefully. That is, caregivers can *set the stage* to promote learning.

Organizing Space Equipment and supplies should be arranged for greatest use by children with least supervision from adults. Consider the following guidelines:

1. Equipment should be placed on low shelves that are open, movable, and not too deep. Children should be able to see and reach the items on each shelf. Shelves on brackets or cement blocks (which can be moved or adjusted from time to time) and open cupboards or bookcases are better than closed, unmovable cupboards. The shelves do not need to be too deep. In fact, when they are too deep, things get pushed to the back and become lost.

2. Shelf space needs to be defined clearly. Items should not be crowded together.

3. Items should be assigned one place on the shelves and should always be stored in their assigned place. Pictures or symbols in different shapes or colors can be used on the shelves and on the equipment that is supposed to be stored on them. In this way, children can match the symbol, shape, or color on the equipment with the shelf that has the same symbol, shape, or color.

4. Items that are used together should be stored together. This is the basic principle of a learning center or activity area. When all the things a child needs for a particular activity are grouped together in one place, the child will be more likely to get, use, and return the items without adult assistance.

5. Learning centers need to have enough space so that activities will not be in the way of traffic. A clear path will help to ensure this.

Planning Schedules. The following guidelines about scheduling are important in developing self-help skills:

1. Alternate active and quiet times in the schedule, to avoid fatigue.

2. Arrange the schedule to allow enough self-help time for each activity.

3. Plan clean-up time—it is an important teaching activity too.

DIRECT ENCOURAGEMENT OF SELF-HELP

As a child care aide your ideas and feelings about young children will affect how you work with them. If you believe they can benefit from helping themselves, you will plan time, space, and activities that encourage self-help skills. On the other hand, if you feel that children depend on *your* nurturing, you will overlook ways to help them learn to help themselves. You can encourage self-help skills directly in the following ways:

1. Do not be in a hurry to help. See what children can do for themselves, but offer help before they fail or become frustrated.

2. Tell children first, show them second, and do it for them last. Describe what happens in words. "Put your sweater in your locker. Hang the armhole over the hook."

3. Set a good example. If you want children to clean up after themselves, let them see you putting things away when you have finished with them.

4. Help children understand that there are three parts to every task. Show them by your example and by having them take part in the following:

   a. Preparing—planning what to do and getting the necessary materials ready beforehand

   b. Participating—letting children know that their ability to take care of themselves lets you participate in their experiences

   c. Following up—evaluating the experience and cleaning up are both part of follow-up activities

5. When supervising self-help activities, put yourself on the children's eye level, give them individual attention, and do not push the children to "hurry up." Use a child-sized chair or sit on the floor and talk or help in a relaxed way. Even though you need to have an overview of the room, give your attention to each child as you help.

SELF-HELP OPPPORTUNITIES IN DAILY ROUTINES

Daily routines provide many opportunities for children to learn and practice self-help skills.

EATING ROUTINES

In most centers, children take turns performing self-help jobs related to food service. Children are not usually forced to take turns in helping with food, but they are invited and encouraged to do so. There will be some children who will want to help all the time and others who try to avoid any involvement at all. Caregivers must make an effort to try to involve as many children as possible in the experience.

Children can perform the following *self-help tasks:*

1. Helping to clean and set the table

2. Helping to prepare the food

3. Assisting in serving the group and serving themselves

4. Helping to scrape their plates and carry dishes and silverware back to the kitchen

5. Clearing and wiping the table.

Further information about self-help activities relating to food appears in Chapter 22, which discusses how caregivers participate in food service.

RESTING

During the rest or naptime, children should be encouraged to do as much for themselves as possible—dressing, undressing, using the bathroom, and helping with the housekeeping.

TOILETING

You will find many opportunities for children to practice their self-help skills during toileting routines.

Figure 6-2. Children should be encouraged to practice such self-help skills as setting the table. (Kenneth Karp)

Signs to Look For. Many young children are likely to wait too long before they stop playing and head for the bathroom. As a child care aide, you will need to watch their actions and faces for signs that they need to use the toilet. Standing and switching from one foot to the other, holding the *genitals* (external sex organs), a flushed face, bowed head, or an anxious, worried look may all be signs that you need to help a child stop playing and go to the bathroom. When you see children who you think need to use the toilet, go to them and make a direct statement such as, "Come with me and use the bathroom." With an older child, you might say, "Go use the bathroom." Do not ask them or invite them to do it.

Getting Ready. Caregivers should first check the bathroom to see that it is clean and has enough supplies (toilet paper, paper towels, soap, and so forth).

Children should be encouraged to handle their clothing when using the toilet. You can help with verbal directions, one at a time.

"Unbutton the top of your pants . . . now pull down the zipper . . . that's good. Now you need to pull down your pants and your underpants."

Some children will want to take their pants all the way off. You can tell them that this is not necessary; but if you do not know the child well, let the child use a familiar routine (unless the child has waited too long before using the toilet and there is not enough time).

You will need to take your cues from the child. Try to match the practices used at the child's home, at least in the beginning. If the child seems to be waiting for you to undress, clean, and dress her or him, encourage and assist with self-help. If the child has put off going to the bathroom too long, help with removing clothing and wait for another time to teach self-help.

Using the Toilet. For boys, the toilet seat must be pulled up. You should encourage them to do it for themselves. If the center is not equipped with potty chairs or child-sized toilets, you should help make children comfortable on the toilet by giving them a step on which to rest their feet and balance themselves. During the toileting routine, you should remain calm and unhurried.

Completing the Toileting Process. When children have finished using the toilet, have them get the toilet tissue and wipe themselves. Teach them to wipe away from the genitals when they are wiping themselves after a bowel movement. Direct them to put the used toilet tissue in the toilet and to flush it when they are finished. The procedure for dressing is the reverse of that for undressing.

Group Toileting. In many centers, children are reminded to use the toilet several times throughout the session and do not use the bathroom as a group at any scheduled time. In other centers, toileting is planned both as a regular routine and in response to an individual child's needs. Group toileting usually takes place in a *transition period* (at a time when there is change from one activity to another). For example, after clean-up, the children use the bathroom and wash their hands before the next activity. Children who do not need to use the toilet simply wash their hands.

When you are assigned the duty of supervising the toileting routine, keep the following things in mind:

1. Arrange for a smooth transition to the toileting routine by being in the toileting area before the children arrive.

2. Try to arrange for several small groups—rather than one large one—to use the bathroom at any one time.

3. Do not make the children wait in line. If it is necessary for them to wait as a group, use the time for quiet talking activities rather than attempting to force silence or stillness.

4. Invite each child to use the toilet. Children who have just used the toilet a short time before probably will not need to use it so soon again. Children who have not *voided* (urinated) after a time on the toilet should not be forced to remain on the toilet. In either case, the children should wash their hands before leaving the bathroom.

5. Give honest answers to children's questions about the differences between their bodies.

6. Avoid using negative words such as *dirty* or *messy* in describing any aspect of the toileting procedure.

7. Help children wipe up spills or clean up toilet accidents: remove the children from the area if an accident requires major cleaning.

8. If you are assigned to the toileting procedure, note individual children's progress.

WASHING HANDS

Children should always wash their hands during the bathroom routine—especially when this routine comes right before snack or eating time. If children tell you that their hands are not dirty, tell them that everyone is washing their hands to get ready to eat. Set a good example by letting the children see you washing your hands as a part of preparing for mealtime.

One problem you are likely to experience during this routine is water play. Children enjoy playing with the water, and you will need to help them understand what is expected of them when they use the bathroom. It will help if water play is included in the overall child care program.

You can teach children to wash their hands by *having them*:

1. Turn on the water in the washbasin. Do not use the hot-water faucet unless you are able to supervise the children closely.

2. Let the water run or use the stopper and turn the water off after a small amount has run into the basin.

3. Put soap on the children's hands. Use either a bar of mild hand soap or liquid soap.

4. Rub the soap over the backs and palms of a child's hands and then over each finger, rubbing until the child "can see the little bubbles."

5. After they are covered with bubbles, rinse and shake the water off of the child's hands.

6. Wash off the bar of soap and put it back in the soap dish.

7. Let the water out of the basin.

8. Dry children's hands with a paper towel and put the used towel in the trash container. If

children use their own cloth towels, they can get them from their nook or locker before the hand-washing procedure begins.

BRUSHING TEETH

In some centers, children brush their teeth as part of the bathroom routine. As with other activities, each child should have a personal toothbrush. Toothbrushes should be stored in a clean place, and individuals' toothbrushes should be kept separate.

Teach children to brush their teeth by having them:

1. Get their toothbrush and toothpaste from the assigned place (in their locker or on a hook in the lavatory).
2. Squeeze at least ½ inch of toothpaste from the tube onto the toothbrush.
3. Brush away from the gums—brush *up* from the bottom teeth and *down* from the top teeth most of the time.
4. Put down the brush and fill a glass or cup with water, turning the faucet off when the cup is filled.
5. Rinse by swishing the water around inside their mouths and then spitting it out.
6. Rinse off the toothbrush, put the cap on the toothpaste, and return both to their assigned places.

You should give children help when you feel they need it. In addition, make simple statements from time to time about the importance of taking care of their teeth. Tell them to brush after every meal, to see the dentist, to learn what the dentist does, and to eat good food.

COMBING AND BRUSHING HAIR

When the grooming process in a center includes combing and brushing the children's hair, make sure that each child uses a personal comb and brush. Have the children remove ribbons or barrettes beforehand and have them look in the mirror as they comb or brush. You can give help when you feel it is needed, but be sure to let the children try to do it themselves first.

Combing and brushing hair should not become a major grooming activity; rather, it should teach children how to keep their hair tidy during the day.

DRESSING AND UNDRESSING

All the different tasks involved in dressing and undressing are difficult for a young child. Caregivers need to remember this when teaching them how to button, zip, pull over, and put on clothing. Directions must be simple. Give directions one at a time, letting children follow one direction before being given another. Some centers have dressing dolls or dressing frames that children can use to learn or practice the different tasks. Table 6-1 shows some ways in which caregivers can help children understand how to perform dressing and undressing tasks.

If you live in a climate where boots and snowsuits are worn, be sure that the children use the bathroom *before* they start to dress for outdoors. Guide the sequence of dressing. Snowsuits or snow pants come first, followed by boots, then cap, and finally mittens or gloves.

When children have reached the self-help stage, parents should be urged to choose clothing that the children can handle easily. Clothing with large buttons and zippers placed where children can see and reach them are helpful.

ASSISTING WITH TEACHING

There are many ways in which children can assist the teacher or the caregiver and learn self-help skills at the same time. As a child care aide, you need to think about ways that children can help themselves, each other, and you.

Group Time. As children help, they gain self-esteem and self-confidence. It is important for caregivers to make certain that every child has an opportunity to participate in these self-help activities. The quiet, shy children may need some special help. Caregivers should not force them to take part but should act as though they expected the children to do so: "Fran, it's your turn now." An invitation put in the form of a question ("Would you like to take a turn, Fran?") will probably be answered with a "No" or a shake of the head.

Table 6-1 DRESSING AND UNDRESSING

Skill	Steps to teach	What to say
Buttons		
To button:	1. Put your finger through buttonhole.	"Look at your bottom button." "Match the bottom buttonhole with the bottom button and put your pointer finger through the hole." "Stop when you can see your fingernail."
	2. Take button with your pointer finger and thumb of your other hand and move it toward buttonhole.	"Hold the button with the pointer finger and thumb of your other hand." "Put the button on top of your pointer finger that is in the buttonhole."
	3. While holding your finger in buttonhole, push button through hole. Grab button with your thumb and forefinger and pull it through.	"Slide the button through the hole with your fingers." "Grab it with your thumb and pointer finger and pull it through."
To unbutton:	1. Grab button with one hand and turn it on its edge.	"Look at your bottom button." "Grab the button and turn it until you see its edge."
	2. Slide your pointer finger (of your other hand) under buttonhole to make the fabric stiff.	"Put your finger under the buttonhole."
	3. Holding buttonhole slightly open, push button through hole.	"Pull it open a little." "Push the button through the hole."
Zippers		
To open:	1. Grab top of material on both sides of zipper with one hand (usually the left one).	"Look at your zipper." "Hold the material at the top like this." (Show the child.)
	2. Pull zipper tab with other hand until it stops.	"Now pull your zipper tab down until it stops."
	3. Pull pin out of the hole by using both hands—one to pull up and the other to pull down.	"Pull up with one hand and down with the other until the pin comes out."
To close:	1. Look at bottom end of zipper.	"Look at the ends of your zipper."
	2. Hold side with hole firmly in place and fit pin into hole by pulling up with one hand and pushing down with the other.	"Grab one side of the zipper with one hand and the other side with your other hand." "Put the pin into the zipper hole." "Push down with the pin side and up with the hole side."
	3. Grab material on both sides at end of zipper firmly and hold it while zipper tab is being pulled up.	"Now pull up the zipper tab as you hold tight onto the material at the bottom."
Sweaters, jackets, coats		
	1. Lay sweater on floor with collar facing the child.	"Put your sweater on the floor with the collar toward you." (Show the child.)
	2. Spread the sweater so that both armholes are seen, and have child put left hand in armhole on left side of sweater and right hand in armhole on right side.	"Put your hands into the armholes." "Put your left hand (that's this one) into the left hole and your other hand (that's your right hand) into the right hole."
	3. When both arms are in armholes,	"Raise your hands over your head." "Now bring

88

Table 6-1 DRESSING AND UNDRESSING (Continued)

Skill	Steps to teach	What to say
	child raises hands over head and sweater slides down and settles onto the child's shoulders. As the child brings arms down, the sleeves will slide down the arms.	your arms down to your sides." "Surprise! You put your sweater on."

Socks

Skill	Steps to teach	What to say
To put on:	Put thumbs in one sock and pull them apart, making a big opening. Put toes of one foot in the opening made when you stretch your sock. Pull on your sock as far as you can (probably to the heel). Ease sock over heel by sliding thumbs down sock, stretching it over heel. Pull it on all the way.	"Put your thumbs in the top of the sock, and stretch it wide open." "Stick your toes into the big opening you have made." "Pull your sock on as far as you can. Reach your thumbs down into the sock and pull it around your heel and up your leg."
To take off:	Slide thumbs down into sock and push down to heel. Pull sock off foot by holding onto toe of sock.	"Put your thumbs in the top of the sock and push the sock down to your heel." "Hold onto the toe of the sock and pull it off your foot."

Shoes

Skill	Steps to teach	What to say
To put on:	Place shoes side by side with straight edges together. Have heels toward toes and away from body. If laced shoe, unlace and pull tongue up. If buckled shoe, unbuckle. Put left foot in left shoe, push and pull on. If possible, lace or buckle. A child can put shoes on alone a long time before he or she can buckle and/or lace shoes.	"Sit down on this small chair (or right here on the floor)." "Put your shoes side by side in front of you." "Unlace (or unbuckle) this shoe." (Point.) "Now this one." "Put your foot, toes first, into this shoe." ("Right foot, right shoe"—say it as you help child do it.) "Now the other shoe"...similar comment. "Push." Help child pull heel of shoe against foot as he or she pushes. You lace shoe for child unless he or she can do it alone.
To take off:	Unlace or unbuckle. Hold onto shoe, and pull foot out of it. Place shoes side by side when taken off (beginning of good housekeeping).	"Unlace (or unbuckle) each shoe." "Hold onto the back of your shoe." "Place your shoes together under the cot."

Boots

Skill	Steps to teach	What to say
To put on:	Place side by side with straight sides together. Put left foot in left boot, pushing against bottom.	"Put your shoes side by side in front of you." "Put this foot in this boot (point)." "Push the boot from the bottom."
To take off:	Sit down. Cross foot over opposite knee and pull boot away from foot at the heel. Child may need teacher's help to pull. If so, have child hold onto chair while someone is pulling.	"Sit down on this chair (or on the floor)." "Pull your boot off at the heel. Try it all by yourself." If difficult, you, the caregiver, pull. Tell the child, "Hold onto the chair while I pull."

Here are some examples of ways children can help:

1. *Leading songs and music.* Child chooses own song and either sings it alone or leads an action song ("Do as I'm Doing," "Simon Says," and so forth).

2. *Turning the pages of a book.* A child is given the chance to turn the pages when the caregiver is reading to the group or when child is reading or looking at a book alone.

3. *Flannel-board figures.* Children help put figures on the flannel board. If possible, have one figure for each child to put up, or have them take turns helping at different times.

4. *Holding charts or objects.* Children help to show an object by carrying it around to the children in the group so that they can see it. Or they may hold up pictures or charts in front of the group.

5. *Dictating stories.* Children may do this as an individual or group project. It will help them to understand that reading is the speaking of written words. The child or children tell the teacher what to write. This kind of activity can also be made a part of the follow-up for a field trip or a visit from a special person—the children can help write the thank-you note.

6. *Finishing stories.* Caregivers read stories without endings, and the children help to finish them. This is a good experience in problem-solving and the use of language skills.

7. *Folding scarves or clothing.* Children help to clean up after using materials in a music or dramatic activity.

8. *Leading activities or games.*

Writing Names. Some children may want to put their own names on their artwork. As a caregiver, you can help them to recognize correct writing by using it on artwork, charts, and labels. Show them how the letters look, but do not scold children if they print the way they were taught at home, which is usually with all capital letters instead of capital (*uppercase*) and small (*lowercase*) letters.

HOUSEKEEPING

You can guide children toward using materials and equipment without help from an adult by arranging the environment so that it encourages children to get and return things by themselves.

The following tasks are specific ways for children to help with housekeeping activities:

1. *Hanging up their own sweaters, coats, and clothing.* Caregivers should encourage children to look at the hook when they are hanging up a coat, and to put the collar or armhole over it. Caregivers can help at first by walking the children to their lockers and watching them hang up their wraps.

2. *Getting out blocks and other materials.* Children can take blocks and materials from the shelves and use them without adult help. When the shelves are marked, they find it easier to put items back in the right places.

3. *Using housekeeping items.* Children can use brooms, mops, and sponges to clean up their own spills.

4. *Helping themselves.* If flour is in a small container, water in a squeeze bottle, paper on the shelf, scissors in a holder, and small items on open shelves, children can help themselves. However, some supervision is still needed to guide the children toward careful and proper use of such materials. Otherwise, the art area may come to look like a battlefield.

CLEANING UP

Caregivers can successfully encourage children to clean up by using the following methods:

1. Give a warning time and a signal to remind children that the activity will soon end. Some centers use a verbal signal, others flicker the lights, and still others ring a bell. Regardless of what is used, it should be the same signal every time. Children often take turns participating. They enjoy ringing the bell, flicking the lights, or striking a piano note.

2. Involve children in specific clean-up tasks. Rather than saying, "Jane, come here and clean up the housekeeping corner," caregivers should give a more specific direction, such as: "Jane, put the fruit into the bowl on the table."

Figure 6-3. Every child should be given a specific task to perform during cleanup. (Jane Hamilton-Merritt)

in this puzzle. Please find it before you put the puzzle away.''

5. Ask direct questions about clean-up. ''Are the flannel-board pieces in their containers?'' ''Are all the books back on the bookshelf?''

6. Help children to understand the steps involved in clean-up. In the art area, children can take off their smocks and hang them up, wash their hands, put the paints away, and clean off the table.

7. Self-help activities take place indoors and out. Ideas about self-help activities outdoors appear in Chapter 13.

When children complain about cleaning up (''I didn't play with anything! Why do I have to pick up?''), caregivers should tell them, ''Everybody helps.'' This statement can be backed up by giving the children a specific task to perform. ''Here is a sponge for you to clean off the table for snacks.''

In some centers, children are assigned to clean up certain areas. This system of ''snack helpers,'' ''art-area helpers,'' ''block-area helpers,'' ''housekeeping helpers,'' and so forth, often works well. Whatever system is used, children should be taught to work together to perform their clean-up tasks thoroughly.

3. Expect children to participate in cleaning up. Instead of asking the children to help you clean up, you should ask the children whether you can help *them* clean up. Caregivers should not rush in and clean things themselves; instead, they should encourage the children to help by calling attention to unfinished tasks. ''John, this doll looks uncomfortable. Let's smooth out the sheet and fold the blanket to make the bed more comfortable.''

4. Help children to get in the habit of putting things away after use. Caregivers should remind children to put toys away before getting others out. Check to see that children have replaced all the parts of a toy and that all the pieces of equipment or materials are in place. ''Marie, the dog's bone is missing

CHAPTER SUMMARY

1. *Self-help tasks* are tasks that children perform for themselves. By learning to take care of themselves, children gain self-esteem and build a good self-concept. Self-help skills help children learn to respect other people, to accept responsibility, and to practice coping skills.

2. When children are able to perform their own routines, teachers have more time to spend interacting with all the children.

3. Caregivers can provide opportunities for children to learn and practice self-help skills in an indirect way by arranging the environment so that it encourages children to do things for themselves.

4. Caregivers can offer children direct encouragement to develop self-help skills by helping them learn to perform the tasks involved

in routines such as eating, toileting, resting, dressing, washing, and grooming.

5. Children should also be involved in housekeeping and clean-up activities, and in helping the teacher in group or individual learning activities.

• WHAT NEW TERMS HAVE YOU LEARNED?

Several new words and ideas were presented in this chapter. To see whether you understand them, match the letter of each term below with the numbered phrases under "Definitions."

Terms

a. Self-help skills
b. Self-esteem
c. Coping skills
d. Self-help tasks
e. Lowercase letters
f. Setting the stage
g. Positive reinforcement
h. To void
i. Genitals
j. Uppercase letters

Definitions

1. How I value myself
2. The recognition of good efforts
3. External sex organs
4. Self-help jobs—responsibility for taking care of yourself
5. Taking care of yourself
6. To urinate
7. Small letters
8. Scheduling and organizing space
9. Finding ways to solve problems
10. Capital letters

• PROJECTS, DECISIONS, ISSUES

1. Select a specific self-help activity, identify the three basic parts of the task needed to carry out that activity, and demonstrate the specific steps to take in accomplishing the task. If possible, participate in supervising the activity with children.

2. Indicate whether you *agree* or *disagree* with the following statements; cite examples to substantiate your answers.
   a. Self-esteem is the value other people place on an individual.
   b. A self-help skill cannot be learned by a team effort, it must be learned by an individual.
   c. Self-help skills are desirable but more trouble than they're worth.
   d. There are different acceptable ways of teaching self-help skills.
   e. Self-help skills must be taught *directly,* so the child caregiver needs to allow time for their teaching each day.

• WHIFS (WHAT WOULD YOU DO *IF* . . .)

1. Becky holds out her arms in a position that indicates "take off my coat." What would you do?
   a. Take it off
   b. Tell her to take it off herself
   c. Ignore her
   d. Tell her to unbutton the bottom button first
   e. Other responses

2. Craig turns the water on full force and stops up the drain with a paper towel. What would you do?
   a. Tell him to stop
   b. Turn off the water
   c. Give him a good lecture
   d. Tell your supervisor
   e. Let him play in the water
   f. Other responses

3. Julia asks you repeatedly whether she can ring the bell for clean-up. (In fact, she's so anxious to ring the bell that she doesn't choose anything or anyone to play with but just stands around watching.) What would you do?
   a. Tell her she can't ring the bell unless she gets busy and plays with something
   b. Tell her "I'll see"
   c. Promise her she can

d. Look at the assignment chart and tell her it's not her turn today

e. Other responses

4. David refuses to help with snack when it's his turn. What would you do?
   a. Insist that he help
   b. Pick someone else
   c. Do it yourself
   d. Encourage him to help
   e. Other responses

• CHECK YOURSELF

Carefully read each item and answer *yes* or *no* in terms of your performance in encouraging young children to use self-help skills.

1. Do you
   a. Arrange equipment and supplies for maximum use by children and minimum supervision from adults by placing equipment and materials in clearly defined spaces?
   b. Allow self-help time in each activity?
   c. Use clean-up time as a self-help activity?
   d. Let the children help you?

2. Do you set a good example by recognizing and using the three basic parts of each task?
   a. Preparation: Do you plan what you're going to do in detail? Do you get all the things you need ready?
   b. Participation: Do you use good supervising techniques? Do you encourage children to use self-help skills?
   c. Follow up: Do you evaluate the experience for yourself? Do you evaluate the experience for the children? Do you clean up and put things away where they belong?

3. Do you encourage self-help in these daily routines and activities?
   a. Eating
   b. Resting
   c. Toileting
   d. Washing hands
   e. Grooming
   f. Dressing, undressing
   g. Clean-up
   h. Group time

• STUDENT ACTIVITIES

1. Define the term *self-help skills*.
2. List four self-help skills young children use daily and give an example of each.
3. List four ways self-help skills benefit young children and give an example of each.
4. Identify two basic ways a child caregiver *indirectly* encourages self-help.
5. List five specific ways that a child caregiver *directly* encourages self-help skills and demonstrate two of them.
6. List at least two self-help opportunities in each of the following routines and demonstrate how a child care aide would supervise them.
   a. Eating
   b. Using the bathroom
   c. Dressing
   d. Undressing
   e. Housekeeping
   f. Assisting with teaching

7 | SUPERVISING EATING ROUTINES

After you have studied Chapter 7, you should be able to:

1. Identify five ways in which eating routines aid children's learning
2. Name five steps necessary to prepare the setting and the children for snack or mealtime
3. Demonstrate five behaviors that a child care aide should show when supervising eating
4. Show two procedures that are usually included in completing the eating routine

Food service in child care centers usually consists of a midmorning snack, lunch, and an afternoon snack. In some places, breakfast is also a part of the day's schedule. When programs end at noon, only a midmorning snack is provided.

The procedure used during any eating time—whether breakfast, lunch, or snack—is called an *eating routine*. As you know, the term *routine* means doing the same thing over and over each day. Eating routines remain the same each day within child care centers. However, eating routines vary from one center to another. Child care aide assignments differ, and routines differ, depending on the size and staffing pattern of the center.

EATING ROUTINES HELP CHILDREN

Whatever your assignment may be in relation to eating routines, you must be aware of how the eating routines benefit children.

Whenever food is served to children, they learn something from the experience. You can affect how much learning takes place. Be alert. Make use of daily educational opportunities connected with your food assignment. You can help the children learn the following things.

ENJOYING FOOD

A national food company claims: "Nothin' says lovin' like something from the oven." Children are comforted by food. It is a symbol of security. Food served with care and delight is an expression of love. Children will learn to enjoy more kinds of food and the many ways it is prepared if you encourage them to talk about the different flavors and other food qualities as you eat with enthusiasm and pleasure.

RECOGNIZING NUTRITION

"It's good for you" is a phrase that can turn children off. Good health can turn them on. You can help children learn that nourishing food helps them grow and to be strong and energetic. Talk about the value of milk in building good teeth. Mention carrots and apples as nature's toothbrushes. Build the idea of "yes" to fruits and vegetables and "no" to many sweets. Discuss how breakfast really can start a good day. From their experiences at the child care center, children sometimes teach their parents about nourishing food.

USING SELF-HELP SKILLS

Consider the many opportunities for young children to use self-help skills when food is served. Before eating, they wash their own hands. They follow a pattern when going to the table and starting to eat. When they serve themselves, they are learning to make decisions about how much or how little of each food to take. They are also learning to use a napkin and food utensils, usually a spoon and fork. Children can pour their own beverage if you steady the glass, fill the pitcher half full, and start the pouring by putting the notch point (lip) over the rim of the glass. As children participate in the clean-up process, they are learning order, care of property, and concern for others.

EXPERIENCING COURTESY

Children learn by doing. Eating time should not be a continuous lecture on manners. But thoughtfulness toward others should be part of the child's experience. When you say "please" in asking for something or "thank you" as food is passed to you, you are setting an example that children will follow.

Practicing Eye-Hand Coordination. Opportunities for coordinating the sight of food portions and small-muscle movement are ever-present as children are involved with food. It's a challenging experience to manipulate peas onto a spoon. Peeling a banana is another example of coordinating both eye and hand movements.

Figure 7-1. Every meal is an opportunity for children to practice their eye-hand coordination. (Joan Menschenfreund)

LEARNING IN OTHER SUBJECTS

Besides the learning experiences already mentioned, eating times provide many opportunities to strengthen subject-matter learning. The following subjects are only a few of the possible examples. How many more examples can you think of?

Language Skills. Talking at mealtimes helps children to relax while they eat. It makes them eat more slowly. You could ask them to comment on the sounds food makes when it is eaten (crunchy or chewy). Or ask whether they enjoy the taste (sweet or sour) of the food. In this way, words become connected with foods and eating activities. For instance, the word *delicious* usually applies only to food.

Math Skills. Encourage children to comment on the number and shapes of food items. For instance, "There are five glasses of milk on the table." "Our plates are round, but the brownies are square." Even the idea of *fractions* is experienced: "You have eaten half of your cookie."

Art Skills. The colors and textures of food should be pointed out to children. Apples are red. Bananas are yellow. Oranges are orange. Putting all these foods together makes a nice combination of colors.

Science Skills. How food is produced and how it changes form when prepared relates to science. The act of making apples (solids) into apple juice (liquid) always interests children. Such ideas help them to apply scientific concepts to real life.

Music Skills. Singing during preparation and clean-up of food makes eating routines fun.

Social Studies Skills. The entire process of producing food—from the farmer, to the trucker, to the grocer, to consumers, and to cooks—is a study of social and economic activities. This can be discussed at the table, especially if the children have taken field trips to a farm or supermarket. Foods from other nations—tacos, matzoh, spaghetti—also make children aware of the differences among the people of the world.

Learning from Special Projects. Besides the daily opportunities to learn, special projects can be planned around eating routines.

Holidays and Birthdays. Holidays set the stage for food customs to be explored. Birthdays are another special time that can include food experiences.

Visitors. Visitors—such as a mother who makes bread with the children, a milk deliverer, or a cook—stimulate interest in food.

Cooking Experiences. Including cooking experiences as a part of the children's eating program wins every time. Who can turn down a serving of applesauce when he or she helped cut the apples and stir them while they were cooking?

Sometimes simple self-help preparation of foods becomes a special project. Peeling an orange, shelling a peanut, squeezing a lemon, or

Figure 7-2. Children are always more enthusiastic about eating food that they have been allowed to help prepare. (Betty Terhune)

spreading peanut butter can give a child the feeling of success and an interest in eating.

Field Trips. Going to a bakery, to a dairy, or to someone's garden can stimulate interest in the eating of various foods. Discussing these events at the table will remind the children of such first-hand experiences for a long time.

PARTICIPATING IN EATING ROUTINES

Plans for getting ready to eat will vary, depending on the setting and resources available.

PREPARING THE SETTING

Whenever possible, the children should be involved in preparing for meals.

Clean the Table. Clean the tables before setting them. Use soap, hot water, and clean sponges that are used only for food service. This is especially important when the play tables are also used as dining tables and when sponges are used for art projects.

Show the children how to wash the tables, squeeze out the sponge, and then rinse the tables. Guide their assignment of wiping the table. You should not use the children to do your job; instead, you want to provide a good experience that, with practice, can become a skill. As children become familiar with the routine, expect them to complete more of the task and to do it better.

Check the Number to Be Served. If the center has a cook, you may be responsible for reporting how many children and staff need to be served. Whether there is a cook or not, someone must decide how many glasses, napkins, and plates will be needed.

Set the Table. You might be responsible for setting the table. Use children to help when you can. If this hasn't been done before, ask your teacher's permission to try it. Taking turns allows each child in the group to benefit from the experience. John and Julie help today; Bill and Sue help tomorrow. They can be called *snack helpers* and wear hats or symbols to identify them as such.

Place the correct number of chairs at the table. Then you can give the snack helpers the experience of matching items (a *one-to-one relationship*). For example, you might tell the children to place a glass on the table in front of each chair and then to put a napkin near each glass. If buffet service is used, set out the number of glasses or dessert dishes needed.

Sometimes large place cards with a picture or name are used to show where children sit. This allows children to recognize their names in print or symbol. It also gives you a chance to have children sit together for different reasons. It may be that a good eater will stimulate a poor eater. A shy child may be helped by a comfortable, outgoing one. You might want to separate two talkers so that they will eat more and talk less.

Don't forget to have serving utensils ready. A tray, to put dirty glasses or dishes on, must be available. Sponges for mop-ups, dishes, and a beverage pitcher are also needed. If children are to help serve, fill serving dishes about half-full. Remember the serving spoons if food is in a serving dish. If the children must keep leaving the table to get food or utensils, the order they achieved in getting to the table is quickly lost and is hard to regain.

When food is ready and the table is set (with serving items available), it's time to invite the children to eat. This may be done with a signal such as a bell or a piano note, or by having a snack helper tell other staff members to bring children to eat.

GETTING CHILDREN READY

Plan a Quiet Activity. Children who are too hungry, too tired, or too excited do not enjoy their food. It helps to have a quiet activity just before the snack or meal. During this time, children who need to use the bathroom may do so. All wash their hands and then join a quiet activity, such as a story, music, or talking time.

Use Interesting Experiences. Keeping order as children approach the table can be accomplished by saying, for example, "All those with blue shoes go first; those with white shoes next."

The way children feel about themselves is often seen in their attitudes toward food. Be sure to keep the children's feelings about themselves in mind as you make choices. For example, if Martin tends to feel left out, look at the kind of shoes he's wearing and call for that kind first.

At times a child is asked to choose a friend to take to snack. Ways of getting to the snack area can differ. One child may want to walk with a friend. Another may want to walk alone while tiptoeing. Whenever possible, however, have the children make choices, because decision-making will help them learn to solve their problems.

Perhaps Ellie has been troublesome all morning because she wanted to be recognized by the other children. You should acknowledge her in a positive way. Ask her to choose a friend to take to snack. When you ask her to decide whether they will skip or hop to the snack area, she can only make a positive decision.

Use Descriptive Language. "Go to the table as quietly as a feather blowing in the wind," is much more effective than the order "No talking." Or ask the children to describe something

quiet. Then encourage them to proceed as quietly as their example.

SERVING THE FOOD

How the food is served will depend on the resources available and the style of food service used in the eating routine.

Resources Available. Food service depends on the resources available, such as facilities and personnel, building, and equipment. Dining facilities affect where the food is served. Play tables may become dining tables for a snack or a meal. Some centers have dining rooms. Others use counters, even though they limit eye contact between children and caregivers.

When there are only a few staff members, children's plates may be served in the kitchen and brought to the table. In small centers, teaching staff may need to help prepare the food, serve, and then join the children at the table to eat it. In other centers, where there are more staff members, a cook may prepare the food and someone else will serve it.

Styles of Food Service. Food may be placed in bowls and platters and served at the table. This is known as *family-style service*. This style of

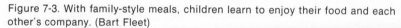

Figure 7-3. With family-style meals, children learn to enjoy their food and each other's company. (Bart Fleet)

food service has advantages: With family service it is possible to *model* (act out) good food habits. Children enjoy each other's company. Conversation is encouraged among children.

Perhaps the most important advantage of family-style service is that it provides many opportunities for self-help. Children can pass the food and serve themselves. With a little help, they can pour their own juice. If the pitcher has a good pouring spout, is small enough, and is not too full, a child enjoys pouring. Very young children need help with aiming the pitcher at the glass, and they do not know when to stop pouring. A child care aide must supervise this kind of activity.

Snacks may also be served *cafeteria style,* which means that the children get their beverage and other food (in individual servings) from a special place. A table, a counter, or a kitchen pass-through window are the usual locations.

Children who get their snack cafeteria-style may not sit down to eat it. In this case, they miss the type of relaxation and talk that comes from sitting together at a table. Enjoyment of food gets mixed up with other activities, and crumbs and spilled juice may cause some problems. Many families use this kind of "eat on the run" approach.

SUPERVISING EATING

Start Together. The children should arrive at the table in an orderly way. As mentioned earlier, some centers *assign* eating places, using symbols. Children will recognize names if they can read. Sometimes a child is assigned the space next to the teacher or between two other children. Some children prefer the security of sitting in the same place each day.

In some private centers, a simple blessing or prayer begins the meal service. A word of caution: You should respect the feelings of parents regarding prayer in the center. If there are no objections, a short, simple prayer of thanks can be given. But such a prayer should not pertain to any one religion. In other centers, teachers begin the meal service by assisting children as they serve the plates or by inviting children to serve themselves from a serving dish.

Children's behavior is related to their stage of development and to what adult supervisors expect. If you balance what you expect of the children with their ability to do it, you will find that children will have more successful experiences.

The eating routine should be the same each day. If you let the children grab their food as soon as they get to the table on one day but make them wait on another, they will become confused. Waiting is a learning experience. In fact, short waits help children learn to postpone gratification of their desires and to work toward long-range goals.

Model Behavior. What does it mean to *model behavior?* It means that what you do is an example for the children who watch you. Suppose you don't like milk. You don't eat liver. Vegetables turn you off. You skip breakfast. Children are good watchers, and they will notice and copy your food habits, good or bad.

During food time, be a good model. Set a good example by serving yourself a portion of each food and eating all you have taken with pleasure. When you enjoy food, children will be more likely to eat it with pleasure, too. Even though there's a tendency for children to choose familiar foods, set an example by eating the unfamiliar, and invite them to join you. Keep the size of servings small. Children may have second helpings if they wish. Introduce new foods one at a time, along with well-known and well-liked foods.

Children may have trouble staying at the table for the entire snack or meal. The length of time young children remain seated may be lessened by having the children carry their dirty dishes to a side table or counter. You can be a model by staying seated throughout the meal, leaving food service from the kitchen to someone else. If you have to serve and supervise at eating time, try to have everything you need on the table before the snack or meal begins. It's hard for children to understand that they must sit throughout the meal if you get up from time to time.

Provide Guidance at the Table. As a child care aide, you set the stage for a pleasant eating time. Talk with the children about the food's

Figure 7-4. Successful completion of self-help tasks leads children to feel more self-confident and to repeat the effort. (Kenneth Karp)

textures, names, and colors. Comment about its flavor: "This fresh pineapple tastes sweet." You might mention where a food comes from. Encourage self-help through simple directions such as, "Pull the paper off before you eat your cupcake." Take advantage of the many learning experiences that are possible at mealtimes.

Notice the good actions and words that children do and say. It's hard for children to enjoy food when you are criticizing them.

Children's appetites may vary from day to day. Some days children may not feel well; they may be tired or simply not hungry. Young children have been known to go on food "jags" (wanting only certain foods for a period of time). Therefore, do not expect the children to eat the same amount of food each day.

Self-help builds self-esteem (that feeling of "I can do it," "I like myself") and self-control. This, in turn, leads to self-respect. All these "self-" developments lead to better eating habits. You can aid this process by making positive statements like "You *did* drink all your milk"; "That's right, take the first cookie you put your

hand on." How good it feels to the children when they can serve themselves and have someone share this success!

Try to Prevent Accidents. Help the children sit comfortably in their chairs. If you see that a small child has a big chair or a large child a small one, try to find a chair that fits the child better. Sitting squarely and comfortably on the chair (rather than on the edge) prevents falls.

Small servings and half-filled glasses help to avoid spills. Staying seated also helps. Passing food, rather than reaching across the table, results in fewer accidents and better manners.

Help Children Learn from Accidents. When accidents happen, use them as an opportunity for children to learn. Milk may be spilled, or a plate may be knocked off the table. Food may be dropped or may overflow because a child has misjudged distance or lacks skill in handling utensils.

Have a clean sponge or cloth ready. Hand it to the children and teach them how to clean up.

If the spill or accident is large, help the children. You must move quickly so that the accident will be kept to a small area. A sponge will stop a liquid from flowing off the table into someone's lap or onto the floor. Focus on helping the children with the clean-up job. Spills are embarassing and make children feel bad enough without scolding. You may want to watch certain children more closely, especially those who have poor motor skills. Remember, your job is to help children succeed, not to point out their failures.

ENDING THE EATING ROUTINE

Procedures for ending eating times vary in child care centers. You and the children need to know what the procedure is and to follow it regularly.

Follow Established Procedures. The procedure may include putting dishes on a tray and paper napkins in the wastebasket or trash can. Chairs may be pushed under the table and sticky hands may need washing. Whatever the procedure, you should give the children directions about the next activity before you leave the eating area.

At its best, the children's help accomplishes the housekeeping chores as part of the meal service. Children scrape their own plates and put their glasses away. Certain self-help jobs—such as cleaning the table, helping to get utensils and dishes back to the kitchen, or wiping off the tables—may be assigned to the children in turn.

Work as a Team Member. Teamwork is needed to accomplish a smooth transition from eating to the next activity. You may be asked to leave the table or food area a short time before the children, in order to prepare the program area to which the children will move. Or your assignment may be to stay with the children. It might even be to follow up in the kitchen, putting food away and starting the dishwasher. Whatever assignment you have, it is an important part of the team effort, and you must do it well.

Evaluate Your Performance. Each time you complete an assignment as a child care aide, you should review the experience and discuss it with your supervisor. After you are comfortable with the assignment, you can give it less thought. But until you are familiar with the methods of helping children learn all they can from the eating experience, your evaluation should be formal and should include a meeting with your supervisor as well as a checklist.

CHAPTER SUMMARY

1. Food is served in most child care centers and usually consists of a midmorning snack, lunch, or an afternoon snack.

2. The type of food service used in child care centers depends on the size of the center. Larger centers usually have more facilities and staff members to help prepare, serve, supervise, and clean up after meals.

3. Eating time is another excellent time for learning. When possible, the children should be involved in the preparation of certain foods and with setting the table. You can help by showing good table manners. Also, you should provide guidance at the table: sit down and eat with the children, using the proper utensils.

4. When accidents happen, use them to teach children how to clean up themselves.

5. Eating time is also a good time to experience learning in other subjects. Math, language skills, and other subjects can be part of the eating routine. For instance, you and the children can talk about how many children are sitting at the table.

6. As with most group activities, teamwork—between you and the children and other staff members—is needed to accomplish a smooth eating routine, including the clean-up part. Teamwork eases the transition into the next activity.

• WHAT HAVE YOU LEARNED FROM THIS CHAPTER?

Several new words and ideas were presented in

this chapter. To see whether you understand them, match the letter of each term below with the numbered phrases under "Definitions."

Terms

a. Eye-hand coordination
b. Eating routine
c. Model behavior
d. Family-style service
e. Snack helper

Definitions

1. The things that are done over and over each day in relation to eating
2. Serving food by placing it in bowls and on platters and serving it at the table
3. Acting out good food habits
4. Coordinating sight of food pieces and small-muscle movement
5. Child who assists with some meal routine task, matching items, such as a glass with a glass

• PROJECTS, DECISIONS, ISSUES

1. Indicate whether you *agree* or *disagree* with the following statements; comment on your answer.
   a. Visitors disrupt eating and should not be invited at mealtimes because they excite the children too much.
   b. Young children should not have to wait to start eating at the same time.
   c. Eating time is a fun time; therefore teaching should be reserved for other parts of the day.
   d. A child care worker does not have to eat the same food as the children, especially if she is dieting.
   e. Since family service provides so many opportunities for learning, licensing standards require this style of service in all child care centers.

2. You have been given the assignment of getting the children ready for snack. How will you do it?

3. Keep a log of your experiences with children's eating routines. Specifically, record the learnings taking place and identify the subject area involved.

4. You are a member of a team. Anticipate what your assignment might be and tell how you would carry it out.

5. Select two classmates and role-play the occurrence of an accident and the desirable follow-up. Do a rerun of the same basic accident situation in terms of how it might have been prevented or minimized. Point out differences in two role-playing skits.

• WHIFS (WHAT WOULD YOU DO IF . . .)

1. Everyone has arrived at the table and Michele quickly drinks her juice, gobbles down her cookies, and says, "I want more." What would you do?
   a. Remind her to share
   b. Tell her to be polite
   c. Give her as much food as she wants
   d. Ask her if she had breakfast
   e. Tell her, "Let's wait until everyone has been served."
   f. Other responses

2. As Karen pours milk into her glass, she misses the glass and pours it on the table. What would you do?
   a. Give her your milk
   b. Go get a sponge
   c. Send her for a sponge
   d. Clean it up
   e. Other responses

3. At lunch, Sandy helps herself to two handfuls of bread sticks. What would you do?
   a. Make her put them back
   b. Take them away from her
   c. Pretend you don't see her
   d. Tell her to share
   e. Make her give one to each child in the group
   f. Other responses

8 SUPERVISING REST

After you have studied Chapter 8, you should be able to:

1. List two reasons why children need rest
2. Identify four things that you should do to get the environment and children ready for nap time
3. Demonstrate ways that child care aides help children to nap
4. Demonstrate ways that child care aides end nap time effectively

CHILDREN NEED REST

Children need rest mainly because they get tired. You will see many tired children in child care centers. Living in a group all day is emotionally and physically tiring for children. In addition, today's busy life of many activities, irregular hours, family mobility, and general lack of routine often causes children's rest to be disturbed or cut short.

EMOTIONAL FATIGUE

The stimulation of group living—with its close contact, noise, and movement—affects children's emotional energy. Tired children in group care may not be relaxed children. Sharing toys, friends, and a teacher can cause *emotional fatigue*, which makes it difficult for the children to unwind.

PHYSICAL FATIGUE

Children use their bodies a great deal in learning and growing. After children have climbed, run, pulled, pushed, lifted, and jumped, they have made themselves physically tired. Children who feel *physical fatigue* find it easier to fall asleep than children who are emotionally tired.

SIGNS OF FATIGUE

As a child care aide, you should always be alert to *signs of fatigue* in the children in your group. Often, you will be able to tell just by watching their eyes. If *eyelids are drooping* or being rubbed, chances are that the children are tired. Other signs of fatigue are *crying*, and *fussing*, or *whining for no reason*. Tired children often show fatigue by their posture—they will lean against things or hang onto the caregiver.

Some children may seem to have extra energy when they are tired, especially when they are emotionally fatigued. Children whose behavior indicates that they are overstimulated (they may be jumping, squealing, or talking in high-pitched voices) are just as likely to be suffering from fatigue as children who look drowsy.

REST NEEDS VARY

Children's needs for rest vary, either because of their basic stamina or because of the state of their health. Some children simply need more rest than others. Children who are ill will be more likely to welcome rest than to fight it.

As a caregiver, you will notice that children find their own ways to rest. One child who has been running may rest by lying on the grass and looking at the clouds; another may sit by the caregiver and talk.

The length of the children's day at the center also affects how much rest they need. The longer the day, the more important it is that rest be part of the regular nap time. Children whose day at the center begins at 7 in the morning and ends at 6 in the evening, for example, need to go to sleep in the middle of the day. On the other hand, quiet times that provide a change of pace may meet the rest needs of children who are in a 3-hour program.

WAYS TO PREVENT FATIGUE

To prevent fatigue and overexcitement, caregivers schedule alternate periods of active and quiet play. They encourage children to pace themselves during free-choice time, both indoors and outdoors. Caregivers know that the comfort and security of a *regular schedule* helps reduce emotional fatigue. Therefore caregivers try to follow a regular schedule that is familiar to the children. In addition, nooks and quiet corners (both indoors and out) help children to enjoy quiet play away from the stimulation of the group.

REST ROUTINES

PREPARING FOR REST

The routine of getting the room ready for rest period should be the same each day. In some centers, an aide puts down cots while children are eating. In others, children unfold their mats in their assigned places.

Day care licensing standards usually call for a certain amount of space and distance between children's faces. If their heads and feet are alternated, the distance between faces is greater, which keeps germs from spreading. Licensing standards also require that exits and passageways be kept clear in case children need to leave the center in an emergency.

The room should be well ventilated but free of drafts. If the room is cold, covers should be provided. Unusual temperatures may make the children restless and may even lead to health problems.

Children should be assigned regular places for taking their naps. They should have their own cots or mats and their own blankets. This is good not only for health reasons but also be-

Figure 8-1. Each child should have his or her own cot and blanket. This gives the child a feeling of belonging to the group. (Kenneth Karp)

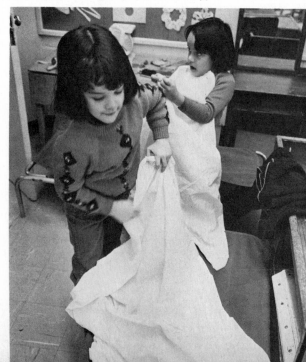

cause it gives children the feeling that they are part of the group, or a sense of *belonging*.

PREPARING THE CHILDREN

Children need to be prepared for rest. When naps are the main part of rest time, children should use the bathroom before settling down. Some children will need to use the bathroom after they have relaxed a little, but many children use a trip to the toilet as a way to stall or avoid going to sleep.

Centers vary with respect to the amount of clothing removed at nap time. Usually, shoes are taken off and are placed under the child's cot or in a locker. Whatever the *rest routine* (procedure that occurs every day), it should not change often.

When children sleep in their underclothing, a cover such as a sheet or blanket should be placed over each child.

Avoid Stimulation. Caregivers should see that there is as little excitement as possible during nap time. Toys should be removed so that children are not tempted to play with them. Caregivers may need to separate friends, since talking is likely when they are near each other.

Caregivers should take advantage of *visual barriers,* which keep children from seeing other parts of the room. Children who become excited as their fatigue increases should be assigned napping places away from the main group (such as behind a table or a bookcase). The other children will benefit from the removal of the active child.

The use of books or toys as a way of making the transition from play to sleep is not a good idea. This kind of play equipment is used to stimulate children at other times.

Drinks of water should be discouraged at nap time. Usually, children have just finished lunch, and they should not be thirsty. Besides, drinks before nap time may lead to bed-wetting.

Lights Out. Turning the lights out and drawing the shades can be the caregiver's *cue* (signal) for "Now it's time to go to sleep." Soft music can also be used as part of a *sequence* (series) *of cues* to which children learn to respond.

HELPING CHILDREN TO NAP

Children cannot be forced to go to sleep, but they can be encouraged to respond to a routine rest procedure. As a child care aide, you need to have a positive, patient attitude toward children's rest. When you are supervising rest time, you should help to set the stage for children to sleep. Assist individual children in relaxing, and show children by your attitude that you know they will be able to go to sleep.

As with all other activities, you need to be in a position where you can see all the children. While supervising, speak softly and only when necessary. There should be little movement, and it should be quiet.

HELPING CHILDREN TO RELAX

Children need time to unwind and to make the transition between activity and sleep. This is part of the getting-ready-to-sleep process. Children may fool with their shoes, tug at the blanket, move around on the cot, or even get underneath it. By allowing this time, a caregiver is more likely to get an effective response to cues such as turning off the lights and saying, "Now it's time for sleep."

As a child care aide, you can help individual children to relax in several ways. While some children are still "unwinding," you can help the child who is almost asleep to be more comfortable by tucking in a cover or adjusting a cot. By helping children who are ready for sleep, you give more time to those who take longer. When you are helping a child get to sleep, you should sit on a child-size chair or on the floor. Children's cots are strong enough for children, but they are *not* made to support adults. You should try to find a comfortable position for yourself, since you will not be able to help a child relax unless you are relaxed. Do not, however, become so relaxed that *you* fall asleep.

Often children will tell you how you can help them to go sleep: "Rub my back," or "Don't touch me. Just stay close."

NURTURING

When children are tired, they need a nurturing person to make them feel safe and comfortable.

They may "want Mommy," especially when they are new to the center and find it difficult to relax. When children get homesick, they may want the comfort and security of sucking their thumbs, twirling their hair, or holding a toy from home.

If a child asks, "When is Daddy coming?" caregivers should give an honest but descriptive answer. In other words, a caregiver should not answer, "When you wake up" unless the child's father *will* be there when the child awakens. Whatever the answer, it should give the time in terms of the routine which the child knows, such as, "Mommy will be here after you get up and have finished your snack."

RECOGNIZING INDIVIDUAL DIFFERENCES

Since children have individual rest needs, they will sleep for different lengths of time. In some cases, it is wise to awaken a child who seems to be sleeping an extra long time. The child's parents will have trouble with bedtime if nap time is too long or occurs too late in the day.

Children should not be punished when they do not go to sleep or when they awaken after a short nap. Sometimes, caregivers can help a child who wakes up early to go back to sleep. But if a child is fully rested, other quiet activities—such as looking at books—can be chosen to fit the quiet period.

SUPERVISING NAP TIME

Once children are familiar with naptime routine, there is less need for individual help. Usually, supervision by one caregiver is enough. When children are settled down, the caregiver may sit in a rocker or a chair and relax. The caregiver should never go to sleep but must always remain alert to the needs of the children.

Children may awaken and be frightened to find that they are not at home; or a cover may get tangled in such a way as to make breathing difficult. All these possibilities require the immediate attention of an alert caregiver.

USING STAFF TIME DURING REST PERIODS

How staff members use nap time is decided by the child care center. Whatever the overall plan for staff time is, at least one staff member must watch each group of sleeping children carefully.

CHANGING PACE

As a caregiver, you should not spend the entire time that the children are resting in working hard yourself. The children will be refreshed and full of energy when they awaken from their naps, and they will need a caregiver who is rested, rather than one who is tired, cranky, and irritable.

A change of pace often meets an adult's need for rest. Most staff members use nap time for group or individual planning sessions as well as for conversation or a snack. Such activities provide enough relaxation to increase the caregiver's emotional and physical energy.

ENDING NAP TIME

During the transition period following nap time, caregivers work as a team. The teacher may stay in the nap area with children who are still sleeping or just waking up, while the child care aide supervises the children who are already up and involved in some activity. If snack time follows shortly after the nap, another staff member may be getting the food ready.

USING WAKE-UP TIME EFFECTIVELY

The period during which children are waking up is an excellent time for a child and a caregiver to get to know one another in a special way. Since children will awaken at different times, the chance for individual attention can take place with several different children, one after the other, during each transition period. You notice that Joe gets his colors mixed up as he names them in the book. You listen to Carla's speech and realize that she doesn't pronounce the *th* sound. Stephanie seems so shy when she has a teacher all to herself, she makes only brief eye contact but mostly drops her eyes when the teacher looks at her. Such important actions may not take place or be noticed when a child is part of a group.

Figure 8-2. Wake-up time is a good opportunity for the caregiver to give the child some individual attention. (Michael Weisbrot)

ENCOURAGING SELF-HELP

Children should be allowed to do as much as they can for themselves before and after nap time. They also should be encouraged to participate in the housekeeping procedures that follow nap time. When they understand that putting cots and bedding back in their assigned places is part of the naptime routine, children usually enjoy getting the room ready for work or play.

EVALUATING NAP TIME

Any significant changes in children's behavior should be reported to the supervisor or teacher. Changes that would be considered significant at nap time include a high fever, vomiting, or other signs of illness, sudden awakening from a nightmare, bed-wetting, and excessive crying. As a caregiver, you will want to tell your supervisor if a child was very restless at rest time or behaved in a way that disturbed the other children during rest period.

Any equipment or materials that need repair (a broken cot, a torn blanket) should be reported to the supervisor or taken care of by the caregiver.

As a caregiver, you should evaluate your performance in supervising nap time. You should ask yourself whether you were comfortable and relaxed enough to help the children get ready for sleep and whether you remained alert and watchful throughout your assignment. Did you do your part as a team worker in the naptime routine? It is important to check your own performance and to talk over your feelings and problems with your teacher.

CHAPTER SUMMARY

1. Children need rest because they can become physically and emotionally tired in group care and because group living uses more energy.
2. Children's rest needs are different, depending on the individual child, his or her health, and the length of the day.
3. A regular schedule and switching between active and quiet periods are two ways in which a good program can help to prevent fatigue in children.
4. Caregivers' responsibilities at nap time include preparing the space and the children for rest, helping the children relax and go to sleep, supervising during rest, and helping to bring the rest period to a close.

● WHAT HAVE YOU LEARNED FROM THIS CHAPTER?

Several new words and ideas were presented in this chapter. To see whether you understand them, match the letter of each term below with the numbered phrases under "Definitions."

Terms

a. Emotional fatigue
b. Signs of fatigue
c. Significant
d. Visual barrier
e. Physical fatigue
f. Rest routine
g. Sequence of naptime cues
h. Regular schedule
i. Belonging

Definitions

1. Rest-time procedure that is the same each day
2. Object which stops child from seeing other parts of room
3. Fatigue from active use of body
4. Something that helps to prevent fatigue
5. Steps taken in getting ready for nap, such as turning off lights, playing records, etc.
6. Fatigue resulting from stimulation of emotions
7. Drooping eyelids, crying, whining, excessive energy
8. Important
9. Feeling that one is part of the group

• PROJECTS, DECISIONS, ISSUES

1. Indicate whether you *agree* or *disagree* with the following statements; comment on your answers.
   a. Children should be awakened from their naps if they sleep too long.
   b. Child care workers can go to sleep when the children do, because it's better to have a rested child care worker than a tired one after nap time.
   c. Looking at books is a good nap or rest time activity.
   d. Tell a child Mommy or Daddy is coming after nap time to comfort him or her, even if you don't know when the parent is coming.
   e. Children require different amounts of sleep at night or rest time.

2. Describe the behavior of a child care worker who has a positive attitude toward nap time.

3. Describe and explain the value of following a sequence of cues from beginning of nap time until it's time to go to sleep.

4. Observe nap time in a day care center. Watch the waking-up transition time and record the one-to-one interaction you see between individual children and the teacher or aide.

5. Check your local day care licensing standards regarding requirements of rest and/or nap. Report to your class what you find.

6. Role-play or carry out steps assigned by your teacher in preparing for rest, supervising rest, or bringing the rest period to a close.

• WHIFS (WHAT WOULD YOU DO *IF* . . .)

1. Leslie wet his bed during nap time. What would you do?
   a. Get the janitor
   b. Leave the room
   c. Scold him
   d. Remove Leslie to the isolation room
   e. Comfort Leslie
   f. Remove bedding and wet clothes and replace with dry
   g. Other responses

2. Brett wakes up screaming. What would you do?
   a. Call your supervisor
   b. Pick Brett up
   c. Rub his back
   d. Tell Brett to be quiet
   e. Talk softly to him
   f. Other responses

3. Kathy wants a back rub, then all the children want their backs rubbed. What would you do?
   a. Tell them no back rubs
   b. Rub Kathy's back
   c. Rub the back of your favorite child
   d. Rub the back of the leader
   e. Other responses

4. Jimmy and Mike are playing with stuffed animals and having a lively conversation as well. What would you do?
   a. Take the toys away with no comment but an angry look
   b. Tell them to put the toys on the shelf
   c. Ignore them
   d. Request that they put the toys away
   e. Other responses

5. Sarah will not take her shoes off at nap time. What would you do?
   a. Let her keep them on
   b. Force her to remove them
   c. Request that she remove them

d. Offer to help her

e. Other responses

6. Dennis has been to the bathroom twice and says he has to go again. What would you do?

   a. Tell him to go on but report his behavior to your supervisor

   b. Refuse to let him go

   c. Tell him he doesn't need to go, he's been twice already

   d. Scold him, but let him go

• CHECK YOURSELF

Carefully read each item and answer *yes* or *no* in terms of your performance in relation to nap time responsibilities.

1. Do you recognize signs of fatigue by noticing children who

   a. Rub eyes

   b. Cry

   c. Are irritable

   d. Whine

2. Do you prevent fatigue by

   a. Alternating active and quiet activities

   b. Using a regular schedule

   c. Providing nooks and quiet spaces

3. Do you effectively prepare for rest by

   a. Preparing the rest room or area

   b. Preparing the children for rest

   c. Minimizing stimulation

   d. Using a sequence of cues

4. Do you effectively supervise nap time by

   a. Choosing a location where you can see all the children

   b. Helping children relax

   c. Helping children feel safe and comfortable

   d. Recognizing individual differences

   e. Following naptime routine

   f. Respecting center policy regarding staff time during rest period

   g. Having a personal change of pace

5. Do you effectively bring nap time to a close by

   a. Using wake-up time effectively

   b. Encouraging self-help

   c. Participating in transition activities

   d. Working as a team member

6. Do you evaluate nap time by

   a. Reporting significant changes in children's behavior

   b. Evaluating your own performance (were you relaxed, alert, successful in helping children rest?)

• STUDENT ACTIVITIES

1. Give two reasons why children in child care centers need rest.

2. List three ways you can tell that a young child is tired.

3. What are three ways to prevent fatigue in young children in child care centers?

4. Name four things you should do to get the environment and the children ready for nap time.

5. Identify five things you can do to help children sleep at nap time and demonstrate them if possible.

6. List three things for you to do at the end of nap time; use them if possible.

9 SUPERVISING HOUSEKEEPING ROUTINES

After you have studied Chapter 9, you should be able to:

1. State four reasons why housekeeping is important to children
2. Name four ways to involve children in housekeeping
3. Demonstrate five ways to create and maintain a responsive environment
4. Prepare a bulletin board to display children's artwork

In child care centers, *housekeeping* refers to creating and maintaining an attractive and safe setting for children. The never-ending process of keeping toys, supplies, and equipment orderly is part of each child caregiver's assignment.

Maintaining an environment that is orderly does not mean keeping it so neat and tidy that children are uncomfortable. Children need to use their hands to feel and enjoy messy things and to handle large and small toys and books. They use their bodies and legs to explore space and to play creatively. The children's classroom may appear to have wall-to-wall supplies, toys, equipment, and children during free-play time. However, when free-play time is over, these items *and* the children should become orderly.

Things that are alike in some way are grouped together. Supplies, toys, and games are put in their assigned places. Children should help to clean up and then should move on to another activity in a familiar and comfortable way.

Are you a good housekeeper? Do you already have the habit of putting things back where they belong when you are finished with them? Do you see that toys, children's clothing, and other objects are picked up? If so, you know where to find things quickly and without frustration when you need to use them. If not, you should start now to develop this habit, which is an important ability for child caregivers.

HOUSEKEEPING IS IMPORTANT TO CHILDREN

Good housekeeping is an important part of child caregiving for several reasons, which are discussed below.

FEELING SECURE IN AN ORDERLY WORLD

Children feel that they are part of the action when they know where things belong and what is expected of them. They feel secure when they know what comes next.

110

Figure 9-1. Children enjoy messy activities like fingerpainting. (Michael Weisbrot)

FREEDOM TO MAKE CHOICES

Children can learn what is available when things are in place. This helps them to make choices. They can choose something to play with, select an object to use in an art project, or find a way to solve a problem. "How can I cover this hole? I'll see what's in the box of lids."

BUILDING A GOOD SELF-CONCEPT

To depend on the environment helps build confidence. When children know where things go, they can help put them there, and they can get them by themselves. They enjoy helping others, both children and adults, by running errands for them. "Let me, I can get it" is an expression of confidence that builds self-esteem.

ENJOYING AN ATTRACTIVE SETTING

Both children and caregivers are pleased by attractive surroundings: "Our room really looks good"; "Our paintings are on the bulletin board"; "That's so pretty. I like flowers on the snack tables."

BETTER CHILD CARE

When things are in order, a caregiver is able to capture the "teachable moment" and add "just the right touch." That is, there may be enough time to find a magnifying glass with which to watch the ants at a newly discovered anthill. Or you may take a moment to nurture a child in a casual but meaningful way by providing a soft, fluffy scarf for the child who is "baby" today.

Children benefit from the teamwork and positive communication that result when each caregiver accepts responsibility for housekeeping. The unpleasant parts of housekeeping are well known. When you are annoyed by trying to find something that was hurriedly tucked away, or by having to clean up another staff member's mess, your annoyance has a "ripple effect." The bad feelings spread like the ripples in a pond when a pebble is thrown into it. For example, you may be annoyed when another staff member leaves the paint supplies on the counter of the workroom. If you are not careful, you may find that your bad feelings about something like this will spread, and you may take your anger out on the children.

WAYS TO INVOLVE CHILDREN IN HOUSEKEEPING

Housekeeping is a self-help skill for young children. Whenever and wherever children can get their own materials or play equipment and put them away after use, they should do so. Open shelves and storage containers marked with symbols help children know where things go. Enough—but not too many—items on a shelf or in the room make things manageable for children. Be sure that objects are not crowded and are easily found. Set an example of good housekeeping habits, and the children will follow your example.

CONTINUOUS HOUSEKEEPING

Have you ever wondered whether you should make the children pick up their toys right after they use them or at the end of playtime? Like many questions about children, the answer to this one depends on the situation.

Table 9-1 CLEAN UP AS YOU GO

Guideline	Things to do
Return small items to assigned places after use.	Return books to shelf; flannel figures and puppets to storage places; puzzle pieces to puzzle pegs; game pieces, crayons, chalk, and small objects to containers.
Protect materials from drying out.	Cover up fingerpaints, clay, and other materials.
Make materials and play or work areas attractive for other children to use.	Roll clay into balls for someone else to use; return art supplies to containers; tidy the art area; tidy other areas if they are uninviting to the children.
Pick up toys that are in the way or in the path of traffic.	Pick up and put in place items such as books, wooden beads, collage pieces, trucks, and dolls, and blocks.

There are some situations in which housekeeping should take place as play is going on. Such a clean-up-as-you-go plan should be used as shown in Table 9-1.

When there is a danger that someone may trip or be hurt, you should pick up small objects and other materials. If you see a child play with or leave something in a *traffic pattern* (the main path where children and adults walk), tell the child to pick it up and put it away. Say, "Stephen, put the truck on the bottom shelf if you are finished with it. Someone may step on it and fall."

If you do not know who left the toy or object in the path of traffic, or if there are no children around, or if the children are busy, pick the truck up and put it away without comment. Good housekeeping is a skill that you can teach by example and by discussion at an appropriate time rather than by scolding and criticism.

CLEAN-UP TIMES

Besides the continuous housekeeping that takes place in child care centers, housekeeping is sometimes done by everyone at the same time. These times usually come at the end of an activity, as after free-play time, after outdoor play, or after projects in music, art, science, mathematics, or language arts. All the children and adults help. Your role is to teach the children how to clean up. This isn't easy, especially with children who are good at avoiding things. To avoid clean-up, they may say that they need to use the bathroom in a hurry. Others may tell you either that they didn't play with anything or that they have already put their things away. A few guidelines for group clean-up follow:

Figure 9-2. Children help with housekeeping tasks at the end of most activities. (Kenneth Karp)

Everyone Helps. Putting things away after each use takes time and often distracts children. When it's clean-up time, all the children should help put items in their proper places. Your willingness to help gives an example for the children to follow. You can encourage children to take part by showing that you expect everyone to help and by praising good work. Let the children know that you will help them put things away, especially if the job is difficult or if the children are tired.

Give Simple, Clear Directions. Clear directions—given one at a time or to each child at a time while demonstrating your instruction—teach children the skills of housekeeping. Say, "Elizabeth, I'll show you how to put the doll to bed," and talk as you show her. "First, put a sheet in the bed and smooth it out. Now put your doll in bed. Cover her with a sheet and blanket. Fold the blanket and put it in the dresser drawer. Do you know how to fold it? I'll help you."

Check the children's work and tell them when the work is well done. If it is not done well enough, considering the age and experience of the children, point out the good part, and show them how to correct their mistakes.

After a child has been given directions and has had time to carry them out, do not go into details. "Josephine, clean up the doll corner please" is direction enough.

Allow Plenty of Time. Housekeeping is part of learning. Time for housekeeping must be part of the daily schedule. You may have to cut back on activity time a bit to allow the children time to clean up. When children are learning how to clean up, do not make them do so many things that they become overwhelmed or confused. At first, for example, you may have them help only with the basic unit blocks, saving all the other block pieces until later, when they can follow the additional instructions.

WAYS TO CREATE AND MAINTAIN A RESPONSIVE ENVIRONMENT

Your housekeeping habits make a difference in the environment, and the environment makes

Figure 9-3. Toys and other things should be stored on shelves where children can reach and use them without adult help. (Bart Fleet)

a difference in children's feelings and behavior.

A *responsive environment* is one that promotes learning. It gives children the feeling that they affect the environment, that what they do makes a difference. Children who live in a responsive environment approach life not only with the curiosity of "Why is it so?" but also with the interested attitude of "We'll find out."

A LEARNING ENVIRONMENT

A responsive environment is a "hands on" environment. In such a setting, children feel free to handle objects, books, toys, and games. They feel free to explore how things work, and they try new ways of putting things together.

You can use good housekeeping to create a learning environment in the following ways:

1. Provide enough items to interest children but not so many that you confuse them.
2. Put things where children can use them with little or no adult help.
3. Keep things in the same place for a while so that the children can get used to the setting.
4. At times, use the walls, floor, shelves, windows, corners, and ceiling for attractive displays. In this way, you can stimulate interest, build self-esteem, and aid learning.
5. Organize the storage space for learning. Besides storing items on open shelves or special places in the classroom, the storage of

materials that you only use once in a while is important. These things—such as extra materials and equipment for replacement purposes or for seasonal use—are usually stored outside the classroom. All items must be marked and stored so that they are kept in good shape and are easy to reach, even in an out-of-the-way place.

Help with Big Projects. Children are tired at the end of activities. Sometimes they need your help to put things away. Add action to your words if the children seem tired or confused: "Edith, please bring me the blocks by your feet; I'll put them on the shelf for you." You may say to several children, "Bring the blocks to me and I will put them on the shelf." If a child has played with the blocks for the first time, do not spoil the experience by insisting on help with housekeeping. Invite the child to help, but don't make a fuss about it.

Keep Standards High. Housekeeping standards should match the children's overall abilities. Do not let the children just stuff things into drawers or throw them onto shelves. You can keep housekeeping standards high by having an occasional "inspection tour." Remember that children repeat successful experiences. Do not turn the inspection experience into a criticism session. You can be the inspector, or you can name a child or a team of children to take turns inspecting the area.

Make Clean-up Fun. Include singing as part of housekeeping. The children enjoy songs that tell them what to do. "This is the way we put up the blocks" (to the tune of "Mulberry Bush") or, "Where, oh where, does this toy go?" ("Paw-Paw Patch") are examples.

Let the Children Teach Each Other. "Many hands make light the work" is a true statement when children help each other. It is especially true when children enter the group at different times. For example, in many child care centers, new children are enrolled throughout the year. To introduce the new child to the idea of housekeeping, ask an old-timer to show the new child where things go.

Save Supplies. You have a responsibility to use supplies wisely. Supplies are sometimes called *consumable materials*; these are items that are used up, such as paint and paper. If such materials are bought only once a year and you use them carelessly, so that they run out, you will hurt the program. Either the children will have to do without supplies or money must be found to buy more. Many centers buy consumable materials in large amounts so that some are always available to the staff. The rest of the supplies are stored for later use.

Use the following housekeeping techniques to save consumable materials and supplies:

1. Use only the supplies you need.
2. Remove materials from their storage place carefully. For example, paper may be torn or bent when you close the closet or drawer carelessly.
3. Pick up materials that drop on the floor and put them where they belong.
4. Use a box for scraps. Lay scraps in the box without crumbling them, and teach the children to do the same.
5. Use scraps first, before using new supplies.
6. Cover materials that may dry out, such as clay, glue, or paint.
7. Put used items in the right place—on open shelves or in assigned places in the storeroom.
8. Label all items in boxes, drawers, or closets.

Find "Beautiful Junk." "Beautiful junk" includes items that have been thrown away and are usually available without charge. They may be found in many places: from stores and rummage sales or from friends of the center. When things are stuffed into paper bags or thrown into large boxes marked "beautiful junk," they tend to be more junk than beautiful. New items may be stored for later use. However, if they are not available when needed, they are of little value. By the time you find the needed item, the children may have lost interest in your project.

It is important for children to see what treasures are available and to understand how they are stored. Things that are alike are kept together. When lids, string, straws, buttons, and cardboard tubes are organized so that they can be found easily, such "junk" becomes not only beautiful but important to a responsive environment.

A SAFE, HEALTHY ENVIRONMENT

Basic care of the center is usually assigned not to child caregivers but to maintenance staff. However, all child caregivers are responsible for a safe, healthy environment. They should regulate ventilation, heat, and lights; wipe up spills and pick up objects in traffic lanes; clean off tables where food is served; and remove toys or materials that need to be cleaned or repaired.

AN ATTRACTIVE ENVIRONMENT

The physical environment of the room affects children's behavior. Bright colors, plants, well-placed pictures and other artwork and displays all make a room more attractive. Keeping it attractive is the goal of good housekeeping. There should be no bottles on the windowsill; plants should be watered and trimmed; and bulletin boards and other displays in the room should be rearranged often.

Displaying Children's Work. Even though young children usually want to take their work home at the end of the day, displaying their work makes the room attractive and builds self-esteem. If you want to create a holiday theme (say at Christmas), have the children make several items, but do not insist that all projects stay in the center. Some children may not want to leave their work behind.

Be sure all the children's work is displayed, not just the pieces you think are pretty. Use the colors, textures, and shapes of the children's work to decorate the room. Pictures, photos, models, and nature items need to be at eye level for children to study and enjoy. Anything within reach of children should be intended for them to touch and look at carefully. Use all parts of the room—windows, corners, shelves, and even the ceilings (for mobiles). Arrange to have private areas (corners) for children to go to when they want to do something alone.

Bulletin Boards. Children, parents, and visitors enjoy and learn from well-designed bulletin boards. Such displays also make the learning environment attractive and responsive.

Here are some basic guidelines about bulletin boards:

1. Identify the purpose of the bulletin board. Label it "The Vegetables We Eat," "Our School Day," or "Families Have Fun Together," for example.
2. Recognize good patterns for display. Use bright colors, unusual shapes, or large words. Prevent clutter; use the space effectively.
3. Use contrast. Attract the eye by combining bright and dull colors, or dark and light tones; use different textures.
4. Create unity. Repeat colors, textures, shapes, or sizes.
5. Select wording carefully. Use questions or problems to create interest; use few words and different kinds of lettering.

To save time in preparing the bulletin board, you can buy lettering. But if it is not available, make your own. Figure 9-4 shows you how.

When you have completed your bulletin board, evaluate it by using this checklist:

· Does the display draw attention?
· Is the lettering clear and easy to read?
· Are large and small letters used correctly?
· Are messages easy to read and understand?
· Do the children like the display (if it is intended for them)?

EVALUATE YOUR HOUSEKEEPING

How do you rate yourself as a housekeeper in a child care center? How does your supervising teacher rate your work habits? Use the following questions to help evaluate your housekeeping performance:

· Do you clean up your own area?
· Do you return things to the right place?
· Do you hang up clothing?
· Do you wipe up spills quickly?

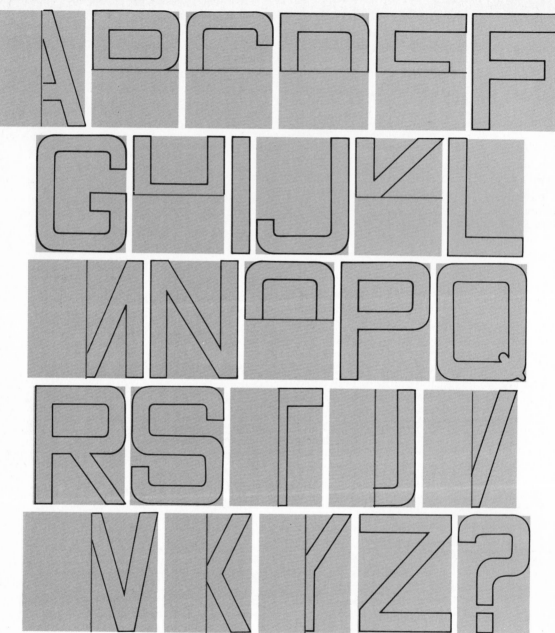

Figure 9-4. To make your own display lettering, fold and cut the paper as shown here.

· Do you protect areas with covers when painting or using other messy materials?

· Do you cover materials that spoil if exposed?

· Do you take care of children's projects so that they can be taken home in good shape?

· Do you encourage children to help with housekeeping?

· Are you a good model housekeeper for the children?

· Do you match your standards with the children's abilities?

· Housekeeping should not be a separate or dull chore. It is an important part of good child caregiving.

CHAPTER SUMMARY

1. In child care centers, *housekeeping* refers to creating and maintaining an attractive and safe environment. But the setting should not be so neat and tidy that children are uncomfortable. Remember that the purpose of housekeeping is to stimulate the children's participation and to promote learning, especially of self-help skills.

2. Housekeeping is important to young children, and they should be involved in it. Your housekeeping habits make a difference in the environment, and the environment makes a difference in children's feelings and behavior.

3. When children help to create a safe and attractive setting by keeping it neat and displaying their artwork, they take pride in the environment. As a result, the child care setting becomes a place they want to be. Usually, this feeling leads to better learning.

● WHAT NEW TERMS HAVE YOU LEARNED FROM THIS CHAPTER?

Several new words and ideas were presented in this chapter. To see whether you understand them, match the letter of each term below with the numbered phrases under "Definitions."

Terms

a. "Beautiful junk"
b. "Hands on" learning
c. Ripple effect
d. Housekeeping
e. Teachable moment
f. Continuous housekeeping
g. Responsive environment
h. Consumable materials
i. Clean-up times

Definitions

1. Keeping things in order
2. A time of discovery
3. The spreading outward of feelings
4. Clean-up-as-you-go process
5. Periods when everyone helps to pick up
6. A setting that invites learning
7. A situation in which children are free to handle things
8. Items that are used up
9. Someone else's discards

● PROJECTS, DECISIONS, ISSUES

1. Select one of the five reasons that "housekeeping is important to children" (listed in the text) and develop either a cartoon or a poster that will illustrate this reason visually.

2. Using Table 9-1, collect the necessary materials and set up a demonstration table that will show the right and wrong ways of doing housekeeping.

3. Choose one of the five ways to involve children in housekeeping activities. Set up and role-play this situation for the class.

4. Make a checklist using topics from the chapter that suggest a responsive environment and how it promotes good housekeeping. Use the checklist to evaluate either the child care laboratory or a community child care center.

5. Prepare a bulletin board for the public library in your community, displaying children's artwork from your school's child care laboratory.

6. Indicate whether you *agree* or *disagree* with the following statements. Be prepared to discuss or defend your decisions.
   a. Children feel more comfortable in a very tidy and neat room.

b. Child care aides are more effective in attractive surroundings.

c. It is easier, faster, and better for all concerned if child care aides do the clean-up without the help of children.

d. Only child caregivers should show new children in the child care center how and where things are stored.

e. Because children produce so much creative work every day, it is impossible and unnecessary to display it.

f. It is more important to send the artwork home with the children than it is to display it.

g. The child care aide's example can make housekeeping a dull chore.

h. Bulletin boards are more useful for adults than for children.

• WHIFS (WHAT WOULD YOU DO *IF* . . .)

1. It is the middle of the free-choice play period and several trucks have been left in the main path. You do not see any child playing with them but they are dangerous because if someone stepped on one they could be injured. What would you do?
   a. Make the nearest child pick them up
   b. Put them on the shelf yourself
   c. Let them alone
   d. Start a search for the offending child/ren
   e. Other responses

2. The parents have been bringing "beautiful junk" for several days. Their contributions are put in the storage room for later use, but it is almost impossible to get anything out of the room because of the quantity of materials that have been brought. What would you do?
   a. Avoid using items from the storage room because you can't find what you want easily
   b. Volunteer to organize the materials
   c. Complain about the disorder
   d. Put all the materials in one big box
   e. Have the children help you classify the materials
   f. Other responses

3. Alice paints at the easel each day. Her work is so much better than the other children's that it is consistently displayed. The children painting color splotches never have anything displayed. What would you do?
   a. Make models for the other children to paint
   b. Help the other children paint pretty pictures
   c. Discuss your concern with your supervisor
   d. Display each child's work at some time and in an attractive way
   e. Remind Alice that she has had a turn to show her paintings and now it is time for someone else to have a turn
   f. Other responses

4. You go in the workroom to prepare materials for your assignment and find that another student has left the vinyl glue jar uncapped. There is vinyl glue on the work area. What would you do?
   a. Report the situation to your supervisor
   b. Cap the jar, wipe up the spills
   c. Say nothing to anyone
   d. Complain to other students
   e. Wait until another time to prepare your materials
   f. Other responses

• STUDENT ACTIVITIES

1. State four reasons why housekeeping is important to children.
2. List five ways a child care aide helps to conserve supplies.
3. Name four ways to involve children in continuous housekeeping.
4. Name three techniques child care aides should use to involve children in clean-up time.
5. Tell what is meant by a "responsive environment."
6. List five ways to create and maintain a responsive environment and carry them out if possible.
7. List five basic principles to be followed when making a bulletin board.

10 | SAFETY RESPONSIBILITIES

After you have studied Chapter 10, you should be able to:

1. List three safety practices child caregivers must follow
2. Identify six precautions necessary to assure safety for young children
3. Identify three ways caregivers teach children the safe way
4. Outline the steps to be taken in case of accident or injury to a child and during an evacuation procedure in a child care center

THE IMPORTANCE OF SAFETY

More children die each year from accidents than from any other cause.[1] Part of the reason for this is that *safety hazards* (dangerous conditions) are not always easy to see and safety measures often do not come to mind until there is an accident. If you do not follow the guidelines of your center, you may be held responsible for the incident. If you have done everything that you should in an emergency, it will be handled as a situation that may occur in any child caregiving setting, and your supervisor will follow up on the situation.

Children's safety has always been the main concern behind child care licensing standards. Even the lowest standards focus on safety. Therefore, safety is a basic part of child care services. Without safety, even a well-planned program may be dangerous to children.

PRACTICING SAFETY

"I care about children enough to protect them from harm" is an essential part of a good child care aide's attitude. It makes the child care aide aware of possible safety hazards.

As a child care aide, you can take steps to provide a safe environment for young children. Remember that it is not enough to think quickly during a crisis. You must think ahead to build safety habits and avoid dangers.

YOUR RESPONSIBILITY

Child care aides have a responsibility to carry out the safety and health guidelines of their center, which are based on licensing standards. A child's

[1]*Your Child from 1 to 6*, U.S. Department of Health, Education, and Welfare, Children's Bureau, Publication No. 30, 1962, p. 74.

119

Table 10-1 CLOTHING GUIDE FOR CHILD CARE AIDES

Do wear clothing that	Do not wear clothing that
Fits well	Is tight enough to restrict movement
Is comfortable	Gets in your way—long skirts, flare-legged pants,
Allows you to focus all your	wide sleeves, dangling jewelry
attention on the children	Attracts attention away from the children—flared
Is washable	pants, high-heeled shoes, clogs, see-through
Is durable	shirts
Is easy to maintain	Is your best or newest outfit that you are afraid to
	get dirty, torn, or harmed in any way

health and safety is a great responsibility that you share with other staff members. As a child care aide, you must do everything you can to keep the children from harm.

Your supervisor will explain your responsibilities regarding safety. If you follow the health and safety guidelines for your center, you will provide safe care for each child. If an accident occurs, report it at once to your supervisor, who will help you handle the emergency.

PERSONAL SAFETY HABITS

Your good *personal safety habits* will benefit both the staff and the children. As a child care aide, your actions should set a good example for the children.

Safe Clothing. When you work with children, choose your clothing with safety and comfort in mind. The following guidelines in Table 10-1 will give you an idea of what kind of clothing is best.

You will find that the most practical way to protect your own clothing is to wear a smock (loose-fitting jacket), preferably one with big pockets that can be used to carry clean tissues, a note pad, and other small items.

Comfortable Shoes. As a child care aide, you will spend much of the day on your feet. Your shoes must be the right size and give good support. Low heels will let you move quickly and safely, and closed toes will protect you when children step on your feet. Avoid high heels, clogs, sandals, and bare feet.

Save Energy. Caregivers need lots of energy to

perform their duties. Therefore, do not waste energy by lifting children who are able to walk. Let the children walk if they can, even if it takes a little longer to get where you're going. You should not try to move large, heavy objects (such as a piano). Lifting and pushing can cause back injuries as well as use extra energy. Remember that, as a child care aide, your responsibility is caring for children, not moving large equipment. Get the custodian for such tasks.

Figure 10-1. Child care aides should wear comfortable and durable clothing. (Kenneth Karp)

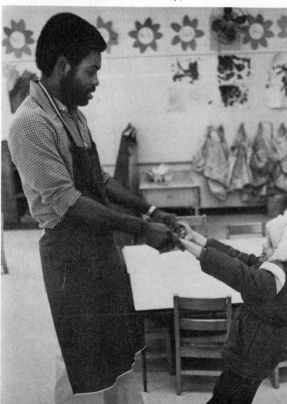

AVOIDING HAZARDS

Possible hazards may be found in all areas of the center—the children's area, the cooking area, the supply closet, the medicine cabinet, the laundry room, or the playground. You can help to eliminate or at least reduce hazards by:

1. Being observant and reporting conditions in the building or on the playground that may harm children
2. Making sure that dangerous items or equipment are kept out of children's reach
3. Using dangerous equipment and materials in a safe way and teaching children to follow your example

Reporting Hazards. As a child care aide, you need to be aware of conditions on the playground or in the building that may harm children. Report such hazards as broken glass, a loose step, a nail that is sticking up, or a broken toy. In some centers, the staff often handles small repairs that can be fixed with a screwdriver or a small hammer.

Spills (water, food, or paint) should be wiped up at once, and any object that can cause someone to trip and fall should be picked up from the floor. It is especially important that traffic ways be kept clear. Closet doors should be kept closed, and doors, gates, and windows should be fastened. Rugs, shelves, and bookcases should be held firmly in place. Caregivers must examine the space and equipment that the children will use and they must remove any potential hazards.

Keeping Danger out of Reach. Child care aides must keep dangerous materials or equipment out of children's reach.

Poisons and Medicines. Young children often put things into their mouths, and so it is important that poisonous items be locked up. Medicines (including aspirin), household products (such as drain cleaners, laundry soap, and cleaning supplies), gasoline, and kerosene should all be stored properly, marked clearly, and kept where children cannot get them. Poisonous items should never be stored in soft-drink bottles or any other container that usually holds food or drink.

Sources of Burns. Licensing regulations require that open flames and other sources of burns be eliminated. Wall heaters, registers, and floor furnaces must have guards on them so that children are not able to touch hot pipes or heating elements. In the children's area, the hot water should be set at a lukewarm temperature or shut off, so that the children cannot be burned by hot tap water.

Children should not be able to reach matches, cigarette lighters, and small appliances like hot plates, toaster ovens, electric frying pans, and so forth. If you smoke, you must see that your matches or cigarette lighter are kept away from curious children. Remember that children move quickly. It takes only a moment when your back is turned for a child to pick up a book of matches or a lighter.

When using small electrical appliances, keep in mind that they can start fires and burn children. Carefully supervise the children when using small appliances. Keep the children away from hot areas or sharp edges. Always make sure that the electric cord is not crossing a traffic pattern, and remember to turn off and unplug the appliances when you are finished with them. Directions for using washers, dryers, and dishwashers should be followed carefully.

Drowning. Even a small amount of water can drown a child. You must be especially careful to supervise children when water activities are part of the day's program. Always be alert and ready to act quickly when children are near water. Licensing regulations are very strict when it comes to the use of pools or other water situations.

USING EQUIPMENT AND MATERIALS SAFELY

Some equipment and materials used in children's activities can be hazardous if they are used improperly or poorly supervised.

Cooking Equipment. There are two main hazards in cooking activities: knives and heat. Cooking experiences, therefore, should be matched to the abilities of the children, and they should always be supervised.

Cooking activities should be planned so that small numbers of children are involved for short periods of time. This will avoid crowding and pushing to see. Children should be allowed to participate, but proper utensils should be used. (Plastic knives are recommended, but small paring knives may be used with cutting boards and close supervision.) Children should be shown how to cut in a direction away from their bodies. You should stress that knives are to be used only when adults are present. Never leave a knife lying around.

When a stove or electrical appliance is used, the number of children participating should be limited. Children should be taught to keep their faces away from the steam and their hands away from hot pots or pans. Always use potholders to prevent getting burned; this sets a good example for the children.

Woodworking Equipment. The woodworking area should provide children with enough space to work without danger. There should be only a few children using the tools at any one time. Children should use goggles. Teach them to clamp wood firmly before hammering or sawing and to use both hands when sawing. (You may need to help a child start the first cut when using a saw.) Nails, wood, hammer, saw, and drill should all be locked up when not in use.

Scissors. The scissors, which children need for art and other activities, should have blunt points. This is essential for safety. But even blunt scissors have sharp blades, so children should learn how to pass them with the sharp edge pointing toward the floor. A scissors rack is helpful in passing and storing children's scissors. Children should not walk or run with scissors in their hands. Both children and caregivers should learn to return scissors to their assigned place after use. Return adult scissors to their storage place at once; do not leave them where the children can reach them.

Paper Cutter. The paper cutter is usually in a service area, away from the children. Sometimes children may go with you to such service areas. When you finish using the paper cutter, put the handle with the cutting blade down and fasten it with a hook, if possible.

Small Objects. Pegs, beads, macaroni or beans, pins, and wire should be used with care. Remind the children that these objects are to be used with hands only. Show them how to use them rather than calling attention to the dangers of putting them in their mouth, nose, or ears.

Glass Objects. Magnifying glasses, thermometers, glass jars, and mirrors can be dangerous when broken or used carelessly. Caregivers must set an example for the children. Call their attention to the need for handling such things carefully. Remember that safe use and good housekeeping practices are the best teachers.

Blocks. By themselves, blocks are not dangerous. But they become a hazard when children build a block structure so high that a chair is needed to continue building it. The chair might slip, or the structure might tumble onto other children. Some centers use the rule that children can stack blocks to their chin level. Caregivers should warn children of danger before the situation is out of hand. Encourage children to build things of manageable size.

Climbing Equipment. Climbing equipment should be securely anchored and free of rough edges and loose screws or parts. Caregivers should check carefully for any of these dangers. Report them promptly. Portable climbing equipment should be set up so that it will not move or sway in use. Boards should be placed so that one end will not pop up when a child steps on the other end.

Climbing requires close supervision by caregivers. Stay close to climbing structures and keep a sharp eye on all children in the climbing area.

Rope. Rope can be used for climbing and for dramatic play, but caregivers must watch children closely. Children easily get carried away during play and can choke each other accidentally, especially if they are imitating something they have seen on television.

Sand. Both sand and the materials used with it can be dangerous. Shovels, buckets, measuring cups, and so forth may have sharp, rusty edges that can cause injury when used carelessly. If the number of children in the sand area is limited, sand will be less likely to get into a child's eyes. Children who throw sand should not be allowed in the sand area with others. Sand can scratch the eyes, especially when children rub them.

Animals. Animals that are suited for children can easily be cared for and are harmless. Children should be taught not to tease or abuse animals. They should learn not to pet an animal that is eating. It is also dangerous for a child to go near an animal while the child is eating, because the animal may go for the food if it is hungry. Use care in removing pet droppings. After handling pets or their feeding equipment, children should wash their hands—especially before they handle food.

SUPERVISING EFFECTIVELY

We have said that supervision is truly "super vision," and that caregivers need to be able to see in several directions at once. As a caregiver, you should learn to watch children from the corner of your eye as well as seeing those directly in front of you. You should always try to position yourself so that there are no visual barriers between you and the children. In this way you can watch several activities at one time.

You should always be aware of where your children are and what they are doing. Count the children from time to time. If you have to leave your group for a while, arrange for someone else to supervise them. Always tell your substitute how many children there are, which program they are on, and when you will return.

At the center, children should have an adult near at hand. On field trips or nature walks, when children are away from the protection of the center, keep track of all the children at all times. You should expect the children to be excited on field trips, because of the differences in routine and environment. Schedule quiet activities before and after the trip. Carefully planned short trips are usually better for children than long ones. Short trips are simpler, the staff and children are more relaxed, and the children become less tired. When supervising field trips or nature walks, some experienced caregivers use a knotted rope to move a group of children through busy areas. Each child holds onto a knot in the rope, and one adult leads the line while another adult brings up the rear.

Teaching Children the Safe Way. As you know, children respond better to directions or instructions that are positive rather than negative. In calling good safety habits to children's attention, remember that they learn more quickly when they are told to *do* something (rather than *not* to do something). For instance, instead of saying "Tommy, please don't bang the blocks together," you can say "Tommy, let's see how high we can pile these blocks."

A good program should include activities that are designed to help children learn how to work and play safely. For example, "Stop, look, and listen" teaches children the meaning of a traffic light's colors and can be learned through a song, a story, conversation, or pictures.

Figure 10-2. For art activities, children should be given scissors with blunt points and should be taught not to run or walk while holding them. (Kenneth Karp)

A Good Match. You have learned that a good program should match children's abilities with their environment. This good match both encourages learning and promotes safety.

When an activity is beyond the abilities of a child, a safety hazard may be created. A toddler will not be able to control a real hammer safely, but a 5-year-old, whose motor skills are more advanced, can use the same equipment with less danger. When children's abilities are well matched with their activities, safety is more likely to result.

Freedom with Protection. We have mentioned several times that children must have the freedom to explore and experience in safe surroundings. Caregivers must provide a good balance between freedom and protection. As a child care aide, you must understand that children sometimes learn through bad experiences. You must use your common sense and good judgment in deciding when something is part of a child's learning process and when it is a danger to him or her.

TRANSPORTATION PROCEDURES

As a child care aide, you should learn your center's procedures for loading and unloading children from private cars and school vehicles. You should also learn any other transportation guidelines used by the center.

For the sake of safety, children should stay in one place with a caregiver while waiting for their rides. This is true whether transportation is provided by the center or by the parents. In some centers where parents provide transportation, a drive-in system is used. The cars line up one behind the other and pull up to the area where the children are waiting. In this way, caregivers can fully supervise the loading of children into cars.

When parents come at different times, they must park their cars and come into the building to pick up their children. Children should never be sent out to the street to meet parents.

Parents also should be made to understand the importance of telling the center who will pick up a child. Caregivers cannot allow a child to leave with anyone who has not been ap-

Figure 10-3. Caregivers should carefully supervise the loading of children into school buses or other vehicles. (Michael Weisbrot)

proved by the parent who enrolled the child or with anyone whose name is not recorded in the child's file. This is especially important when the parents are separated or divorced, since the child may then be in danger of emotional or even physical harm. In some cases, a legal liability may be involved, and the child care aide may be cited as part of the legal action taken.

When the center provides transportation, the standards and procedures set forth in state licensing regulations should be followed. The driver of the school vehicle carrying the children should have a chauffeur's license. The children should be supervised, so that the driver is not distracted. Supervision needs depend on the number, age, and special problems of the children being transported and on the time of day and the traffic.

Children should be seated and doors should be locked before the vehicle is put in motion. The children should be delivered safely to the right address and into the care of a responsible person before the bus or car drives on.

TAKING STEPS IN AN EMERGENCY

As a child care aide, you will face emergency situations. It is important that you remain calm so that you can decide what help is needed and see that it is provided.

ACCIDENT OR INJURY

If an accident occurs and a child is injured, send word to your supervisor or a responsible staff person at once. Do not leave the scene of the accident: instead, send another adult with the message. If no adult is close by, send a responsible child.

As a child care aide, you will have completed a first-aid course and will be able to follow standard procedures in case of an accident. Review the first-aid techniques with your teacher or supervisor from time to time, so that you will be able to handle an emergency situation.

Remember these basic rules of first aid.

First aid is the "immediate and temporary care given the victim of an accident or sudden illness until the services of a physician can be obtained."[2] The first objective is to save life. To do this, you must

· Prevent heavy loss of blood
· Maintain breathing
· Prevent further injury
· Prevent shock
· Call a physician

The first aider must also:

· Avoid panic
· Inspire confidence
· Do no more than necessary until professional help arrives

While you wait for help, use first-aid precautions and techniques. Encourage the other children in the group to continue their activities by behaving in a *calm, confident* way. If you need to explain to curious youngsters what has happened, keep your voice low and steady. Give the impression that everything will be all right by keeping your body and face calm and relaxed.

When a supervisor or director arrives, you will have help in deciding what steps to take. If the injury is slight, a substitute will supervise your group while you give follow-up first aid. If the injury is great, medical help will be needed at once, and the parents will be notified. Caregivers will work as a team in such situations. One staff member will care for the injured child, another will make any needed telephone calls, and a third will care for the other children. You should learn the location of the *first-aid kit* and manual. Every so often, check what is in the kit to make sure it includes needed first-aid materials.

PROCEDURES FOR LEAVING THE CENTER

To meet licensing standards, every child care center must have a plan for getting children out in the event of fire, gas leak, bomb scare, hurricane, or tornado. This plan must be approved

[2]American Red Cross, *Standard First Aid and Personal Safety*, Doubleday, Garden City, N.Y., 1973, pp. 13–17.

Figure 10-4. By taking roll call during a fire drill, the caregiver can make sure all the children are evacuated from the building. (Kenneth Karp)

by the fire department. Licensing regulations require that the plan be posted in the center and explained to all staff members. It should be practiced often, without warning.

The plan should specify the area to which children and staff must go, the route they must take to get there, and the responsibilities of staff members regarding safety. They should check bathrooms and other places where children may be hiding. A roll call should be taken when everyone is out of the building to find out whether anyone is missing.

Fire drills should be called often enough so that all staff members will know and be able to carry out their responsibilities. Fire drills also help the children to learn about the emergency alarm and how to leave the center. In this way, they will not be so upset by an actual emergency.

WEATHER EMERGENCIES

Sometimes, storms such as hurricanes or blizzards may require emergency measures. A plan for gathering children in a safe, protected part of the building (away from windows and glassed-in areas) should be set up in case of tornado warnings.

The rule that requires a child to be picked up by a known adult is always in effect, whether the weather is stormy or fair. The same applies when the center provides transportation: the child must be delivered to a responsible adult no matter what the weather is like. Caregivers cannot take shortcuts with safety procedures.

CHAPTER SUMMARY

1. Protecting children is a main concern of any child care program. Interest in children's safety is an important part of a child care aide's attitude. Caregivers must teach children good safety habits by their example.
2. Child care aides must also be alert to safety hazards in all areas of the center. Safety measures include good supervision, proper use of equipment and materials, and removal of hazards.

3. Child care aides should know about first-aid procedures and should be calm and effective in case of an accident.
4. Every child care center must have a plan to leave the center in case of fire, bomb scare, gas leak, hurricane, or tornado. Staff members and children should practice the plan so that they will know how to act in an emergency.
5. Safety measures may vary with the age of the children (who have different motor skills) and the types of play equipment.

• WHAT HAVE YOU LEARNED FROM THIS CHAPTER?

Several new words and ideas were presented in this chapter. To see whether you understand them, match the letter of each term below with the numbered phrases under "Definitions."

Terms

a. Personal safety habits
b. Safety hazards
c. Calm and confident
d. First-aid kit

Definitions

1. Modeling behavior that prevents accidents
2. Those things in the child's environment that can be identified as dangerous to safety
3. A box containing the items necessary to give treatments for an injury
4. How a caregiver should feel in an emergency situation

• PROJECTS, DECISIONS, ISSUES

1. Develop a checklist of safety hazards in your child care center. Then ask your supervisor whether you may suggest safety measures that might be adopted to reduce or eliminate the hazards.
2. Enroll in and complete the Multimedia Red Cross First Aid Minicourse. Select one part of the course and give a demonstration or report to your class.

3. Develop two posters, each illustrating a safety practice. Display them on the classroom bulletin board.

• WHIFS (WHAT WOULD YOU DO IF . . .)

1. A child falls and cuts his hand on a piece of glass from a soft-drink bottle. What would you do?
   a. Faint
   b. Call your supervisor
   c. Talk softly to the child while you examine the wound
   d. Wash the cut
   e. Put a bandage on the cut
   f. Call the parents
   g. Take the child to the hospital
   h. Other responses

2. You see smoke coming around the edges of a closet door. What would you do?
   a. Open the closet door
   b. Ring the fire gong
   c. Say nothing . . . you don't want to alarm anyone
   d. Run out of the building
   e. Tell your supervisor
   f. Have the children use the fire drill procedure and leave the building
   g. Pour some water on the door
   h. Other responses

3. The fire bell rings during naptime. What would you do?
   a. Ignore it, the children need their naps
   b. Get the children up and out in a hurry
   c. Complain about the noise
   d. Shout "There's a fire, the gong is ringing!"
   e. Other responses

4. You see a loose board on the outdoor playhouse. What would you do?
   a. Pull it off
   b. Tell the children the board is loose
   c. Get a hammer and fix it
   d. Tell your supervisor
   e. Complain to the janitor
   f. Other responses

5. A rusty nail is protruding from a climbing ladder. What would you do?
   a. Ignore it, that's not your job
   b. Pull it out
   c. Hammer it in
   d. Tell your supervisor
   e. Tell the janitor
   f. Other responses

6. Name three safety practices that should be followed in a child care center.

7. Place the following steps in the sequence you would follow in handling a child's injury.
   a. Administer first aid or get medical help
   b. Assist supervisor in deciding further steps
   c. Use first-aid precautions
   d. Send child or teacher to tell supervisor
   e. Encourage children to continue their activities
   f. Stay calm yourself
   g. Move the child if advisable

8. From the following list, select the terms or phrases that represent good personal safety habits:
   a. Enjoying dangling jewelry
   b. Picking up toys
   c. Wearing washable clothing
   d. Locking up poisons
   e. Wearing comfortable shoes
   f. Closing cupboard doors
   g. Carrying children
   h. Having household products handy
   i. Moving pianos
   j. Unplugging appliances

• STUDENT ACTIVITIES

1. Name three key safety practices to follow in a child care center.
2. List at least two personal safety habits of child care aides.
3. Identify six precautions necessary to assure safety for young children.
4. Name four kinds of equipment or materials that can be dangerous and describe safety measures to use with each.

11 | HEALTH RESPONSIBILITIES

After you have studied Chapter 11, you should be able to:

1. State three measures a child care aide should take to prevent disease
2. Name four specific ways that your health habits affect children
3. Demonstrate what you need to know and do in order to assist with the health supervision of children
4. Outline the steps to be taken when a child becomes ill

Each adult in a child care center has the great responsibility of guarding the health of the children. As a child care aide, you have three basic responsibilities for children's health:

1. Preventing disease from spreading
2. Teaching good health habits to the children
3. Recognizing and responding to disease symptoms and other health problems of children

PREVENTING DISEASE

The best way to fight disease is to take measures that will prevent it. Children in group care are more likely to be exposed to disease than those at home, who have less contact with other children their age. So it is important for caregivers to take measures that will prevent germs from spreading. Caregivers must also understand the importance of immunization shots in preventing disease.

KEEP GERMS FROM SPREADING

The following practices will help to keep germs from spreading in a child care center:

1. Use tissues (not handkerchiefs) for runny noses. Throw them away right after use. Place them in a proper container and do not leave them lying around or put them in your pocket.
2. Turn your head away and cover your mouth when coughing or sneezing. Use a tissue if you can. Set a good example for the children.
3. Remove soiled clothing or bedding quickly and place it in the proper container. Do not leave it lying around.

4. Report any infections or illnesses you have to the supervisor, who will decide whether or not you should be near the children.

5. Wash your hands with soap and water and dry them thoroughly before you touch food and after toileting or any activity that is dirty or messy.

6. Put children's names on their own items and give them an assigned place.

7. See that the children use their own wash-clothes, towels, toothbrushes, sheets, blankets, and cots.

8. Keep sick children away from others.

SET A GOOD EXAMPLE

You already know how important it is for caregivers to have good health habits *and* to be in good health. Your health affects the way you behave, and your behavior is an example that children will copy. A caregiver who enjoys good health has the patience and energy to care for children in a cheerful, warm way.

PHYSICAL CHECKUPS

Many centers require or prefer caregivers to have regular medical checkups or at least chest x-rays. In this way, health problems can be found early and corrected. This benefits the caregivers as well as the children.

MEDICAL HISTORY

Can you say which childhood diseases you had? You may not remember all of them, but there may be some that you can still catch. Try to learn which diseases you had (such as measles or mumps). Check with your doctor about immunization against other diseases. This is important not only to keep disease from spreading but also because some childhood diseases can be more harmful to adults than to children.

STAYING HOME WHEN SICK

Although you may not feel too bad when you have a sore throat or a very slight fever, it is wise to stay home until you are well. Then you cannot infect the children or other child care workers. If you wait until you are very sick before you stay home, it will take you longer to recover and you may spread germs around the center. When you *are* ill, take enough time to get well before you return to work.

Some illnesses are common among children, and you can expect to have a number of coughs, colds, and sore throats until your body has built up defenses against them.

PERSONAL GROOMING

As a caregiver, you can practice good personal hygiene (cleanliness) by making sure that your body, hair, nails, and clothing are clean and neat. Your hair should be cut or clipped so that it does not get in your eyes or get in your way when you are working with children. If your hair is long, you should put it up or pull it back. Fingernails should be trimmed, clean, and short so that you don't scratch children by accident and spread germs.

TEACHING GOOD HEALTH HABITS

Caregivers teach children good health habits by their example. But there are also other ways that you can stress good health practices with children.

Figure 11-1. As a caregiver, you are responsible for teaching children good health habits. (Bart Fleet)

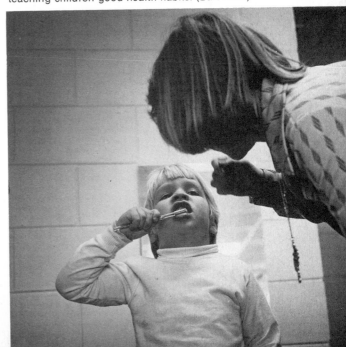

Table 11-1 COMMON COMMUNICABLE DISEASES OF CHILDREN

Disease	First signs	Incubation period*	Prevention	How long contagious	What you can do	Keep at home†
Chickenpox	Mild fever followed in 24 to 36 hours by small raised pimples which become filled with clear fluid. Scabs form later. Successive crops of pox appear.	2–3 weeks; usually 13–17 days	None. Immune after one attack.	1–2 days before and 6 days after appearance of rash. Scabs are not infectious.	Not a serious disease; trim fingernails to prevent scratching; a paste of baking soda and water, or alcohol, may ease itching.	For 6 days after rash appears.
Rubella	Slight fever, mild cold symptoms or sore throat may precede tiny, rose-colored rash. Enlarged glands at back of neck and behind ears are usual.	2–3 weeks; usually 18 days	Vaccinate children 1 year to puberty (12 years of age)	Until rash fades. About 5 days.	Not a serious disease; complications rare; give general good care and rest.	For 5 days after beginning of disease.
Mumps	Fever and nausea followed by painful swelling of glands near ear and about the angle of the jaw. Other parts of body may be affected also.	12–26 days; usually 18 days	Immunize children prior to school entry if recommended by your doctor.	Until all swelling disappears.	Keep child in bed until fever subsides; indoors unless weather is warm.	Until all swelling disappears.
Measles (rubeola)	Sore throat; red, watery eyes; running nose; fever. Red rash or blotches appear in 3 to 4 days. Small red spots with white centers in mouth appear before rash. Eyes sensitive to light.	Usually 10 to 11 days	Immunize all children 10 mo. to 12 yr. of age who have not already had measles. Recommend immunization earlier than 10 mo. of age when and only when measles is	4 days before rash and 5 days after rash appears.	May be mild or severe with complications of a serious nature; follow doctor's advice in caring for a child with measles, as it is a most treacherous disease.	During catarrhal symptoms and for 7 days after rash appears.

			present in community. Repeat pre-10- mo. immunization at 12–18 mo.			
Roseola	High fever which drops before rash or large pink blotches covering whole body appear. Child may not seem very ill despite the high fever (103°–105°F), but he or she may convulse.	About 2 weeks	None. Usually affects children from 6 mo. to 3 yr. of age.	Until child seems well.	No special measures except rest and quiet.	Until child seems well.
Strep throat (septic sore throat) and scarlet fever (strep throat with rash)	Sometimes vomiting and fever before sudden and severe sore throat. If followed by fine rash on body and limbs, it is called scarlet fever.	1–5 days; usually 2–5 days	Antibiotics may prevent or lighten an attack.	7–10 days. When all abnormal discharge from nose, eyes, throat has ceased.	Frequently less severe than formerly; responds to antibiotics, which should be continued for full course to prevent serious complications.	As long as physician advises.
Whooping cough (pertussis)	At first seems like bad cold with sneezing and dry cough. Changes at end of second week to spells of coughing accompanied by a "whoop."	7–21 days; usually under 10 days	Immunize all children at 2 months of age. Usually given with immunization for diphtheria and tetanus (DPT).	At least 4 weeks. Exposed children should be kept at home as soon as cold symptoms appear.	Child needs careful supervision of physician throughout this taxing illness.	For 3 weeks after the "whoop" is first heard. Exposed children should be kept at home if cold symptoms appear.

Source: From information in *Communicable Diseases of Children,* Georgia State Health Department, and *Your Child from 1–6,* U.S. Department of Health, Education, and Welfare, Children's Bureau, Publication No. 30, 1972.

*Incubation period is the usual amount of time which elapses between exposure to the disease and onset of the first symptoms.

†Consult your physician before allowing child to return to school after having had any of these communicable diseases.

PLANNED EXPERIENCES

Planned activities are one way to help children learn the basic rules of good health. For example, washing hands, brushing teeth, eating good food, and covering coughs or sneezes with a tissue can all be part of music or story time. Cooking experiences can include learning about the importance of cleanliness when cooking and about the kinds of foods needed for good health. In dramatic play, you can use doctor's and nurse's equipment to make points about health care.

Audiovisual materials such as puppets, filmstrips, and activity charts can be used to help children learn about practicing good health habits. A set of scales and a growth chart (or simply marks on a wall) will show children that they are growing.

TEACHABLE MOMENTS

There are moments that especially lend themselves to teaching about health, just as there are good times to stress other areas of learning. Caregivers should watch for times when children are curious and eager to learn about health. You should realize that illness is a very personal experience. Help the children to put their feelings about being sick into words. These moments offer caregivers the chance to help children build a good attitude toward health, and to correct any mistaken ideas children may have about illness. Children often associate doctors, hospitals, and nurses with "being sick" or "hurting." It is important to show them that these people and places help to get rid of pain and illness rather than cause them.

RECOGNIZE COMMUNICABLE DISEASES

Most *communicable diseases* (diseases that spread easily) have early warning signs or symptoms. Often, different diseases may have the same symptoms at the beginning. Caregivers should know the symptoms of illnesses as well as their contagious period (the time period during which a sick child can infect other people). Children should stay home during the contagious period. Table 11-1 lists this information; you should study it carefully. Most centers have such a table or chart posted, so that staff members can check it when they think a child may be sick. When one child gets a communicable disease, the parents of all the children in the group should be told at once.

IMMUNIZATION

There are two ways to *immunize,* or defend, the body against communicable diseases. In some cases, the body builds up a *natural defense* against the germ. This is why many childhood diseases can be caught only once.

The kind of immunization which doctors give when they *vaccinate* children or adults takes advantage of the body's ability to develop its own defenses against a disease. A very small amount of a particular disease germ (measles, for example) is injected into the bloodstream, so that the body begins to produce the type of cells needed to fight the germ.

By learning a few facts about the common communicable diseases a child may have, you may be able to prevent the disease or hasten the recovery period. (*Always follow a physician's advice concerning the care and treatment of any of the diseases listed in Table 11-1.*)

Immunization helps to prevent such childhood afflictions as diphtheria, whooping cough, polio, rubella, tetanus, and mumps. All children should be immunized against these diseases by the time they are 2 years old, because they are more dangerous to infants, toddlers, and preschoolers than to older children. Polio and diphtheria are especially dangerous to children less than a year old. The American Academy of Pediatrics advises the schedule of immunizations shown in Table 11-2.

It is not up to the caregiver to take children for immunizations. That is the parents' responsibility. You may, however, be asked to check the children's health records to see that all the immunizations are up to date. If they are not, the center must remind the parents to finish the immunization series or get the recommended *boosters* (the shots that boost, or increase, the body's ability to fight germs). In Table 11-2, you will notice that the immunization known as

Table 11-2 SCHEDULE OF IMMUNIZATIONS

Immunizations	Age		
	Months	**Years**	
DPT	2 3 4 6	1–1½ 5 12	
	X X X	X X X	
OPV trivalent (polio)	X X X	X X	
Live measles	X		
Mumps	X		
Rubella	X		

Source: Day Care Health Services, A Guide for Project Directors and Health Personnel, U.S. Department of Health, Education, and Welfare, no. 1791-0162, Washington, D.C., pp. 37–38.

DPT is recommended beginning the second month after birth. DPT immunizes against three diseases—diphtheria, pertussis (whooping cough), and tetanus—so it is an important shot. DPT boosters are given at 3 to 6 months, at 1 year, at 5 years, and at 12 years. But parents sometimes forget to take their children for DPT boosters (or other immunizations) unless they are reminded.

RESPONDING TO HEALTH NEEDS AND PROBLEMS

Children's health needs are not limited to protection from communicable diseases, of course. Caregivers must always be on the lookout for signs of all types of health problems.

HEALTHY CHILDREN

Before you can understand how to recognize signs of health problems, you need to know how children look and behave when they are in good health. Healthy children show it in their physical appearance. They have clear skin, bright eyes, shiny hair, and straight posture. And they gain in height and weight.

Healthy children behave as you might expect. They have lots of energy, so they are usually active and often noisy. They have good appetites. They do not have to be urged to eat, but they do not stuff themselves either. Healthy children have strong, white teeth. Their bowel movements are regular and normal. And they are able to relax and sleep soundly when it is time to rest. When they are awake, healthy children are interested in what they are doing and what they are going to do. They meet new experiences with curiosity and excitement, and familiar things bring them the happiness and contentment that comes from security.

SIGNS OF ILLNESS

Sick children have little energy and short attention spans. They are often cranky or irritable. As a result, they may get into fights or minor conflicts more often than healthy children do.

Here are some specific signs to look for when you think a child is becoming ill:[1]

1. Flushed face and hot, dry skin; or unusual paleness or coldness
2. Unexpected, profuse sweating
3. Drowsiness, especially when the child is usually wide awake
4. Watery or glassy appearance of the eyes
5. Runny nose, sneezes, coughs
6. Sore throat, hoarse or husky voice, swollen glands
7. Nausea, vomiting, diarrhea
8. Stiff back or neck
9. Pain in ear, head, chest, stomach, abdomen, or joints
10. Rash, bumps, or breaking out of skin
11. Convulsions, fits, or spells during which a child stiffens and twitches

It is important to notice these first signs of illness so that children can receive care quickly and can be kept away from other children. When the early symptoms of illness are ignored, the illness may last longer and other children may be exposed to it.

[1] *Your Child From 1 to 6,* U.S. Department of Health, Education, and Welfare, Children's Bureau, Publication No. 30, 1977, p. 77.

DAILY HEALTH CHECK

Child caregivers watch each child carefully for signs of illness as the children arrive at the center each morning. This is often called a *health check*. It alerts the child care staff to any symptoms that should be watched during the day. A health check can be informal (included in a caregiver's greeting of each child) or formal (the caregiver may use a flashlight to check for sore throats and may feel under children's ears and chins for swollen glands). Whether formal or informal, a health check should not be frightening to children. It should be done in such a way that children see it as a good way to start the day.

Children have other health needs too. Caregivers must watch for signs of all types of health problems, including trouble with the teeth, eyes, or ears; physical handicaps; and emotional disturbances. The signs or symptoms of problems must be recognized and understood in order to correct the problems. You should therefore report any behavior that is unusual or not normal to the supervising teacher. For example, if you, as a child care aide, notice that some of the children in your group always hold picture books a few inches away from their faces, you should call your supervisor's attention to it. Probably the children should have their eyes examined. Or you might notice that a child in your group is unusually shy and perhaps slow in developing language skills. You should watch the child carefully and then tell the supervisor what you have noticed about the child's behavior.

Be alert both for changes in children's behavior that may signal the early stage of illness *and* for behavior that is abnormal and may indicate a health problem.

Usually, when problems are suspected, parents are referred to a health agency where their child can be checked. Sometimes, problems can be found and corrected by the child care center, especially if it is one that provides health and social services.

Family health problems may affect children in a child care center; therefore caregivers should report to their supervisors when a health need is mentioned by a parent or family member. In many cases, the center can arrange for families to get help from a local agency that provides health services in the community.

WHEN CHILDREN BECOME ILL

When children do become ill, caregivers must work as a team. While you are comforting the sick child, other staff members will supervise the children you had to leave, or it may be the other way around. When children do not feel well, they do not want a substitute caregiver. They want their parents or their main caregiver, who provides nurturing ways with which they are familiar.

ISOLATE THE CHILD AND PROVIDE COMFORT

By keeping sick children away from others, you reduce the danger of spreading germs. You also provide a more comfortable environment for those who are sick.

A center should have a special area that is used only for sick children. This should have a toilet, running water, and good ventilation. It should also be attractive and cozy, so that children will find it comforting.

Soon after you bring a sick child to the isolation area, remove his or her shoes and outer clothing. Help the child onto a cot and encourage relaxation, especially if the child is lying in a cramped position. Call the child by name; use a comforting voice and a gentle touch. Use your judgment about covering the child. If the child has an upset stomach, place a container near the cot in case of vomiting. If possible, darken the room.

Caring for sick children requires a caregiver who can *empathize* (understand how it feels to be sick).

WATCH CAREFULLY

The behavior of sick children should be watched carefully. You should be quick to notice any changes in the illness.

REPORT YOUR OBSERVATIONS

Your observations of a sick child's behavior should be reported to your teacher or supervi-

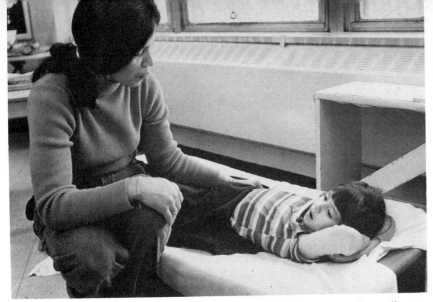

Figure 11-2. If you are put in charge of a sick child, encourage him or her to lie down and relax. Call the child by name, talk in a comforting tone, and use a gentle touch. (Kenneth Karp)

sor, who will decide what steps need to be taken. If the child's parents must be called, the supervisor will take responsibility for this.

LOCATE HEALTH AND FAMILY INFORMATION

In large centers, a secretary or a social worker will keep records of family histories and medical information. These records must be kept up to date. As a child care aide, you can help by mentioning any changes you may learn about during your conversations with parents. Parents' business and home telephone numbers should be available quickly when caregivers need them. Immunization records, information about the health services to be used, and which parent or relative will pick up the child in an emergency—all these things should be up to date and near at hand.

DO NOT GIVE MEDICATION

Regulations for 3, 4, and 5-year-old children usually require that the caregivers have written permission before medicine can be given. Normally, the teacher in charge will handle this. But you should know the regulations under which your center operates, in case your supervisor asks you to give medication to a child.

PRACTICE SANITARY HOUSEKEEPING

After a sick child has left the isolation room, you should change the sheets and towels that have been used, bringing dirty linens to the laundry quickly. Anything used by the sick child must be cleaned thoroughly. The area itself should be cleaned, disinfected, and made ready for future use.

RECORD AND EVALUATE

When you have finished caring for a sick child, you should take two additional steps before ending your assignment:

1. Make a report to your supervisor. A written report or a short conference may be necessary, depending on your center's standard procedures.

2. You should evaluate your performance in health emergencies as well as your health practice skills. A checklist is usually helpful. When you have taken a look at yourself, discuss your evaluations with your supervisor. Discussing an assignment right after it is completed is the best way to improve your performance.

CHAPTER SUMMARY

1. Caregivers have the important responsibility of guarding the health of children at a child care center. They should prevent disease by following practices that keep germs from spreading, by serving as good models, and by teaching children good health habits through planned activities or moments that lend themselves to teaching.

2. Caregivers must know about communicable diseases—their early symptoms, their contagious periods, and their recovery times.

3. An immunization schedule helps to prevent communicable diseases. Child care aides are sometimes expected to check children's records to see that they receive their immunizations.

4. Caregivers need to know how healthy children look and act, so that they will be alert to signs of illness or health problems. By being sensitive to small changes in children's behavior and by noticing unusual behavior, caregivers can help to correct health problems.

5. When a child becomes ill, caregivers must respond quickly by isolating and comforting the child. The child is watched carefully for signs that the illness is growing worse, and the caregiver reports any changes to the supervisor. The caregiver's report will help to decide whether the child's parents must be called.

6. Medication should *not* be given to children unless written permission has been given by the physician. Medical and family histories for each child should be kept up to date and should be easily available to caregivers.

• WHAT NEW TERMS HAVE YOU LEARNED?

Several new words and ideas were presented in this chapter. To see whether you understand them, match the letter of each term below with the numbered phrases under "Definitions."

Terms

a. DPT shot
b. Contagious period
c. Empathy
d. Symptom
e. Isolate a child
f. Medicine
g. Immunization
h. Boosters
i. Communicable diseases
j. Health check

Definitions

1. A sign of illness
2. Immunization against diphtheria, pertussis, and tetanus
3. Keep a child away from other children
4. Recognizing someone else's feelings
5. Time during which a communicable disease can be caught from the sick child
6. Shots which are part of an immunization schedule and strengthen previously given ones
7. Something that should not be given without written permission
8. Using a vaccine to make the body build up defense against a disease
9. Mumps, measles, chickenpox
10. Daily observation of children's health by caregivers

• PROJECTS, DECISIONS, ISSUES

1. List the basic immunizations required of children under 6 years of age in your community and/or those recommended by the American Academy of Pediatrics.
2. Name at least three agencies which provide health services to young children and their families in your community.
3. Inquire of a large and a small child care center what health agencies they use as part of their child care services.
4. Role-play or carry out four actions you need to take when assisting with health supervision of children.

• WHIFS (WHAT WOULD YOU DO *IF* . . .)

1. You wake up feeling terrible; you have a stomachache, fever, and a runny nose. Yesterday, two child caregivers were absent and you know that you are needed at the child care center today. What would you do?
   a. Call in sick
   b. Get dressed and go to work
   c. Wait to see if you feel better in an hour
   d. Go back to sleep
   e. Other responses

2. Johnny's older sister brings him to the child care center and hands his medicine to you with the comment that his mother said to give the medicine to Johnny every 4 hours. What would you do?
   a. Hand it back to her and tell her it's against the rules to give medicine at the child care center
   b. Thank her for bringing Johnny and the medicine
   c. Tell her to take the medicine to the supervisor
   d. Accept the medicine, get Johnny settled, and talk with your supervisor
   e. Give the medicine as requested
   f. Other responses

3. Susie falls asleep during group time. You feel her forehead and it is hot to the touch. What would you do?
   a. Let her sleep
   b. Carry her to the isolation room
   c. Comment that her mother gives her aspirin
   d. Tell your supervisor
   e. Force her to wake up and listen
   f. Other responses

4. Kenneth vomits on the playground and looks like he is going to faint. What would you do?
   a. Have him sit down
   b. Send the other children inside
   c. Take Kenneth inside
   d. Ask the other teacher on the playground to watch your children while you take care of Kenneth
   e. Carry Kenneth to the isolation room
   f. Other responses

• CHECK YOURSELF

Carefully read each item and answer *yes* or *no* in terms of your own performance in relation to health responsibilities.

1. Do you keep germs from spreading by
   a. Using tissue when needed?
   b. Turning head away and covering a cough or sneeze?
   c. Placing soiled clothing and bedding in the proper place?
   d. Reporting exposure to infection?
   e. Washing hands before touching food and after toileting?
   f. Seeing that children are assigned items?
   g. Isolating sick children?

2. Do you promote good health habits by
   a. Getting a regular medical checkup?
   b. Staying home when sick?
   c. Practicing good personal hygiene and grooming?

3. Do you teach good health habits by
   a. Planning health experiences?
   b. Recognizing moments of teaching?

4. Do you acknowledge and minimize the spread of communicable diseases by
   a. Knowing where the communicable disease chart is located?
   b. Studying the communicable disease chart?
   c. Referring to the communicable disease chart when a child has symptoms of communicable disease?

5. Do you respect immunization by
   a. Assisting in checking children's immunization records?
   b. Having the necessary immunizations yourself?

6. Do you recognize signs of illness and/or health problems by
   a. Noticing changes in children's behavior?
   b. Noticing behavior indicative of health problems?

7. Do you report signs of illness and/or health problems to your supervisor?

● STUDENT ACTIVITIES

1. Identify three measures a child care aide should take to prevent disease.
2. List four specific ways that your health habits affect children.
3. Identify signs of illness for each of the following parts of the body: eyes, nose, throat, and skin.
4. Referring to a communicable disease chart for information, identify the first signs of three communicable diseases.
5. Name at least four actions you need to take when assisting with the health supervision of children.
6. Outline the steps to be taken when a child becomes ill.

12 GUIDING CHILDREN'S BEHAVIOR

After you have studied Chapter 12, you should be able to:

1. State four reasons why children need guidance
2. Identify five key concepts to keep in mind when providing guidance
3. List four kinds of problem behaviors and demonstrate ways to handle each
4. Exhibit three ways that caregivers' personal behavior affects guidance

CHILDREN'S NEED FOR GUIDANCE

Guidance and *discipline* mean different things to different people. Let's look at these terms and others relating to guiding children's behavior.

DEFINING THE TERMS

Guidance and *discipline* are terms that are used often in relation to guiding young children toward desirable behavior. Their meanings (when used in relation to children), are similar, and the terms are often used as one. *Guidance* and *discipline* both describe how adults help children learn to control their actions and make their own decisions. Discipline is considered a desirable guidance technique because it represents behavior that children can follow. When child care aides use discipline, their behavior is imitated by children. Good discipline recognizes positive actions and clearly defined rules. This kind of discipline benefits young children and helps them achieve *self-discipline* (self-control). Child care aides set an example for children. Discipline is considered a desirable guidance technique because it represents behavior that children should imitate.

Punishment is a penalty for doing something wrong. Punishing a child focuses on behavior that an adult considers not acceptable. While this points out the wrongdoing, it may not be related to the wrongdoing. It may stop the behavior for a while, but it seldom corrects or changes it for long. *Guidance* may also include paying a penalty for undesirable actions. However, guidance usually relates to the wrongdoing *and* includes suggestions about changing the behavior in the future. For example, a 3-year-old girl who has marked the wall with a crayon may be spanked, so that she stops. But later she will probably mark the wall again, when an adult is not nearby. Punishment has stopped the unacceptable behavior one time, but it has not

139

guided the child toward acceptable behavior. Guidance would stop the unacceptable behavior and guide the child toward something acceptable. For example, the child care aide might ask for the crayon and then have the child help clean the wall. Then the child might be helped to use the crayon on a large sheet of paper and encouraged to "keep the crayon on the paper."

WHY CHILDREN NEED GUIDANCE

Why do children need guidance? Here are four reaons why guidance should be provided:

1. Children need guidance in order to be safe. Caregivers need to provide guidance quickly when a child is in danger of being harmed or of harming someone else. Little children need protection from scratches, bites, cuts, burns, poisons, falls, drowning, suffocation, and automobile accidents.

2. Children need guidance in order to stay physically and emotionally healthy. Providing good supervision, nourishing food, and protective health measures such as shots and visits to the doctor and dentist are essential in guiding children to physical and emotional health.

3. Children need guidance in order to develop social awareness and to interact effectively with others. Children's growing awareness of others—and their clumsy attempts to get along with other children—need the guidance of a caregiver who can help the children play together successfully. Coming to know and respect the rules that will benefit each person is part of this learning. Through guidance, children learn to consider others, to respect social customs, and to obey laws.

4. Children need guidance in order to develop a good self-concept and self-control. Self-confidence leads to *self-respect* and to self-control. It begins with the feeling, "I can do it. I like you. You like me." These feelings show a good self-concept. Caregivers who guide children to gain self-respect and self-control encourage them to try out their talents, to use their abilities, to ask questions, to seek answers, to express their feelings, and to listen to and become aware of the feelings of others.

PROVIDING GUIDANCE

When you have the responsibility of providing guidance for young children, you must consider the following: aspects of growth and development; the behavior observed; the *limits*, or rules, of the child care center; factors that provide direct and indirect guidance; and positive and negative guidance techniques.

ASPECTS OF GROWTH AND DEVELOPMENT

It is important for those who work with young children to recognize the *aspects of growth and development*—the general characteristics of the various age groups and stages of development. Table 12-1 shows average characteristics of children by age and behavior. The abilities listed represent the average of many children's

Figure 12-1. An important first step to observing children objectively is to learn what behaviors are "normal" for a child's stage of development. (Kenneth Karp)

TABLE 12-1 ASPECTS OF DEVELOPMENT OF PRESCHOOL CHILDREN

Aspect of Development	Age Level			
	2 years		3 years	
	Abilities	Implications	Abilities	Implications
Physical	Balances forward	Hits forehead in fall-ing	Balances erect	Fall may break tooth
	Can kick object	Kicks big ball	Alternates feet	Climbs stairs
	Steps in place	Climbs by restep-ping	Stands on one foot	Learns to hop
			Developing coordi-nation	Jumps, walks, and runs with music
	Pats, pokes	Enjoys clay		Unbuttons buttons
	Runs, lugs, pushes, pulls	Enjoys action toys		Rolls ball
		Pulls or carries a load		Throws underhand
		Likes to fit pieces		Toilets self during day
				Talks, or eats, or plays
	Rotates forearm; has voluntary muscle control	Opens doors		
		Fills and empties		
		Learns to toilet self		
		Likes water play		
Social	Must possess	Holds and hoards	Learning to share	Shares toys
		Does not share		Not able to share workplace
	Slow in relating to new adults	Wants familiar adult		Brings possession to share
	Does not cooperate in play	Prefers solitary play	Sensitive to people	Tries to please and conform
		Watches others		Feels sympathetic
				Likes simple guessing
				Enjoys dressing up
Emotional	Likes to touch	Can be moved to new location	Shows some self-control	Rests for 10 minutes
	Likes people	Watches others		Waits until it is time
		Imitates		Takes turns
		Understands "He needs it"	Proud of what he or she makes	Likes to take it home but often forgets to
	Dependent on mother	Plays with baby doll	Developing independence	Leaves mother for nursery school
		Plays house		Plays alone
Intellectual	Increases control of language	Learns words easily	Is attentive to words	Responds to adult suggestions
	Has short attention span	Talks as part of play		Likes to talk with adults
		Has brief snatches of play		Listens longer to stories

(Continued next page)

TABLE 12-1 ASPECTS OF DEVELOPMENT OF PRESCHOOL CHILDREN (Continued)

Aspect of Development	Age Level			
	2 years		3 years	
	Abilities	Implications	Abilities	Implications
Intellectual	Attends to words spoken a few at a time	Responds to brief commands		Enjoys praise and simple humor
			Compares two objects	Builds a three block bridge
			Counts to three	Points out three objects in a picture
			Uses words more	Talks about proposed study trip
			Participates in planning	Tries out words dramatically

Aspect of Development	Age Level			
	4 years		5 years	
Physical	Climbs easily	Learns to use a fire-man's pole	Has more motor control	Able to sit longer
	Actively runs, jumps, hops	Covers more ground	Crosses street safely	Explores neighbor-hood
				Does simple errands
	Has more motor control	Learns to skip	Has more even hand control	Learns to lace shoes
		Saws		Learns to use over-head ladder
		Cuts on a line		Learns left from right
		Throws overhand		Uses bathroom alone
	Has more coordina-tion	Talks and eats	Self-sufficient in personal care	
		Talks and plays		
Social	Continuing sensitivity to people	Quotes parents as authorities	Is social	Has more operative play
		Dislikes isolation from group		Likes to play house and baby
		Learns to express sympathy		Gets along well in small group
		Likes to dress up and play dramatically		Conforms to adult ideas
				Asks adult help as needed
	Likes birthday parties	Talks about inviting, not inviting, someone		
	More cooperative	Plays with small group		
		May not take others into group		

(Continued next page)

TABLE 12-1 ASPECTS OF DEVELOPMENT OF PRESCHOOL CHILDREN (Continued)

Aspect of Development	Age Level			
	4 years		5 years	
	Abilities	Implications	Abilities	Implications
Emotional	Goes out	Likes to brag Likes freehand drawing (not coloring books)	Poised and in control Proud of what he or she has and does	
	Is learning limits	Likes to go on excursions Runs ahead but waits on corner Interested in rules Plans ahead with adults Acts silly if tired	Likes to have rules Responds to feasible challenge	Learns what is right to do and say
Intellectual	Experiments	Makes up words and rhymes Likes new words, big ones Listens to stories longer	Interests	Recognizes some numbers and letters Interested in the clock and time
	Asks why and how	Runs a topic to the ground Likes to have explanations	Thinks accurately	Asks what and how Learns own address and telephone number
	Likes to imagine	Does much dramatic play	Has purpose	Draws what he or she has in mind at the moment
		Learns to distinguish fact and fancy	Is flexible	Is not concerned with inconsistencies
	Has fluid thought	Interested in death Changes title of his drawing as he or she draws		

Source: V. E. Todd and H. Hofferman, *The Years Before School*, 3d ed., Macmillan, New York, 1977, pp. 41–44.

behaviors. These are sometimes called *norms*. Since norms are average behaviors, no single child has all the characteristics of a particular age group listed on the chart. For example, a 4-year-old may have the physical abilities of a 5-year-old, the social and emotional abilities of a 4-year-old, and the intellectual abilities of a 3-year-old.

OBSERVING CHILDREN'S BEHAVIOR

By watching a child carefully and writing down what you see, you may gain some understanding of that child's behavior. When you review what you have written, you may find that there is a pattern in how the child behaves.

Table 12-2 GUIDELINES FOR OBSERVING CHILDREN AND RECORDING OBJECTIVELY

1. Observe without being obvious.
2. Treat all observational material as confidential.
3. Record date, place, time, situation, activity accurately to make observation more meaningful, whether recording a specific instance or giving a summary of what you have observed about the child.
4. Give your name or initials to show who did the recording.
5. Describe the child's behavior with words that tell how child acts rather than judgment on your part.

   Example: 6/9/76 Paul does not talk much and when he does it is hard to understand what he says. When he wants something, he motions to the teacher.
   Note: Paul is slow and dull (judgment on observer's part).

6. At the end of your descriptive record, a paragraph marked "opinion" is all right. To give your feelings about a child is helpful. Many times it is hard to describe or identify a child's problem, but when the observer "feels" or "senses" it's there, intuition is a valid basis for making judgments and helps in securing additional or special help for the child. Be sure to distinguish between facts, feelings, and interpretations.

Recording Children's Behavior. *Objective recording* involves a written description of what and how a child does. Personal opinions and judgments are not included in an objective record. A record with judgment in it is called a *subjective record*. Objective records are desirable because they describe behavior. Table 12-2 presents guidelines for recording objectively.

Here is an example of objective and subjective recording:

Objective Recording
(Stating *what* and *how*)

Mary slammed the door and stamped her foot.

Subjective recording
(Indicating judgment of recorder)

Mary was angry.

Observation Record. Different forms are used for observation records, depending on the purpose of the record and the amount of time there

Figure 12-2. An objective record is a description written by the caregiver of how a child behaves. (Kenneth Karp)

is for recording. As a child care aide, you may be asked to keep two kinds of records that take little time but require accurate, careful observation: the anecdotal record and the checklist. An *anecdotal record* (see Table 12-3) is a report of an important incident that does not necessarily include every detail. It is usually written at the end of the observation or work period, and facts are separated from opinions or interpretations.

A *checklist* lists various possible behaviors, and the caregiver checks the ones observed over a certain period of time. A checklist is often used as a *pretest* and *posttest*: that is, the same checklist is used to record behavior at the beginning and at the end of a certain period. In this way, changes in children's behavior are easily noticed.

A good checklist is descriptive; the items are defined objectively rather than subjectively (that is, facts, not opinions, are called for). Table 12-4 shows two samples of portions of objective checklists. While both describe behavior, the second sample gives more specific details.

LIMITS IN GUIDANCE

Limits are the rules or the boundaries relating to acceptable behavior that adults use in guiding children. Not all adults see limits and guidance in the same way, and they also differ in the amount of guidance they provide. Some set up too few limits or rules, while others insist on too many. Still others achieve a good balance between adults' rules and the feelings and behaviors expressed by children.

Few or No Limits. Some adults set few, if any, limits or rules. Instead, they allow the children to make all the decisions and set all the limits. These adults are tolerant of all behavior. The trouble with this "anything goes" attitude is that it doesn't work. Children really *do* need the security and protection of well-defined, fair rules—especially in a child care group. Without limits or boundaries, children think that no one cares enough to guide them. They do not have the feeling of "belonging" and the comfort that comes with guidance. A child without consistent limits has to test each limit or rule each time to see if it will be enforced that particular time.

Table 12-3 AN ANECDOTAL RECORD

Name of child Rob Jones		Name of observer Ron Wing
Child's birthdate January 3, 1975	Date of Recording April 10, 1977	Topic Play

Time	Descriptive behavior objectively recorded	Comments (interpretation or opinion)
10:30 a.m.	Throughout free-play time today Billy sat on the floor and poured the wooden cubes in and out of the dishpan. Sometimes he would stack one cube on top of another. He put the red ones in one clump and the blue ones in another. He did not seem to pay attention to the other colors. He made no signs that indicated that he was aware of other children in the play area.	The description recorded is typical of Billy's play at free time. He usually spends his time manipulating small objects, sometimes carefully placing them vertically on top of one another or sorting out red or yellow ones. He appears to be unaware of other children close by.

Table 12-4 SAMPLES OF OBJECTIVE CHECKLIST

Sample 1: Achievement Checklist
      (This is a list of items that may be achieved by some 3, 4, and 5-year-olds.)

Child's name _____   Birthdate _____

Date of enrollment _____   Observer's name _____

Date observed _____   Position _____

Section I	Yes	No	Sometimes	DNA
Eats with spoon				
Eats with fork				
Holds silver correctly				
Holds cup with one hand				
Spills food or drink only once during meal				
Spills food or drink more than once during meal				

Sample 2: Motor-area portion   Child's name _____

            Motor area   Child's birthdate _____

Age	Behavior	Date achieved	Comments
3–4 yr	1. Stands on each foot 4–8 seconds. (R__L__) 2. Throws ball accurately, can bounce and catch ball with both hands. 3. Skips on one foot (alternates feet when walking). 4. Copies † and □. 5. Draws a recognizable man with four to six parts (e.g., head, eyes, legs, feet). 6. Copies a three-block bridge from model. Imitates a five-block bridge gate. 7. Cuts along an already drawn straight line with scissors.		
4–5 yr	1. Stands on each foot more than 8 sec. (R__L__) 2. Bounces ball (dribbles) at least three times with each hand. (R__L__) 3. Skips on alternate feet. Hops on one foot (10–12 feet). 4. Copies △ and □. 5. Draws a recognizable person with eight to ten parts (e.g., mouth, nose, eyes, body, arms, legs, feet, head). 6. Copies a five-block gate from model. Builds two steps after model is removed. 7. Cuts out simple objects such as ○ and □.		

Source: Adapted from United Cerebral Palsy, Inc., Lexington, Kentucky.

Figure 12-3. When disciplining children, the caregiver accepts a child's feelings while dealing with his or her behavior. (Betty Terhune)

Unfortunately, some adults, including parents, think freedom and creativity mean that the child makes the decisions and that limits are confining rather than helpful. It is true that children test limits, but they do so because they have to find out what kind of behavior adults expect and will accept. Without limits, children are unable to gain the inner controls that help them learn self-control.

Too Many Limits. Some adults approach discipline with many rules that are strict and even harsh. Children's behavior is guided by *don'ts*—"Don't ask questions," "Don't get your shoes wet," "Don't talk when we have company," "Stop it," "Leave that alone." You have probably heard the expression "Children should be seen and not heard." Some adults take this point of view and usually make decisions for children. They often respond to children in a negative way.

Children who experience this kind of discipline are usually so pressured by adults that they become withdrawn and often turn their feelings inward. They think to themselves, "I can't do anything right," "I can't do it—I'll be punished," or "I won't try—I'll only get into trouble." These children are not only developing poor self-concept but they are learning through fear, not understanding.

Consistent, Clearly Defined Limits. When the limits are *consistent* (unchanging) and clearly defined, children can count on the rules to stay the same for similar behavior. They know that the rules will be enforced today the same way

as they were enforced yesterday. They do not need to test rules, because they already know what is expected of them.

Caregivers find this approach to guidance helpful in working with young children. When freedom to choose or decide is appropriate, children have the chance to practice decision-making. During the times or activities when children must follow adult rules, they learn to respect limits and develop self-control.

Effective discipline does not restrict children with too many rules, but it does not leave them so free that they have no limits. When rules are necessary, they are firm. Whenever freedom is possible and beneficial to children, it is allowed and encouraged.

DIRECT AND INDIRECT GUIDANCE

Guidance can be provided in either a direct or an indirect way. *Direct guidance* occurs when caregivers give children direct verbal and physical directions, telling a child what to do and showing how to do it. *Indirect guidance* is provided when caregivers make decisions and prepare a setting that affects children's behavior.

Direct Guidance. Direct guidance involves techniques that you use to guide children's behavior. This includes the way you speak and act with children. The techniques you use to guide children are based on your understanding of children, on how you believe children should be disciplined, and on indirect guidance factors in the environment.

147

Table 12-5 ENVIRONMENTAL FACTORS THAT PROVIDE INDIRECT GUIDANCE

Environmental factor	Positive	Negative
Organization of space	Enough room for movement without interference; well-defined learning areas, clear paths or traffic lanes	Not enough room; children disturb each other; paths and learning areas not well defined
Program activities	Planned to meet individual needs; a balance of familiar and new experiences	No advance planning—too much or too little stimulation; custodial care rather than enriched programs
Daily schedule	Enough time allowed for activities and transition periods; alternating active and quiet periods—change of pace when needed	Too much or too little time scheduled; active and quiet periods not alternated, causing fatigue or overstimulation
Equipment	Adequate amount and appropriate selection of equipment and materials, matching individual and group needs	Inadequate in quantity, quality, and variety
Staff	Appropriate number of qualified staff for the children enrolled	Too many children; too few or unqualified staff
Children's home and family	Strong family ties; adequate parenting, with values and limits well defined; good home–center communication	Family crises related to health, housing, money, and communication; values and limits not defined; little stimulation; poor home–center communication

Indirect Guidance. Many environmental factors of a child care program provide indirect guidance for children. Organization of space, program activities, daily schedule, equipment, staff, and the children's homes and families affect the techniques used in guiding young children. (See Table 12-5.)

POSITIVE GUIDANCE TECHNIQUES

Children are able to gain self-respect and learn self-control when the emotional environment in a group is friendly and when the supervision makes them feel confident and encouraged.

You help to provide this kind of setting by acting in a way that makes children feel that you like them, that you want them to have fun, and that you expect them to follow the rules. It is difficult (and often impossible) to communicate this kind of security by using negative guidance techniques.

Positive techniques stress the kind of discipline that guides children toward desirable behavior. When children learn to respect rules or limits, they also learn to respect themselves and others. Table 12-6 lists some positive guidance techniques and ways to apply them when working with young children.

Table 12-6 POSITIVE TECHNIQUES OF GUIDANCE

Positive guidance techniques	Applying positive techniques
Use positive statements when giving directions or making corrections.	"Zip up your jacket and put on your cap. It's very cold outside."
Use your voice as a teaching tool. Speak firmly, yet with friendliness. Use short, clear, meaningful sentences.	Let the children know that you mean it when you set a limit or give a direction: "It's time to go in now."
Back up directions or suggestions with actions.	Start walking toward the door as you give the signal that it's time to go inside.
Give one direction at a time.	"Put the doll in the doll bed." When this is done, then give another suggestion or direction: "Do you think she'd like to be covered up? Put the blanket on her."
Give children a choice only when the choice is actually left up to them.	"Do you want to paint at the easel or fingerpaint?"
Respond to dangerous situations immediately.	"Joel, put the scissors in their holder *before* you get up from the table." Words are not enough sometimes. Move *quickly* to prevent harm to a child. Grasp a block before it's thrown; catch a child before the child falls; and hold a child's hand when another is about to be hit.
Place yourself where you can see the whole room and be alert to everything that is happening.	Face the children. Be careful not to watch one child so intently that you concentrate only on that child.
Give help when needed. Treat the children fairly, avoid favoritism, and give approval when deserved.	Allow children a chance to try for themselves. Before stepping in, try verbal guidance by suggesting one simple step that will help. If a child wants you to make something, indicate your willingness to help the child make it.
Use body language to communicate.	Smile sincerely. Touch children. A pat on the shoulder, a quick hug, or holding a hand on a nature walk all suggest that you care.
Help children understand the limits or rules. Make them simple and clear, and match them to the children's stage of development.	"It's time to . . ." "Let's listen to . . ." "Remember the rule: Only one person talks at a time." "Don't forget our rule: Stay at the table until we've finished eating."
Enforce limits consistently, yet be flexible when you need to.	"We don't usually run inside, but today it's raining, and we're going to run to the sound of music."

(Continued next page)

Table 12-6 POSITIVE TECHNIQUES OF GUIDANCE (Continued)

Positive guidance techniques	Applying positive techniques
Redirect (suggest other activities) *when children are becoming excitable, tense or negativistic.* Alternatives should be related to the children's interests and needs of the moment.	If the children are getting tired from active play, start quieter play.
Watch and anticipate need for change of pace.	"Let's get the tumbling mat out and do some somersaults."
Speak to children at their eye level when close to them. Don't shout across the room.	When you look children in the eye, often in a squatting position, they feel that you have something important to say and that you want to hear what they have to say.
Match what you expect with a child's ability. Don't expect too much too soon—or too little too late.	"I knew you could do it, Debbie."
Accept children's feelings even though you may not accept their behavior.	"I know you'd like to hold the flag, Joanne, but it's Irene's turn today."

Adapted from Kathryn Reed, *The Nursery School: A Human Relations Laboratory,* Saunders, Philadelphia, Penn. 5th ed., 1971, pp. 88-89.

HANDLING PROBLEM BEHAVIORS

There are some special problem behaviors that all child caregivers face. They are not easy to handle, and the situations that come up will be as different as the children involved. Guidelines for these behaviors may help you face problem behaviors in the future. Table 12-7 suggests solutions, but they are not always easy or simple, and as we have said, each situation is different.

BEHAVIORS THAT AFFECT GUIDANCE

The personal behavior of a caregiver affects how he or she guides children.

PUTTING CHILDREN'S NEEDS BEFORE YOUR OWN

As an emotionally healthy person, you think of the children's needs before you think of yourself. You are able to separate what is best for children from their impulses, or what they want

Figure 12-4. When talking with children, get down on their eye level and listen carefully to them. This gives them the feeling that you think what they have to say is worth listening to. (Bart Fleet)

to do just at that moment. You build a warm, trusting relationship with individual children that tells them you care enough to let them try out things and ideas for themselves, and that you will help if they need help. The children can count on your feelings and behavior to be the same—accepting and nurturing, yet firm and correcting in a kind way. They know that there will be trouble if the limits or rules are not followed.

Table 12-7 HANDLING PROBLEM BEHAVIORS

Problem behaviors	Ways to handle
Using swear words	Ignore if seldom heard. If used often, indicate that "We don't use those words here. There are other words that tell us how you feel. You could say 'I'm angry; I don't like it when . . . .'"
Disrupting group time	Improve group time to hold children's interest. Give a child something to hold or to do. Give child attention at other times so that it is not as needed at group time. If necessary, remove child from group. If child is younger provide something for him or her to do quietly. If child is older, "time out" may be effective.
Separating anxiously from parents	Give special attention to this child. Stay with child until involved in an activity or with someone else. Reflect feelings: "It's hard to leave Mommie, but she has to go to work. She'll be back to get you after playtime this afternoon."
Avoiding involvement	Plan something this child will like. Assume that child will participate, and involve yourself as well as the child in getting started. Ask questions that keep the child doing the activity. "Are there enough pegs in that dish to fill all the holes in the pegboard?" Arrange uninterrupted time between the child and the caregiver.
Disturbing other children	"I will not let you knock down Jan's block building. You may build one and knock it down when no one is nearby to get hurt." Use techniques mentioned under avoiding involvement if child is bored or disinterested.
Hitting others	"Hitting hurts. I will not let you hit. You can tell Barbara that she made you angry or that *you* want to play with the boat. Say it in words." Redirect to pounding clay, digging, or punching a bag.
Spitting	"Spitting is to be done in the toilet." "There are a lot of germs in spit, and I will not let you spit on anyone."
Biting	"Biting hurts. We must take care of the place you bit Frank. Let's wash it and put some medicine on it." "You may bite this carrot or get a doll to bite, but

(Continued next page)

Table 12-7 HANDLING PROBLEM BEHAVIORS (Continued)

Problem behaviors	Ways to handle
	you may not bite children or teachers." Biting back sets a wrong example and caregivers do not use this technique with children.
Waiting turns	Make children feel that waiting one's turn is an accomplishment. It's a sign of growing up. "It's hard to wait, but I know you can do it." Take special care to see that each child has a turn at favored activities—holding the flag, being first, choosing songs. Keep a record if you can't remember.

SETTING AN EXAMPLE

The children use caregivers as *models*. How you relate to children is how the children tend to relate to each other. For example, when you listen carefully, you give children the feeling that what is being said is worth listening to. Later, children listen carefully to what you say.

When you accept a child's feelings—even though you may not accept the behavior involved—you help children become aware of the cause and effect of their actions. Children with consistent adult models learn to say: "I'd like to (feeling), but I shouldn't (the action)"; or "I don't want to, but I should."

LEARNING ABOUT CHILDREN'S GROWTH AND DEVELOPMENT

Your willingness to keep on learning about children's growth and development affects the way you guide them. For example, when you learn that 4-year-olds often exclude another child from group play, you help both the group and the rejected child find ways to play together. You might suggest that the "intruder" make believe that he or she is a service person who needs to read the water meter. This gives the child a useful role in relation to the group. A child caregiver who does not understand this about 4-year-old social play might scold those who were excluding the child.

EVALUATING YOURSELF

Children are always changing, and so is the guidance they need from caregivers. As a result, caregivers must always evaluate their performance in handling children's behavior.

As a child care aide, you need to talk about your feelings—guidance problems and successes—with your supervisor as often as possible. Identify the things that went well for you during the day. Talk about how you handled behavior problems positively. Then talk about your feelings in situations when negative techniques were used. Child care aides sometimes make mistakes. There may be times when you are not feeling well, when there is a personal problem, or when you just do not see the whole picture and have the wrong idea of what the problem is. It's dangerous to make judgments in the middle of a crisis. To ask the misbehaving children who started it is to encourage them to make excuses or put the blame on someone else. Handle times like these as best you can. But review the experience with your supervising teacher when things are quiet and you can think through all the parts of the incident—who was involved, what the circumstances were, what you did and said, and ways you might handle a similar situation next time. Be specific. Talk about individual children or incidents. Ask for advice about how to handle similar situations in the future.

Do not wait to talk about guidance problems

and successes. What seems important to you today may not be easy to remember tomorrow. Or you might be faced with a similar situation tomorrow and will have missed a chance to change your views and your technique in handling the problem. Remember that no one has all the answers to children's behavior. Your supervisor will be willing to share with you insights that have grown out of work with children. These will be most helpful. Listen, and use this advice with appreciation and with sensitivity to each child's needs. In this way, you can improve your understanding and your guidance techniques.

CHAPTER SUMMARY

1. *Guidance* and *discipline* describe how adults help children learn to control their actions and make their own decisions.
2. Children need guidance in order to be safe, to stay physically and emotionally healthy, to develop social awareness, and to develop a good self-concept and self-control.
3. When providing guidance, a child caregiver must consider the aspects of child growth and development, the limits of the child care center, factors that provide direct and indirect guidance, and the use of positive and negative techniques.
4. The personal behavior of the caregiver affects the way in which he or she guides children.
5. In handling children's behavior, it is very important for caregivers to evaluate their performance and to discuss it with their supervisors.

• WHAT HAVE YOU LEARNED FROM THIS CHAPTER?

Several new words and ideas were presented in this chapter. To see whether you understand them, match the letter of each term below with the numbered phrases under "Definitions."

Terms

a. Subjective recording
b. Impulses
c. Checklist
d. Punishment
e. Self-discipline
f. Self-respect
g. Objective recording
h. Pretest, posttest
i. Ancedotal record
j. Guidance
k. Consistent limits
l. Indirect guidance

Definitions

1. Recording of personal opionions
2. First thoughts or wishes
3. Self-appreciation
4. Same checklist used at the beginning and end of period
5. Guiding children
6. Behaviors listed and checked off
7. Paying a penalty for wrongdoing
8. Self-control
9. Report of important incident
10. Recording of facts
11. Environmental factors which affect children's behavior
12. Rules that are enforced the same way each day

• PROJECTS, DECISIONS, ISSUES

1. Pretend you are a news reporter and write a news article for the local newspaper, listing the four reasons children need guidance. Take pictures with your camera to accompany the story.
2. Make a scrapbook and divide it into five sections, each section dealing with one of the five key concepts to keep in mind when providing guidance. Use pictures from magazines to illustrate all the points you want to make.
3. Visit two different child care centers and interview the directors. Find out what kinds of problem behaviors are observed in the

center and how the center staff handles them. Compare your findings with Table 12-7. Are the problems the same or different? Are the ways they are handled similar to the one suggested in Table 12-7? Discuss your findings with your teacher.

4. After you have read about how the personal behavior of caregivers affects their guidance of children, write a paper describing why *you* think one of the following is more important than another: (*a*) putting children's needs before your own; (*b*) setting an example; (*c*) learning about children's growth and development; (*d*) evaluating yourself.

• STUDENT ACTIVITIES

1. List four reasons children need guidance.
2. Give five positive guidance techniques and list ways to apply them.
3. Define *direct guidance* and *indirect guidance*; give examples of each.
4. Role-play three personal characteristics of child caregivers that affect guidance.

5. Explain why it is important to observe, record, and report children's behavior objectively.
6. What are four problem behaviors of young children? Demonstrate ways you would handle each.
7. Identify three different limits adults use in guiding children. What are the advantages and disadvantages of each?
8. Respond to the following agree-disagree statements. Give examples to support your answers. You may prefer to respond to these as a group choosing one or two other students to participate.
   a. Punishment, while unpleasant, is necessary to guide young children.
   b. Easygoing children do not need discipline.
   c. Recording of children's behavior, to be complete, should be both objective and subjective.
   d. Indirect guidance factors make direct guidance difficult.
   e. Caregivers' personal behavior is the key factor in guiding children.

13 | SUPERVISING OUTDOOR PLAY

After you have studied Chapter 13, you should be able to:

1. State four benefits children derive from outdoor play
2. Identify three things to consider when planning a good outdoor program
3. Demonstrate four ways a child care aide should supervise outdoor play activities
4. Show the steps that child care aides take in ending outdoor play

Outdoor experiences are part of any good child care program. The learning environment outdoors can be just as good as the indoor environment, and not just for "letting off steam," amusing oneself, or passing time.

As a child care aide, you may help another staff person supervise outdoor experiences. Or you may be directed to "take the children outside" while your supervisor stays inside to work with an individual child or to get ready for program activities.

OUTDOOR PLAY

To appreciate how important outdoor play is to a young child, one must consider each word separately. *Outdoor* refers to a location and a setting. *Play* refers to how children learn; it is often called a "tool of learning."

BENEFITS OF OUTDOOR PLAY TO YOUNG CHILDREN

Outdoor experiences require extra effort from the caregiving staff. You may be asking yourself, "Why take small children outdoors? Can't they learn the same things indoors?" To find the answers, consider the following benefits that children receive from outdoor play.

Enough Space. Children need plenty of space. To master heights and overcome fear, children must have space to climb and jump safely and to move around freely.

Children also need to play with one another without conflict. Indoors, fights between children may arise when too many share too little space. They disturb one another, often unintentionally, and emotions flare up when space is limited.

Fewer restrictions are needed when more space is available. Messy activities involving sand, mud, and water play can be carried on more freely

Figure 13-1. Outdoors provides children with the space they need for running, jumping, and playing together without conflict. (Michael Weisbrot)

outside. Hosing down a table that has been used for wet-clay activities is both fun for children to do and an efficient housekeeping procedure.

Fresh Air and Sunshine. The combination of fresh air, sunshine, and exercise increases children's alertness and leads to good health.

As children exercise their bodies in such activities as backing down a ladder, pushing a barrel, or crawling up a hill, their *large muscles* are strengthened. Large muscles are those found in the trunk of the body and in the neck, arms, and legs. When children use these muscles, tensions are eased and their bodies work more efficiently.

The Chance to Express Feelings and Relax. There are many opportunities to express feelings in outdoor play. Children's tensions ease when outdoor activities such as pounding nails, digging in the ground, or playing in the snow are available. Carrying small buckets of water from the outside faucet to the sandbox, trip after trip, seems like a waste of time to an adult, but it seems delightful and satisfying to young children.

The Chance for Child-Initiated Activities. Outdoor play encourages *child-initiated* and *unstructured activities*.

Child-Initiated Activities. These are activities that children begin by themselves without

directions from teachers. When children are free to choose and carry out their own activities, they learn to make decisions and to manage time and resources. Most outdoor experiences give children this freedom. When outdoors, they choose what they want to do. Often, during this time, children relive their earlier experiences. After a trip to the fire station, the hollow blocks are used to make a fire engine. Digging a garden may follow a visit to a farm. Or a towel fastened on the shoulders may enable a child to play the hero of a favorite television show.

Children receive satisfaction from having chosen and completed an activity. When children begin something on their own, they become involved, and their *attention span* (time spent with an activity) is lengthened. One child may sit and watch the clouds float by. Another may ride the tricycle. A third may choose to walk the balance beam over and over. If a foot slips off, it's easy enough to try again. A child care aide may call this practice, but children call it fun when it is their idea. And they will be interested in it longer because the activity holds some special challenge for them.

Unstructured Activities. In *unstructured activities,* children are not organized or directed by teachers. Unstructured activities sometimes take place during play. For example, the children are building with hollow blocks when one child says, "Let's build a bridge." Now bridge play captures the children's interest until it's time to go inside.

For some children, the environment alone suggests the play theme. For example, Eric notices that his shadow is long and narrow. He and Bill begin to explore other shadows on the playground.

A balance between structured (teacher-directed) and unstructured (child-initiated) activities is desirable. Some children want to be left alone to carry out their own ideas. Others may need help getting started, and they will welcome ideas from adults. In these situations, child caregivers plan activities with some structure. For example, the children may be given the choice of climbing through a maze or following a trail. In both activities, the concepts of *over* and *under* are emphasized.

Enough Time. Outdoor play is usually scheduled in a large block of time (an hour or longer). This is good for children, because it gives them enough time to finish what they start. They are also able to play long enough to be satisfied with their experiences. A child who has just learned to climb the jungle gym wants to show others "what I can do." There is enough time to do it over and over again, until the newly learned skill becomes easier to perform.

A Good Learning Environment. Outdoor play provides an excellent environment for learning experiences because:

1. It can strengthen concepts children learn indoors.
2. It gives children the chance to discover and observe the natural world.
3. It lets children compare natural objects and conditions.

Children sort leaves by color, size, or shape. A ball and a bean bag are thrown up into the air, and both come down again. Children learn to see likenesses and differences and to group things according to their similarities.

The Chance to Develop Physically. Outdoor activities benefit children's physical development in the following ways:

1. Children improve their coordination and are better able to balance themselves.
2. Children learn basic motor skills, such as jumping, pedaling, balancing, crawling through a tunnel, and turning a somersault.
3. Children develop body control through outdoor activities. They learn how low they need to bend in order to go under a tree limb or through a tunnel and where to put their hands in order to catch a ball.
4. Children improve their *sensorimotor skills* (use of the five senses and muscles) outdoors. Use of the five senses and the muscles of the body to gain knowledge first-hand is encouraged outdoors.

The Chance to Develop Speech. Outdoor play encourages children to use language and to increase their vocabularies, because:

1. They have the freedom to talk or call loudly.
2. When children are playing with friends and enjoying activities that they have initiated themselves, language flows freely.
3. Children are inclined to ask questions and to make comments about their outdoor experiences. This enlarges their vocabularies and makes them more aware of feelings and things around them. It also helps them think more clearly and develop a better memory of their experiences.

THE OUTDOOR SETTING

Outdoor play will certainly be easier to plan and supervise if the physical setting of the area is near or next to the classroom and if there is a covered patio or porch off the classroom. A mild, sunny climate will also make your teaching job simpler. But outdoor experiences are valuable enough to be included in any program, regardless of the climate or the location of the playground.

Just as indoor programs must be planned to fit the physical setting of the room or the building in which a child care service is located, outdoor programs must be designed for the kind of play area available.

Figure 13-2. Outdoor skills like tricycle-riding allow children to develop their motor skills. (Michael Weisbrot)

Essential Characteristics. Safety, space, variety in the landscape, and adequate equipment are essential characteristics of a good outdoor setting for children's activities.

Safety. The outdoor setting should be free of safety hazards:

1. The grounds and equipment should be clean and well kept.
2. The play area should be fenced or enclosed by something that children cannot climb easily and possibly hurt themselves.
3. The fence should have a *child-proof gate*, with a latch at adult height.
4. The sandbox should be kept clean and should be covered when not in use.

Space. Plenty of space is very important in a good outdoor program. About 100 square feet of space for each child is considered the minimum but as much as 300 square feet is desirable. Only those areas that the child can use are figured.

Good organization of space is important. Equipment should be arranged so that children can move freely and quickly from one part of the play area to another. It should be possible to see all parts of the playground when supervising outdoor play. There should be no visual barriers. Climbing structures, such as the slide and jungle gym, should be grouped together so that one person can easily supervise climbing activities.

Areas where children are involved in quieter projects like painting, building, or woodworking should be protected from running and throwing activities. Areas where infants or toddlers are playing should be separated and protected from older children. Space should be assigned for special activities such as digging, planting a garden, raising small animals, and so forth.

Variety. The physical setting of an outdoor play area should offer variety by including:

1. *Both sunny and shady areas.* If there are no trees on the playground, beach umbrellas, awnings, or shrubbery can provide shade.

2. *Different heights.* If the playground is flat, you can use equipment, posts, boards, and boulders to provide a variety of heights.
3. *Different surfaces.* Activities that involve wheel toys and building blocks work out better on hard-surfaced areas. On the other hand, rolling, crawling, and tumbling are more safely and comfortably done on grassy surfaces.

Equipment. A good outdoor program provides a sufficient amount and variety of equipment to stimulate physical development, creative and dramatic play, and both individual and group play. Permanent equipment, movable equipment, and small items or accessories are essential.

Desirable Characteristics. Desirable characteristics of outdoor settings include nearby bathrooms, water, and storage facilities. Such things reduce the need for close adult supervision for some routines, and they encourage children to be self-reliant. However, exciting outdoor learning can take place without these facilities.

Storage. A storage area for outdoor equipment and accessories near the playground reduces preparation and clean-up time. This area should be large enough for equipment that is best stored indoors because it might be stolen or ruined by rain or snow. The storage area should have a lock on it.

Buckets, large baskets, and wagons make it easier to move equipment and accessories to and from the play area. As always, children should be encouraged to help with housekeeping routines.

Bathrooms and Water. A desirable feature of a good outdoor play area is a nearby bathroom that children can use with little supervision. A drinking fountain is also useful because it allows children to get a drink without help. Both these features let teachers and aides spend more time helping the children with outdoor activities. An outdoor faucet provides children with water for such activities as water play, sand play, gardening, taking care of animals, and housekeeping.

OUTDOOR PROGRAMS

The following guidelines will help you recognize the qualities of good outdoor programs.

Qualities of Good Outdoor Programs. Outdoor programs should provide a balance between structured and unstructured activities, just as indoor programs should. Too many structured activities keep children from enjoying child-initiated activities. But too much unstructured time and too little stimulation may cause children to use outdoor play simply as a way to let off steam.

Some children may need help getting started when activities are not scheduled or structured. You need to be available to make suggestions or give directions. Children may vary from day to day in their responses to unstructured activities, and child care aides should be alert to their changing needs.

Outdoor programs require careful planning ahead of time if they are to provide a good learning environment. Movable equipment, accessories, and indoor activities to be used outdoors must be set up before outdoor play begins. If the outdoor experience is taking place away from the center's playground (a nature walk or a field trip, for example), plans for supervision must be made.

Outdoor play should be scheduled for the same time each day, so that children can look forward to it. The daily plan may depend on the weather, the time of year, and the number of children and staff at the center, but the scheduling of outdoor play should be as consistent as possible. When playground space is limited, outdoor time must be scheduled carefully to give all age groups a chance to use the area. Although freedom is still important within the scheduled block of time, the beginning and ending times need to be enforced firmly when the schedule is tight.

Indoor Activities Brought Outside. Outdoor activities should include some indoor activities brought outside. Messy art activities—such as fingerpaints or working with clay and also woodworking activities—will work well in the outdoor setting, especially since clean-up will be much simpler. Quiet activities are also enjoyable outdoors. Fresh air and sunshine often make looking at a book, playing a musical instrument, or story time even more pleasant than they are indoors. As a caregiver, you should be aware of the added benefits to be gained when some indoor activities are brought outdoors.

PLANNING OUTDOOR PLAY

As a child care aide, you need to talk over outdoor learning objectives with your teacher. You can learn why certain activities are planned, what equipment and materials will be needed, how much time is scheduled, and what you are expected to do.

THINGS TO CONSIDER IN PLANNING

In planning outdoor activities, the same guidelines that are used for overall program planning should be followed. As you plan with your supervising teacher, discuss ways to provide:

1. An environment in which children can start things on their own and can respond to ideas suggested by the setting
2. A setting that will encourage children to play together as a group
3. A setting that will stimulate dramatic play
4. Adequate amounts of equipment and materials so that children will not have to wait too long for a turn and so that every child will have something with which to play
5. Activities for children who need help getting started
6. Activities to test strength and skill
7. Variety in activities, accessories, equipment, and location

PREPARING FOR OUTDOOR PLAY

In addition to planning, there are three more steps involved in preparing for outdoor activities. Caregivers need to prepare themselves, the children, and the equipment and materials.

Preparing Yourself. How much or how little the children in your group will enjoy outdoor activities depends a great deal on your attitude.

What is more, how much you enjoy the outdoors yourself will be determined by how positive your attitude is.

Show the children that you look forward to going outdoors, and, once you are there, let them know that you are enjoying the fresh air and sunshine. Be a good observer and take advantage of learning opportunities on the playground. Try to be alert to children's needs and learn to anticipate them.

Caregivers need to dress properly for outdoor activities. You should wear comfortable clothing that will let you enjoy the children without thinking about how hot or how cold you are and without worrying about getting your clothes dirty or torn.

Preparing the Children. When caregivers are getting children ready to play outdoors, they need to check the weather and then decide how the children should dress. Is it cold enough for jackets? Should they be buttoned? Once the decision is made, children should be told how to dress: "It's cold today, and so you will need to wear your jackets zipped or buttoned up." For health reasons, do not give children a choice. But remember that children are very active and may not need as much clothing as adults.

Figure 13-3. Encourage self-help in dressing; only help the child with those details that he or she simply can't manage. (Kenneth Karp)

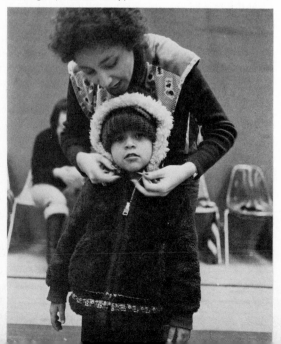

Expect and encourage self-help in dressing for outdoors and take advantage of opportunities to teach children self-help skills.

Children should use the bathroom before going outdoors, especially if winter clothing is worn. In this way a staff person will not have to leave the playground to take a child to the toilet, leaving too few adults to supervise the children.

Preparing Equipment and Materials. As for all other activities, the equipment and materials that will be used outdoors should be prepared before the activity begins. Careful planning will help you to know what measures to take and the best time to apply them. Remember that you should be giving all your attention to the children during outdoor activities—not to the equipment and materials.

You already know that it is important to have a sufficient amount and variety of equipment and materials, but it is just as important not to have too much. Too many pieces of equipment may cause the children to go from one item to another without getting involved in anything. Besides, unnecessary equipment can take up the empty space needed for active play.

You may find that you need to give children fewer choices in order to encourage them to try something new or to get more involved. If the children have not been using the sandbox, for example, you may want to cut down on the small equipment you put out. Then, by adding a variety of sand toys, you will stimulate their interest.

When you are setting up portable equipment, remember the guidelines for good organization of space. Group together such equipment and materials as are used together, avoid visual barriers and crowding and make sure that there will be clear paths and enough empty space. Children should be encouraged to help get things out and put them away.

SUPERVISING OUTDOOR PLAY

When you are supervising outdoor play, you must be aware of two important things: (1) what you can do to provide safe and enriching experiences for the children and (2) the choices and actions of the children.

SAFETY

It is especially important that safety precautions be followed outdoors. Children run fast, climb high, and talk loud on the playground. Some children, because of their stage of development or handicaps, may not be able to use the equipment with as much skill as others. All these factors can cause accidents. You must be extra alert and always watchful. The following situations require safety responses from a child care aide:

An Injury from a Fall

· Notify the teacher at once by sending a reliable child.
· Do not move the child if the fall involves a head injury or broken bones.
· Keep the child warm.
· Remain calm; help the injured child and other children not to panic.
· Once the teacher has arrived to take care of the injured child, take the group of children to another area of the playground.
· If necessary, have another staff person care for your children while you help the teacher with the injured child.

An Injury Involving Cuts

· If the cut is *slight,* wash it with soap and warm water. Apply a sterile bandage such as adhesive gauze.
· With *excessive bleeding,* notify the teacher at once by sending a reliable child.
· Keep the child lying down and quiet.
· Cover the wound with a sterile bandage or gauze.
· Apply pressure over the area with your hand.
· Elevate the wounded part.
· Remain calm; help the injured child and other children not to panic.

Other Accidents

· Refer to a first-aid chart.

· Always remember to notify the teacher at once; remain calm and help the children not to panic.

If a Child Leaves the Playground

· Notify the teacher that you are leaving the playground so that the teacher can supervise your children. Go after the child. In a calm manner, help the child to return to the play area. Don't run after the child, as that may trigger a chase. Watch the child's behavior. The child may only be curious and want to explore something on the ''other side of the fence.'' Or the child may be challenging the system or seeking attention. Watch from a distance and see whether the child is in danger. If the child is testing the rules, continue to watch, preferably without being seen. When the child returns, review the rule of staying inside the fence and why. Explain what will happen if the child breaks the rules—probably the withdrawal of some privilege. Interest the child in some new activity that can be used on the playground. Stimulate the child's curiosity.
· If the child is impulsive and may be in danger, quickly advance to retrieve him or her. Try to stay calm as you invite the child back into the yard to participate in another activity.

SUPERVISION

As a child care aide in charge of a group of children during outdoor play, you must *never leave the children unsupervised.* If you need to use the bathroom or if you are called to the telephone, ask another caregiver to look after your children for a few minutes. With two groups of children to look after, the substitute caregiver can provide only custodial supervision. Take care of your personal needs quickly and return to your group as soon as possible.

There are so many things going on outdoors that it is easy for a caregiver to be distracted. You will need to make a special effort to concentrate on your supervising tasks during outdoor play if you are to provide an effective, stimulating program. Keep in mind that when you are on duty, the children in your group are your first responsibility.

Figure 13-4. As a caregiver, you should help the children get their game started, then let them carry on. (Kenneth Karp)

You must use positive guidance techniques in setting and enforcing rules and in dealing with problem behavior during outdoor play. Remember that when a child is in danger, a caregiver must act first and explain the rules to the child later.

OUTDOOR ACTIVITIES AND YOU

In the outdoors, you will have the chance to enjoy many different activities, both with individual children and with groups. You can help children learn in the following ways.

Using Equipment. As a child care aide, you will help children learn how to use outdoor equipment by your verbal directions and your encouragement. In teaching children the skills needed to use equipment, make sure that they learn the rules for its care and use: "Sand toys stay in the sandbox," "Stop the tricycles before they hit the fence," "Fill your buckets half full," "Come down the slide one at a time," "Bean bags and balls must be put in the storage shed, not left outside."

Getting Started. At the beginning of outdoor play, take a careful look at the children and decide which ones are comfortably involved and which ones may need help in getting started. Make a suggestion, add an accessory, or participate yourself for a few minutes. In short, give just enough help for the children to become independently involved; then leave them alone, giving support only if needed.

It is always a good idea to start with simple activities at which children can succeed easily. You can lead up to more complex and challenging activities as the children gain confidence and increase their involvement.

Using Words. Caregivers help to add new words to children's vocabularies during outdoor play. As you put children's actions and experiences into words, the children are able to relate your words to what they are doing, seeing, and feeling. Always use the correct terms for labeling actions and experiences, and be alert to children's comments. If, from children's comments, you learn that they have a mistaken idea about something, explain the correct idea and help them to understand it.

Extending Concepts. Normal outdoor experiences provide children with many opportunities to see the relationships between things in the natural world and to classify objects and occurrences according to their likenesses and differences. Children often classify things or occurrences. ("Today is cold and windy; yesterday was too.") Caregivers can provide experiences in classification by suggesting activities that involve classifying items. ("Let's sort the leaves we collected on our nature walk. Put red leaves in one pile and yellow in another. Now let's separate the big leaves from the small ones.")

Caregivers need to use concepts to help children understand natural relationships. For example, space relationships—such as *over* and *under, in front of* and *behind*; texture relationships such as *rough* and *smooth, soft* and *hard*; and temperature relationships such as *hot* and *cold*—are just some of the ideas that can be applied to actual events.

Integrated Activities. When several subject-matter areas are used together in one activity—such as science, mathematics, art, music, dramatic play, and language arts—it is called *in-tegrating activities.* As a child care aide, you can use various kinds of outdoor learning at one time. Here are some examples:

Outdoor Experience	Subject-matter Areas
1. Comparing different qualities of sand or dirt; fine or rough texture, color, qualities such as crumbly, dusty, hard, soft, smooth	Science—observation and experimentation Art—sand painting and collage Language—talking about different textures, colors, etc.
2. Using measuring cups, spoons, dippers, bowls, and funnels in water	Mathematics—feeling weight, counting Language—describing activity Science—observation, experimentation
3. Moving outdoors to music—imitating trees moving in the wind	Music—creative expression Science—natural force, weather Motor development—control of muscles Dramatic play—creative role-playing

Using Resources. The center where you work may have too little equipment and materials for outdoor use. When resources are limited, caregivers have to *improvise* (find a substitute). Listed below are some helpful suggestions for improvising equipment.

- Burlap bags or laundry bags stuffed with leaves or grass may be used for punching bags.
- Wooden soft-drink cases may be used for hollow blocks.
- A baby-bed mattress or foam rubber makes a fine tumbling mat.
- A blanket or a sheet over a fence, a table, or a line of cord makes a tent.
- Wooden steps, to go up and down on, may be built.
- Old tires can be used for jumping, stacking, rolling, or as a tire swing.
- Large drums can be rolled, straddled, or crawled through.
- A real steering wheel can be mounted on a wooden box or large drum.
- A boat provides many hours of role-playing.
- A partial shelter built with a wooden frame and a cover provides shade in the yard.

- Cardboard boxes can be used to build playhouses or just to crawl into.
- A balance beam is used for walking and maintaining balance.
- Styrofoam is used for carpentry, water play, and art activities.
- A net may be used as a rope ladder and for climbing.
- A rope may be knotted and hung from a tree branch for climbing hand-over-hand; or tie it to a sandbag to make a seat for swinging.
- The fence should be used as a piece of equipment. Fasten a large piece of cardboard or plywood to the fence and use it as an easel. Hang finished paintings on the fence.
- Tubs and basins set up near the painting activity provide an opportunity for water play, science experiments, or clean-up from art activities.

Since the setting of each center is different, resources will not always be the same. Use your imagination, and put your own ideas to work. Collect "beautiful junk" that can add to children's outdoor experiences. Cardboard boxes, dress-up clothes, pieces of hose, styrofoam, and tires are a few examples of the beautiful junk that can extend outdoor learning.

ENDING OUTDOOR PLAY

Like all good experiences, outdoor play must end. You can make it a good ending by using the transition procedures established by your center. Evaluate the experience with your supervising teacher soon after the outdoor play period is over.

TRANSITION PROCEDURES

Your way of moving from one activity to another is called a *transition procedure*. The following procedures apply to transition from outdoor to indoor activities in child care centers.

Give a Short Notice. When children are enjoying themselves, they are often unwilling to stop what they are doing. If you let them know that outdoor playtime is almost over, you will prepare them for bringing their activities to a close and for getting ready to help with the clean-up.

Let Children Help. Guide children's participation in cleaning up and putting things away as part of learning self-help skills. Trash must be picked up and put in containers. Doors on outdoor equipment must be closed, covers must be put in place. Equipment and materials must be returned to the storage area, and this area must be locked. The principles of maintaining order and sharing housekeeping jobs apply outdoors as well as indoors.

Taking Outdoor Activities Inside. Outdoor activities can be brought indoors by using outdoor experiences in charts, during talking time, in painting activities, and in making collections of things picked up outdoors. One teacher, Cheryl Corbette, utilized outdoor activities in this way:

> We sometimes keep a weather chart, and we put the things the children collect on a "science table." We have brought chipmunks and field mice indoors for short periods of time. Children like to bring flowers and fruits indoors to enjoy. One year we planted sunflower seeds in the spring, and then we picked the seeds out in the fall. We had enough sunflower seeds to treat our guinea pigs all year.

Leaving the Playground. With enough staff members, the children can leave the playground over a period of time rather than all at once. One staff member can accompany each small group indoors. The last caregiver to go in should check the playground to see that all pieces of material and equipment are stored properly or brought inside.

EVALUATING OUTDOOR ACTIVITIES

Once the children are inside, activities will continue as planned. As soon as possible, you should share with your teacher any significant events that took place outdoors—especially if accidents or fights led to injury or problems. Your teacher will share such information with parents when it is appropriate.

Report pleasant events, too: Jody learned to skip; Leslie walked on the balance beam. Sharing information about good and bad events will help both staff and parents in planning future activities.

Another part of evaluating the children's experience is looking at your own performance during outdoor play. Did your supervision help children to grow and learn, or did it get in their way? Did you know how far to get involved and when to remove yourself from the children's activities? Did you prepare yourself, the children, and the equipment effectively? Did you extend children's learning? Were you alert to safety hazards? Did you carry out steps of the follow-up? Your skill in supervising outdoor play will grow if you evaluate yourself and use what you learn to improve your planning and performance.

Figure 13-5. Growing plants is an example of an outdoor activity brought indoors.
(Kenneth Karp)

CHAPTER SUMMARY

1. Outdoor experiences should be part of any good child care program. The outdoors can be just as good a learning environment as the indoor classroom if caregivers take advantage of the opportunities available.

2. Outdoor programs can include any experiences that benefit children, including indoor activities that are brought outside. Outdoor programs benefit children's health and stimulate speech, motor skills, and social development.

3. A good outdoor program should have the same basic qualities as an overall child care program. The environment should be safe as well as stimulating. Activities should be planned ahead of time, and the needs of individual children and groups of children should be considered.

4. In preparing for outdoor play, caregivers need to take three steps: (a) to prepare themselves, (b) to prepare the children, and (c) to prepare the equipment and materials. This preparation is necessary if children are to have meaningful experiences outdoors.

5. In supervising outdoor play, caregivers must remember that safety always comes first. There are many opportunities for accidents in the freedom of the playground. The most important outdoor rule for caregivers is *Never leave children unsupervised.*

6. Caregivers need to use positive guidance techniques in supervising children, enforcing rules, and handling problem behavior.

165

7. Caregivers need to enjoy outdoor activities and make use of the many moments of teaching that occur during outdoor play. Helping children get started in activities, teaching them how to use and care for equipment, adding new words to children's vocabularies, helping to extend children's concepts, and integrating subject areas during learning experiences are the main ways that caregivers can provide meaningful outdoor experiences for children.

8. The two main steps in following up outdoor activities are (a) clean-up and (b) evaluation of the children's experiences and the caregiver's performance.

• WHAT NEW TERMS HAVE YOU LEARNED?

Several new words and ideas were presented in this chapter. To see whether you understand them, match the letter of each term below with the numbered phrases under "Definitions."

Terms

a. Improvising
b. Child-initiated activities
c. Integrating activities
d. Large muscles
e. Transition procedures
f. Permanent or stationary equipment
g. A fence with a childproof gate

Definitions

1. Fixed swings, climbing structures, or slides
2. The way that caregivers change from one activity to another
3. Muscles of trunk, neck, arms, and legs
4. An important safety feature of a playground
5. Activities which children begin by themselves
6. Using materials at hand to make your own equipment
7. Using several subject areas together

• PROJECTS, DECISIONS, ISSUES

1. Prepare a bulletin board illustrating what you think are the four most important benefits of outdoor play to children.

2. Visit two child care centers to observe their outdoor play areas. Compare the settings. Identify three things that contributed to good planning for the children's outdoor program.

3. Pretend you are a 3-year-old child and write a story in your own words about what a child care aide should do to make outdoor play a good experience.

4. Prepare a chart listing the steps, in sequence, for ending outdoor play. Tell what the child care aide does in each step.

5. Identify activities and equipment that encourage:
   a. Use of large muscles
   b. Prescience relating to outside environment
   c. Premath outdoors
   d. Language development as part of outdoor play
   e. Improvising with limited equipment
   f. Improvising with limited staff
   g. Integration of subject matter areas
   h. Effective use of the immediate environment

6. Make a collection of photos or pictures showing different kinds of outdoor programs.

• WHIFS (WHAT WOULD YOU DO IF . . .)

1. A child opens the playground gate and leaves the play yard. What would you do?
   a. Look the other way
   b. Run after him or her
   c. Call to the teacher
   d. Send another child after the first
   e. Other responses

2. You have worn a long dress to school, forgetting that supervising outdoor play was part of your assignment. What would you do?
   a. Trade assignments with another student
   b. Ask the teacher to be relieved of the assignment
   c. Supervise outdoor play in your long dress

d. Find a friend who was your size and switch clothes

e. Other responses

3. You're the only caregiver on the playground and you're called to the phone. What would you do?

   a. Tell them to take the message

   b. Find out who it is

   c. Go to the phone

   d. Get another teacher or student to substitute

   e. Other responses

4. A child falls off the top of the slide and lands on his head. What would you do?

   a. Pick him up

   b. Call the teacher

   c. Call an ambulance

   d. Run and call a doctor

   e. Other responses

5. You see a wounded bird on the playground. What would you do?

   a. Put it in a low shrub

   b. Kill it and bury it

   c. Comment on its injury and nurse it

   d. Hide it

   e. Other responses

6. A child finds a snake on the playground. What would you do?

   a. Examine it carefully

   b. Scream and run

   c. Pick it up

   d. Kill it

   e. Other responses

7. It's time to go and the portable playground equipment has not been put away. What would you do?

   a. Stay and put it up

   b. Tell the teacher it's still out

   c. Catch your bus

   d. Tell the children to put it up

e. Other responses

8. A child comes out on the playground on a cold day and takes off her coat. What would you do?

   a. Put it on for her

   b. Decide she's warm enough

   c. Tell her to put it on or she'll have to go inside

   d. Other responses

9. A child climbs high on the jungle gym and is afraid to come down. What would you do?

   a. Climb up after him

   b. Coax him down, saying, ''You're a big boy, you can do it''

   c. Tell him, ''Turn around and back down''

   d. Leave him up there, he'll come down when he's not the center of attention

   e. Have another child climb up and help him down

   f. Other responses

• STUDENT ACTIVITIES

1. Give four ways outdoor experience benefits children.

2. Name three things you should do to get ready for outdoor supervision.

3. Identify the *most important* part of supervising outdoor play.

4. Summarize four essential characteristics of a good outdoor setting.

5. Identify three things to consider when planning a good outdoor program.

6. Role-play four ways a child care aide supervises outdoor play activities.

7. Show one method of moving children from outdoor activity to indoor activity.

8. What kind of evaluation should you make regarding your outdoor teaching experience? To whom should you make it, and when?

14 | ENCOURAGING MOTOR DEVELOPMENT AND CREATIVE MOVEMENT

After you have studied Chapter 14, you should be able to:

1. Identify four reasons why movement is important to young children
2. Compare the stages of body awareness and management of young children and give examples of activities useful in each stage
3. Demonstrate five ways to stimulate motor development and creative movement using opportunities available in the daily schedule
4. Use procedures that child care aides should utilize to make manipulative play effective

Motor development refers to muscle and body development and control. *Movement* refers to children's use of their muscles and body to change positions and location. Because the terms *motor development* and *movement* are related so closely, they are used as one in this chapter.

MOVEMENT AND LEARNING

Movement is natural for children. In fact, it is difficult to keep children still. Effective child care aides encourage young children to move and to handle objects because they know that movement is an important part of physical development and that young children learn as they move. If children don't move, there are things they don't learn.

BODY MESSAGES

Children receive messages from outside and inside their bodies. Outside messages, received through nerve endings, make up the *senses of taste, touch, hearing, smell, and sight*. The more senses used in an experience, the better. When children handle, see, listen to, smell, and taste something, they are getting much information at one time from many different nerve endings. For example, when they climb the ladder of a treehouse, they may:

· *Feel* the pull and push of their bodies against the ladder rungs
· *See* the ground from way up high
· *Smell* the pine needles or other natural tree smells
· *Taste* the saltiness of perspiration from active play
· *Hear* the wind rattling the leaves or branches

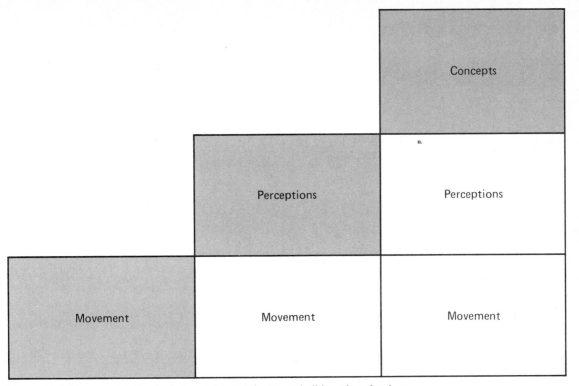

Figure 14-1. Movement is the first step children take toward all learning. As shown here, movement provides the foundation for later perception and concepts.

Messages Inside the Body. These messages help children become aware of the position of their bodies in space and the ways in which they must use their muscles to control and balance themselves. For example, if you place your arm behind your back and balance on one foot, you are using your muscles, tendons, and joints to help you move and to balance yourself. This awareness of muscles and balance is referred to as the *kinesthetic sense*.

THE IMPORTANCE OF MOVEMENT

In a young child's world, movement is essential. It is the basis for children's readiness for other important learnings. Movement is the first step children take toward understanding concepts. As they move, children discover what they can do with their bodies. The ability to use muscles to control movements is called *motor skill*. When children use their muscles and their five senses to get information about themselves and the world, they take part in *sensorimotor learning*. Figure 14-1 shows three stages in developing concepts; each is built on the others. Note that movement provides the foundation for later *perception* (understanding of what one sees) and *concepts* (meanings or ideas).

Movement, then, is important to young children because:[1]

1. It develops strong muscles, which are important to normal growth and good health.
2. Motor skills are learned and practiced through movement.
3. The kinesthetic sense is developed through movement.
4. Sensorimotor learning takes place during movement.

[1]Jeanie B. Finnell, *The Tuscumbia Physical Activity Program*, Tuscumbia Head Start Program, Alabama.

Table 14-1 BASIC MOVEMENT PATTERNS ACHIEVED BY 3-, 4-, AND 5-YEAR-OLDS

Basic pattern	Age achieved
Ascending stairs	3 years
Walking	
Pushing small bench	3½ years
Standing broad jump	
Climbing	4 years
Descending stairs	
Galloping	
Hanging	
Hopping	
Pulling	
Running	
Walking balance beam	
Bouncing large ball	4½ years
Bouncing on board	
Running high jump	
Forward roll	5 years
Throwing	
Sliding sideward	5½ years
Kicking ball	

Source: Caroline Sinclair, *Movement of the Young Child*, Merrill, Columbus, Ohio, 1973, pp. 28–30.

MOTOR DEVELOPMENT SEQUENCE

Like other areas of development, motor development has a sequence, or a predictable set of stages. By recognizing the stages of body awareness and management and development of motor skills, you are better able to provide the kinds of activities that will encourage the growth of children's motor development.

STAGES OF BODY AWARENESS AND MANAGEMENT

In young children, motor development centers on becoming aware of and learning to manage one's body. Body awareness and management occurs in three overlapping stages.

Stage 1. Children first become aware of themselves in terms of their bodies. They learn to distinguish the different parts of their bodies, and they develop general muscle coordination. This allows them to manage their bodies well enough to walk, run, achieve bowel and bladder control, and stop and start movement at will. In the last part of this first stage of development, children are able to manage their bodies well enough to move different parts of their bodies in such activities as hopping and jumping on one foot.

Stage 2. In the second stage of motor development, children become aware of their bodies in relation to other people and objects. (This is called *spatial awareness*.) Now, children are able to manage their bodies well enough so they can move without bumping into something or someone. They also become aware of the position of their bodies in space. They are able to manage themselves well enough to step over something that is in their way or to bend down in order to walk underneath something. They become aware of direction, size, and height.

Stage 3. In the third stage of body awareness and management, children are able to manipulate objects within their environment. This involves coordination and control of small and large muscles in activities such as threading beads and kicking balls.

DEVELOPMENTAL SEQUENCE OF MOTOR SKILLS

As children grow, they gain more and more control over their muscles. The first muscles to develop are those of the trunk (back and neck). Following this, the large muscles of the arms and legs develop. The last muscles over which children gain control are the small muscles of the hands, feet, and eyes. This means, then, that children's muscles develop from the trunk outward, with large muscles developing ahead of small ones.

Gross Motor Development. The development of large muscles is called *gross motor development*. What kind of activities stimulate gross motor development? You already know quite a few—climbing, running, jumping, pedaling a tricycle, and so on. In short, any activity that involves the use of large muscles will encourage gross motor development. Skill in using large muscles is called *gross motor skill*.

Figure 14-2. Music periods encourage children to practice creative movement—dancing, singing, hopping, clapping. (German Information Center)

Fine Motor Development. The development of small muscles is called *fine motor development*. Skill in using small muscles is called *fine motor skill*. How do children learn and practice fine motor skills? Again, you should be able to name a number of activities that encourage fine motor development—stringing beads, putting pegs in a pegboard, picking up small objects. These activities require children to use *eye-hand coordination*, which means using their eyes and hands together. The ability to coordinate the movement of the eyes, hands, and fingers is an important skill for children to develop; it is used in putting puzzles together, painting, cutting, and many other activities.

MOTOR DEVELOPMENT
IN A CHILD CARE PROGRAM

Motor development in a child care program focuses on identifying *basic movement patterns* and using them in the daily schedule. *Creative movement* emphasizes the movements created by the children.

BASIC MOVEMENT PATTERNS

Basic patterns in motor development that 3-, 4-, and 5-year-old children can achieve have been identified by Caroline Sinclair and are listed in Table 14-1. Activities using these basic patterns, along with variations, provide a good basic movement program for young children.

BASIC MOVEMENT PATTERNS
IN THE DAILY SCHEDULE

As a child care aide, you should become aware of chances to encourage motor development in the course of the day. Although the daily schedule differs in each center—depending on program resources, the weather, and the needs of the children—there are many activities that involve movement and many opportunities for you to encourage motor development. To give you an example, the following daily schedule suggests some movement tasks:

171

Daily Schedule	Basic Movement Patterns
Greeting (arrival at center)	Walking, running into center
Free-play activities	Walking, pushing and pulling a wagon, climbing up and down steps, carrying objects
Group time	Creeping, galloping, hopping, sliding, skipping during an activity, a song, or in acting out a story
Outdoors	Pushing, pulling, walking, running, climbing up the slide; hopping, sliding, kicking, throwing, catching, hitting; standing broad jump; running high jump; balancing beam; tumbling

Table 14-2 ACTIVITIES THAT ENCOURAGE CREATIVE MOVEMENT

Objectives	Learning experience and materials
To develop the ability to move comfortably through	
Walking	Play "Simon Says"; walk fast, slowly, quietly, like a duck, like a giant.
	Walk with eyes on a fixed target.
	Form a circle, drop hands, turn to side. Walk and sing "Let's Go Walking, Walking, Walking" (from *Make Music Your Own*, Silver Burdett Company).
	Walk through a path made of chairs, tables, furniture.
	Walk through a path made by two rows of tape on the floor.
	Walk like a camel, bear, elephant.
	Walk hands and feet on the floor, face down, same hand and foot moving together.
Running	Run to a designated place.
	Run fast, quietly, on tiptoes, like an animal.
Jumping	Jumping game: "Who would like to jump with me? Here's a card. *Jump* what you see." Hold up numbered card, and children jump the number of times that card shows. Use numerals as far as children are able to recognize.
	Rope games: jump *over* the rope, jump *into* the rope circle, jump *beside* the circle, etc. Jump rope with two people swinging the rope; with child swinging own rope.
	Play "Jack Be Nimble" with a stack of blocks to jump over.

Table 14-2 ACTIVITIES THAT ENCOURAGE CREATIVE MOVEMENT (Continued)

Objectives	Learning experience and materials
Hopping	Hop like a rabbit, kangaroo, frog, etc. Hop on two feet.
To develop the ability to move efficiently through space and to change directions	On the playground, encourage running, hopping, skipping, jumping freely. Use all activities in movement and add directions to change and go another way, such as "Let's go walking—let's go back again, back again, back the same day." Play hopscotch.

Source: Adapted from JoAnne K. Tucker, "Creative Movement" *Children Our Concern*, vol. 2, no. 1, p. 5, January, 1977, The Florida Association on Children under Six.

CREATIVE MOVEMENT

Creative movement takes place when children create the movement. When they move as they feel, or as the music tells them to, or as they tell a story, they are moving creatively.

As a child care aide, you encourage creative movement by moving yourself. Make large and small movements, then make slow and quick ones. Consider how your body can give the message of a shape—such as a circle, a square, or a triangle. Think of animals (such as a hippopotamus) or big machines (a bulldozer). Then think of small things (butterflies and snowflakes). Stimulate movement with direct requests, such as "take giant steps"; or use stories, poems, pictures, and music that involve movement.

There are four different qualities of movement, based on the manner in which energy is released. They are:[1]

1. *Sustained:* Moving in a slow, continuous manner
2. *Percussive:* A sudden, strong burst of energy
3. *Staccato:* Quick, short movement
4. *Swinging:* Moving back and forth or from side to side

[1]JoAnne K. Tucker, "Creative Movement" *Children Our Concern*, vol. 2, no. 1, p. 5, January, 1977, The Florida Association on Children under Six.

Children should have experiences in moving all four ways.

Useful materials which motivate movement are scarves and streamers, rhythm sticks, hula-hoops, blocks over which to leap, and elastic with which to stretch.

If you are shy about moving creatively, you might start with some of the activities listed in Table 14-2. As you become more comfortable, you will feel freer to encourage children's creativity in movement.

MANIPULATIVE PLAY

To handle an object is to *manipulate* it. Children use their hands, fingers, and eyes as they manipulate objects. Examples of play equipment and materials that encourage handling are pegs, puzzles, interlocking shapes, dough clay, sand, and crayons. *Manipulative play* is composed of experiences in handling things.

Besides stimulating the development of fine motor skills and eye-hand coordination, manipulative play offers several other benefits to young children. It involves them in sensorimotor learning experiences. As they poke, push, sort, arrange, and compare objects, they make observations, gain information, and solve problems. Manipulative play also allows children to feel more in control of their environment. Items small enough for children to pick up and handle are less likely to overwhelm them.

Language should go along with the handling of items. You help children remember and identify what they are doing and how it is done when you label objects and talk about size, shape, location, what is happening, shadows, color, what is alike and different, and so on.

The manipulation of objects and materials allows children to control their environment, to simplify concepts, and to sort out stimuli that may be bombarding them and preventing them from paying attention to any one part of their environment. Too much excitement, too much confusion, too many things to choose from, and people and things that are too big for a small child to take in must be given in small doses. A child can handle only one concept at a time. One sensorimotor experience to explore and enjoy can be managed, but too much stimulation leads to confusion.

PREPARING FOR MANIPULATIVE PLAY

You can promote manipulative play in these ways:

1. Provide space for a few manipulative items. Too many are confusing. Store spare items for later use.

2. Place items on open shelves at children's height so that they can see the items and choose one.

3. Arrange the items clearly. Each item should have a place, and each should be returned to its place after use.

4. Select manipulative equipment that will help reach identified program objectives.

5. Use *self-correcting* toys (toys that work in only one way) whenever possible, such as nesting cups, puzzles, and graduated items.

6. Provide variety. Change equipment from time to time, but not so often that children cannot repeat experiences. Children gain feelings of achievement as they put familiar items together one more time. "I can put this 'Little Boy Blue' puzzle together" may be heard from a child who has done it before. Repetition is a form of practice.

7. When putting manipulative items out on tables, put like things together. For example, set out pegs and pegboards one day and knob puzzles another day. Match items and accessories. For instance, place a small bowl or box of pegs by each pegboard. Place the set of pegs and pegboard in front of each chair at the table. This arrangement clearly defines the work space for a child to use. It sets a pattern for the child to maintain after using the manipulative item.

SUPERVISING MANIPULATIVE PLAY

Here are some things to keep in mind when supervising manipulative play:

1. Allow children to explore and experiment freely with materials, especially if they are new to the children.

2. *Verbalize*—that is, use words—to describe what a child is doing or has done.

3. Simplify difficult concepts. Deal with one concept at a time. When one characteristic is to be emphasized, other things should remain constant. For example, when teaching the color red, don't introduce the concept of shape or size. *After* one concept is understood, other ideas can be mentioned, and concepts can be extended or combined (after color is understood, shape can be taught). This helps children to become more sensitive to ideas received through the senses and muscles. For example, consider the concept of *sense of touch*. You might use one of several approaches: Isolate sense of touch from other senses, especially the sense of sight. Feel objects in a bag without seeing them or use a blindfold to cover the eyes while touching objects. Run the fingers around the edge of letters or objects. Another example would be *visual-kinesthetic-tactile sense*. This relates to experiences (using sight, muscles, and touch for sensory input). Feel objects and see them at the same time.

4. Watch how children handle materials. Are they exploring and manipulating only? The materials and equipment can be used to solve problems.

FOLLOWING UP AND EVALUATING MANIPULATIVE PLAY

After manipulative play, do the following:

1. Remind the children to leave the equipment and materials as they found them, either on the table or on the shelf.

2. Discuss individual children's use of manipulative items with your supervising teacher.

CHAPTER SUMMARY

1. Effective child care aides encourage young children to move and to handle objects because they know that movement is important to physical development and that young children learn as they move.

2. Movement is important to children because it develops strong muscles, motor skills, kinesthetic sense, and sensorimotor learning.

3. Physical development and motor skills differ from child to child, but they follow a sequence in all children. Motor development centers on children's growing awareness of and ability to manage their bodies.

4. Basic motor patterns have been identified for children between the ages of 3 and 5. Activities using the identified basic motor patterns are provided in daily schedules. Child care aides need to use routine activities to encourage motor development. They should also participate in planned activities that increase motor skills.

5. Creative movement emphasizes movement created by the children. As children grow, they learn to control their large muscles first, then their small muscles. Large-muscle activities may be provided both indoors and outdoors. Small-muscle activities usually center on manipulative play, which focuses on handling small objects that require the use of small muscles.

6. Procedures for manipulative activities emphasize self-help skills and housekeeping. Verbalizing (or talking about) activities helps to increase the effectiveness of the learning related to motor development.

• WHAT NEW TERMS HAVE YOU LEARNED?

Several new words and ideas were presented in this chapter. To see whether you understand them, match the letter of each term below with the numbered phrases under "Definitions."

Terms

a. Manipulative play
b. Fine motor skills
c. Eye-hand coordination
d. Motor development
e. Creative movement
f. Basic movement pattern
g. Sensorimotor learning
h. Gross motor skills
i. Kinesthetic sense
j. Perception
k. Concepts
l. Spatial awareness

Definitions

1. Using the five senses and the muscles to gain information
2. Balance and awareness of the position of one's body in space
3. To understand what one sees
4. Movement created by children
5. Basic pattern of walking, galloping, or climbing, etc.
6. Ideas
7. Using hands and eyes together
8. Body development and control of muscles
9. Skill in using the large muscles of the trunk, arms, neck, and legs
10. Skill in using the small muscles of the hands, feet, and eyes
11. Handling pegs and small interlocking blocks
12. Aware of one's body in relation to other people and objects

• PROJECTS, DECISIONS, ISSUES

Divide into small groups and discuss the following "agree-disagree" statements. Report your findings to the class with explanations for your answers. Change "disagree" statements so that you can agree with them.

1. Since children learn as they move, rest periods should be of short duration.
2. There are enough opportunities for motor development in the daily schedule without planning special activities related to motor development.
3. *Body awareness* and *motor development* mean the same thing.
4. Since children need fine motor skills to write, development of the small muscles is more important than that of the large muscles.
5. Manipulative play is taught by showing a child how to use small toys such as pegs, puzzles, and Lincoln logs.

• WHIFS (WHAT WOULD YOU DO *IF* . . .)

1. All the children are moving like tired camels except Kerri. She says she's tired and doesn't want to move that ''silly way.'' What would you do?
   a. Ignore her
   b. Insist that she participate
   c. Sit beside her and watch the other children walk
   d. Tell her to watch, she may want to participate next time
   e. Make her stand in a corner
   f. Other responses

2. Joey avoids manipulative activities where he needs to use his small muscles. You have watched him carefully for the past 2 weeks and he has not put a puzzle together, put pegs into a pegboard, or used a crayon in that period of time. What would you do?
   a. Mention your observation to your supervising teacher
   b. Deny him use of the blocks, which he loves, until he participates in manipulative play
   c. Make him put a puzzle together before he does anything else
   d. Give him a choice of several manipulative activities before he can participate in large-muscle activities
   e. Ignore the situation; he'll do it when he wants to
   f. Other responses

3. Laurie does not know the names of the parts of her body. What would you do?
   a. Provide a mirror for her to use
   b. Put labels on her body parts
   c. Have her draw a picture of her body
   d. Send a note home that requires that her parents teach her what parts of her body are called
   e. Use songs that name parts of the body
   f. Look at picture books with her that identify the parts of the body
   g. Other responses

4. George was playing with the puzzles. He dumped six puzzles out of their frames into a pile, then left them to go to the easel to paint. What would you do?
   a. Make him go back and pick them up
   b. Insist that he put each puzzle together
   c. Put the puzzles together when the children have gone home
   d. Put the puzzles together but let the other children know that ''George made this mess''
   e. Overlook the situation; all children do the same thing at one time or another
   f. Other responses

• STUDENT ACTIVITIES

1. The following activities foster muscle development in children. Identify those that focus on large-muscle as opposed to small-muscle coordination: playing tag, skipping rope, putting pegs in pegboards, swinging, writing, putting a puzzle together, climbing ladders, playing the piano, following the leader, doing finger plays.
2. List one activity which will enhance body awareness for a 3-year-old, one for a 4-year-old, and one for a 5-year-old.
3. Demonstrate five ways to stimulate motor development and creative movement from opportunities available in the daily schedule.
4. Use at least three procedures child care aides should utilize to make manipulative play effective.
5. Name four reasons why movement is important to young children.

15 | ASSISTING WITH SOCIAL LEARNINGS

After you have studied Chapter 15, you should be able to:

1. Identify four basic goals related to social learnings
2. Name four kinds of daily social learning experiences for young children
3. Provide three different kinds of social learning experiences for young children and evaluate performance by using a checklist

GOALS RELATED TO SOCIAL LEARNINGS

The four basic goals related to social learnings in a child care program are to help children:

1. Develop a positive self-concept
2. Get along with others
3. Become aware of basic personal needs
4. Become aware of how society is organized

In schools these social learning goals are identified as part of the social studies curriculum. In child care centers they may be referred to as *social experiences* or *social learnings*.

DEVELOPING A POSITIVE SELF-CONCEPT

A *self-concept* is the impression that people have of themselves. Children build their self-concepts from how "significant others" treat them. Good experiences with important people in their lives lead to positive self-concepts, while poor experiences lead to negative ones. A positive self-concept is sometimes called a positive *self-image*; it gives children *self-confidence*. In addition, children with positive self-concepts develop

· Faith in themselves and others
· Creativity and enthusiasm for learning
· Perseverance, which enables them to finish the things they start and therefore leads to accomplishment
· Honesty, including recognition of the difference between fact and make-believe

You can help children build positive self-concepts in the following ways:

1. Use children's names when talking to them.

2. Show children their reflections in a mirror. Photographs also help children feel that they are important.

3. Listen carefully to children—they should feel that what they are saying counts.

4. Take your time and give your attention to children, even if only for a short time. Even a few minutes of individual attention helps children feel that they are important.

5. Take children seriously, without thinking of their behavior as "cute" or funny.

6. Value children's favorites. When you value a child's favorite toy or food, the child feels valued.

Self-Concepts Affect Behavior. Children with positive feelings about themselves are likely to behave in a desirable way. A positive self-concept helps children to accept responsibility, develop coping skills, and build respected values.

Accepting Responsibility. Children with positive self-concepts accept rules or limits set for them. They also accept responsibility for their own behavior.

Developing Coping Skills. The *ability to cope* is the ability to meet and solve problems. Problem-solving skills are therefore called *coping skills*. Children with positive self-concepts are able to develop coping skills. The world today is complex and always changing. Therefore it is important that children learn coping skills early in life. Child care aides can help children to learn the basic process of coping with problems in the following way:

1. *Identify the problem.* "What is wrong?" "What has happened?" "What needs to be changed?" "How can we get the job done?" By such questions, you can help children figure out what the problem is.

2. *Look for solutions.* "How can we solve the problem?" "What are some different ways to find the answer?" "How can we get the job finished?" You will need to ask questions or make suggestions that encourage the children to think of possible solutions. You can help them see that there are different ways to solve problems.

3. *Decide on a solution.* "Which way is best?" "Which way is easiest?" "Which way is fastest?" "What can we really do?" Help children decide on a reasonable solution. Their imaginations often lead them to unrealistic solutions.

4. *Form a plan.* "What should we do first?" Ask questions or make suggestions that encourage the children to plan the order in which things should be done. In some situations, you may let the children try various solutions until a workable one is found. Talking about difficulties that arise with this *trial-and-error method* will help children see that it is not the most efficient way to solve problems.

5. *Act on the plan and follow through.* Help the children follow the plan and not lose sight of their goal. Help them overcome any difficulties they meet along the way.

6. *Evaluate your action.* "Did it work?" "Did we accomplish our goal?" "Did we solve the problem?" If the children did well, recognize their accomplishment. If the problem was not solved, help the children figure out what went wrong. Help them decide what to do next.

Building Values. Child care aides have many opportunities to help children build values by making experiences meaningful to each child. Your actions help children to become aware of and appreciate

· Beauty and order in the natural world
· Cleanliness in the natural world as well as that made by humans
· Needs of plants and animals
· Family, friends, the community, and the country
· The special and individual value of each person they meet
· Cooperation and loyalty—recognition that people can do things together that one person cannot do alone

The ability to accept responsibility, to cope, and to maintain values are social learnings that children will use throughout life.

Figure 15-1. Good child care programs help children learn how to get along with others. (Menschenfreund)

GETTING ALONG WITH OTHERS

Children learn to get along with others in the family before they extend their social experiences outside the family. Child care centers often provide the setting in which children practice getting along (interacting) with others outside the family.

As young children have their first contacts outside the family, they are likely to build a relationship with a nurturing adult before becoming aware of other children. When children are comfortable with the setting, they feel less of a need to be near to or to show an adult everything they do. Their attention then turns to other children. However, they still want assurance that important adults are available when needed. During this time, it is enough for children to see their nurturing adults somewhere nearby.

In the beginning years, children are not aware of other children. They are content to play alone, a phase of play known as solitary play. When two children play near each other but not together, it is called parallel play. This phase of play follows solitary play and seems to be an experience that children must have before they are able to play together. When children do play together, often assigning roles, it is called cooperative play. For example, in playing "family," Linda is the baby, Joe is the brother, and Mark is the daddy. As with other skills, children must practice getting along with other children in order to become successful at it. Their first attempts at cooperative play will probably not be smooth. They may push, call each other names, tattle, and perhaps even fight.

In child care centers, children within a group depend on each other as they play together. If Ruth takes the tape away from the art table when the children need it for an art project, she stops the project. If this happens often, she may find that the children do not welcome her when she wants to play with them. A group may help a shy child. For example, one day David brings a collection of shells to the center. The children enjoy the shells at group time, and they tell him so. This group experience helps David overcome his shyness. At the same time, the group benefits from seeing the shells.

GAINING AWARENESS OF PERSONAL NEEDS

Basic Personal Needs. Basic needs involve things people need in order to survive. Everyone needs water, food, air, clothing, shelter, protection, and love. As a child care aide, you can help children to understand the idea of personal needs by starting with the things children know. Then you can add to their information with enriched experiences. Table 15-1 gives some examples of experiences in the child care program that relate to personal needs.

Young children understand the concepts when you relate them to their own experiences. For example, after a power failure during a hurricane, the children tell about how their families prepared their food. After seeing, on a television show, how tortillas are cooked on a simple outdoor fire, the children may be interested in how the Indians cooked their food. After a vacation trip, a child may bring some pine nuts to share, which may lead to a study of different kinds of edible nuts. Through such experiences, eating is identified as a basic personal need of all human beings and animals. Children come to realize that while food may be prepared in different ways, it nourishes everyone similarly and tastes good to those who eat it.

Table 15-1 HOW PERSONAL NEEDS RELATE TO THE PROGRAM

Basic need	Key concept	Experiences in program
Food, water air	People, animals, and plants need food, water, and air to live; without them, they die.	Naming and tasting foods; studying water and air—how they move, what they do for us.
Shelter, protection	People, animals, and plants need protection from weather, animals, machines, and people.	Becoming aware of different kinds of homes; naming items of clothing and their uses; saying how animals and plants are protected; naming safety measures for people, animals, and plants.
Love, acceptance, belonging	Everyone needs to be cared for, loved, and accepted and to have loved ones and friends.	Seeing ways people take care of each other; taking care of pets.

BECOMING AWARE OF HOW SOCIETY IS ORGANIZED

Young children need to develop awareness of how society is organized to satisfy personal needs. They think in terms of themselves rather than in terms of social groups or units. There is plenty of time in the future for them to learn about the governmental structure of their community, their country, and the world. Yet children's present experiences relate to the group. In a child care center, children experience being part of a group, listening when someone else is talking, and sharing the feeling of success when several children push and pull a heavy load from one part of the yard to another.

You can help children appreciate the individuality of families. Some children have grandparents who live nearby. Others go on long trips to see theirs. Some do not have grandparents. Joshua and his mother are a family all by themselves. Suzanne has four brothers, and she is the youngest in the family. Neal's mother is expecting a new baby; he hopes it's a brother. All the children can be helped to see how their families care for them. While each family is different, children begin to see how most families provide food, clothing, and shelter for their members.

Pride comes from knowing the name of one's town and some of the places in it. The park, the library, the post office, the grocery store, and the drive-in hamburger stand all become familiar places when children have visited them.

Communication tends to help people feel closer to one another. Today's children—through television, travel, and perhaps personal experience—have contact with many cultures and customs. You can help children recognize the personal worth and cultural heritage of each individual as you work with them daily.

Table 15-2 DAILY SOCIAL LEARNING EXPERIENCES

Experience	Social concepts children may learn
Arriving transition from home to child care center	Families do different things at home. Children come to the child care center in different ways. People exchange friendly greetings when they see each other.
Relating to one another, individually and as a group	Sharing, planning, making and following rules, expressing ideas and feelings, and solving problems are part of group experiences.
Getting help from staff members	Each person has a job to do. These jobs may be done by men or women. Each job is important.
Taking care of toys and equipment	Part of being a good citizen is taking care of things that belong to the group.
Enjoying children who may look different or have different customs	Each human being is a person of unique worth. There may be more than one way to do something.
Participating in snack time, mealtimes, rest periods, and playtimes	There are special times to do certain things. There are approved ways to behave at these times.
Solving problems	Problems may be solved in different ways.

PROVIDING EXPERIENCES FOR SOCIAL LEARNING IN DAILY ACTIVITIES

Daily activities and routines include many social learnings. When child care aides use these experiences effectively, they provide children with a good foundation for personal and social awareness and interaction (Table 12-2).

Planning Activities for Social Learnings. Routines and daily activities provide experiences in social learning for young children. It is also possible to plan special activities or provide useful accessories that will help children extend their awareness and understanding of their immediate community as well as the larger world.

DRAMATIC PLAY

Dramatic play helps children learn about feelings, roles, and society. Dramatic play can be *spontaneous* (started by children on the spur of the moment) or part of the planned activities.

Spontaneous Dramatic Play. Spontaneous role-playing is one of the most natural ways children learn. They try out how it feels and what it's like to be someone or something that they know and have strong feelings about. Play that the children start themselves is usually done on a plan-as-you-go basis. In fact, a child or two may begin their role-playing in the kitchen and end up with a supermarket sale!

While the most obvious area for dramatic play tends to be the housekeeping learning center, you find children trying out their imitative skills with blocks, sand, and other materials also. The entire outdoor area lends itself to "trying out how it feels" or "let's build it this way." Equipment such as playhouses, slides, or climbing structures become forts, bridges, tunnels, or other items of fantasy. This is especially so if the children's experiences are richly stimulating and can be relived later (example: a trip to a farm).

How Child Care Aides Enhance Dramatic Play. Children usually start the action in dramatic play, especially if their experiences lend themselves to imitation, so that they can see, through role-playing, how it feels to be someone else for a while. You can help children benefit from dramatic play by doing the following things:

1. *Provide time and space.* It takes time for children to interact, and for role-playing to evolve. The large blocks of time usually allowed in preschool schedules provide enough time for children to play without being rushed by the clock. Space is another basic requirement of dramatic play. Children need room to walk, strut, give orders, tend to the sick, cook supper, and imitate the ways of grownups.

2. *Provide a variety of objects.* Children may need props to get started, but too many may confuse them. Props that suggest roles or ways to behave but do not define roles are best. For example, a man's shirt turned backward makes a fine doctor's coat, a nurse's white uniform, or a barber's smock. If the prop is too exact, it may be limited. Use real items rather than toys wherever possible. Unbreakable, real salad plates and cups are better than play tea sets. Items of various sizes and shapes lend interest to block, sand, and woodworking projects.

3. *Help only when needed.* Children often have trouble getting along in their first experiences in dramatic play. If the children need help in working out a plan or idea, you may need to redirect their interest or to add something else that can be shared. Don't intervene too soon. Give children a chance to work out their own problems. Often what seems like a big problem to an adult is easily and creatively resolved by the children if adults do not interfere. If children are full of ideas, stay out of their way and let them carry them out. If children have trouble getting started, try some of the following:

   a. Raise questions that stimulate their thinking ("Do you need to call the doctor?"). Or extend sick-baby play by adding a phone, a bottle, or a blanket.

   b. Involve yourself in role-playing for a few minutes ("What are you cooking for dinner?"). Be careful to take your cues from the children, and remove yourself from their play as soon as their own interaction has started.

4. *Don't get in the way.* Place yourself where you can see and redirect play or stimulate it if needed, but do not get in the way.

Planned Dramatic Play. Besides the spontaneous play that children start, you can help them learn by acting out stories or role-playing situations that show relationships. You may set the stage for these activities by reading a story without an ending, so that the children discuss and play out how it ends. Children enjoy planning and collecting props for their favorite stories. For example, "The Three Bears" is easy for children to play, and they like to do it again and again. Props may be *very* simple; three different-sized bowls, three items to sit

Figure 15-2. Child care aides should help children learn how to think through and solve their own problems. (Mimi Cotter)

on, and three on which to lie down. Be sure everyone has something to do. Besides Goldilocks and the three bears, children can be stagehands, or on the prop committee, or trees in the forest, or part of the audience. Everyone should have the chance to get in the act in one way or another. Rearrange assignments so that each child experiences lead roles as well as supporting ones. For example, Marie is Goldilocks one time and impersonates a tree in the forest another time. Talk about the feelings of the characters involved. Plan together and evaluate the performance in a relaxed way. When the activity becomes one of practice and learning lines, adults take over the children's play; that is not good for little children.

Materials That Encourage Dramatic Play. The selection, use, care, and storage of materials for dramatic play set the stage for children's experience.

Choose items that are familiar to the children from their home experiences. Ask yourself, "What experiences have the children had? Is the community rural or urban? Who lives at home? How does the family travel? What means of communication are used? How is the cooking done? Who comes to visit? What items does the family spend money on?"

Besides things that are familiar to the children in their home life, consider items that are brought into their lives through television, movies, and books. Also use items and topics experienced at the child care center.

Include all sorts of props and accessories. Give the children opportunities to try out roles without sex labels. Make a special effort to include male clothing and accessories along with those for females. Boys will enjoy dressing up in girls' clothes and girls enjoy trying on men's clothing.

Puppets and Puppet Stage. Puppets can help children say things they are too shy or too afraid to say themselves. Puppets encourage dramatic play and let children have fun while learning social concepts.

Puppets to be used by children should be attractive but sturdy. Children enjoy several kinds of puppets:

- *Finger puppets* are made from felt, from pictures pasted on cardboard or stiff paper, or from plastic hair rollers or small Styrofoam balls. These puppets can be made by constructing a band or cone which slips over the child's finger. Finger puppets are small and easily manipulated, and they can be used either in solitary or cooperative play or during group time.

- *Hand puppets* are the most common kind of puppet children use. They can be made from a variety of materials. The heads can be made from papier mache, Styrofoam balls, or small paper bags. Another kind of hand puppet can be made from a sock with a face drawn or painted on it. Stick puppets, face puppets, and body puppets are still other kinds of puppets.

- *Coat-hanger puppets* are made by stretching a coat hanger into a diamond shape and putting a nylon stocking over the hanger frame. This mask is then decorated with bits of ribbon, cloth, yarn, and so forth. Cover the hook part of the hanger to protect hands and to provide a hand hold. This is an enjoyable project for the children, who can use their finished puppets to play with one another.

A *puppet stage* may be made from an overturned table or chair, or a more formal stage can be made from a large cardboard box. Cut one side of the box completely away, and cut a large rectangular area away from the top of the side opposite the one you have just removed. Cover the remaining part of the box with vinyl adhesive paper, or paint it. Stretch a curtain rod across the top of the rectangle and hang curtains on it. Presto! You have a puppet stage to use with the puppets!

Care and storage of materials. Launder or clean and mend clothing as needed. Be sure fastenings are large and in good repair. Put them in locations that children can manage easily. If not on front of garment, where the child can manage it alone, put it where a friend can help.

Spray hats, shoes, and wigs with disinfectant. Brush or wipe them once in awhile to keep them attractive.

Check accessories for broken parts, splinters, and loose or sharp edges. Repair them as needed. Throw broken items away.

Clothes should be hung on hangers or hooks, where children can use them. Shoes should be placed together on a rack.

Props should be stored in boxes, well marked. Placing items together in a kit (such as a medical kit, a hairdresser kit, and so on) makes it easy for the children to get what they want.

If items are grouped together and regularly stored in clearly defined places on open shelves, teachers will encourage self-help, good work and play habits, and use of accessories to expand creativeness of the play. Blocks should be sorted according to size and shape. Patterns on the backs of the blocks or on the shelves help children put them back into their assigned places. Woodworking tools should be stored in a safe place, with each tool placed in its assigned location so that children can identify the tool needed, use it, and return it to its place.

Dolls, bedding, and household items should be stored in an attractive manner that invites dramatic play to begin again another time. When playtime is over, the children must be helped to put the dolls to bed, fold the clothing that should be put in a drawer or on a shelf,

and hang other items on the hooks provided. Children tend to take off doll clothes but not put them back on. They will need some help from you to develop the habit of putting dramatic play items in their assigned places or storage areas.

FIELD TRIPS

Visits to see people at work and play, machinery being used, and others are helpful to children's social development.

Some important guidelines to remember when planning and taking field trips follow:

1. *Choose simple trips.* Examples include a visit to the grocery store, a trip to see workers put in drainpipes at the end of the street, a visit to the fire department, or even a visit to the kitchen to watch the cook prepare lunch.

2. *Clear your plans with your supervisor.* Let your supervisor know the day, time, and place of the visit. Then make sure that you have all the necessary clearances before you tell children and parents about the trip.

3. *Take the trip yourself beforehand.* Talk to the person in charge and explain that the children will want to be involved in "hands on" experience if safety rules permit. Sometimes you may need to arrange two separate trips, so that the children may have the chance to find out "how it's done" and "what it feels like." You may want to show a filmstrip before or after the field trip.

4. *Arrange for supervision.* Field trips are a good way to involve parents and ensure that the children will be well supervised when they are away from the center. When you plan the details of the trip, let parents know what time you are leaving, which children they are responsible for, where you are going, how you are going to get there, and when you plan to be back.

5. *Return on time.* When you have informed your supervisor that you and the children will be back by a certain time, be sure that you are. Otherwise, everyone at the center will become worried about you and the children you're supervising.

Figure 15-3. Field trips to see people at work enhance children's social learnings. (Kenneth Karp)

6. *Safety on field trips.* See Chapter 6 for safety guidelines regarding field trips.

7. *Follow-up.* Talk about the trip and have children help you to write a thank-you note to the person whom you visited. You can invite another group or teacher to come to see pictures and items collected on the trip and to hear the children's thoughts about it. Stories, songs, and art activities are coordinated with the field-trip experience.

Here's what one teacher, Cheryl Corbette, has to say about field trips:

We use audiovisual materials in conjunction with field trips and visitors. We might show a film about a farm the day before our field trip to the farm. If the farmer gives the children fresh eggs, we save them to let the children hard boil them the next day for snack. If he gives them some wool from a sheep, we might use it in an art activity the next day. Also, a lot of times we'll set up the dramatic play area to represent the place we've been. If we've been to the grocery store, we'll set up the folding play screen and get out the toy cash register, play money, plastic fruits and vegetables, scales, empty food cartons, and sacks. The children will almost always role-play what they saw or did on their field trip.

Sometimes the children do not role-play their field trip experience the next day. Instead, they relive it a week or two later.

VISITORS

Ellen's father is a carpenter. George's mother decorates cakes in a bakery. Leslie's cousin is a nurse. Ken's big sister makes flowers out of silk and wire. Each of these people become special visitors when they come to share their talents with the children.

It is important that each visitor, whether a relative of a child in your group or just a friend with something to share, understand that children need to get close to the action. They want and need to participate as much as possible.

To make the visit most effective, check plans well in advance. Find out whether your visitor needs special equipment: an extension cord, a stove, a slide projector to show slides, or a chair placed in a certain location. Plan the schedule and how the children will be arranged or involved. Stories, songs, conversation, and dramatic play experiences help children remember the visitor.

Audiovisual Materials. It is not always possible or safe for children to experience all learning first-hand. Filmstrips, movies, slides, transparencies, cassettes, and tapes can all help children to understand social concepts which are not available at first hand and to reinforce field trip and visitor experiences.

To use audiovisual materials effectively, caregivers should look at or listen to them before using them with the children. Before presenting the material, caregivers should talk with children about things to look and listen for.

In the follow-up discussion, caregivers should try to relate the material to children's personal experiences.

Caregivers should use audiovisual materials along with stories, songs, art activities, and props, so that children receive the greatest benefit from the experience.

EVALUATING YOUR PERFORMANCE

How would you evaluate your participation and contribution to the children's learnings related to *social studies* (how people get along together). Answers to questions such as the following may help you to understand your participation in young children's beginning social studies experiences:

· Was I aware of individual children's feelings about themselves?

· Did I give each child a chance to make his or her own decision?

· Did I give each child enough time to work out a solution to the problem?

· Was I aware of the "happenings" that help children understand ways people work? The janitor changing a light bulb, the street sweeper going by, the helicopter flying overhead?

· Did I find ways to extend this meaningful experience and others by talking with the children or using a story, song, poem, or picture to help them think about the experience?

· Was my involvement with the children helpful? Or did I get in their way?

CHAPTER SUMMARY

1. The goals related to social learnings in child care centers are to help children develop a positive self-concept, to learn and practice getting along with others, to become aware of basic personal needs, and to recognize how society is organized.

2. Children need to learn the important life skills of accepting responsibility, coping with problems, and building values.

3. Children have social experiences at a child care center as a part of the daily schedule, during child-initiated dramatic play, and through planned program activities such as field trips, planned dramatic play, visitors, audiovisual materials, and the use of puppets.

• WHAT NEW TERMS HAVE YOU LEARNED?

Several new words and ideas were presented in this chapter. To see whether you understand them, match the letter of each term below with the numbered phrases under "Definitions."

Terms

a. Positive self-image
b. Building values
c. Coping skills
d. Interacting
e. Self-confidence
f. Spontaneous
g. Parallel play
h. Cooperative play
i. Social studies
j. Basic personal needs
k. Society
l. Solitary play

Definitions

1. Ability or skill to meet a problem and select and carry out appropriate solutions
2. Learning to understand the worth and importance of people and things
3. Two children play near each other but without interacting
4. Program activities related to social learnings in school
5. Those things required for a person to survive
6. Unplanned
7. An acceptance and liking of self
8. Comes from a positive self-concept
9. A phase of play when children play together and assume assigned roles
10. Getting along with others
11. The system of community, state, nation, and world living together
12. A phase of play when children are content to play alone

• PROJECTS, DECISIONS, ISSUES

1. Make at least three kinds of puppets and use them with the children at a later date. For extra credit, make a puppet stage and use it, too.

2. Make a sketch of five circles in the form of a bullseye target. In the center, place the word *child*. Label each surrounding band to show the child's expanding awareness of the ways society is organized.

3. Using the questions asked in the evaluation section of this chapter, answer each question with regard to your own performance in providing experiences for social learnings.

4. Group living in a child care center places responsibilities on young children. Give an example of ways a child care aide helps young children learn about each of the following areas of responsibility.

**Area of
Responsibility**

a. Limits
b. Schedules
c. Taking turns
d. Sharing
e. Putting things away
f. Respect for prop-
   erty and materials

● WHIFS (WHAT WOULD YOU DO *IF* . . .)

1. Gregory is using a big bad wolf puppet to scare the other children. What would you do?
   a. Snatch the puppet away from him
   b. Ask him to stop
   c. Look the other way
   d. Tell your supervisor
   e. Call to him to stop
   f. Other responses

2. Eddie, Teresa, and Marjorie are playing house. Teresa wants Eddie to be Daddy and Marjorie wants him to be the baby. What would you do?
   a. Round up another boy to play one of the roles
   b. Ignore the situation
   c. Tell them to work it out themselves
   d. Lecture them on the importance of being kind to one another
   e. Other responses

3. Arthur and David are playing monster. Beth and Peggy are squealing and enjoying being chased. What would you do?
   a. Tell them to use their inside voices
   b. Send them outside
   c. Make them sit on chairs and calm down
   d. Pick a favorite story and read it to them
   e. Other responses

4. You are ready to go on a field trip to a farm. Sam's 12-year-old brother brings him to the child care center along with a note from home saying that Sam has been sick all night and requesting that you call his mother at work if he gets sick again during the day.

What would you do?
   a. Leave him at the center
   b. Take him on the field trip and keep him with you
   c. Send him home with the 12-year-old brother
   d. Call your supervisor
   e. Hope he stays well and go on about your business
   f. Other responses

5. Rachel didn't bring her permission slip for the field trip that you are about to take to the fire station. What would you do?
   a. Leave her at the child care center
   b. Call her mother at work
   c. Sign her mother's name on a permission slip with your initials
   d. Ask you supervisor what to do
   e. Stay behind with her while the others go
   f. Criticize Rachel's mother in front of the children
   g. Other responses

6. Larry likes to play with dolls and dress up in long dresses and high heels. His father becomes very upset when he sees Larry playing this way. What would you do?
   a. Agree with the father that Larry should not be playing with girls' things
   b. Explain that many little boys do this
   c. Tell the father to talk with your supervisor
   d. Excuse yourself and leave the room
   e. Ask the father what's wrong with such play
   f. Give him a lecture on not being sexist
   g. Other responses

● STUDENT ACTIVITIES

1. Name four basic goals related to social learnings.
2. Identify four ways a child care aide can help children build a positive concept.
3. Name three values you want children to develop.
4. List three basic needs everyone has and identify a key concept for each.
5. List three questions you would ask yourself as you choose items to use in dramatic play.

6. Name four kinds of daily social learning experiences for young children.

7. Arrange the following steps in the order you would use them to solve a problem.
   a. Evaluate
   b. Look for solutions
   c. Decide on a solution
   d. Form a plan
   e. Identify the problem
   f. Act on the plan

8. Name three ways child care aides encourage dramatic play.

9. Put the following steps to having a successful field trip in the proper order.
   a. Provide safety on field trips
   b. Clear your plans with your supervisor
   c. Choose simple trips
   d. Take the trip yourself beforehand
   e. Arrange for adequate supervision
   f. Return on time

16 | ASSISTING WITH LANGUAGE EXPERIENCES

After you have studied Chapter 16, you should be able to:

1. Identify terms and goals of a good language arts program
2. Name at least four ways to increase children's language skills
3. List five language arts duties that child care aides are responsible for, and describe how they should be performed

THE LANGUAGE ARTS PROGRAM

The experiences and activities related to language development in a child care center make up the children's *language arts program*. A good language arts program provides children with a variety of *first-hand experiences* that stimulate their language development. (First-hand experiences are those in which children handle, smell, taste, or do something for themselves.)

LANGUAGE AND COMMUNICATION

In simple terms, *language* is made up of words. *Language arts* refers to the ability to use language to communicate. *Communication* is sending a message and having it understood. It is not limited to using words. Babies communicate. They send messages and receive them. Caregivers can communicate warmth and love to babies, without using words, long before the babies can understand language. Here are examples of verbal and nonverbal communication:

Verbal Communication	Nonverbal Communication
With words (speaking, labeling, reading, listening)	Without words (facial expressions, posture, gestures)

When words are used to communicate, the communication is said to be *verbal*. When other means are used to communicate—such as facial expressions and gestures—it is said to be *nonverbal*. Although language focuses on verbal communication, nonverbal communication is essential for full understanding of a message. Young children and adults use verbal *and* nonverbal communication together to communicate.

Verbal communication includes the *language skills* of listening, speaking, writing, and reading. With young children, the focus is on listening and speaking. Children learn to listen before they learn to speak. Interest in writing and reading comes later.

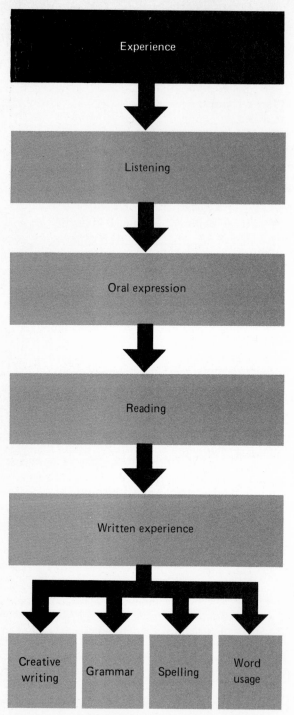

Figure 16-1. Here you can see the sequence of language development. Listening and speaking are important intermediate steps to reading and writing.

GOALS OF LANGUAGE ARTS PROGRAM

A good language arts program for young children includes activities and experiences that help them develop in *all* language skills. Figure 16-1 shows the sequence of language development. Special emphasis is placed on listening and speaking, which precede the later language skills of reading and writing. In addition, opportunities are provided for children to realize that what is said (spoken words) can become what is read (written words). Children connect spoken words with printed ones when they see their names on their pictures or when they watch a child care aide print the words of a story as they say the words. Experiences such as these help children think of words as "talk written down."

The following overall goals for a language arts program are appropriate for all child care centers:

· To provide experiences which encourage children's progress in learning to use language effectively (1) as a means of communication, (2) as a tool for thought and learning, (3) as a resource for self-expression
· To develop beginning understanding of the relationship between the written and the spoken word[1]

Why are experiences so important in developing language skills? Children learn to use and develop their language skills *through their experiences*. If their experiences are limited, their language development will also be limited.

LANGUAGE EXPERIENCES

Children's language experiences can be direct or indirect.

Direct Experiences. As you learned earlier, direct experiences are first-hand experiences because they enable children to handle, see, smell, or taste something themselves.

[1]Mary Alice Mallum, *Curriculum Guide*, California Children's Centers. Directors and Supervisors Association, Hawthorne, Calif., 1970.

Direct experience is the most effective way for children to learn the accurate meaning of words. For example, children may see pictures of horses in books and thus gain a general idea of what a horse is; however, when they actually *see* a horse, they experience its size and smell, the sounds it makes, how it moves, and what its skin feels like. After this experience, they have an accurate mental picture of a horse.

Indirect Experiences. It is not always safe or possible for children to experience things directly. Indirect experience can help children learn when direct experience is not available or desirable. When a first-hand experience is shared with others by writing about it, drawing a picture, taking a snapshot, or talking about it, the others are offered an *indirect experience*. For example, children who live in a farm community may not have the chance to actually ride on a subway, but they can learn a great deal about what a subway is like by seeing pictures or a movie and listening to a story.

Reading Readiness. It is important to let children's interest in the printed word develop naturally in response to a stimulating environment. The phrase *reading readiness* refers to children's ability to begin learning to read. Children show their readiness for reading when they become interested in the sounds of letters and meanings of words. The best way to "get children ready" for learning to read is to give them meaningful experiences.

LANGUAGE ACTIVITIES

Language activities help carry out the goals of the language arts program. They can be classified as planned or spontaneous and as individual or group activities.

Planned Language Activities. Activities planned to encourage children's language development are called *planned language activities*. Examples are the use of puppets, a flannel board, reading or telling stories, or talking with a special visitor.

Spontaneous Language Activities. These language activities are not planned—they just happen. When you take advantage of moments that are suited for teaching to help children develop language skills, you are carrying out spontaneous language activities. Child care aides stimulate language development in everyday situations and routines. These can also be considered spontaneous language activities, regardless of when and where they occur and how long they last. Remember that whenever words are used—to listen, to speak, or to think—language development is being affected.

Group Language Activities. Group language activities are often called *group time* or *story time*. In some centers, both group time and story time are scheduled. During these times, a teacher or child care aide directs group language activities. Group time is an important part of a language arts program. However, because it may be the only *planned* language activity, it can become *too* important. Keep in mind that group time is only a part of the overall program.

Individual Language Activities. Language activities in which only one child is involved are known as *individual language activities*. Because they are often unplanned, they are easy to forget or overlook. Individual language activities are essential to language development. Any time a child's interest is stimulated, you have an opportunity to encourage language development.

INCREASING CHILDREN'S LANGUAGE SKILLS

Child care aides have many opportunities to help young children develop language skills. The following guidelines will give you an idea of how you can encourage children to develop the skills of listening and speaking. They will also help you see how you can encourage children to use language to solve problems, to communicate with others, and to be creative.

INCREASING CHILDREN'S LISTENING SKILLS

Listening is an essential part of language development. Children achieve skill in listening as they (1) hear sounds and spoken messages, (2) learn that they don't need to listen to everything, and (3) learn to understand what is heard and to respond.

Listening to Sounds and Messages. Children must become aware of sounds before they are able to hear the difference between one sound and another.

To stimulate children's awareness of sounds, you must first encourage them to *listen* to sounds. Begin by setting the example of being a good listener yourself. When children talk to you, look at them—eye to eye—and listen carefully; ask questions and be responsive. Provide a relaxed, friendly atmosphere in which chil-

dren feel free to listen and talk to each other. Plan a variety of listening activities. You can use nature sounds, sounds from daily living, and animal sounds. Help the children identify words that sound alike as well as those that sound different.

When giving children directions, get their attention first; then, keep the directions short and simple. Giving children simple directions and seeing that they follow them helps them to remember what is heard.

Once again, here's how *you* can help young children hear likenesses and differences in sounds and help them to listen to what is said:

1. Be a good listener and set a good example.
2. Create a friendly, relaxed atmosphere in which children feel free to talk and listen to each other.
3. Plan a variety of listening activities.
4. Give children directions that they can follow: then see that the directions *are* followed.

Listening Selectively. You can help children learn the important lesson that they do not have to listen to everything. Table 16-1 lists ways to help children listen to appropriate sounds and messages at the right times.

Responding to Spoken Language. Children learn to listen and respond to what they hear when you:

1. Give them a reason for listening and responding. The reason might be to find out something—so they'll know what to do next ("Music time comes next; go sit near the piano") or how to do something ("Turn this screw to make the clamp tight"). The reason might be to get recognition from the caregiver for being a good listener. It might be self-satisfaction, which comes from knowing that the correct response was given. Children feel a sense of accomplishment when they have followed directions successfully.
2. Have them participate in group discussions and language activities. Games such as "Simon Says" (for younger children) and "Did you every see a Lassie?" stimulate participation. Encourage each child to join

Table 16-1 WAYS TO ENCOURAGE SELECTIVE LISTENING

Children learn *that they don't need to listen to everything when they*	Ways you can help
1. Are encouraged to work on projects without interruptions	Respect each child's use of time and interest. Don't interrupt when children are enjoying each other or are busy with a project.
2. Are able to tune out background noises	Provide stimulating activities that children want to hear.
3. Are given freedom and opportunities to use their own time	Within limits, give children time to select their own activities and to get used to many different things going on in the room at the same time.

Source: Adapted from Mary Alice Mallum, *Curriculum Guide*, California Children's Centers Directors and Supervisors Association, Hawthorne, Calif., 1970, p. 71.

Figure 16-2. Games like "Simon Says" help children practice their language skills. (Kenneth Karp)

group discussions, but do not force a fearful child to do so. Groups should be kept small so that all children have time to say what they really think or feel.

Understanding Spoken Language. Children learn to understand spoken language when you:

1. Name things and point to them or hold them as the children talk about them.
2. Demonstrate as children talk about actions or activities.
3. Use pictures, posters, flip charts, flash cards, and models of objects and people when the real object or person is not available.
4. Sit down and just talk with the children, both individually and in groups.
5. Answer all their questions in simple, familiar terms.
6. Explain new words and expressions in simple, familiar terms.
7. Use new words and terms over and over until they become familiar to the children.
8. Provide opportunities for children to practice language as they learn it. Children often repeat a word or phrase over and over while they are playing. Allow children to play with language—to chant and say silly things.
9. Provided *planned* language activities, such as learning a new finger play, describing ob-

jects, picking out words that rhyme, answering questions ("What if . . . ?"), telling what's wrong with a picture, telling a story about themselves.

INCREASING CHILDREN'S SPEAKING SKILLS

After children have developed the ability to listen, they develop the ability to express themselves. With stimulating language experiences, children learn to speak freely and to use language correctly.

Speaking Freely. Table 16-2 lists the conditions that encourage children to talk. It also describes how child care aides can help children speak freely.

IMPROVING VOCABULARY

Table 16-3 lists ways you can help children improve their vocabularies (increase the number of words whose meanings they understand correctly).

USING LANGUAGE CORRECTLY

Children pronounce words in the right way and use proper grammar when they do things listed in Table 16-4.

USING LANGUAGE TO THINK

Table 16-5 highlights how children use language abilities to develop and improve their thinking; it also suggests ways you can help.

USING LANGUAGE AS A SOCIAL TOOL

One of the most important uses for language is as a *social tool*. Children must learn to use language to get along with each other. You can help them by following the procedures listed in Table 16-6.

USING LANGUAGE CREATIVELY

Children learn to use language creatively when they have opportunities to hear all kinds of words, as identified in Table 16-7.

Table 16-2 WAYS TO ENCOURAGE SPEAKING SKILLS

Children learn to speak freely when they	Ways you can help
1. Have something to say	Provide experiences to talk about: cooking, pets, gardening, visitors. Ask about family and personal experiences.
2. Have to put their wants and needs into words	Require that children tell you with words. Don't be in a hurry to respond to children's gestures or facial expressions.
3. Are comfortable with themselves	Provide many opportunities for success. Introduce new things, one at a time, along with familiar ones.
4. Are understood and taken seriously	Catch the meaning behind the words and nonverbal behaviors. Express children's feelings in words and accept those feelings as important.
5. Are free to talk with each other and their teachers	Focus on what children are doing, how they are getting along with each other, rather than concentrating on how quiet or noisy they are.
6. Have someone who will listen when they have something to say	Give your complete attention to what children are saying—to the meaning of and behind their words. *Paraphrase* (say the same things in different words) their thoughts to see whether you "heard them right." Ask questions to explore their messages and to encourage further speech.

Source: Adapted from Mary Alice Mallum, *Curriculum Guide*, California Children's Centers Directors and Supervisors Association, Hawthorne, Calif., 1970, p. 71.

Table 16-3 WAYS TO IMPROVE CHILDREN'S VOCABULARIES

Children improve their vocabularies when they	Ways you can help
1. Imitate a child care aide who uses vivid descriptions	Use new words along with familiar ones and with colorful descriptions. Describe actions, objects, feelings and experiences in an accurate, meaningful way.
2. Hear stimulating stories, good literature	Select stories, books, poetry, pictures, filmstrips and movies to read or show to the children.
3. Hear terms used correctly	When you describe objects, use exact terms (*the big red ball*) instead of pronouns (*it, that, this*).

Table 16-3 WAYS TO IMPROVE CHILDREN'S VOCABULARIES (Continued)

Children improve their vocabularies when they	Ways you can help
4. Have unfamiliar words defined clearly and simply for them	When you are explaining a new word to children, make sure you use words that are familiar to them. Keep the definitions simple and appropriate to their stage of development.
5. Use words to talk about their experiences in detail	Ask questions that encourage children to describe their observations and conclusions.
6. Are given recognition when they use new terms and descriptive language	Recognize and encourage children's use of new words and clear description.

Source: Adapted from Mary Alice Mallum, *Curriculum Guide*, California Children's Centers Directors and Supervisors Association, Hawthorne, Calif., 1970, p. 66.

Table 16-4 USING LANGUAGE CORRECTLY

Children use language correctly when they	Ways you can help
1. Hear correct speech	Be a good speech model by speaking clearly and distinctly, by pronouncing words correctly, and by using *standard English* (that is, English that is grammatically correct, such as that used in schools). Talk slowly and use a low voice.
2. Are not hurried when they have something to say	Be a good listener and give children who are talking your full attention.
3. Are accepted as individuals	Do not call attention to children's errors, but use words so that children can hear the correct use and pronunciation. Language abilities will vary with the individual. They are, in fact, part of each child's uniqueness. Accept these differences as you would any others—physical differences, cultural differences, and so forth.
4. Are encouraged to speak in complete sentences	Encourage children to speak in complete sentences. Use complete sentences in response to one- or two-word sentences used by children. For example, if a child says, "Drink," the caregiver should say, "You would like a drink of water."

Source: Adapted from Mary Alice Mallum, *Curriculum Guide,* California Children's Centers Directors and Supervisors Association, Hawthorne, Calif., 1970, p. 67.

Figure 16-3. Use exact terms and correct grammar when describing an object to a child. (Kenneth Karp)

Figure 16-4. Young children enjoy making discoveries: tasting, smelling, touching, and learning new things. (Mimi Cotter)

Table 16-5 USING LANGUAGE TO THINK

Children use language abilities to improve their thinking when they	Ways you can help
1. Have correct vocabulary and meaningful explanations applied to what they are learning	Use proper terms, verbalize actions, use labels.
2. Have opportunities to discover, to see likenesses, and to talk and reason about experiences	Provide tools for discovery such as magnets, magnifying glass, scales, books for reference, informal discussion spaces, and enough time. Provide materials and objects to see, touch, taste, smell, hear. Add new props and materials to extend attention span and to deepen understanding and discovery. Help children to organize their thoughts and record their experiences. Record experiences—use paintings, drawings, tape recordings, labels, and experience charts. Enjoy learning yourself—keep on learning, take courses, read personal as well as professional literature.

Source: Adapted from Mary Alice Mallum, *Curriculum Guide* California Children's Centers Directors and Supervisors Association, Hawthorne, Calif., 1970, p. 68.
Ibid., p. 68, adapted.

PREREADING AND PREWRITING SKILLS

As children's listening and speaking abilities develop, their interest in the printed word usually increases. There are specific ways that you can help them develop prereading and prewriting skills:

1. Children need to have many different *first-hand experiences* (handling real objects). You will learn about the kinds of first-hand experiences that caregivers can provide for children a little later in this chapter.
2. Caregivers should provide children with a variety of books, pictures, and stories to experience. You will learn how caregivers select books, use pictures, and read and tell stories in the section about group time in this chapter.
3. Children need to develop *visual discrimi-*

nation (the ability to see differences and likenesses) and *visual memory* (the ability to remember what has been seen). Play materials and simple games in which objects are classified, put in sequence (first, second, third, and so forth), or must be remembered will all help children to develop visual memory and visual discrimination.

4. Caregivers can help children to connect spoken words with written symbols by teaching them to identify shapes, sort objects, and see the differences in the shapes of letters and the shapes and sounds of words.
5. Children must come to feel that reading is useful before they will be interested in learning how to read. Caregivers should let children see them reading for a variety of purposes—reading directions for how to make a cake, how to play a game, how to grow a plant, and so forth—as well as reading during story time.

Table 16-6 USING LANGUAGE AS A SOCIAL TOOL

Children grow in ability to use language effectively as a social tool when they	Ways you can help
1. Are encouraged to express their thoughts, ideas, desires, and feelings	Provide a comfortable, accepting atmosphere. Use questions: "What do you think? How does it feel to . . . ? What would you like to do? Would you like to ____ or ____?"
2. Recognize ways to hear and be heard	Establish some rules that children can abide by: · One person talks at a time. · Raise your hand when you want to speak, don't call out. · Listen while someone else is talking. · Wait until others are listening and you have their attention before you begin to talk.
3. Carry on conversations with each other and with you	Answer or reply to what you have been told or asked. Help children to do the same.
4. Are given opportunities to question, give directions, relay simple messages, explain something to others, tell about personal experiences, and assume leadership	Provide opportunities for these experiences at group time, in learning centers, during activity periods, and in personal conversations. Listen before interrupting children's conversations. Respect children as people, just as you would respect adults.
5. Are encouraged to talk things over and to listen to another person's opinion or point of view	Allow time for talking things over. Stay on target, bring children back to main subject if they get off it. Help children express their views. Support the fact that each one is entitled to his or her opinion whether you agree or not. "That's Janie's opinion. That's how Frank feels, and Sue agrees but George feels differently." Separate feelings from facts. "You'd like to go outside without your sweaters, but it's too cold to do so today."

Source: Adapted from Mary Alice Mallum, *Curriculum Guide*, California Children's Centers Directors and Supervisors Association, Hawthorne, Calif., 1970, p. 68.

Table 16-7 USING LANGUAGE CREATIVELY

Children learn to use language creatively when they have opportunities to	Ways you can help
1. Try out the sounds and rhythms of words	Provide all kinds of words for children to hear—nursery rhymes, poetry, stories, calling attention to words that sound alike in conversations with children.
2. Learn what words mean	When new words are used during an activity, talk about them. Ask children questions to see whether the children understand what the word or words mean. Use colorful descriptions when you speak, and encourage children to "say it another way."
3. Use words to express feelings and imagination	Encourage children to "say it in words." Tell Jim you get angry when he hits you, and to stop it. Create dramatic play situations where children express feelings. "Let's imagine you are the biggest child in the class. What would you do?"

Source: Adapted from Mary Alice Mallum, *Curriculum Guide*, California Children's Centers Directors and Supervisors Association, Hawthorne, Calif., 1970, p. 65.

AFFECTING CHILDREN'S LANGUAGE DEVELOPMENT

Child care aides stimulate children's language development by serving as *language models* for the children and by using language throughout the day.

SERVING AS A LANGUAGE MODEL

What you say and how you say it makes a difference in children's experiences. Children will imitate the way you pronounce your words, and they will get many of their first meanings of words from you. It is most important to serve as a good model for them. How do you feel about reading and about talking? Are you afraid you can't say the words right, or that you don't know what they mean? Does it scare you to think that you may not be able to hold children's attention because you can't read a story with expression while you are also holding a book so that the pictures face the children?

Being afraid is natural. You must take steps to get over this feeling. Practice reading stories aloud—to yourself—if you are embarrassed to read to someone else. Record your voice and play it back. Ask someone whose opinion you trust to make suggestions about your reading and speaking. Attend reading improvement classes in school. Work at getting better. Practice and do a good job of reading a few stories that you like before you tackle some more. When you are sure of yourself with these few, read one of them to the children. You will find that children respond to your improved reading, and you will want to work even harder to read with ease and skill.

There are three steps you can take with children before you read them a story. First, use nursery rhymes you enjoy. Second, look at pictures with the children and identify what the pictures say. Third, use a familiar story such as "The Gingerbread Man" in telling a flannelboard story. Concentrate on the sequence in the story and encourage the children to help you tell it. This will help you to forget the fear you have of words. As the children participate and enjoy it, you will begin to enjoy the experience too.

Perhaps you are a person of few words. You will have to make an effort to put children's experiences into words. Children would not learn to talk if no one talked to them or if there was nothing to talk about.

If you are going to be a language model, you should:

1. Speak clearly and slowly enough for children to understand what you are saying to them.
2. Pronounce words correctly.
3. Use standard English.
4. Listen to children and sense the meaning behind their words when the words alone do not make the message entirely clear.
5. Know how to print quickly and accurately, using accepted manuscript lettering.
6. Enjoy reading and communicating.
7. Describe actions and objects to children as they are experiencing them, using accurate, colorful words.
8. Use new words in expressive, descriptive ways—ways that will help children to understand, enjoy, and imitate your speech.
9. Use props and accessories while telling stories to children.
10. Tell stories without using any props at all—and keep the children's interest while you are doing it.
11. Be able to use poetry spontaneously and during group time in order to call children's attention to likenesses in the sounds of words.

If all these requirements scare you, you are very much like many other caregivers who were shy about using words around children in the beginning. As you develop more confidence in your own abilities, you will discover that you are beginning to enjoy telling stories, using words and poetry, learning new words yourself, and helping children to understand words that are new to them.

USING LANGUAGE THROUGHOUT THE DAY

Earlier it was said that you serve as a language model for young children. Specifically, children will learn to enjoy *poetry* if you do. They will enjoy your use of poetry during various activities other than group time. When you are outside and the wind blows, it is a good time to say, "Who has seen the wind?"—reciting the poem by that name. Call attention to words or names that sound alike, such as "pound the clay, and make a mound," when talking together at the clay table. *Listen attentively* while a child tells you something. *Use new words*, and give simple explanations of what they mean to help enlarge children's vocabularies. Helping with direct experiences, including field trips, is part of language arts activity. *Use good grammar* and speak clearly—not too fast or with too high-pitched a voice. This makes it pleasant for children to listen to you.

LANGUAGE ARTS DUTIES OF CHILD CARE AIDES

You already know that you are an important part of the language arts program because what you say and how you say it affects the language experiences of the children in your care. You may be asked by your supervisor to participate in planning language experiences for the children. Here are the specific duties you will perform in helping to carry out a language arts program:

1. You will prepare and use materials for language arts activities.
2. You will carry out language arts activities using filmstrips, movies, recordings, story records, overhead transparencies, and finger plays.
3. You will read or tell stories to individual children or during group time.
4. You may be asked to set up the language arts center.
5. You will write down messages or stories told by an individual child or by a group of children, using approved manuscript lettering.

Figure 16-5. Listen carefully to children. By using new words and giving simple explanations of what they mean, you will help children enlarge their vocabularies. (Kenneth Karp)

PREPARING AND USING MATERIALS IN LANGUAGE ARTS ACTIVITIES

Materials used in language arts activities are called *props* or *accessories*. Caregivers use props to make the story more interesting and more easily understood. They also add variety; sometimes, they even give the storyteller more confidence.

Some of the different props that are used to tell stories are flannel and magnetic boards and figures, sequence pictures, and puppets. As a caregiver, you will need to know how to prepare these props.

Making Flannel Boards. A *flannel board* is a large panel of plywood or other stiff material. It is usually about 2 or 3 feet tall and 3 or 4 feet wide, and it is covered with flannel, felt, or any

fabric with a nap (velveteen or corduroy, for example). The nap on the fabric is what helps flannel-board figures stick to the board. The color of the fabric covering the board is usually a soft or dark one (light blue or dark green, for example) rather than bright (bright red or yellow). The soft or dark color of the board helps the figures to stand out, so that they can be seen easily by the children.

Flannel boards can be bought, or you can make your own with a piece of heavy cardboard or plywood and some napped material. To make a flannel board, select the board you want to cover and measure the fabric so that 2 inches overlap on each side. Then staple or firmly tape the edges on the back side so that the fabric is smooth on the side that will be seen.

Flannel boards can be of different sizes. Large ones (at least 2 feet by 3 feet) are needed for use with a group of children, and small ones can be used for individuals. Figures should be placed on the flannel board with enough space around them so that the children can see each figure clearly.

You can make a slipcover flannel background in the shape of a pillowcase if you want to change the color of the background from time to time. One side of the slipcover might be a light color and the other a dark color. Both sides will contrast with the flannel figures.

For variety, try making individual flannel boards by covering the top of a cigar box, the top of a carry-out box from the drive-in, or the side of a soap box. You can also tape flannel to a file folder or a piece of cardboard.

Making Flannel-Board Figures After a story has been selected for use on the flannel board, read it carefully and pick out the key points and figures in the story. For example, if a dog is clean and then gets dirty, you will need two flannel figures: one for the clean dog and another for the dirty one. Use only key figures. Make them large, attractive, and free from detail that gives a busy look. Place animals, people, and objects with parts that stick out (ears, arms, legs, etc.) against a background, so that the figure will not tear or bend in use and storage.

Felt Figures. Felt figures stick easily to flannel. You can cut them out without worrying about fraying edges, and they stick to the board without additional backing. To get contrasts or detail on the figures, cut and glue smaller pieces of felt with vinyl glue, or use a marking pen. Use simple details when decorating them, emphasizing the shape of the figure rather than the decoration.

Printed Fabric Figures. Printed cotton flannel may be used without backing. Look for designs and prints that will help children see likenesses and differences.

Nonwoven Fabric. The kind of nonwoven fabric used for interfacings can be used for flannel-board figures as well. Colored pens or pencils can be used to decorate them. Like the felt and cotton flannel, no backing is needed.

Paper Figures. Paper needs some kind of backing in order to stick to the flannel board. Cotton flannel, felt, nylon net, or sandpaper may be used. Another effective method is to spray the backs of paper figures with dressmaking pattern spray; then dab them with lint from the clothes dryer while they are still sticky. This makes a nap that adheres to the flannel well.

In adding something that adheres you do not need to cover the entire figure. Small pieces of felt, flannel or sandpaper distributed evenly over the figure will do. If the nap becomes flattened as a result of storage or use, take a suede or metal clothes brush and brush against the nap to make it stand up again. The figures will stick to the flannel board better if you do this.

Paper figures may be laminated (covered with protective film) or covered with clear vinyl paper before applying the flannel, sandpaper, or lint. This is a good idea for items you use often. They will then be firmer, will not wrinkle in storage, and will last much longer.

Effective flannel-board figures may be made by using film web (polyethylene film) that sticks two surfaces together when it is melted by using steam. The simplest way to do this is to use the steam iron. Select a print fabric that tells a story or can be used for classifying likenesses and differences such as left and right. Place the film web between the fabric and the flannel. Then place this "sandwich" in a paper folder to protect the ironing-board cover from any melted plastic that may squeeze out along the edges. Use the steam iron to press the fabric "sandwich" inside the folder. After a minute or so, remove the fabric from folder and cut out the figures. The iron must actively steam, since it is the steam that melts the fibers. Following the same process, this film web can be used to stick paper and a napped fabric together.

There are several ways to get figures for a flannel-board story. Buy two inexpensive picture books and cut the figures from them. (You need two books because you will need figures from both the front and the back of the page.) You may use the whole page or cut out the figures. Use the procedure described earlier for preparing paper figures for the flannel board. If the figures are small but look right for the story, use an opaque projector to enlarge them. Or, if you have an overhead projector, you can trace the figure onto acetate film and then project it on the wall, making the figure as large as you want.

Coloring books also have figures that can be used. Make a habit of examining them in the stores from time to time. Printed fabric may also be used for flannel-board figures. Pattern books, catalogs, magazines, wallpaper, and wrapping paper are other sources of sketches or pictures that can be used. The secret of a good collection is to keep relating things you see to ways they can be used. Store materials you find in an organized way so that you can find them when you or your supervising teacher wants them.

Storing Flannel-Board Stories. To prepare a flannel-board story, you must do more than just make figures. You need a system for storing them and for finding them for the story when you're ready to tell it.

Figure 16-6. Use a flannel board to involve children in telling a story. (Bart Fleet)

File folders, especially legal-sized ones, make good storage folders for flannel-board stories. The ends of the folders may be taped with masking tape to make an envelope. If the figures are prepared for a special story, the title should be typed on the file folder. Some teachers put the figures in an envelope in the folder and attach the story to the folder, leaving the ends open. Your supervising teacher may have a favorite way of doing this, and you must prepare the items as instructed.

Telling a Flannel-Board Story. A flannel-board story is told by placing figures onto the fabric-covered surface of the board. The figures represent the key persons, animals, or objects in the story.

When you are asked to tell a flannel-board story, you will need to practice ahead of time, just as you would if you were telling or reading a story using a picture book. Put the figures face-down in a stack in the order in which they appear in the story. As you tell the story, you place the figures on the board as they enter the story. If the figure you have placed on the board is not involved in the following scene, you should remove it. If it *is* involved with other figures entering the story, you should leave it on the board and simply add the new figure or figures.

Make sure that you limit the flannel-board figures to the main persons or objects in the story. If there are too many, you will have to spend most of your time putting them on and taking them off the board. Place the board itself at a slight angle. This will help the figures stick. When you place a figure on the board, put it on squarely and press down before taking your hand away.

It is important to develop a certain amount of skill in using flannel-board figures. If figures fall off the board or if you have trouble making them stick, the children will become restless and lose interest.

Magnetic Stories. *Magnetic stories* are similar to flannel-board stories. Magnetic tape is put on the backs of figures, and a chalkboard or any metal surface is used as a background. Magnetic tape will stick to most chalkboards with a metal base; a small piece (1/4 inch) of tape on the back of a figure will make it stick easily. The procedures for making magnetic figures and telling magnetic stories are like those for flannel-board figures and stories.

Puppets. There are so many kinds of puppets! Finger puppets, coat-hanger puppets, sock puppets, lightbulb puppets, papier-mache puppets, Styrofoam puppets, paper-bag puppets. (Refer to Chapter 15 for details on making and using puppets.)

Using puppets to enhance language arts is very practical. A child will often listen more carefully to advice from a puppet than from the teacher. A puppet can speak in a special small voice and get a response from good listeners. A child may use a puppet and speak before the group with less fear than without such a prop. The children will enjoy using puppets to speak to each other.

Sequence Pictures. It is important that children learn to tell you what happened in sequence—in the order in which it happened. They need to see and hear stories in sequence. You can buy sequence pictures or you can make your own to show the key ideas in a story. Often, the sets you buy have the story printed on the backs of the pictures. You can do the same with a set you make. This lets you read from the back of the picture while you hold it up for the children to see.

You can make sequence pictures by using pictures as they appear in picture books, coloring books, and appropriate comic strips. Cut the pictures apart and place them on individual cards or a board. (If you use a book with pictures on the back and front of each page, you will have to get two books, so that the pictures can be taken from both sides.)

You can develop a sequence-picture story without an ending and encourage the children to finish the story. After using the pictures in sequence at group time, you may want to display them at the children's eye level so that they can retell the story to each other or enjoy it alone.

AUDIOVISUAL MATERIALS

Recordings. Children enjoy hearing stories read by an adult who is close to them. They can also enjoy hearing a story that is recorded on a cassette or tape—especially when they can look at the matching pictures in a book at the same time. Record, cassette, and tape stories can be bought, or they can be made. In some child care centers, headsets are available. With these, several children can listen to a recorded story without disturbing others.

Filmstrips and Movies. Filmstrips and movies are audiovisual materials that can be used as teaching tools. They allow children to experience things that they cannot see first-hand, and they can help to strengthen first-hand experiences. A variety of audiovisual materials are available for sale, but caregivers can use home movies and make slides into filmstrips when it is necessary to improvise audiovisual materials. You should learn how to use the filmstrip and movie projectors.

Overhead Transparencies. Try telling a story and sketching as you go. You can do this on a large piece of paper attached to the wall or placed on a chart holder. It's also fun to do this with an overhead projector. If you are not an artist (and most of us aren't), sketch the figures lightly on the acetate, then go over the lines with a dark marking pen or pencil. This is an especially good way to tell a story that is full of suspense.

Figure 16-7. Children who enjoy having stories read to them usually also like to talk about the pictures and point out details. (Kenneth Karp)

READING AND TELLING STORIES

Reading and telling stories is an art that each child enjoys at one time or another. Some children will ask you to "read this book to me." Others will avoid books or storytelling except as part of group time. You may read the story from a picture book or tell it with or without props.

Selecting Books. Books that you choose for children should have certain characteristics. They should:

· Be attractive in design, color, and illustration
· Deal with experiences familiar to the children
· Challenge a child's imagination and stimulate creativity
· Give new ideas and information
· Deepen children's understanding of people and things
· Have meaningful illustrations, words, and phrases
· Be comfortable to hold and well made, with good bindings

Selecting Stories to Read or Tell. Preschoolers enjoy stories

· About things that go—trains, fire engines, boats
· About animals
· With jingles
· About themselves
· About things they know—the grocery store, the farm
· Told in small groups for short periods of time

Use the following guidelines when you select stories to read or tell. Select stories that have:

· A simple, logically developed plot
· Repetition, catch phrases, and/or rhymes
· A familiar setting and events
· One main character
· Plenty of conversation

²*Child Care Aide*, Instructional Home Economics/Materials Center, Texas Tech University, Lubbock, Texas, p. A122, September 1969.

· Language which is familiar and colorful, that flows easily and simply
· A simple, satisfactory climax
· A length suited to a child's attention span and the purpose of the story

Reading Stories to Individual Children. Children who enjoy having stories read to them individually want to be close to you and the book. They want to be able to talk about the pictures and to point out things that they see. Take time to study each picture; encourage the child to see the details and get the message of the pictures. Ask questions that increase the children's interest in what they see. If a child brings you a book that is too difficult for the child, simplify the story or help the child choose another book.

Reading Stories to Groups of Children. Often your supervising teacher will read a story to the children while you help them to be comfortable and to listen. You may sit beside a restless child or place yourself between two who are disturbing each other.

When you are asked to read a story to the children, you must choose a book that you enjoy. If you like it and read it with pleasure, the children are more likely to enjoy it. Practice reading it several times. Know the story well enough that you do not have to look at the book but can look at the children instead. You should hold the book so that the pictures face the children. Hold it to the side so that you can glance at it in order to tell where you are and when to turn the page. Hold the book at the bottom of the center binding, with your thumb behind the book and your fingers supporting it in front. When the group is large, you will need to move the book slowly from one side to another so that all the children can see the pictures. When the group is small, each child can see the pictures as the story is being read. In turning pages, use your other hand to turn the upper right-hand corner toward you, over to the upper left-hand corner. This keeps you from tearing a page during turning, which may happen if you pull the bottom corner. You should relax the fingers with which you are holding the book as you turn the pages. Practice this until you become comfortable enough that you can keep your mind on the children and the book and can forget about how to turn the pages.

Read the story with feeling—for example, use a deep voice for Papa Bear, a wee-sized one for Baby Bear, and so on. Make the characters in the story seem real and "come alive" for the children.

There are some variations for reading or telling a story. Consider the following:

1. Read the story as the author wrote it, using exact words and showing pictures as you read.
2. Tell the story in your own words while showing the pictures in the book.
3. Tell the story by using a flannel board, pictures, puppets, or transparencies.
4. Tell the story without a book or props. This is hard to do, but it is worthwhile to practice because it lets you have full eye contact with the children. You can also change details as the group responds, making the story more exciting as it unfolds.

Telling a Story. Just as you carefully select a book to read to a group of children, so should you carefully choose a story to tell. Pick one that appeals to you. Read it over and over until you know it well. Practice telling the story in front of a mirror, varying your voice and facial expression as you act out the story for yourself. Do not tell a story that you don't know well. If you are nervous about telling the story, consider the following ways to make storytelling effective and exciting:[3]

· With a stick or wand, draw a circle around the group and sit in the magic ring.
· Bring a long, bright-colored ribbon and have everyone grasp the magic cord.
· Wear a special hat, putting it on only when the story starts—a tall, black witch's hat, a "royal crown," or a party hat.
· Consult a "magic mirror" to decide what story to tell.
· Use a tape recorder to provide sound effects for your story.

[3]Ibid, p. A123.

· If you feel self-conscious, use a doll, a hand puppet, or a stuffed animal and pretend that it is telling the story.
· Try variations, such as felt cutouts, flannel boards, or sketching with chalk or crayons on a large piece of paper as the story develops.
· Do not be afraid to pause, whisper, or yell if the story demands it.
· Seat the group so that they face away from distractions and late joiners.
· If sudden distractions come up, have the children close their eyes for a few moments during the story.

GROUP TIME

Group time is like any other activity in that it has three steps: preparation, application, and follow-up.

Preparing for Group Time. Preparing for group time involves the following things:

1. You must select the method (a picture book, puppet, flannel board, etc.) to present the story or information you wish to use. You must make decisions about the interests and abilities of the children in the group when you do this. Select something you enjoy using. Consider the guidelines for good stories and books and choose one that fits the method of presentation and will appeal to the children.
2. Practice presenting the story until you know it well enough that you can watch the children's faces as you tell it instead of looking at the words.
3. Plan other activities to use. For example, you may decide to use finger plays to get the children's attention and give them a chance to settle down. Activity songs are another way to switch between active and quiet periods. If you have selected a flannel-board story, you must get the flannel-board figures ready and collect any other props you want to use. In planning, you should figure how much time the activities will take. You might want to prepare a few extra activities to use in case you need them.

4. Set the stage so that there are no distractions in the physical setting during group time.

In planning for group time, caregivers need to consider what resources are available in the center and the community. Then you can use the equipment, materials, and personnel which those resources can supply.

Carrying Out Group-Time Activities. When supervising group time, you should begin by gathering the children together and directing them to sit where they can see you easily. Allow them to relax and be comfortable, but enforce the rules for acceptable behavior such as "Stay in one place." To get children's attention, use finger plays, or a puppet, or an activity song.

When the children are interested and quiet, begin the story. If you are using a picture book, hold it so that the children can see it, and turn the pages as the story unfolds. It is important to tell the story with enough dramatic feeling to keep children interested. Try using different voices for the different characters in the story.

If the children know the story, you may encourage them to help tell it. Until you are experienced at this, however, it is better to wait until you have finished before involving children in a discussion about the story. If a child asks a question or makes a comment, acknowledge it simply and return to the story. Ask questions that relate the story to the children's experiences. You might ask, "What do you have in your pockets?" (following the story *Willie's Pockets*), or "What can you do?" (following *Is It Hard, Is It Easy?*).[4] Or you might ask the children to help by showing you and the group where a certain object is located in a picture in the book. At first, call a child by name and ask him or her to find a certain object: "Mary, find the wheelbarrow in the picture." If you ask a question such as "Who can find the wheelbarrow?" you will have the whole group trying to answer at once. If you want to get the children into the act, you might say, "Each of you will have a turn to point out something in the story. I will call on each one

of you before the story is over to show us something you see." Regardless of how and when you choose to involve the children, make sure that you call on each over a period of time. Of course, you will not be able to use this method if you do not know the children very well. It is a good way to give individual children recognition and practice in responding in front of a group. If you are not able to do it now, make it a goal and work toward it.

Following Up Group Time. Your assignment is not finished until you have returned all the equipment and materials you have used to their proper places. When you have completed these housekeeping duties, evaluate the group-time experience on the basis of the children's involvement and your performance. Discuss your evaluation with your supervising teacher as soon as you can.

Other Interest-Getters for Language Development. There are some other techniques to create interest in language that may be used at group time, with individual children or in small groups. *Toy telephones* stimulate conversation between one child and another or between a child and the teacher. *Finger plays* involve the children as they are repeated. (Details about finger plays are given in Chapter 20.) Children may be encouraged to *"listen and help tell the story,"* either by saying phrases and words that the author has used over and over—such as hundred and thousands—or by filling in words that sound alike: "Fred likes the color *red*. Sue likes the color *blue*."

Acting out stories. Another way to extend children's language learning is to have them act out a story they know and like. Caregivers can provide suggestions, encouragement, and a few props to make this form of dramatic play successful.

A paper-bag puppet and a bench make good props for acting out the nursery rhyme "Humpty Dumpty." A candlestick, or something like it, will give the children enjoyment as they play "Jack jumped over the candlestick." Repeat the nursery rhyme, but substitute a child's name in it each time before that child does "jump over the candlestick."

[4]Mary McBurney Green, *Is It Hard, Is It Easy?* Scott, Foresman, Glenview, Ill., 1960.

SETTING UP A LANGUAGE ARTS CENTER

Your supervising teacher may ask you to set up the language arts center for the day. When you are given this assignment, remember that the items included in the center should be appropriate for the children and the center's program. Follow these guidelines for setting up a language arts center:

1. A language arts center should include picture books, flannel-board stories, pictures, and props which have been used recently during group time. Audiovisual materials such as tape recorders, a record player, and a television set may be placed in the center. Letters and symbols that can be handled are also placed there.

2. Relate items to the current program and children's ability and interest level. For example, if you are talking about family, place family stories on the table, family pictures on the wall at child's eye level, etc. Place where children can use them recent stories read at group time or flannel-board stories that have been told.

3. Make the center attractive. Place some things on the shelf for children to select. Put some on the table where children can see them.

Figure 16-8. Printing words carefully for children helps them to learn that speech can be written down. (Kenneth Karp)

4. Combine several different learning areas from time to time. For example, place the aquarium and books about fish close together.

5. Select activities that children can *do* as well as *see*. For example, if you have been using the nursery rhymes, put some nursery-rhyme puzzles in the language arts learning center, or have sequence pictures for children to use regarding the sequence of the story.

6. Your goal is to make the center inviting and for children to be able to use it with as much self help and as little supervision as possible.

PRINTING MESSAGES AND LABELS

Recognizing letters and seeing written words are prereading skills. You can set a good example for children by printing messages and labels correctly and by using these for communication. (Chapter 6 tells you how to use manuscript lettering.)

Writing Children's Stories or Messages. To help children understand that reading is the ability to understand talk which has been written down, caregivers can let children see that their own speech can be written down. Child care aides do this by *recording* (writing down) what children dictate (say) and then reading it back to them. Children can dictate stories, messages, or descriptions for an *experience chart* (a poster that tells what the children have to say about an experience). Experience charts help children to see words and talk as part of reading. Manuscript lettering should be used when you write children's comments down. If you cannot print the message as fast as they speak it, ask them to go slower, so that they can see the words being added to the paper as they are said. (You should practice this skill at home.) Encourage the children to use complete sentences and descriptive phrases. Ask questions that will help them fully understand an action, object, experience, or person. For example, "How did the fireman's boots feel when you put them on?"

Writing *thank-you letters* or *messages to parents* (such as a Mother's Day card) make the experience personal and strengthen the idea that words are recorded so that other people can read them.

Using Labels. Labels give messages too. Be sure to use manuscript lettering as practiced in your community school district. You will use labels on children's artwork and on bulletin boards, displays, materials in learning centers, and directions.

PROBLEMS RELATING TO LANGUAGE ARTS

Problems may arise in relation to the learning of language in a child care center. Following are some examples and how to handle such difficulties.

1. *Baby talk:* If children use baby talk, don't correct them but use the word or words that the baby talk represents, pronouncing them correctly.

2. *Mispronounced words:* Do not call attention to a child's error, but use *correct* words after a child has used them incorrectly.

3. *Single words rather than complete sentences:* Use complete sentences yourself. Avoid use of *this, that, it;* instead, use the names of the objects or persons referred to. For example, don't refer to a color shape as "the red one," but say, "the red circle," "Put the one red circle on top of another red circle."

4. *Stuttering:* Young children increase their understanding of language and their vocabularies at a very rapid rate. Sometimes they think faster than their mouths and tongues can form the words. The result is a number of "false starts." This is not true stuttering. Don't correct children when they are doing this or appear to be stuttering. Speak slowly yourself; give a child your complete attention, looking at him or her eye to eye; and listen carefully. *Paraphrase* (rephrase) what has been said, speaking slowly and distinctly. You may ask him or her to "Tell me more slowly, I want to hear what you have to say."

5. *No language:* Help a child feel comfortable. Build self-esteem whenever and wherever possible. "You finished the puzzles all by yourself." Ask questions that invite answers "What is the puzzle about?" Don't anticipate and respond to gestures; expect a child to *tell* you what is wanted or needed. Spend time with the child individually to build a trusting relationship. Provide many experiences to talk about. Let the child hear and participate in many language arts experiences without pressure to perform. Never force a child to speak or perform in front of the group until the child's behavior indicates readiness.

6. *Home language:* Respect the language used in the child's home. If a curse word is used, do not criticize him or her; simply say, "We don't use that word here." Listen carefully to get the meaning of the approximated sounds the child is using, then paraphrase them using the pronunciation considered standard English. For example, respond to "Wa dat?" with "This is a ball."

7. *Using name rather than pronoun:* "Dan do it" is often the way a young child refers to himself at first. Don't insist that the child use the pronoun. As children hear language and come to understand the use of pronouns as referring to themselves, they will make the change. Activity songs where pronouns are used give children some experience in hearing pronouns and using them as references. For example, use the song "You sing a song, and I'll sing a song" and tell the children, "When the song says 'you,' I'll point to you and you will point to me. When it says 'I,' I'll point to myself and you point to yourself." Allow time to let children acquire these concepts.

8. *Show-and-tell group time:* Teachers of young children often encourage them to express themselves in front of a group. If the experience is a gradual one where children point to pictures in a book, volunteer to lead a following-the-leader type of activity, answer questions, or put figures on the flan-

nel board, the children acquire confidence slowly and comfortably.

Some teachers use a show-and-tell period as a sharing time that helps children express themselves in front of the group. It is wise to limit the amount of time spent with show-and-tell experiences or objects. Watch the children and stop when they are losing interest. Have only a few children showing and telling at group time. If children bring objects from home, have a special arrangement for their security. Say, "Put it in your locker" or "Put it on our show-and-tell shelf." If a child is about to tell family secrets, thank the child for what has already been said, ask a question, or change the subject.

9. *Children disturbing each other:* Before the group activity begins, be sure each child is comfortable. Remind the children of the group rules. ("Be sure you can see; stay in one place; if you have something to say, raise your hand; listen when someone else is talking; only one person talks at a time.") If two children who are likely to disturb each other are sitting together, move them apart before the group activity begins. Don't tell them you are separating them because they will get into trouble, just rearrange their seating by giving firm but kind directions. ("Jim, you sit over here. Mary, come sit by Jane.") If a child keeps bothering another child, describe the action. ("Joe, Bill wants to hear the story and he is disturbed when you poke at him. Keep your hands in your lap.")

10. *Calling out during group time:* One child dominates the session. Remind the children of the listening rule that "Only one child talks at a time. Raise your hand and we'll know you have something to say." Use a soft, firm voice in giving directions and reminders. Make an extra effort to call on each child or to recognize each child from time to time. Balance volunteering with being called on. ("Today I'm going to call on. . . ." "Who would like to. . . ?")

11. *No books, pictures, or props* for language arts in the child care center: Get busy and make some.

CHAPTER SUMMARY

1. *Language arts* refers to the abilities involved in using language to communicate. A good language arts program includes activities and experiences that help children in all language areas. However, in a child care program for young children, language arts focus on listening and speaking.

2. The overall goal of a language arts program in a child care center is to provide experiences that encourage children to use language for communicating, thinking, and learning and as a resource for self-expression.

3. Child care aides have many opportunities to help children develop language skills. They stimulate language development by serving as language models and using opportunities to increase language skills throughout the day. Their responsibilities in a language arts program include planning with the supervisor or teacher, preparing and using materials for language arts activities, supervising group time and other activities when assigned, and setting up the language arts center.

• WHAT NEW TERMS HAVE YOU LEARNED?

Several new words and ideas were presented in this chapter. To see whether you understand them, match the letter of each term below with the numbered phrases under "Definitions."

Terms

a. Listening skill
b. First-hand experience
c. Reading readiness
d. Language arts
e. Paraphrase
f. Language model
g. Language
h. Standard English
i. Verbal
j. Social tool
k. Communication
l. Flannel board

Definitions

1. Pertaining to words
2. The skills involved in using language to communicate
3. Sending a message and having it understood
4. Words used to communicate
5. Direct experiences
6. Children's interest in the sounds of letters and meaning of words
7. The skills used to hear sounds and spoken messages
8. To say the same things in different words
9. English that is grammatically correct
10. The use of language to get along with people
11. Someone to imitate
12. Panel of plywood covered with napped fabric

• PROJECTS, DECISIONS, ISSUES

1. Record in writing or on tape a child's conversation. Compare your recording with that of another student in class and note likeness and differences.
2. Using a tape recorder, read a children's story out loud and note whether you speak distinctly and pronounce words correctly. You may choose a partner for this activity to evaluate your performance.
3. Develop a card file of children's books.
4. Make a flannel-board story.
5. Set up a language arts center for preschool children.

• WHIFS (WHAT WOULD YOU DO IF . . .)

1. You are telling a flannel-board story and the figures keep falling off the board. What would you do?
   a. Stop the story and tell the children you'll fix the figures and tell the story another day
   b. Slant the flannel board more
   c. Tape the figures on with masking tape
   d. Slap them hard against the board
   e. Push firmly with a downward motion
   f. Other responses

2. Matthew is telling you something as he plays with play dough. You listen carefully but do not understand a word that he says. What would you do?
   a. Guess what he's saying
   b. Tell him "OK," "Yes," or "That nice"
   c. Listen carefully, without comment
   d. Find a child who can interpret
   e. Nod your head but say nothing
   f. Tell him you do not understand what he's saying and ask him to tell you again.
   g. Start talking about what he's doing
   h. Other responses

3. Emily wants to write her name. You print it in manuscipt lettering but she says that is not her name. You suspect that she recognizes her name in capital letters only. What would you do?
   a. Print it in capital letters
   b. Tell her she is too young to print
   c. Get her a crayon and unlined paper and help her with the first letter in her name
   d. Show her her name and have her copy it with play-dough rope
   e. Give her a pencil and print her name for her to trace
   f. Other responses

4. You are reading a story to the children at group time and 2-year-old Lydia keeps getting between the book and the children as she points to pictures in the book. What would you do?
   a. Stop reading until Lydia is sitting down
   b. Hold the book above her head
   c. Call for help
   d. Put her on your lap
   e. Other responses

5. You ask the children "Do you have a pet?" and they all shout out their answers at the same time. What would you do?
   a. Outshout them
   b. Cover your ears
   c. Whisper to the group
   d. Remind them of the rule that only one person should speak at a time
   e. Say "Shhhhhh!"
   f. Other responses

6. During free-choice time, Nell asks you to read her a story from the book she brought from home. What would you do?
   a. Read it immediately
   b. Tell her to wait until group time
   c. Tell her you can't read it, you're too busy
   d. Read it as soon as you can
   e. Other responses

• STUDENT ACTIVITIES

1. Name four language skills.
2. List two goals for a language arts program.
3. Describe four ways child care aides help young children *hear* likenesses and differences in sounds.
4. List four things child care aides do to help children learn to understand *spoken* language.
5. List five things child care aides should be able to do in order to be good *models* for children to imitate.
6. List five *specific duties* that child care aides may be asked to do in a child care center.
7. List six important steps used to read a story.
8. List four of the six criteria for setting up a language arts center.

17 | ASSISTING WITH ART EXPERIENCES

After you have studied Chapter 17, you should be able to:

1. Name three benefits of art experiences for young children and identify four ways to encourage creativity
2. List four different types of art activities for young children
3. Compare art activities used with different age groups
4. Summarize and demonstrate at least five ways to provide meaningful art experiences for young children

CREATIVE ART EXPERIENCES

The freedom to decide what color and materials to use, how to arrange one's artwork, and when to start and finish an art activity stimulate small children to be creative. Art experiences with this kind of freedom allow children to change their minds and to follow their own ideas.

BENEFITS OF CREATIVE ART EXPERIENCES

Why should creative art activities be included in a children's program? Art activities are messy, and the materials are expensive. It takes time to prepare for art activities, and clean-up is a chore. Do children benefit from creative art experiences? Yes, they do. Creative art experiences stimulate young children in the ways listed in Table 17-1.

WAYS TO ENCOURAGE CREATIVITY

You can help children toward success or failure in freely expressing themselves by how you encourage or discourage creativity in art experiences. Table 17-2 shows some ways in which creativity is encouraged.

TYPES OF ART ACTIVITIES

Art activities can be classified in many different ways—according to how much supervision they require, how much preparation must be done, or how they involve children.

213

Table 17-1 BENEFITS OF CREATIVE ART EXPERIENCES

Creative art experiences stimulate children to	Examples
Use original ideas, be creative, learn that there may be more than one way to do something.	Jamie may paste circles around the edge of the paper; Johnnie may clump his in the center.
Be independent.	Susan gets her own crayons from the shelf, uses them, and returns them.
Gain confidence as they use their own resources.	"Look what I did."
Express personally meaningful ideas and feelings. Young children may not be able to put their feelings into words. Negative emotions may be released.	Pounding a ball of clay flat may help a child ease tensions. Messy fingerpaint helps children who are always being told, "Don't get dirty." The teacher helps to provide the time and place to be messy without getting clothes dirty. Smocks help; so do sponges, water, and soap.
Accept themselves as unique and valuable as the teacher values their ideas and thoughts.	"I can paint it the way I want to. It's mine. I can change it, too."
Clarify ideas and concepts. Children often talk to each other and to the teacher as they involve themselves in art activities.	"Your red circles match your red paper—and the red bow in your hair."

Source: Adapted from Evelyn Goodenough Pitcher, Miriam G. Lasher, Sylvia Feinburg, and Nancy C. Hammond, *Helping Young Children Learn,* Merrill, Columbus, Ohio, 1966, p. 17.

SELF-HELP OR SUPERVISED ACTIVITIES

Some art activities require the caregiver to provide a great deal of help and direction. Others allow a considerable amount of self-help and do not require caregiver involvement. Which kind of activities are more valuable and enjoyable for children?

Activities that encourage exploration and discovery—that bring out the fun, relaxation, and stimulation of art experiences—provide greater benefit and enjoyment to children. If *you* have to do most of the work, the activity is not a good choice for the children. For example, suppose you plan an art activity about spring. You cut out flowers, stems, and leaves ahead of time. This takes a lot of preparation. The children are assigned the task of pasting the flowers together. You supervise closely to see that the precut items are used as planned. A better way would be for you to make the supplies available to the children and let them cut out their own flowers. If they are too young to cut things out, choose another cutting-and-pasting activity or simplify the one you have selected. You may have very young children decorate large flower shapes with paper collage, gummed paper, or designs made with crayon, chalk, or objects that can be used as stamps.

To involve children in self-help during art activities, make the art equipment and materials

Table 17-2 ENCOURAGING CREATIVITY

Do	Don't
Provide a setting in which children are free to use art materials in their own way, within basic limits that recognize the rights of others.	
Guide in terms of basic limits such as "keep the crayons on the paper" rather than exactly how to reproduce a pattern, design, or object.	Use patterns or models and give directions on how to use them.
Provide support and encouragement; don't criticize.	Give outlines to fill in; this is called "dictated art" and stifles creativity.
Protect children from the criticism of others.	Make objects for the children. In response to "Make me a turtle," help children think about what a turtle looks like and encourage them to make their own.
Provide plenty of time, space, and materials as well as storage places for everything. This will enable children to use things by themselves.	Watch the clock and hurry the children. Don't interrupt them.
Protect tables, floor, and children's clothing, from paint, paste, clay, and other messy materials.	Start an activity without proper protection of clothing, furniture, and floor.
Keep thinking of ways you can arrange the art area so that children can help themselves.	Put equipment and supplies "just any old way" in the art area.
Value the child's feelings and the meaning of the experience for the child.	
Understand and respect different stages in children's art.	Push for a product or criticize children who scribble or do not make recognizable products.
Recognize that, through art experiences, children may express feelings that are otherwise unacceptable.	Give extra recognition to the children when they make a product and overlook those who are enjoying the process of using materials.
Display each child's artwork at one time or another.	Be an instant psychologist who analyzes emotional health.
Recognize that children grow socially through art experiences.	Isolate children as they do their artwork.
Place easels side by side. Arrange art materials on a table large enough for children to gather round and talk with each other and to work without disturbing each other.	Tamper with a child's artwork. It doesn't need your extra brush stroke or cut.

(Continued next page)

Table 17-2 ENCOURAGING CREATIVITY (Continued)

Do	Don't
Value the child's feelings and the meaning of the experience for the child.	
Recognize that children become more creative through art experiences.	Require that certain objects or themes be carried out.
Make the children comfortable and help them to be free to "do it their own way."	Recognize and compliment only those children who are interested in products and follow your directions.
Report a child to your supervisor if you think the child's artwork is different enough to be considered "strange."	Display only the art items that are easily recognized products.
Recognize each child's effort.	
Give individual attention. Listen to the unusual questions children ask. Respect their unusual ideas.	Require each child to do the same thing at the same time in the same way. Materials teaching that there is only one right way to do it hinder creativity and artistic expression in young children.
Select activities that children can do themselves, rather than having you do most of the work. Involve those children who express interest in projects (involving products); others can continue to work individually—folding, pasting, cutting, and painting as they wish.	Ask children what they have drawn. Label the children's emotional health on the basis of their artwork. Ask the children what they have made.
Watch carefully to see whether the children might like to comment on their artwork. "Would you like to tell me about your picture?"	Rush the evaluation of what has been done. The child may merely be exploring materials and may not want to talk about it.
Provide rich experiences that stimulate creative expression and self-discovery.	
Make a variety of materials available.	Use the same old dough clay or the same old paint (particularly if it is a muddy color or too watery because it has dried up and you have hastily tried to revive it).
Talk about feelings, role-play them, use movement for expression and self-discovery.	Use the same size, the same shape, and the same kind of paper all the time.
Discuss how things looked or happened, such as the color of the ground when the water was put in the holes when the tomato plants were planted.	Clutter the area with art materials, piling "beautiful junk" in a corner, paper on a shelf, and other materials and equipment in a haphazard, disorderly manner in the art area.

Table 17-2 ENCOURAGING CREATIVITY (Continued)

Do	Don't
Help parents understand and appreciate children's creative art.	
Protect clothing, use smocks, put soap in the tempera paint.	Let children use messy paints without protection to clothing.
Teach parents about developmental stages in children's art; the importance of process to the child, and the child's feelings toward expression.*	Provide patterns and objects to take home "because the parents want it."
	Talk to parents about their child in front of the child.
Make creative art part of the child's entire day.	
Encourage creative experiences all day long and in all areas.	Limit creativeness to a certain time and place.
Integrate—which means to put together art and music, science, physical education, and dramatic play. For example, let scarves float in the wind; later, notice that children may identify the wind and how it blows the scarves in their paintings.	Limit creative experiences to art.
	Separate art from other creative experiences.
	Limit art experiences to formal instruction periods.

Source: Adapted from Evelyn Goodenough Pitcher, Miriam G. Lasher, Sylvia Feinburg, and Nancy C. Hammond, *Helping Young Children Learn,* Merrill, Columbus, Ohio, 1966, p. 17.
*Good Schools For Young Children, p. 340.

Figure 17-1. Displaying each child's artwork is one way to encourage children to express themselves and be creative. (Kenneth Karp)

Figure 17-2. A caregiver must realize that a child's drawings reflect his or her stage of emotional and physical development. (Michael Weisbrot)

easily available. Encourage the children to learn where things are and how to use them. Then let them be free to use the equipment and materials within the limits they have been taught.

FREEING OR CONTROLLING ACTIVITIES

Some art activities free children to relax and enjoy their experience, while others tend to control or restrain them.

Since young children's large muscles are more developed than their small muscles, art activities that use the gross motor skills tend to be more relaxing for them. Specific art activities that use the gross motor skills include fingerpainting; clay molding; painting at an easel; using large pieces of paper for painting, tearing, pasting; and painting large boxes.

Activities that require the use of fine motor skills and careful control of movement tend to restrain children. Cutting; putting together small, complicated shapes in a certain way; threading straws or macaroni; gluing objects such as seeds and beads; and using a pencil are examples of art activities requiring control.

MESSY OR NONMESSY ACTIVITIES

Children are likely to relax and become actively involved in messy activities. A good child care program allows and encourages children to use materials that are messy—especially when they are involved in art activities. Messy activities release tensions and help children to work out negative feelings. Some examples of messy art activities are fingerpainting, working with wet clay, using chalk with buttermilk, and pasting. Nonmessy activities include working with crayons or a pencil, handling plasticine clay, and simple cutting activities.

A good art program should balance messy and nonmessy activities. When enough staff members are available, messy activities can be planned. When supervision is limited, nonmessy activities might be scheduled most of the time, with some of the messy ones planned only occasionally.

PROCESS OR PRODUCT

The term *process* refers to the actual "doing" part of an activity, while the *product* is the object that results from the activity. Young children enjoy experiencing art activities. They focus on the process of an activity. For example, they may fingerpaint directly on a table, painting a design with their hands and then changing it with a sweep of the hand or a movement of the finger. When the activity is finished, the table is cleaned off. The child has had a good experience, yet there is no product. Beginning art experiences for young children usually deal with processes rather than with products.

Products can be seen and are easily identified. When a child paints a picture of a tree, you can look at it and think "Sam painted a picture of a tree." Products can be displayed, carried home, handled, or moved about.

Young children may produce pleasing products without trying. They may enjoy the process and just accidentally produce a pleasing picture or design. In fact, sometimes a child will paint a delightful picture or design and within a few minutes cover it with another color of paint. Don't criticize this. Parents and sometimes also child caregivers value products and give children the idea that it's good only if it looks like something; otherwise, it isn't good. As a child care aide, you should value children's experiences more than their products.

Sometimes you may help children to create products, but this will be done for adult reasons. For example, if gifts are to be made for parents at Christmas or for Mother's or Father's Day, the children will have to prepare specific, recognizable items. The important thing is to choose a project that will match the child's interests and abilities. Younger children should make very simple gifts that can be completed in a short time. Such projects should require only basic skills (for example, decorating a bookmark with crayon or marking pen or decorating a candle, pencil holder, or jewelry box with collage materials). Even though the process is simple, some children will not be interested in it. Some may even refuse to take part.

INDIVIDUAL OR GROUP ACTIVITIES

For preschool children, most art activities are individual experiences—even though children may be enjoying each other's company as they paint at easels or sit at a table pounding clay.

Some art activities encourage children to work as a group on something that doesn't belong to any one child but to the group as a whole. Painting boxes that become train cars or a fire station is a good project because all the children can use what is painted. In such an activity, there is no defined "territory" over which a child feels ownership. Decorating a Christmas tree for the holidays is another group art project.

Making a *mural* (a large picture or design that can be displayed on a wall or a window) is a good group art activity. However, since very young children are self-centered, they may have difficulty working as part of a group. Caregivers should invite them to join but should not force them to do so. After children receive attention for their individual efforts, they need to learn how to join a group project. When they are old enough, they will enjoy group activities. Help those who want to join the mural activity by finding a place where they can paint. After the mural has been displayed for a while, you may cut it apart and give each child a piece to take home.

ART ACTIVITIES FOR DIFFERENT AGE GROUPS

How do you know which art activities to select for different age groups of young children? You have learned that children are individuals and that they pass through several stages of development in various ways and at different times. However, some general characteristics of the various developmental stages in young children can be identified. And there are some art activities that match those stages. (See Table 17-3).

As mentioned earlier, children around the world show similar stages of development in art. Likewise, they go through stages in working with various materials. When given new materials or tools, children tend to take the following steps in using them:

· *Exploration:* The children play and experiment with the material to see what it will do and what they can do with it.

· *Chance design:* As the children experiment, they may accidentally produce an object, shape, or design that looks like something to them.

Table 17-3 ART ACTIVITIES SUITABLE FOR DIFFERENT AGE GROUPS

Developmental level	General characteristics	Art activities and materials
2-year-olds (children new to art experience)	Manipulative activities Materials used as toys Markings not confined to paper Large muscles used Alternate use of both hands Process important Short attention span	Scribbling—large crayon, chalk, large soft pencil Dough clay Tempera paint—few colors, large brushes, large paper Fingerpaint on table, tray
3-year-olds	Exploratory activities Process-oriented Short attention span Shape and form appearing Increasing control Advancing skill for those with experience	Same as 2-year-olds for beginners Various drawing materials, large crayon, wet chalk, felt pens, scribbling, printing, fingerpaint, clay More colors, paint brushes Some cut, most tear Dough clay still a favorite
4-year-olds	Longer attention span More control, circle or design appearing Socialize during art activity Interested in color and texture Process still important May talk about art activities, sometimes before starting, during, or after finishing Tensions often worked out with messy activities May begin group activity if experienced with technique	Tempera paint—variations desirable Large paper, various size brushes Collage, construction objects Children like to help get ready, make recipes, clean up, talk about paintings and artwork If not controlled, messy activities enjoyed Murals, decorating for holidays are fun Want to take things home
5-year-olds	If experienced, product becoming important Children identify what they are doing or painting Enjoy socializing May criticize others' work Call attention to own successes Can participate in group	Carpentry, printing with various materials and tools Interested in three-dimensional objects of clay, "beautiful junk," or collage materials More colors and various shades of colors Mixing paints to get own color, various techniques for discovery

Simple symbolic: The children have an idea when they start to paint or draw, but the form tends to be symbolic rather than looking like something. For example, a boat may be simply three lines on the paper.

PROVIDING ART EXPERIENCES FOR YOUNG CHILDREN

Child care aides help to provide art experiences for young children by knowing what equipment

Table 17-4 ART EQUIPMENT AND MATERIALS

Equipment	Where to put them	How to care for them
Easels should have painting surfaces and paint trays with clamps or hooks to hold paper; two-sided easels are preferable; easels are desirable for painting but not necessary—floor or table surfaces can be used for painting, too.	Near water and good light and out of traffic areas; should be close to art materials and smocks.	Wipe up spills while they are still moist; wash paint trays thoroughly; store where children can help themselves. Cover sides of easel with paper to catch spills.
Tables and chairs used in art activities should have waterproof surfaces, be free of rough edges, and of a comfortable height for children; tables should have square edges to help children align their paper.	In art area—near water, etc.—see *easel.*	Wipe with soap and hot water to clean; cover tables with plastic or newspaper when working with messy materials.
Storage equipment— containers used for storing paint, clay, paste should be coded to promote self-help and housekeeping; shelves used for storing art materials and equipment should be waterproof and at a comfortable height for self-help.	Near areas where items are used; in assigned places on open shelves. Near art area.	Replace tops and lids after use, wash off with soap and water. Wipe off if messy, and clean regularly.
Paper—newsprint, construction paper, rolls of paper, tissue paper, drawing paper.	Stored with art materials near art area.	Store flat unless on rolls.

(Continued next page)

Table 17-4 ART EQUIPMENT AND MATERIALS (Continued)

Equipment	Where to put them	How to care for them
Tempera paint can be purchased in liquid or powder form to be thinned or mixed with water; should be thick and creamy.	Should be mixed and kept in wide-mouth small jars with straight sides. Stored with art materials.	Containers should be airtight, kept clean; use alum to keep paint fresh-smelling.
Library paste may be bought in large amounts.	Store on shelves in art area in containers which are well marked and have lids which children can remove themselves.	Replace lids or tops before putting away.
Homemade paste	Store in refrigerator.	
Vinyl glue is cheaper when bought from a building supply store in gallon containers.	Store in large container in staff area; keep small containers in art area for children's self-help use.	Wipe container and opening carefully, seal tightly; wipe up spills while still moist.
Rubber cement requires a special thinner.	Store in staff area and carefully supervise children when using it.	Same as above; remove spills with thinner or alcohol.
Clay—wet clay comes in powdered form or in mixed form; water must be added to soften mixed clay before it is used.	Store in art area on shelves.	Make into 3" or 4" balls; before storing in airtight containers, make a thumb hole in each ball and put water in hole.
Oil clay (plasticine) cannot be used with water.	See above.	Store in airtight containers, soften by working with hands.
Dough clay or play dough can be cooked or uncooked, homemade or purchased commercially.	Stored in refrigerator.	Remove from refrigerator in time to soften; add flour if sticky, oil if crumbly.
Crayons and chalk should be large and flat-sided; chalk should be artist's chalk, not chalkboard chalk.	Store in small containers on open shelves near art area; caregivers may want to store chalk in staff area and bring it out when supervision is available.	Remove paper covers from crayons and oil-based chalk; with chalk, wipe off after use, scrape if buttermilk has dried.

Table 17-4 ART EQUIPMENT AND MATERIALS (Continued)

Equipment	Where to put them	How to care for them
Collage materials and accessories— buttons, ribbons, string, pebbles, etc., sponges, marking pens, masking tape.	Store with bristles up in separate containers or in staff area—may want to bring out when supervision is available.	Keep in good order—clean after use when necessary.
Paintbrushes should have stiff bristles and be in various sizes (½″, ¾″, and 1″).	Store in container near easel.	Rinse in lukewarm water until water rinses clean; lay flat to dry; when storing, store with bristle end up.
Miscellaneous equipment— woodworking tools, stapler, mixing spoons, ice pick, electric iron, hot plate, hand and electric beaters, and utility knives.	Should be kept in the staff area and used with close supervision.	Clean after using and store properly.

and materials to use and how to care for them. They also know how to prepare and supervise many art activities and how to guide an art activity so that it relates to other subject areas. When an art assignment is finished, a child care aide evaluates the performance with the help of the supervising teacher.

EQUIPMENT AND MATERIALS FOR ART ACTIVITIES

To prepare for and supervise art activities, you need to know what kinds of equipment and materials are used, when they should be used, and how to care for them. Table 17-4 lists various art equipment and materials and should help you to understand their use and maintenance.

PREPARING FOR AND SUPERVISING ART ACTIVITIES

Only basic art activities for young children are included in this chapter. These activities may be varied from time to time.

☐ **Painting with Brushes.** Tempera paint, whether in powder or liquid form, can be used in many activities. Very young children enjoy the primary colors—red, yellow, and blue— even before they are able to name the colors they see.

This activity

· Gives large-muscle enjoyment of broad, sweeping strokes with big brushes on big paper
· Gives enjoyment and relaxation in placing color on a surface, exploring wetness and stickiness of paint

Ages:
Two years and up.
Location:
At easel or on protected area of floor or table; inside or outside.

Figure 17-3. Children enjoy making broad sweeping strokes with paintbrushes. (Kenneth Karp)

Items needed:

- Easel—self-standing; wall or table; protected area on floor or table.
- Paper—newsprint, construction, want-ad section of newspaper, cardboard, wallpaper, wrapping paper.
- Paint—ready to use; 1 inch in each container, add more as needed; start with two or three primary colors.
- Smocks—one per child.
- Paintbrushes—one per container; may use sponge on clothespin.
- Sponges or cloths for spills.
- Squeeze-bottle with water for thinning paint.
- Marking pen to put child's name on painting.
- Place with clothespins or clamps to hang pictures or flat surface to put paintings that are covered with paint and are wet and heavy.

Preparation:

- If on carpet, floor, or table, protect with plastic, large cardboard, or newspaper; use container to hold jars so that they won't spill on floor or table.
- Prepare paint the consistency of thick cream; test by stroking paint on upright paper at easel; if opaque, good consistency; if you can see through it or it drips, too thin; add extender, soap, or liquid starch if too thin; add water from squeeze-bottle if too thick.

- Children wear smocks; help if needed, but allow children to help themselves as much as possible.
- At first provide one primary color; later, add variety.
- Put brush in each paint container (if children are beginners); if children are experienced, let them get their own brushes and put them in paint.

Supervision:

- Put child's name and date in upper-left corner in manuscript lettering before painting begins.
- If on floor or table, space children so that they have enough room.
- Watch carefully, but do not hover or interrupt children with questions and comments.
- If children seem hesitant to start, give them time; later, if still not using paintbrushes, show them how to push brush against side of container; then hand brush to child with paint in it, saying "See what you can do with this paintbrush on the paper." Stand back and let child explore.

Guidance:

- "Put a smock on before you start to paint so that you won't get paint on your clothes."
- "Put the same brush back in the same container each time."
- "The brush with the red paint goes in the red paint jar."
- "Cover your paper"; "Use another color."
- "Keep the paint on the paper."
- Encourage child to take time; ask, "Would you like to tell me about your painting?"
- Encourage exploring: "What happened when you painted red and blue in the same spot?"

Follow-up:

- Have child help unclamp painting from easel and hang it up; help only where needed; guide child to do it: "Squeeze the clothespin at the top."

· Paintings heavy with paint must be laid flat.

· Tell child to take off and hang up smock; help if needed.

· If paint gets on child's hands, remind child to wash.

· Place clean paper on easel for next child.

· See that spills are wiped up; encourage child to do it.

Variations:

· Variations of surfaces:

· Paint papier-mache egg cartons, cardboard boxes, wooden structures, dried clay, rocks, windows, etc.

· Variations in paint:

· Add small amount of color to white for pastel; add black to darken; add sand, salt, grits, soap, liquid starch to vary texture; add evaporated milk to give gloss; add soap to adhere to waxed surface such as printing on cardboard boxes; use plain water and large brush; paint walk, walls, fence outside.

After art activities:

· Remove brushes from paint containers.

· Wash in lukewarm water. First rinsing may be saved to use as a wash with other artwork.

· Rinse until no more paint comes from bristles; shake out excess water and lay on side to dry; store with bristles up.

· Cover each paint container with lids, aluminum foil, or plastic.

· Discard muddy paint or paint that is too watery and weak in appearance; if containers are reusable, wash them.

· See section on equipment and materials for further comments about their ongoing care.

☐ **Fingerpainting.** Children differ in their response to using fingers, hands, feet, or elbows as brushes for painting on a smooth surface. Some will delight in the free feeling of gliding across the smooth surface. Others will reject the idea or be afraid of "getting dirty." Your job is to make the experience a good one for each child.

This activity helps children

· Express ideas and emotions—it encourages spontaneity and frees inhibited children

· Experience "messy" materials and enjoy tactile (touching) pleasure

· Use large muscles rhythmically

· Enjoy experimentation

Ages:

Two years and up.

Location:

Indoors or outdoors; on table, floor, or ground.

Items needed:

· Homemade or commercial fingerpaints; liquid starch or wheat paste may be used as a homemade paint (see page 226 for recipes).

· Large sheets of firm paper with slick surface—shelf, freezer, butcher, or commercial fingerpaint paper; beginning experiments with fingerpaint may be done on trays or on waterproof counters or table tops.

· Smocks, aprons, or shirts to protect children's clothing.

· Space that is removed from traffic pattern, preferably near water.

· Dishpan and paper towels.

· Water for dunking hands in immediately after painting; final cleanup can be done in bathroom.

Figure 17-4. Most children delight in using, fingers, hands, and elbows to glide paint onto paper. (Kenneth Karp)

- Water in squeeze-bottle to add to paint that is drying too fast.
- Sponges or cloths to wipe up spills; clean up afterward.
- Powdered or liquid tempera paint to add to uncolored fingerpaint base.
- If outside, use a hose to wash surfaces used.
- Newspapers, plastic sheets, or other protective covering to put on floor where fingerpaintings will dry and to protect surface and area where fingerpainting is done.

Preparation:

- If on carpet, protect floor with plastic, cardboard or newspaper. Have children wear smocks to protect clothing, push long sleeves up.
- Have materials listed ready to use.
- Prepare place for fingerpaintings to dry—out of traffic, where painting can be laid flat or, if held upright, will not blow so

Dough Clay (uncooked)

4 cups plain flour
2 cups salt

4 tablespoons oil
water and food coloring or
  tempera paint

Mix salt and flour together thoroughly. Add food coloring to water (or powdered tempera to dry ingredients). Add water gradually to flour and salt mixture, enough water to make a doughy consistency. If it is sticky, add more flour. Add oil and knead until smooth and elastic. If you feel the salt grains, it must be kneaded some more. When finished, it should be soft, smooth, and nonsticky. The flour and the weather will determine how much water to add, so add water gradually. Store in plastic bag in refrigerator. Before using, allow dough clay to reach room temperature. If cold, it will be hard and resistant to handling and will tend to crumble.

Dough Clay (cooked)

Combine 1 cup flour, ½ cup salt and 2 teaspoons cream of tartar in a large saucepan. Gradually stir in 1 cup water mixed with 2 tablespoons oil and 1 teaspoon food coloring. Cook over medium to high heat, stirring constantly until a ball forms. Remove from heat and knead until smooth.
  Store in plastic bag or airtight container.*

Paste

1 cup plain flour
2¼ cups boiling water
¾ teaspoon oil of wintergreen
  or cloves

1 cup cold water
1 teaspoon powdered alum
  from drugstore

Mix flour with cold water, stir until smooth. Add boiling water, stir. Cook in double boiler over low heat until smooth (will look shiny and slightly bluish-gray). Add alum to help preserve the paste. Stir until smooth. Remove from heat, add oil of wintergreen or cloves for pleasant smell. Store in covered jars in cool place. Baby jars work fine.

*Doreen Croft and Robert Hess, *An Activities Handbook for Teachers of Young Children* 2 ed., p. 93. Copyright © 1975 by Houghton Mifflin Co. Reprinted by permission.

Fingerpaint

1½ cups laundry starch (kind to be cooked)
1 quart boiling water   1 cup cold water
1½ cups soap flakes
½ cup talcum (optional)—buy at drugstore in bulk

Mix laundry starch and cold water. Add boiling water and cook until clear,
stirring constantly. Remove from heat and add soap flakes and talcum.
Store in plastic container in refrigerator.

that painting folds back on itself and ruins design.

· Have a pan with water ready for children to dip hands and wash off excess fingerpaint; wipe with paper towels, then wash hands thoroughly in bathroom.

Supervision:

· Limit number of children fingerpainting to four or five at a time, fewer if you are supervising the entire group without help; it's good to have volunteers or older children help when little ones are fingerpainting.

· Plan other art activities that take little supervision.

· Two children work together as partners, or the teacher serves as a partner for each child, squeezing water from squeeze-bottle, adding color, removing fingerpainting when on paper, and placing in a prepared place to dry.

Fingerpainting Directly on Smooth Surface. Here are some suggestions:

· Place about 2 tablespoons of fingerpaint on surface.

· Have partner add water from squeeze-bottle if paint "drags" and does not slide easily across surface.

· Add color—one color at first, if a variety is available. Ask child for preference of color and location on paper.

· Add another color and even another as child gains confidence and skill in using hands and mixing colors.

· Color may be added by sprinkling dry tempera or dripping a few drops of

liquefied tempera onto surface.

· Talk about changes in colors as they are mixed.

· Design may be "lifted" by rubbing newsprint over design on counter or table; have partner or teacher do this and place design in prepared place to dry.

Fingerpainting on Paper: Here are some suggestions:

· Put child's name on upper left corner of paper in manuscript.

· Wet table or counter surface with sponge or squeeze-bottle.

· Place on wet surface with shiny side of paper up, about 3 to 4 inches from table edge.

· Wet shiny side of paper all over.

· Place about two tablespoons of fingerpaint in middle of paper.

· Encourage child (who is standing) to put both hands in fingerpaint and make designs with fingers.

· Have partner squeeze some water from squeeze-bottle onto paper if paint does not move easily over paper (it will dry out as used).

· Add color as mentioned above; sometimes try using two colors, placing one on the left and the other on the right; child will discover a new color as mixed.

Guidance:

· "See what you can do with your fingers"—or fist, arms, elbows (even toes and feet when planned for—especially if out of doors).

- "Make your hands move in big sweeps across your paper."
- "Keep the fingerpaint on the table" (or the paper).
- "We'll have a place for you soon, Jamie. It's hard to wait, but you can do it." (A child wants to fingerpaint but has to wait his turn.)
- "What happens when you mix yellow and green fingerpaint together?"
- After finishing—"Rinse your hands in the pan before you touch anything, then wash your hands in the bathroom."

Follow-up:

- Have children rinse hands in pan, then wash them in the bathroom.
- Place fingerpainting in prepared area to dry.
- Clean table with sponge or cloth—children can help.
- Remove protective surfaces—throw away newspapers on floor; wipe plastic with sponge or cloth and fold.
- If outside, hose down table and area when fingerpainting ends; children can help.
- Wipe off jars; wash tablespoons and store in assigned places.
- Store homemade fingerpaint in refrigerator.

Variations in fingerpainting:

- Fingerpaint over crayon design.
- Fingerpaint on one side of paper, fold over to make design.
- Play music while fingerpainting.
- Warm weather—fingerpaint outside in bathing suits, hose children and fingerpaint area down when through.
- Add glitter to wet fingerpainting, especially if wheat paste is used as base.
- Try different textures; add soap or use whipped soap (equal parts soap and water) as fingerpaint base; add grits, sand, liquid soap, liquid starch; use talcum for smoother fingerpaint and a good smell too; one teacher uses Christmas talc and toilet water to make fingerpainting a special, good-smelling experience.

☐ **Printing with Sponges and Gadgets.** This activity gives children

- Freedom to explore
- Experience in using various materials
- The opportunity to combine different shapes and textures
- The chance to create designs
- A subject for conversation
- The opportunity to decide when to start and when to stop

Ages:
Two years and up.

Location:
On table, counter, or floor; indoors or outdoors

Items needed:

- Container with paint or paint pad on which to push gadget to pick up paint before printing.
- Container may be small bowl, muffin tins, or pad made from sponge or layers of soft fabric; if you place a sponge in a plastic tray and add tempera paint, the amount of paint picked up from sponge or gadget will be just about right.
- Sponges, gadgets, vegetables, cut to make interesting shapes.
- Construction paper, want-ad section, telephone-book pages, soft-surface cardboard.
- Gadgets—bottle caps, corks, erasers, hair curlers, pipe cleaners, spools, crumbled paper; vegetables (green pepper, onion, carrots, potato, okra)—most can be used to make attractive designs by just cutting across them; in addition, carrot and potato may be cut to make a design.
- Smocks for children.
- Marking pens.

Preparation:

- Collect items needed as mentioned above.
- Protect table surface with newspaper.
- Have children put on smocks.
- Put paint in containers that won't spill.

· Have several containers at one table so that children can use their own as long as they like.

Supervision:
· Put name on paper before child starts to print (in manuscript lettering, upper left-hand corner).
· Place gadgets or sponges in containers with paint pad (made of sponge or several thicknesses of soft, absorbent cloth) nearby; use thick paint to coat pad; put in container if pad is not used.
· Have children put on smocks.
· Encourage experimentation—overlapping using different colors, making different designs, etc.
· Have children dip gadgets in paint or push against sponge pad.
· Print design on paper by pushing painted gadget against paper.
· Return gadget to container.
· Continue until finished.

Guidance:
· "How many colors do you have?"
· "What are the names of the colors?"
· "Which ones do you want to work with first?"
· "See whether you can cover your paper" (use more than one, use them all, use several colors, etc.).
· "When you are finished, put your paper here." (If wet, put in protected place to dry.)

Follow-up:
· Children put finished design in locker or assigned place to dry; or they store artwork until they go home.
· Children are given opportunity to make more than one.
· Children remove smocks and hang them up.
· Children put gadgets in containers.
· Children wash hands.
· Teacher covers paints or paint pads so that they will not dry out.
· Put materials in assigned place.
· Throw newspapers away.

· Wipe off table if food service follows.
· Note any unusual printing or behavior and tell your supervising teacher about it later.

Variations:
· Cut carrots with design; potato design may be cut out or background may be removed, leaving design raised for printing.
· Use cotton balls with dry tempera.
· Use cotton swab, tongue depressors, dried-up marking pens, roll-on deodorant bottles.
· Use sponge or gadget, printing shapes such as flowers, fish, items firefighters use. Use stencil and press sponge over entire stencil shape; when removed, designed shape will appear.
· Use different textures, including fabric, cardboard, and cardboard boxes.

To print with string:
Use pieces of soft, absorbent string 8 to 12 inches long; may be attached to popsicle sticks or tongue depressors; dip short lengths into container and press against side while removing; let fall on paper that has been folded in half; fold over and press; pull string out and let dry.

To use straws for painting:
Cut straws into 4- or 5-inch lengths. Dip straws into fingerpaint and drop paint from straw onto smooth paper; blow to make interesting designs; do not share straws—one clean straw per child.

To use paint blobs:
Drop a blob of paint from spoon, eyedropper, straw, popsicle stick, or brush on soft paper (like construction paper); fold paper in half or any way that child would like to fold it; press and unfold to see pretty-colored magic picture.

To spatter paint:
Use thinner paint than easel paint; use vegetable brush, wire frame, spatter pan, construction paper, and object or design that can be used as stencil.
Dip brush into thin paint; shake off excess paint (this is very important—otherwise there is too much paint, and instead of

Figure 17-5. Drawing with crayons gives children the opportunity to practice using their small muscles. (Kenneth Karp)

getting a lot of tiny spatters, you get a runny puddle); younger children cannot understand the process of spattering and removing the stencil to get a design—they usually scrub the design used as stencil.

☐ **Crayon, Chalk, and Pencils.** This activity

· Encourages use of small muscles, fine manipulation
· Enables children to move from scribbling to exploratory representation
· May release tension if used in relaxed way
· Allows children to control an art material
· Encourages independence—children can get and use materials and return them to their places

Crayons. Children always enjoy this activity.
Materials needed:
Crayons (paper removed; sometimes in containers by color, other times in individual boxes). One color crayon of each color or in large containers like baskets for several children to use at once. Construction paper, various colors; newsprint, drawing paper, interesting papers such as news ads, telephone book, wallpaper, books, cardboard.

Preparation:
Crayons in assigned place on shelf—children get their own; sometimes set up crayons on table ahead of time; good experiences throughout day.

Supervision:
· Allow children to use crayons with freedom; do not hover.
· Encourage child to make choices; don't require or request certain objects to be drawn.
· Ask child if he or she wants to comment on what has been drawn.
· Help children keep crayons on paper; use large paper.
· Provide relaxed atmosphere in which children enjoy each other as they use crayons.
· Allow plenty of time, space.

Guidance:
· "Which crayon is the same color as Mary's dress?"
· "Do you want to tell me about your drawing?"
· "I like the way you are using large strokes."
· "What happens when you use the side of your crayon?"

230

- "When you are finished, put your drawing in your locker and put the crayons back on the shelf."
- "John, will you collect the papers? And Sue, will you put the crayon baskets where they belong on the shelf?"

Follow-up:
- Crayons, paper, unused paper, and drawings in place.
- Opportunity for children to talk about their work if they wish.
- Display of children's work from time to time; each child has a turn to see his or her work displayed at one time or another.
- Continued experiences planned to stimulate thinking and encourage expression of ideas and objects through drawing with crayons.

Variations:
- Mostly for older children (4 years and above).
- Paint over crayon work with wash-thinned tempera paint.
- Fingerpaint over crayon work.
- Crayon rubbing—over textured paper and/or objects; rubbing crayon over wire screen and gives experience of "feeling" letters.
- Use crayons on fabric; iron on.
- Use pressed crayons made of chips melted together, either homemade (do-it-yourself) or purchased.

Chalk. Chalk is an interesting change.

Ages:
Three years and up.

Materials needed:
- Large art chalk (chalk for chalkboard is too little and fragile, and colors are not bright).
- Absorbent paper such as construction paper, firm paper towels, newsprint if chalk used is dry. (Newsprint is too thin if chalk is used wet.)
- Moisture—water, liquid starch, or buttermilk.
- Smocks to protect children's clothing.

- Chalk in small containers so two children can share; one large container forces children to reach and encourages grabbing rather than a relaxed atmosphere.
- Chalkboard at children's height; use ordinary chalk for chalkboard, not art chalk.

Preparation:
- Children put on smocks.
- Table is prepared; may be covered with newspaper if clean-up time is limited.
- Chalk is set out in small flat containers so that it can be seen easily.
- Paper is placed on table; sometimes use manila paper and sometimes use assorted colors.
- If children want to do this as an individual project, they get their own smocks, paper, and chalk container and return them to their places when finished.

Supervision:
- Same as for crayons.
- Younger children will scrub when using chalk with liquid; experience becomes almost one of fingerpaint; be sure they wear smocks.

Guidance:
Same as for crayons.

Follow-up:
- If chalk is used dry, put fixative on it to keep it from rubbing off (use cheap hair spray, plastic spray, or commercial chalk spray).
- If chalk is used wet, place artwork in prepared place to dry; if very wet, artwork will have to be laid flat.
- Children wash hands, remove and hang up smocks; chalk is put on shelf; table is cleaned by removing protective paper, wiping with sponges.

Variations:
Dip chalk in water, buttermilk, or liquid starch on dry paper; use dry, then brush with liquid; if firm paper, dip in water, use dry chalk or brush with water and use dry chalk; use chalk board—see above.

Pencils. This is a familiar medium.

Ages:

Four years and up.

Materials needed:

· Large soft-lead pencils; primary colors.

· Manila or construction paper, newsprint, or manuscript paper.

· Comfortable place to work.

Preparation:

Children get own pencils and paper and draw what they like.

Supervision and Follow-Up:

Same as crayons.

Variations:

May be used with other materials—crayons, paint, paste.

Children's work will vary greatly with age; encourage enjoyment of process rather than required product; use marking pens, colored pencils, or recycled deodorant bottles with roll-on attachment (use as crayons). Be sure marking pens are watercolor, not permanent ink. If marking pens are dried up, use with tempera paint by dipping pen in tempera. Fill deodorant bottles with tempera by removing ball, filling, and replacing for use.

☐ **Paper, Paste, and Scissors.** This activity

· Lets children cut, paste, tear

· Allows children to enjoy the fun of pasting— also the feel, smell, and taste of the paste

· Enables children to produce a finished product

· Provides a social activity—much conversation

Paper:

Younger children enjoy feeling of achievement that comes with making tears in paper and creating pieces; the tearing experience itself is the art activity for these children.

Ages:

Two years and up.

Materials needed:

Paper that tears easily, imagination, fingers; comfortable area to work.

Preparation:

Wastebasket nearby, variety of paper to use; may be followed with pasting.

Supervision:

See that each child has enough space and that he or she has a place to put torn pieces, especially if they are to be pasted later.

Guidance:

"Put the paper between your thumbs and forefingers. Twist your hands back and forth to pull it apart." "See how the paper tears." There is more control with the thumb method, but younger children will want to tear quickly and with big paper. Have plenty available.

Follow-up:

Put scraps in wastebasket; children may want to keep their torn pieces; put in paper bag, or make a simple envelope by folding paper and stapling ends together.

Paste: Using paste gives children a chance to practice their fine motor skills.

Materials needed:

· Paste—homemade or commercial (sometimes called library or school paste).

· Paper—construction, manila, newsprint, wallpaper, magazine pages, telephone-book pages, want ads, lightweight paper, and materials for collage (such as wrapping paper and pictures, tissue paper).

· Scissors—child-sized, blunt-point, good-cutting ones; do not buy cheap scissors, as poor cutting action frustrates children.

Preparation:

· Paste in small containers (or on jar lids, squares of cardboard, or small pieces of aluminum foil).

· Sponges or wet paper towels if children use fingers.

· Paste brushes or popsicle sticks are sometimes used, but fingers are better.

· Paper available as mentioned above.

· Smocks, since children tend to wipe hands on clothes.

· Comfortable place to work; space and time allowed.

Supervision:

· Children may be shown how to put

paste on back of object to be pasted and how to turn it over and press it on paper.

- Younger children will build up paste and paper stacks, pasting one piece on top of another; paste is used almost as fingerpaint.

Guidance:
- "Turn your paper over and put paste on the back of it."
- "Rub it until it's shiny."
- "Now turn it right side up and press it on your big paper."
- "Wipe your hands on the sponge or on the wet paper towel."
- "Paste another one; put as many as you like on your paper."

Follow-up:
- Children wash hands, take off and hang up smocks.
- Materials are put in place; wipe off jars throw away small amounts of paste; put large amounts back into larger container.
- Wash lids, wipe off jars, and put on lids; store in right place.
- Wipe off table; put paste pictures in place to dry (if much paste is used); if little paste was used, paper can be put in children's lockers.

Scissors: Using scissors gives children a chance to practice eye-hand coordination. At first, the cutting experience alone is enough of an achievement.

Ages:
Three years and up.

Materials needed:
- *Paper*—firm enough to hold without bending.
- *Cloth*—lightweight and firm for cutting (for experienced cutters).
- *Scissors*—child-sized, blunt-pointed, good-cutting ones; do not buy cheap scissors, as poor cutting action frustrates children.
- *Paste*, if children want to paste what they have cut.
- Container (bag or envelope) for taking cut pieces home.

- Container for holding scissors—rack, can, or egg carton.

Preparation:
- Place scissor container on table or in area to be used.
- Put paper on table.
- If individual project, child gets paper and scissors from assigned place, uses them, and puts them back.
- Wastebasket near table.
- Plenty of space; comfortable height for chairs and tables.

Supervision:
- Children may be shown how to hold scissors and paper.
- Watch carefully to see who needs help; recognize achievement.
- Have children collect pieces as they cut and put pieces in a stack or pile.

Guidance:
- "Let's cut this big piece of paper into little pieces."
- "Cutting looks easy, but it's not as easy as it looks."
- "Put your thumb in this hole and your finger in that one."
- "Hold your paper in one hand and the scissors in the other."
- "Make your thumb go up and down; see the scissors opening and closing. Now open your scissors, put the paper into the opening, and close your scissors by pushing your thumb down. Do it again."
- At first, children will half tear, half cut; let them experiment, and don't stop this tearing-cutting action—it produces a smaller piece of paper from a bigger one, and that's the first achievement for young children.

Follow-up:
- Put pieces into container if taking home; otherwise put in wastebasket.
- Replace scissors in container; put in assigned place.

Variations:
Created by variation in materials cut; use variety of papers; use both thin and firm materials.

Figure 17-6. Working with clay satisfies the desire children have to manipulate and smear something messy and thick. (Etienne Marcel)

Folding Paper. Very young children will enjoy doing this activity.

Ages:
Four years and up.
Materials needed:
Paper that will hold crease.
Procedure:
Have children fold paper, matching corners or creating own method as they go; do not push for product but talk about what they're doing.
Follow-up:
Put unused paper in assigned place; put folded paper in locker to take home or in wastebasket if child does not want to keep it.

☐ **Play Dough and Clay.** This activity

· Provides opportunities for exploration, self-expression, and manipulation.
· Assures success; a child is free from failure when enjoying play dough or clay.

· Provides an opportunity for friendly activity with others.
· May provide a finished product for an older or experienced child.
· Drains off aggressive feelings.

Play Dough: This activity helps children develop their manipulative skills.

Ages:
Two years and up.
Materials needed:
· Homemade play dough (see page 226) or commercial play dough.
· Accessories—rollers (can be large dowel sticks, cut into 6-inch lengths), cookie cutters, popsicle sticks.
· Plastic bag to store dough in.
· Smocks for children.
· Small amount of flour if clay is sticky.
· Comfortable space to work.
Preparation:
· Children put on smocks.
· Check play dough to see if workable (becomes hard in refrigerator; should be room temperature).
· Break into softball-sized pieces; work with hands until soft, working in flour if sticky.
· Put accessory box on table or put a roller by each clump of play dough.
Supervision:
· Sit with children and listen to their conversation.
· Talk with them as they work.
· Don't push for products or hurry the children.
· Use play dough without accessories at times, encouraging children to manipulate it with hands and fingers.
Guidance:
· "How does the play dough feel? Cold? Why do you suppose it's cold?"
· "What color is it?" "See what you can do with your hands."
· "Make a fist and pound the play dough." "Use all ten fingers and roll the play

234

dough back and forth. What's happening?'' Squeeze it.

· ''Jim, Mary needs some play dough; would you share some of yours with her? Thank you. You are very kind.''

Follow-up:
· Roll play dough into large ball; put in plastic bag and store in refrigerator if it is not to be used for several days.
· Have children help. Wipe off table, wash accessories and put in container or on counter to dry.

Variations:
Have children help make play dough. Sometimes dough differs in color, thickness, stickiness.

Wet Clay. This can be a messy activity.

Ages:
Three years and up.
Location:
Indoors or out; on table or floor; protected area.
Materials needed:
· Wet clay.
· Squeeze-bottle with water to add when clay dries as children work with it.
· Clay boards (about 12 inches square, made of masonite).
· Container for storing clay—plastic pail or crock that is airtight.
· Rollers, flat sticks, cookie cutters.
· Smocks for children.
· Water in pan for rinsing hands.
· Cloths and sponges for clean-up.
· Protection for table—plastic or newspaper.
Preparation:
· Prepare area to be used with protective cover—spread newspaper or plastic.
· Get pan for water to rinse hands afterward.
· Put water in squeeze-bottle.
· Place clay boards around table where children will sit or in area to be used.
· Put clay ball on or by each clay board.

· Have accessories close by, but do not use every time.
· Children put on smocks.
· Work clay a short time so that it is soft enough for children to use.

Supervision:
· Clay is to stay on clay boards, not to be thrown.
· Use little water inside; when outside, children may and probably will want to add more water—they like to see clay ''melt away.''
· Children may like to stand up to work clay; they can get better leverage as they pound, poke, or squeeze it.
· Don't hurry children or require products; enjoy the experience.

Guidance:
· ''Keep your clay on the clay board.''
· ''Throw the clay against the board.'' (Push it, roll it, etc.)
· ''Rinse your hands in the pan, then wash them in the bathroom.''
· ''When you are finished washing your hands, take off your smock and hang it up.''
· Stay close to children who may use clay to release tension; give freedom within limits; encourage release of tension; clay is a messy, tension-releasing experience and you plan the setting for it.

Follow-up:
Children help wash clay boards in water pan, remove protective cover from table, wipe off smocks before hanging them up; they can help hose down a clay area used for clay work in the playground—this is part of the clay experience outside; roll clay into baseball-sized clumps; put thumb hole in each ball and fill with water; store in airtight container for later use.

Variations:
Use natural clay with bits of stones and twigs in it; vary amount of water; use accessories.

☐ **Three-Dimensional Materials.** These are materials that have shape and the third dimension of depth. Clay objects, Styrofoam, wood and box structures, and collages made with objects having depth (such as beads, seeds, and twigs) are examples. Whenever glue is used for these structures, use the white vinyl type, not paste. Paste will not hold anything that has weight.

White Vinyl Glue. Sometimes called white glue, vinyl glue usually dries clear. It is an excellent binder of objects. When using it with objects that do not stick to each other at first, hold the spot to be glued together and count to ten. This usually gives enough time for the binding process to begin. Place objects in a protected place where they dry horizontally (lying down). If vertical (up and down), objects will fall off because of their weight.

When finished with glue, put the cap back on the jar and wipe it. If glue is in a large container such as a gallon jar, cover the glue's surface with a thin layer of water to prevent glue from hardening. Always wash the glue out of brushes before storing them. Never leave white glue uncovered, as it will harden and become unusable.

Collage. The French word for pasting, *collage,* refers to a pasted picture made of lightweight fabric or paper. Use paste rather than glue for binding items to a flat surface. When working in three dimensions, use vinyl or white glue. The following items are examples of three-dimensional objects that can be used in collages: string, seeds, nuts, buttons, acorns, shells, pieces of wood, beads, and pebbles. The procedure for three-dimensional collage is the same as for using paste. See the earlier discussion of supervision, guidance, and follow-up.

Making Structures. Constructions made from paper-towel rollers, toilet-paper rollers, various-sized boxes, interesting shapes, and other "beautiful junk" are limited only by children's imaginations and, perhaps, by the storage space needed. Masking tape and staples are helpful building materials in making structures out of boxes and other interesting objects and shapes. Use vinyl glue to stick things together.

Styrofoam may be used for printing, creating constructions made by gluing, and for first experiences with hammer and nails. Large roofing nails and a small hammer make it easier for children to hit their first nails properly on their heads.

Figure 17-7. Woodworking provides an opportunity for children to release tension and to produce a functional object. (Kenneth Karp)

Working With Wood. This activity

· Appeals to all the senses
· Provides an enjoyable experience in using tools
· Gives children the satisfaction of producing an object
· Releases normal tension through sawing and pounding
· Helps children become skillful in eye-hand coordination
· Gives children practice in solving problems
· Provides good social experiences

Ages:
   Four years and up.

Location:
   Indoors or outdoors, in a space away from traffic lanes and uninterrupted by other activities.

Materials needed:
   · Heavy table, bench, or sawhorse on which to work.
   · Various pieces of soft wood (pine is good)

- Nails—roofing, 2-, 4-, 6-penny nails, tacks, brads
- C-clamps to fasten wood to table
- Cross-cut saw—14 inches long (may be 16 or 20 inches if 14-inch is not available)
- Screwdriver
- Soft-lead pencil, ruler, washers, bits of interesting junk
- Rack for storing tools
- Container for nails, sandpaper, assorted wire, tacks
- White vinyl glue
- Tempera paint and shellac for painting finished objects
- String or yarn for decorating or creating objects
- Vise to clamp wood*
- Brace and bit*
- Hand drill*
- Plane*
- Goggles*

Supervision:
- Limit number of children who are working at workbench or table to one or two at a time.
- Supervise closely.
- Demonstrate the proper use of tools.

Guidance:
- "Keep both hands on the saw."
- "Joe will be finished soon, and then you will have a turn."
- "Watch what you are doing. Push the saw back and forth."
- "Hammer one nail at a time."
- "To start sawing, put the end of the saw nearest the handle on the line and pull toward you. One, two, three times and you have a groove. Get a rhythm as you push hard—pull easy."
- "Hold a hammer where the handle begins to get fat. To pull out a nail so it doesn't bend, put a scrap of wood against the nail almost to the head; rest

hammer on this as it grips the head and then rock it back."

Follow-up:
Put children's work in their lockers; place tools and materials in assigned places; put unfinished work where it will be protected.

Variations:
Combine glue and woodwork experiences; paint completed objects; for experienced children, plan work ahead of time; for beginners, manipulating things is the important experience.

PROVIDING POSITIVE GUIDANCE IN ART EXPERIENCES

Children will react differently to art experiences. As a child care aide, you will sometimes face situations that require special handling. Your response should be based on the situation and the individual child. Remember that your goal in trying to solve a problem is to help the child to get as much benefit as possible from art experiences. Table 17-5 lists the possible causes and solutions for problems that may arise.

RELATING ART TO OTHER SUBJECT AREAS

Art experiences can become even more meaningful if they are related to other subject areas or other parts of the program. Here are some examples of how to integrate art activities with the total program:

1. *Art and music.* Play music while the children paint.
2. *Art and language arts.* Identify words that describe an art activity.
3. *Art and social studies.* Children learn to help one another and be partners during fingerpainting; they experience social interaction and art; they may talk about different jobs that involve art and art materials.
4. *Art and mathematics.* Counting designs children have drawn, calling attention to *greater-than* and *less-than* concepts, geometric shapes, and so forth during art-mathematics experience, classifying items such as collage

*For experienced children

Table 17-5 PROBLEMS AND SOLUTIONS RELATED TO ART ACTIVITIES

Child's behavior	Possible causes	Possible solutions
Child always draws the same thing.	Using the same supplies. The same experiences. There is an adult or older sibling to model. Anxious for praise from adults.	Vary materials and supplies. Add new experiences. Help the child feel comfortable and free to draw something else. Build the child's self-confidence.
Child never talks about his or her art.	Not interested in product. Is shy and afraid to express feelings. Is working out negative feelings.	Let him or her alone. Become the child's friend; invite trust, but do not push. Respect the child's feelings, especially if it seems that anger, frustration, or fear is being released through the art experience.
Child does not know how to draw or paint.	Has not had the experience. Interested in process only.	Typical for age when preschoolers have had no experience. Choose process activities— play dough, crayons, one or two colors of tempera.
Child paints sloppily.	Are your standards too high? Are the child's feelings being expressed? Is the child in a hurry to finish and start some other activity?	Let the child enjoy painting, do not expect too much. If releasing tension, let the child alone after protecting his or her clothing and the area. Simplify the experience, concentrate on process, and suggest things to extend interest.
Child is afraid to put pressure on crayons or to use paint freely.	Is the child tense? Is the child's clothing protected? Has the child been scolded for getting paint on clothing? Is the child worried? Are there family problems?	Provide a relaxed atmosphere; suggest nonfail activities such as dough clay. Use smocks. Put a comfortable, free child near a tense one. Casually sit and visit with the child.
Child wants everything to look real.	Is there an older sibling to model?	Provide process materials like dough clay and fingerpaint.

Table 17-5 PROBLEMS AND SOLUTIONS RELATED TO ART ACTIVITIES (Continued)

Child's behavior	Possible causes	Possible solutions
	Do parents want products? Has the child's experience been limited to dictated art (stencils, patterns, coloring books)?	Same. Put a comfortable, free child nearby and provide time, space, and a variety of materials for the two children to use.
Child draws or paints very small things, using only a small part of the paper.	Is this a new experience or is the child very young? Does the child seem worried or anxious? Are materials and tools suitable? Is child unaware of how large the paper is?	Let the child be free to explore. Help the child feel more relaxed and comfortable. Provide large paper and brushes; suggest art activities that use large muscles. Invite or challenge child to cover the paper.
Child loves clay and does not want to paint.	How old is the child? Does the child need to release tension? Has the child discovered painting yet? Is the child avoiding painting?	If child is young, wait until he or she is interested—clay is often the beginning art experience. Leave child alone if he or she is enjoying the experience. Invite a child to paint. Don't put clay out, have each child paint instead; do not invite, *assume* that the child will participate.
Child does not want to put whole hand in paint or use both hands in fingerpainting.	Is the child afraid of getting messy? Is the child tense? Is the experience unpleasant for the child?	Use smock to protect clothing. Match with a child who is free and give time to explore and discover. Value individual differences, some enjoy messy activities more than others.
Child wants to use art materials to paint shoes or clothing.	How old is the child? Does the child need to explore? Does he or she want attention?	Establish limits about where paint is used. Provide big paper and brushes, lots of space to use big muscles. Use positive reinforcement.

materials when they are sorted and put away.

5. *Art and science.* Calling attention to the properties of art materials—what paint looks and feels like when it is wet, what happens when it dries, how fast clay gets hard. Making a nature collage and forming new shapes and colors combines scientific observation and art experiences.

6. *Art and outdoor experiences.* Painting outside or building wooden structures is a form of art.

As concepts are related to different subject areas during different activities, children's understanding of them is strengthened and increased.

EVALUATING ART ACTIVITIES

During your supervision of art activities, you are making observations about the children's response to their art experiences. Often these observations will give you insight into a child's feelings and frustrations in general, even though you are supervising in a specific activity.

When you are helping children to evaluate their own art experiences, encourage them to tell you or the group how they feel about their art *only if they are interested in doing so.* Do not make children evaluate their experiences.

As you know, the final step involved in following up any activity is to evaluate your own performance and the experiences of individual children. Be prepared to share your observations with your supervising teacher.

CHAPTER SUMMARY

1. Art activities can be classified in many different ways for young children—supervised or self-help, freeing or controlling, individual or group, product- or process-oriented, messy or nonmessy. Different types of art activities are better for children in certain stages in development. Art activities should be matched to the developmental level of the children involved.

2. Art experiences benefit children in many

ways. They encourage children to be independent and creative. Art activities allow children to express their feelings, build self-confidence, and clarify ideas and concepts.

3. Carrying out art activities includes preparing the children, materials, equipment, and space; supervising the activity; cleaning up; and evaluation.

4. Caregivers should relate art experiences to other subject-matter areas in order to strengthen the concepts that children are learning.

Your observations about the children's art experiences and your own performance should be discussed with your supervising teacher.

• WHAT NEW TERMS HAVE YOU LEARNED?

Several new words and ideas were presented in this chapter. To see whether you understand them, match the letter of each term below with the numbered phrases under "Definitions."

Terms

a. Creativity
b. Exploration
c. Product
d. Process
e. Tempera paint
f. Three-dimensional
g. Newsprint
h. Craypas
i. Dough clay
j. Easel brush
k. Plasticine
l. Wet clay
m. Integration
n. Symbolic

Definitions

1. The "doing" or actual experience of an art activity
2. Using your imagination
3. A picture easily identified as a tree or a house
4. Playing and experimenting with material to see what it will do

5. Combining an art activity with music and science
6. Poster paint in liquid or powder form
7. Unprinted newspaper
8. A representation which may or may not look like what it is supposed to be
9. Homemade flour and salt mixture
10. Commercial oil clay
11. Trade name for oil-based chalk
12. Natural clay used with water
13. Stiff-bristled brush
14. Combining several materials in layers to create a design on a sheet of paper

• PROJECTS, DECISIONS, ISSUES

1. Choose three benefits of creative art experiences listed in Table 17-1 and tell why each one is important to the child. You may choose to do this in the form of a bulletin board or as a written paper.
2. Develop a creative mobile using only the key words related to each of the ways listed in Table 17-2 to encourage creativity. Use at least four or more ways. The more you use, the more exciting the mobile.
3. Volunteer to set up an exhibit for showing four different types of art activities that can be used with young children.
4. Collect one example of a creative art activity completed by a 2-year-old, a 3-year-old, a 4-year-old, and a 5-year-old. Mount each one on poster board and describe why they differ.
5. Prepare and give a demonstration that illustrates five ways to provide meaningful art experiences for young children.

• WHIFS (WHAT WOULD YOU DO IF . . .)

1. Patty is painting at the easel and paints the easel and her fingernails red before you discover it. What would you do?
   a. Call your supervising teacher
   b. Ignore it, it will wash off
   c. Have her clean up the mess
   d. Scold her soundly
   e. Other responses

2. Teddy is fingerpainting with one finger. He has a pained look on his face. What would you do?
   a. Insist that he use all his fingers
   b. Ask him whether he can make circles with his fingers
   c. Have another child who fingerpaints freely work alongside him
   d. Let him alone, he'll use all his fingers when he's relaxed enough
   e. Other responses

3. Judy has just learned to use scissors. In fact, she tries them out on Joanne's hair and cuts off a 3-inch swatch. What would you do?
   a. Tell your supervisor
   b. Cry
   c. Tell Joanne's parents
   d. Tell Judy's parents
   e. Other responses

4. Andy and Tammy are building a castle out of small boxes. They need more masking tape. When you go to get some for them, you find that there is no more. What would you do?
   a. Let them figure out a solution
   b. Have them put their project away until masking tape is available
   c. Use scotch tape, pins, stapler, vinyl glue
   d. Discuss other solutions over with the children
   e. Other solutions

5. Bart is hammering for the first time. This new experience delights him and he wants to hammer a long time. What would you do?
   a. Tell him he has to take turns
   b. Let him hammer until he stops
   c. Give him a time limit
   d. Take the hammer away
   e. Other responses

• STUDENT ACTIVITIES

1. List three benefits of creative art experiences for young children.
2. Identify four ways to encourage children's creativity.
3. In a child's experience, what is the difference between painting at an easel and painting on a mural?

4. Describe two reasons why messy art activities help children.

5. Describe the difference between process and product.

6. What are materials called that have shape, length, and the third dimension of depth?

7. What opportunities for learning would young children miss if they were not exposed to creative art experiences?

8. Name four different types of art activities for young children.

9. With regard to the use of art materials, what is the major difference between very young preschoolers and older preschoolers?

10. Discuss why you would or would not support the idea of children making an art activity "gift" for parents at Christmastime.

18 | ASSISTING WITH MUSIC EXPERIENCES

After you have studied Chapter 18, you should be able to:

1. Name four values of music for young children
2. Identify three personal qualities of a child care aide that affect children's music experiences
3. Describe three ways that child care aides provide each basic type of music experience in child care centers

THE VALUE OF MUSIC

Music has many values for young children. It brings them enjoyment and builds self-confidence. It helps children to communicate, to express their feelings, and to release tensions. It helps them to learn.

THE SOCIAL AND EMOTIONAL VALUES OF MUSIC

Children's attitudes toward music depend on how much they enjoy their music experiences. Besides being enjoyable, good experiences with music build self-confidence and help children to express thoughts and feelings.

Enjoying Music. Music experiences are fun. Formal instruction and correction are not stressed. Joy comes from taking part. When children are enjoying familiar, favorite music activities, they are relaxed and happy.

Building Self-Confidence. Whether it's singing a song, being a leader, or handing out musical instruments, music involves children and helps them build self-confidence.

Leading a song can be a game. "Did You Ever See a Lassie?" calls on children to set an example that others can follow. "I know a song" is a phrase that confident children use when they feel comfortable enough to want to sing in front of other children.

Watching and enjoying the other children's singing is a first step toward involvement for those who are shy. In time, shy children will respond to a chance to join music activities—if they are not rushed. Nor should any child be overlooked.

Communicating through Music. Children communicate through music. They express thoughts *verbally* (with words) and *nonverbally* (without words) as

Figure 18-1. Singing allows children to release tension, helps them express their feelings, and encourages them to relax. (Michael Weisbrot)

INTELLECTUAL VALUES OF MUSIC

Children learn as a result of music activities. Their vocabularies grow. Concepts are strengthened. Prereading skills are practiced.

Building Larger Vocabularies. Words and music go together, especially when caregivers help children to hear and understand new words. Talking about words helps to build children's vocabularies and makes the songs more meaningful. For example, "You'll Sing a Song and I'll Sing a Song"[1] mentions "warm and wintry weather." To make the song meaningful, you need to talk about the weather, about differences between warm and cold weather, and especially about the word *wintry*, which is a delightful word but one that many children have not heard before.

Pronouns are difficult for children to understand and use correctly. A song such as "You'll Sing a Song, and I'll Sing a Song" helps children to understand the concept of pronouns as they point to others and then to themselves.

Strengthening Concepts. Music can help children to understand many different concepts. For example, the concepts of *up* and *down* can be stressed in a song like "Jack and Jill." Children can increase their understanding of numerical concepts through music. They can learn about holiday customs, animals, the seasons, and colors. Songs can even teach good safety and health habits!

Practicing Prereading Skills. Children gain experience in listening, following directions, and both hearing and remembering different sounds as they enjoy music.

Children learn to hear likenesses and differences in sounds—soft and loud sounds, high and low sounds, and fast and slow sounds.

Listening skills are developed by activity records and songs that give children directions to follow. Such directions may be as simple as "stand up and sit down," but they require children to listen carefully and respond as directed.

When singing a song or playing a musical

they experience music activities. Children often respond to the rhythm of music before they are able to use words in songs. Music may help children who do not talk or who come from homes in which a foreign language is spoken. It teaches them to communicate with peers and caregivers. Music also helps children who talk very well, because they like to sing words that they know. They also like to learn new words.

Through music, children can play roles and try out how it might feel to be another person or an animal. Anger and fear can be released through the motion and involvement of good music activities. Lullabies and songs about families can bring comfort and security. When children sing about their flag or their country, they learn to feel pride in the nation.

[1] Ella Jenkins, "You'll Sing a Song and I'll Sing a Song," Folkways Records, 701 Seventh Avenue, New York, FC7664, band 1.

game, children use repetition with a definite sequence ("The Farmer in the Dell," for example). Remembering a sequence is an essential prereading skill—one that children can learn naturally through music.

CHILDREN'S MUSIC AND YOU

What happens to children in regard to music depends on *you*. The personal qualities of a child care aide that affect children's music experiences are (1) your feelings about music, (2) your assigned role, and (3) your ability to use music throughout the day in guiding children.

YOUR FEELINGS ABOUT MUSIC

Do you like music? Do you enjoy singing or playing an instrument? Was music part of your childhood? The answers to these questions affect your feelings about music experiences for young children.

You may want to avoid music activities with children if you know little about music or if someone has made fun of your singing in the past. The best way to overcome your embarrassment or shyness about music is to enjoy the children's involvement in music activities. As the children sing and explore sounds, you will forget your shyness and begin to enjoy the experience too.

Start with nursery rhymes, childhood songs, and folksongs that you already know. Change them to include children's names. Use records and cassette tapes to help build your confidence.

YOUR ASSIGNED ROLE

What role does a child care aide play in making music meaningful to young children? Your basic responsibility in any part of a child care program is to assist your supervisor or teacher, who will be responsible for planning the children's program.

Specifically, your role in assisting with music activities includes the following:

1. Planning with the teacher or supervisor and selecting music to be used with the children as assigned. Before choosing a song or record, listen to it. There are many versions of favorite songs, especially nursery rhymes. Pick one that has a good beat and is not too fast. If singing is on the record, be sure that it is clear and pleasant to hear.

2. Enjoying music *with* the children. You are not performing for children, but helping them to enjoy and learn from their music experiences.

3. Strengthening what the teacher has taught. During music time, you will find many ways to strengthen what children have learned. They can sing a new song during outdoor play or free play. Or you can repeat what they have learned during group time while the children are waiting to use the bathroom.

4. Knowing what equipment and materials provide meaningful music experiences for the children and knowing how to prepare and use them effectively.

Even though you will be carrying out plans that are, for the most part, made by someone else, you should have a good collection of music activities to use on short notice in response to children's requests. Use music to guide their behavior during transition times. You will have to plan ahead so that you will be prepared for these times. You can begin by starting a collection of finger plays, musical games, songs, poems, and even props.

USING MUSIC THROUGHOUT THE DAY

Children enjoy music both at music time and throughout the day. When they are relaxed and happy, they use and are interested in the sounds of music all day long. You will find children humming as they paint, singing as they pump themselves on the swings, and discovering sounds as they clap blocks together or listen to the wind in the trees.

Calling Attention to Musical Sounds. You can help children become more aware of sounds by calling attention to sounds and talking about and imitating them. A sensitive, alert child care aide will discover many musical experiences in daily activities—such as listening to bird songs on a nature walk, counting the times that a

Figure 18-2. The caregiver should encourage children to discover the different sounds that can be made with musical instruments. (Kenneth Karp)

church bell rings or a clock chimes, or noticing the sound of water as it splashes against a windowpane or drips from a faucet.

Putting Children's Actions into Song. If children are confident and have had a variety of music experiences, they will put their own actions into song, making up the words and the melody as they go along or making up words to go with a tune they already know. Child care aides can encourage this kind of music activity by starting the humming or singing with children who do not usually do it themselves. If you are not sure of how to do this, start by using tunes that the children know. Put their actions into words and the words into song. For example, "Five Little Speckled Frogs" can be used with five children on a "log," which may be a bouncing board, a step, or the balance beam. This experience often captures the children's interest and lengthens their attention span while they play. Other children will see the enjoyment and wish to become involved. Work time, playtime, outdoors, indoors, field trips, birthdays, and holidays are all occasions when you can express children's actions and feelings with music.

Making a Music Table or a Music Box Available. Exploring sounds takes time. It is often something that children need to experience as individuals rather than as part of a group. Caregivers need to make music experiences available by providing instruments and items for children to manipulate, shake, pound, and listen to. Individual music activities allow children to start and continue their exploration of sound for as long as they are interested.

How do you organize a music center or a music table? Begin by putting out a few items—not too many. Put items that make the same kind of sound together. For example, put out objects and instruments for beating: drums, cans with metal and plastic lids, and boxes with cardboard lids. Let the children discover the different sounds that can be made with these items. Encourage them to talk about how the sound is affected by the materials that the items are made of, by how they beat them (using one finger, the palm of the hand, the fist; beating quickly or slowly, softly or loudly).

Using Music during Transition Times. You learned earlier that music can be used to make transition periods go more smoothly. Children enjoy it and it also provides guidance. What are some specific ways to use music in transition times?

Music may be used when children have to wait for something (to use the bathroom or to be picked up at the end of the day), during finger plays, while children are singing or listening to a musical story, or when using musical instruments. Children often become anxious during transition periods; music can help them to relax.

Using Music to Guide Behavior. Music has many uses as a tool for guiding children's behavior. You can probably think of different ways to use music as a guidance technique. For example, you know that soft music or a lullaby helps children to quiet down and get ready for rest or nap time, or for a quiet activity.

Here are some other ways to use music to guide behavior:

1. *Changing pace*. When children are restless during an activity that requires listening (group time, for example), a song may allow them to "get the wiggles out." Jumping, wiggling, or hopping to music will help them to get ready for the quiet activity.

2. *Transition*. Music can be used to signal the beginning of an activity such as clean-up or nap time.

3. *Releasing tensions*. When children express negative or aggressive feelings through music, they are learning to cope with those feelings. Once they are expressed, children feel better and more relaxed. Music, therefore, allows children to explore feelings by playing them out or by using their bodies and their voices to act out disturbing thoughts and feelings.

4. *Increasing self-esteem*. Music encourages successful involvement, which builds self-esteem and self-confidence. Children who are sure of themselves respond to guidance more easily than those who doubt their value and abilities.

5. *Following directions*. Helping children learn to follow directions is an important part of guidance and discipline. The first step in following directions is to listen to what you are being told to do. Music is a listening art. Make it fun for the children to listen to music and to do what it says.

PLANNING AND CARRYING OUT MUSIC ACTIVITIES

There are several different types of music experiences for young children—singing, listening, body movement, and using rhythm instruments. These may be used together or by themselves.

SINGING ACTIVITIES

Your responsibility for singing activities may include choosing familiar songs, adding and teaching new ones, and supervising singing at group time.

Choosing Songs. As a child care aide, you may select songs for children to learn and sing. When choosing songs, consider the following guidelines:

1. Songs for preschoolers should be short—two lines is a good length for beginners. Short songs are learned quickly and are easy to remember, especially when they are about familiar things.

2. Songs should be about subjects that interest children—family, animals, nursery rhymes, ways to travel, weather, and so forth.

3. The words or phrases of songs and their melodies should be short, clear, and often repeated. Children should get the feeling that they know what comes next after they have sung the song a few times.

4. The rhythm, or *beat*, of songs should be catchy but simple, and not too fast or slow. It helps if the rhythm of the song is related to its subject (an Indian song with a drumbeat, for example).

5. The range of notes should be *between middle and upper C*, and the range between notes should not be too wide. Children do not sing very high or low, and songs should allow them to sing in a comfortable range.

6. Try for a balance between songs that the children know and new ones. Make songs up by substituting names and activities for the words in familiar songs.

Adding New Songs. While children do enjoy familiar songs, they can become bored with them if the same ones are used over and over again. Many teachers try to add a new song regularly—perhaps one each week.

Make a practice of collecting new songs to use with your children. Songs come from many sources: records, songbooks, caregivers, and children's favorite television shows.

Teaching a New Song. When you are trying to teach children a new song, begin by singing it all the way through. When you have sung the song once, encourage children to join in, but stop if they get restless. When you teach children a song phrase by phrase, they will probably get bored and lose interest. Watch the children's responses to determine how much to teach them at one time. During singing activities, it is a good idea to sing some familiar, well-liked songs along with those they are still learning.

Parents often enjoy hearing their children sing, and special programs are sometimes scheduled for this purpose. However, a program should not be the only reason why new songs are introduced, nor should practicing for special programs be the main goal for singing activities.

Supervising Singing Time. When you are supervising singing time, be sure that children are comfortable and can see you. Background noise should not distract the children. A musical instrument may be used, but children are able to hear the words and the melody better when you sing without one. Do not drag out the song or race through it. Do not distract children by using hand motions to lead their singing unless you are comfortable in doing so. Keep your attention on the children and respond to them.

Encouraging Children to Sing Alone. When children are self-confident and know songs, they will want to sing for the group. This is an opportunity to help children build self-esteem.

Take advantage of it by making children feel that their efforts are enjoyed. Welcome children's offers and remind the group to listen while others sing. You can provide support by putting an arm around the child's waist, having the child stand close to you, or encouraging the child's efforts with a smile.

LISTENING ACTIVITIES

Listening to music takes several forms: comparing sounds, following directions in songs, and listening to mood music, musical stories, singing, or musical instruments. Each activity has a place in a program for young children.

Children listen when what they hear is interesting or pleasurable to them. Though good music is available, children cannot be forced to listen. They may be made to be quiet, especially if they fear the consequences of misbehavior. But the child caregiver who sets the stage for effective listening does so by giving the children something they want to hear.

THE MUSIC LISTENING CENTER

Everyday materials that make different sounds (such as beans in a jar, pebbles in a pie plate, tapping with sticks against various surfaces) help children become involved in the music of sound. This activity calls for close supervision at first. As with other first experiences, young children need to handle objects and listen to changes in sounds before they can listen closely.

When children come to a *music listening center* (place where sound can be explored) on their own, they are likely to be interested in hearing likenesses and differences that they create. Rhythm-band instruments, a xylophone, or an autoharp may be placed in the listening center at different times. Children may make up their own songs as they explore sounds. The experience may develop into one of listening first and singing second.

USING MUSICAL INSTRUMENTS

Letting them hear an instrument played by a teacher or a visitor is a good way to help children enjoy listening. When children can get close to the instrument, to touch it and perhaps even create music, they gain first-hand experience. If children are shy or frightened by the volume or the sound of the instrument, help them get used to it from a distance. Then provide support and encouragement when they show interest.

Piano. By using a piano, you can offer more kinds of music activities. Children enjoy listening to the piano as long as they are able to identify with and respond to the music played. For example, they can identify with "The big truck that slowly pulls up a hill" if you use the piano to play heavy, loud, slow chords. If you are playing for the children, do not play complicated pieces.

Have the children sit where you can see them as you play (to the side of the piano is better than behind your back). You should be able to see their faces as you play so that you can tell whether they are interested or whether they are restless and bored.

When teaching a new song, do not use the piano until the children know the song. Play only single notes of the *melody* (tune), and respect the timing of the music.

You also can use the piano to give children signals. By playing a few chords on the piano, you can get children's attention. For example, one series of notes can mean that it is time to clean up, while another can tell children that you have something to say to them and want their attention. Once children learn to associate a certain message with a specific signal, they will respond in a positive way.

Autoharp. The autoharp is shaped like a small harp (about 2½ feet long). It has a chord (a bar that presses down strings to produce different chords) and strings that are played with a pick or with the player's thumb. You can place an autoharp flat on your lap when you play it, or you can stand it on end on your lap.

The autoharp has several advantages. It can be played by caregivers and children without fear of its being harmed. It can be kept in tune by checking the pitch with a piano, pitch pipe, or tuning record. And it is not difficult to play. To be effective in using an autoharp with children, you must practice playing it until you can do so without having to think about it.

Figure 18-3. Children enjoy listening to and singing with the piano or organ. Have them sit to one side or around you so you can see if they are interested and responding as you play. (Jane Hamilton-Merritt)

Guitars, Banjos, and Ukeleles. Other *stringed instruments* that use chords are the guitar, the banjo, and the ukelele. The banjo and the ukelele are inexpensive and can be learned in a short time. Guitar music is good for folksongs because its soft sound does not drown out children's small voices.

If you plan to use a stringed instrument such as an autoharp or a banjo during singing activities, it is a good idea to keep a file of songs and the key in which you should play them to accompany the children's singing.

Listening to Tapes and Records. There are many opportunities for using records and tapes during music activities. *Activity songs* tell children what to do and give them the chance to follow directions while using their bodies. Mood music encourages rhythm and body movement without verbal directions. Both these activities will be explained in detail later in the chapter.

Musical story records provide other listening opportunities. Mother Goose stories and other tales that are put to music give children a great deal of enjoyment. They are helpful during transition times because they encourage quiet involvement. If your child care center has headsets so that more than one child can listen to a record without disturbing other children, you are fortunate.

Like piano music, records and tapes can be used to gain children's attention and give them a signal or a message.

Selecting Tapes and Records. Before you use a record or tape with the children, listen to it yourself. The description on the package or album cover will not tell you enough. You must hear what it sounds like in order to decide whether the song, story, or music fits your group. Although there are many records and tapes with children's songs, Mother Goose story-songs, musical finger plays or marches, not all of them will match the needs of the children with whom you are working. You must evaluate them, keeping in mind the kinds of songs and music that your children enjoy most. Spoken records should be pleasant to hear and easy to understand. Directions for activity songs or musical games should be short, simple, and clear. The comments made on the record or tape should be directed to preschool children.

After you have listened to a record or tape, you may decide that you want to use some of the music but not all of it. Or you may select certain songs or pieces of music for particular activities. Mark down the ones you want to use and the activity for which you will use them. If it is a record album, note on which side and band the selection is. If it is a tape or cassette, use the numerical gauge on the tape or cassette player to find out where the selection you want is located. Mark down the number where it begins so that you can find it easily when you are ready to use it with the children.

Listening to Singing. When children are confident enough to sing in front of the group, they should be allowed and encouraged to do so.

Other children should be taught to show appreciation and respect by listening quietly. Another experience that delights children is listening to their own singing after it has been recorded on a tape or cassette player.

MUSIC ACTIVITIES AND MOVEMENT

Activity and music go together. Children naturally move when the music starts, especially if it has a catchy tune or a lively beat. The forms of this music activity range from activity songs, finger plays, and musical games to rhythm and creative movement.

Activity Songs. *Activity songs* direct the children to make certain movements as they listen to the music. Children sing these songs or follow directions given on record or tape. Activity songs often contain a story or theme that is repeated. Records that give too many instructions before the song begins will bore children and should be used as resource material for child caregivers rather than activity records for the children.

Musical Finger Plays. Music will get children's small muscles moving. The fingers can dance, keep time to music, and dramatize a poem, story, or finger play. In *finger plays*, the fingers are used to show an idea, story, poem, or song. Finger plays are often done as a part of singing or music activities, but they can be used without music.

Children are manipulators of objects, including their fingers. If you watch a little child try to put one finger up at a time while singing "John Brown had a little Indian—one little Indian, two little Indians," and so on, you will see a child concentrating on which finger and when to put it up. The activity is a manipulative one, truly sensorimotor in nature.

What is easy for an adult is not so easy for a young child. For example, "Where Is Thumbkin" is a favorite finger play that needs to be simplified for young children. A customary part of this finger play is identifying each finger as it is mentioned in the song. It is difficult for little children to grasp three fingers with a thumb so that the ring finger sticks up.

Start with simple finger plays. "Open, Shut

Figure 18-4. Children like to do finger plays to and act out songs. This kind of activity stimulates their imagination. (Kenneth Karp)

Them'' is a good one because the children put all their fingers up at once and shut them together. They listen and respond to "Give a Little Clap." "Put Your Finger in the Air" is another favorite of very young children. Children do not have to practice managing their fingers to follow this song. Parts of the body are emphasized, and this gives each child a feeling of self-esteem. In contrast, "Itsy-Bitsy Spider" uses more difficult finger motions unless you simplify them for the children.

Finger plays are good tools to use for transition from one activity to another. They may be used when children are waiting—to go home, or at bathroom break, or when assembling for group time. The children will have their favorites, and they like to repeat familiar ones. Teach them new finger plays from time to time, so that their list of favorites grows.

Musical Games. Children enjoy simple *musical games* ("London Bridge," for example) that involve everyone in the action. "Ring around the Rosie" and "Here We Go 'round the Mulberry Bush" are other games that children like. In choosing musical games for preschoolers, it is important to use only a few simple rules. And there are no winners or losers in musical games.

Sometimes, activity songs and musical games will be combined; "Five Little Chickadees" and "Hokey Pokey" are two examples.

If there are many children and more than one caregiver is working with them it may be a good idea to divide the children into smaller groups for musical games. The children's attention span is usually not long enough to allow you to go around a large circle so that each child will get a turn.

Teaching Musical Games. To teach a musical game, start with a small group. Walk through the movements and the sequence of the game before the music starts. Use a child or children to show how it's done and what happens next. For example, if the children have partners, you will want to use two children and show how they are to hold hands, to stand together, or to move in a certain direction. If you have taught a small group in an informal setting such as outdoors or during free-choice time, these children can serve as models for other children. Just tell the children to "Watch Lorraine, Eleanor, Ken, and Christopher," for example.

251

Don't try to teach too many concepts as part of a musical game. For instance, don't try to teach *right* and *left, sliding,* and *hands over the head* all at the same time. Tell the children to watch those who are the leaders on that day. Then use yourself as a model, or let the children who have learned the game set the example. If you are not participating, you have a better chance to see which children need help; you can then provide it when it is needed. Match your choice of games with the children's development, abilities, and interests. Children get frustrated if a game is too difficult. Remember that successful experiences build self-esteem.

Rhythm and Creative Movement. After children have learned to respond to directions as part of songs, they are ready to respond to music without directions. Let the music guide their movements while you encourage them to use their bodies in dancing, telling a story, expressing a feeling, or playing a role. Scarves, streamers, and other props help them to become involved. You may have to make suggestions and ask questions to get things started. ("See whether you can hop like a bunny." "How does a bear walk?")

Mood music without words also gives direction. The beat and tempo of the music itself carry a message for children. They get better at responding to "what the music tells you" if they are encouraged to listen to it and move as they feel. Verbal directions from you or a narrator on the record are not necessary.

RHYTHM INSTRUMENTS

Rhythm instruments are used to help children explore sound. Drums, bells, tambourines, and maracas are all considered rhythm instruments. They can be used by individual children or by groups.

When children are first introduced to rhythm instruments, they want to explore them and the kinds of sounds they make. When children are ready to use the instruments as a group, provide only one or two kinds of instruments at first. Have the children play the instruments as they sing or listen to a song.

Unless rhythm instruments are made available regularly, children may become overex-cited with this type of activity. By following these few basic rules, the caregiver can keep order and ensure a positive experience for the children:

1. The children wait their turns to receive an instrument.
2. Children keep their instruments quiet until everyone in the group has received one.
3. Children find their own ways to play each instrument as they handle them with care. Good examples of careful use by caregivers teaches respect for the instruments. In this way, destructiveness tends to be eliminated.
4. Children who do not wish to play an instrument are invited but not forced to do so.
5. Instruments are put away carefully in their assigned places after the activity.
6. Positive guidance techniques are used to handle problem behavior.

When children are playing instruments as a group, you must make them aware that the music has a beat. Many children are easily able to match their playing with the rhythm of the music. If a child does not seem to be aware of the beat or is having trouble keeping time to it, help the child by marching or standing alongside and clapping your hands to the music. Do not do this in an obvious way that may embarrass the child; instead, be casual about it.

Do not make the use of rhythm instruments a formal lesson. Children may march in different directions at first, making their own music and enjoying it on an individual basis. When they are ready to march as a group, set the stage by giving them specific directions about where and when to march. You may have to act as the leader until the children get the idea of marching as a group. Make the path for marching clear and go only in one direction. March around the table, behind the chair, and between the bookcases, for example.

There are many rhythm instruments that children can use either individually or in groups—triangles, wooden blocks, wooden sticks. Some instruments suggest songs by the sounds they make. But do not limit children to certain instruments for certain songs. Let them play the instruments freely, listening and learning.

Table 18-1 HOMEMADE RHYTHM INSTRUMENTS

Instrument	Materials	Method
1. Tambourine	Pie plates Flattened bottletops Spool of thin wire Paint	Paint designs on pie plates, flatten bottletops, attach to plates after stringing wire through tops.
2. Maracas	Ice-cream cartons Pebbles Paint	Decorate cartons. Fill with pebbles. Tape closed.
3. Tennis-ball maracas	Tennis ball Pebbles Smooth stick	Cut small hole in ball. Insert pebbles. Place stick in hole for handle.
4. Drum	Oatmeal box Paint String	Decorate box. Tie string around it to hang from child's neck.
5. Drum	Large no. 10 can Old inner tube Heavy cord	Cut out ends, stretch inner tube over ends, lace with firm cord.
6. Drumsticks	Broom handles or wooden spoons	Sand smooth and paint.
7. Bells	Elastic Jingle bells	Attach bells to a ring of elastic.
8. Bells	Paper cups Bells Scotch tape	Place bell inside cups. Fasten two cups together with scotch tape.
9. Horns	Paper roll Construction paper Wax paper Rubber band or paste	Cover paper roll with construction paper. Cover one end with wax paper and hold in place with glue. Punch three or four holes down the middle. Blow on open end.
10. Triangle	Large nails of different sizes String	Tie nails with string. Leave some space between nails.
11. Sand blocks	Two wooden blocks Sandpaper	Glue sandpaper to one side of each of the blocks.

Drums are especially useful rhythm instruments. Children enjoy listening to them, and they respond easily to the beat of a drum. Caregivers can use a drum to introduce children to other musical instruments and to accompany many music activities.

Improvising Rhythm Instruments. Rhythm instruments can be purchased, or they can be made from everyday materials. Instruments that caregivers make may be sturdier and more interesting to children than those bought in a store. Table 18-1 gives some ideas for making your own rhythm instruments from inexpensive materials. Remember that you are not limited to these suggestions—the best part of improvising equipment is that you can use your imagination.

EVALUATION

How do you feel about using music with young children? Are you comfortable singing to them and with them? Playing for them? Are you learning new songs? Are you learning to play new instruments? Are you listening carefully to children's singing and playing? Listen to records and tapes with the attitude "I can use that with the children" or "I think the children would enjoy that song."

Unlike adults, children are not self-conscious. They enjoy involving themselves in doing something rather than in the product that may result. They are not disturbed if they hit a wrong note or if their singing or playing does not sound attractive.

As an adult, you are much more aware of the results of your efforts, and you are likely to feel embarrassed or silly if other adults listen to your performance and make fun of it. As a caregiver who is trying to provide good musical experiences for the children in your group, you must forget about other adults and concentrate on the children's enjoyment. You will find that it is much easier to become involved and to enjoy music activities if you follow this advice.

CHAPTER SUMMARY

1. There are many reasons for including music in a child care program. Music gives children pleasure, helps them to learn, allows them to express their feelings, and even guides their behavior.

2. The personal qualities of a child care aide that affect children's music experiences are (1) your feelings about music, (2) your assigned role, and (3) your ability to use music throughout the day in guiding children.

3. Music can be part of the total program if it is used during transition times, caregivers call attention to sounds, and caregivers verbalize children's actions in songs. A music activity center should be available so that children can explore music and sounds freely.

4. Your assignment as a child care aide in carrying out music activities will depend on the planning of the supervisor or teacher.

5. There are four different types of music experiences available for young children—singing, listening, music activity and movement, and using rhythm instruments. These may be used together or by themselves.

6. Singing should be an enjoyable experience for children, not a formal lesson. Songs that are used with children should be carefully selected and taught a little at a time as the children hear you or someone else sing them. Music and activity are brought together in activity songs, finger plays, music games, and rhythm and creative movement.

7. Children have music experiences when they explore musical instruments and sounds on an individual basis, when they listen to a musical instrument (such as the piano, guitar, or autoharp), and when they listen to music or songs on records and tapes. Caregivers should listen to records and tapes before using them with children.

8. Rhythm instruments help children to explore sound. Caregivers can help children learn to use and enjoy these instruments on a group or an individual basis.

9. When evaluating your music experiences with children, concentrate on the children's enjoyment. Do not focus on your own insecurity or feelings of embarrassment.

• WHAT HAVE YOU LEARNED FROM THIS CHAPTER?

Several new words and ideas were presented in this chapter. To see whether you understand them, match the letter of each term below with the numbered phrases under "Definitions."

Terms

a. Activity songs
b. Music listening center
c. Finger play
d. Rhythm instruments

e. Beat
f. String instruments
g. Melody
h. Musical games
i. Between middle and upper C
j. Verbal
k. Nonverbal

Definitions

1. Tune
2. Using fingers to tell a story, describe a sound or an action, etc.
3. Guitar, ukelele, banjo
4. Songs that tell children what to do
5. Location where items enabling children to explore sound are placed
6. Tambourines, bells, and drums
7. Without words
8. "London Bridge" and "Ring around the Rosie"
9. Rhythm
10. With words
11. Singing range of young children

• PROJECTS, DECISIONS, ISSUES

1. State three personal qualities of a child care aide that affect children's musical experiences.
2. List four values of music in children's lives.
3. Describe four different types of musical experiences for young children.
4. List five points to be considered when choosing songs for preschoolers.
5. List five homemade rhythm instruments for children.
6. Name four instruments that can be used to accompany children's singing.

• WHIFS (WHAT WOULD YOU DO IF . . .)

1. Dorothy covers her ears and sits bent over when the children sing in a group. What would you do?
   a. Force her to sing
   b. Take her outdoors to play with something she likes
   c. Ignore her

   d. Go sit beside her
   e. Tell the children, "Dorothy isn't happy"
   f. Report her behavior to your supervisor
   g. Other responses

2. Steven is using the wooden mallet from the pounding bench to beat the drum. What would you do?
   a. Snatch the mallet away from him
   b. Take the drum away
   c. Tell him he can't play if he doesn't stop
   d. Explain that the mallet can damage the drum
   e. Call to him across the room
   f. Other responses

3. The children are not listening to your directions regarding use of the rhythm instruments. They are seeing what sounds they can make without waiting to start with the music. What would you do?
   a. Stop talking
   b. Start the music and follow the children's lead
   c. Take the instruments away and tell the children "If you can't play them as I tell you, you are not allowed to play them at all"
   d. Shout "Be quiet!"
   e. Begin playing a rhythm instrument yourself
   f. Other responses

4. The children are playing "Pop goes the Weasel." David and Barbara are not "popping." What would you do?
   a. Watch them but say nothing
   b. Send them away from the group
   c. Tell them to do what the song says
   d. Change locations and go stand between them in the circle
   e. Other responses

5. You are teaching the finger play "Where Is Thumbkin?" Three-year-old Jimmy is using his pointer finger for each family member mentioned in the finger play. What would you do?
   a. Tell him he's using the wrong finger
   b. Watch but make no comment
   c. Show him each time which finger to use
   d. Simplify the finger play
   e. Change finger plays

19 | ASSISTING WITH SCIENCE EXPERIENCES

After you have studied Chapter 19, you should be able to:

1. State four goals of science experiences for young children
2. List three ways science experiences help young children
3. Demonstrate five ways to provide meaningful science experiences for young children
4. Define and identify parts of the scientific process as related to young children's experiences

Very young infants seem programmed to "find out." Watch them examine their fingers, follow light with their eyes, and respond to loud sounds. Infants who have stimulating experiences become more aware as they grow. They become more aware of the person who feeds them. They know the touch, smell, and sound of this person.

In science, awareness and curiosity come first. When children do not have opportunities to touch, smell, hear, see, or taste, they lose whatever awareness or curiosity they might have had as infants. As a child care aide, you can help children become more aware and curious about their surroundings.

GOALS OF SCIENCE EXPERIENCES FOR YOUNG CHILDREN

The goals of science experiences for young children include helping them to:

1. Become more aware of themselves and their environment and to develop a curiosity, sense of wonder, and appreciation of the world around them
2. Seek first-hand experiences that encourage self-discovery and a scientific attitude
3. Develop skills that will help them find answers to the questions raised by their curiosity
4. Evaluate the information they collect in bits and pieces and put it together to form concepts

There are many opportunities for personal discovery—the basis of the scientific process—in a well-run child care center. As children discover one scientific concept, they become stimulated to find more. Science experiences help young children to:

Figure 19-1. The caregiver should try to make science experiences meaningful to children. They like to become involved by seeing and touching. A science activity such as gardening may encourage the child to develop an inquiring attitude. (Jane Hamilton-Merritt)

· *Promote a positive self-image.* Linked with personal discovery and involvement is an increased feeling of self-esteem. As children become familiar with their world through discovery, they gain self-confidence and a positive self-image.

· *Develop problem-solving abilities.* The need to solve problems appears daily for children as well as adults. Coping skills depend on the ability to solve the problems one faces in life. The scientific process of observing, classifying, and drawing conclusions is an effective tool in solving problems.

· *Increase vocabulary.* Words increase communication. With your help, children learn many new words as they actively explore their world. The words may label objects they use or describe actions they observe. When children discover things together, they talk together. This gives them the chance to use the words they are learning in the process of discovery.

· *Foster an inquiring attitude.* Children with an *inquiring attitude* are curious—they look, wonder, and experiment. They want to find answers. The more they see, the more they want to see. The more they classify, the easier it becomes for them to group things together.

· *Build concepts and encourage intellectual growth.* As children are helped to put the bits and pieces of their discoveries together, they form concepts. As they inquire and experiment with new ideas and discoveries, concept is added to concept, and these are linked together to form an overall view of a topic.

MAKING SCIENCE EXPERIENCES MEANINGFUL TO CHILDREN

Science experiences become more meaningful to children when (1) sensory experiences are provided, (2) child caregivers improve their knowledge of science, (3) questions stimulate discovery, and (4) opportunities for science experiences are recognized throughout the day.

BUILDING AWARENESS BY PROVIDING SENSORY EXPERIENCES

Science experiences begin with curiosity. Children must be aware of their environment before they become curious about it.

How do children become aware of their world? They build awareness by using their senses. They gain information by seeing, touching, tasting, smelling, and hearing. Therefore caregivers should provide intense and varied sensory experiences for them. Cooking, water play, gardening, caring for pets, listening, walks, and carrying things are experiences that involve the senses. (See Table 19-1).

Experiences that use more than one sense at a time strengthen the child's awareness of the experience. Cooking is a good example. It includes taste, touch, sight, smell, and maybe hearing—especially if what is cooking is popcorn! Have the children identify or match smells, sounds, or textures.

Occasionally, use only one sense at a time. For example, put an apple or some other fruit or object in a "feelie bag," a bag containing objects that may be felt without being seen. Have a child identify the object inside by the sense of touch only. This experience helps children become more responsive to the sense of touch.

Table 19-1 INVESTIGATIVE SKILLS

Process	Materials suggested	Activities
Observing: seeing	Colors (paints, crayons, food coloring), living plants, seeds, leaves, rocks, minerals, pieces of wood (sawdust from the wood), small animals, fish.	Opportunities to examine objects visually; look for general and specific properties, changes in appearance.
Observing: smelling	Perfumes, fresh-cut flowers, plants, common household products with distinctive odors, fresh fruits, fresh vegetables.	Describe smells; use the sense of smell to identify and describe objects.
Observing: touching	Cloth material of varying textures, wood of varying grains, various grades of sandpaper, objects of various temperatures.	Use the sense of touch to increase the quality of observations.
Observing: tasting	Variety of foodstuffs, harmless drinkable liquids.	Taste a variety of edible products to increase the accuracy of observations. Identify characteristics of objects on the basis of taste.
Observing: hearing	Musical instruments, variety of noisemakers, phonograph records (music and sound effects), tape recorder.	Identify voices and commonly heard sounds. Identify degree of loudness, pitch, quality. Increase child's awareness of environmental sounds and how they can be used to make better observations.

Table 19-1 INVESTIGATIVE SKILLS (Continued)

Process	Materials suggested	Activities
Inferring	"Gift box," sealed bags of materials.	Infer what is in the gift box or sealed bag without looking inside.
	Variety of clear liquids.	Infer which liquid is water without smelling or tasting the various liquids.
	Closed container with small living insect inside.	Is the object inside the container alive?
	Sound effects (record or tapes).	Infer whether noise is being made in the city or in the country; describe object making noise from its sound.
	Hot and cold objects.	Infer how objects became hot or cold. Is entire object hot, or only part of it?
Classifying	Bags of buttons, bags containing a variety of materials; sandpaper squares consisting of a variety of grades and painted a variety of colors; tagboard pieces in a variety of shapes, sizes, and colors; bags of rocks; shells.	Have children sort materials according to properties of their own choosing. Encourage children to think about and tell why they sorted objects in the way that they did. Also encourage them to try to find another way to sort their objects.
Communicating	Any and all the materials used in developing the skills of observing, inferring, and classifying can be used to develop this process skill. In addition, small sets of objects with specific properties can be used to help children develop a useful vocabulary for communicating. The sets may include the properties of shiny and dull, hard and soft, rough and smooth, heavy and light, hot and cold, fat and thin, noisy and quiet.	Describe materials and/or recognizable objects; name materials and objects; tell about perceived relationships among materials and objects. Learn descriptive terms.

Source: Adapted from Donald Neuman, "Sciencing for Young Children," in Katherine Read Baker (ed.), *Ideas That Work with Young Children,* National Association for Education of Young Children, 1972.

IMPROVING YOUR KNOWLEDGE OF SCIENCE

What is *your* attitude toward science? Are you afraid of it, thinking that children may ask questions you can't answer? Get busy and learn with the children. Discovery is a big part of science experiences for young children. "I don't know—let's find out" and "I'm not sure—let's look it up" are replies that involve children in finding their own answers. No matter what, don't make statements that are not accurate.

The first step in making science meaningful to children is to make it meaningful to yourself. Children's science questions should be answered accurately. Improve your interest in and knowledge of science concepts in the following ways:

1. Ask resource people—science teachers, veterinarians, doctors, nursery personnel, and librarians. Borrow materials they are willing to share.
2. Read children's encyclopedias, elementary science textbooks, nature magazines, and teachers' reference books.
3. Look more closely—be more observant. You encourage children to take another look—do the same yourself. Describe what you see.
4. Keep learning about everything. Share your learning with the children. If you are interested in many different things, both you and the children will make many more exciting discoveries.
5. Ask questions—the kind that get you and children looking more closely, thinking of reasons, and improving your skill in finding answers.

ASKING THE RIGHT KINDS OF QUESTIONS

There are different kinds of questions. Some can be answered by replying yes or no. For example, "Can you see your shadow now? Yes or no." Some questions must be followed by other questions or comments that arouse curiosity. Use questions that make children look more carefully, think, wonder, or make guesses and comparisons. For example, "When do you see your shadow?" This question requires further observation before it is answered. "What do you think will happen to your shadow if you run under the oak tree?" Now the children make a guess. The question has stimulated their curiosity. "Let's find out," they say.

If a question can be answered as children look at what has happened or is happening, it will be a good question to stimulate discovery. In general, ask questions that describe situations. For example, "Which objects float? Which ones sink?"

Questions that may have several answers are called *divergent,* or open-ended, questions. For example, "What do you think will happen?" Questions having only one answer are called *convergent* questions. For example, "What color is the ball?"

Children who hear good questions learn to use questions to gain information for themselves. At times, ask the children a question that cannot be answered with the information on hand. Encourage them to say they don't know when the information is not available, and to seek further information. Children ought to discover that some questions cannot be answered without further information. Stress finding out rather than guessing.

The following ways will help children learn:

1. *Recognize true and false statements.* Using a picture, make statements about things in the picture and ask the children to agree or disagree.
2. *Recognize available information.* Ask children questions that can be answered by looking at a picture. Then ask occasional questions that cannot be answered in this way and have the children justify their answers. Prepare pictures with missing parts, so that children have to draw conclusions from partial information. For example, two apple cores, a pile of apple peelings, and a paring knife may be shown to the children. From the picture, can they answer such questions as, "How many apples were peeled?" "Who peeled the apples?" "Were they made into applesauce?"
3. *Locate an object by asking questions.* The idea is to help the children ask questions that

will give them information. Encourage the children to ask broad questions at first; then, from these questions, narrow things down bit by bit until they arrive at the answer. This is a classifying game. Match the items to be grouped together or classified with the ability of the children who are to group them together.

Questioning is not an easy skill to learn, and many children take a long time to learn it. As with most things, children gain questioning skill as they experience success. If children are having trouble questioning, make the task easier. Simplify it so that they can succeed in finding answers through questions that are meaningful to them.

THE SCIENTIFIC PROCESS

The *scientific process* is an orderly way of discovering how things are put together or changed. By using the scientific process, children develop skill in finding answers to questions that arise from their curiosity. The process a child uses to find answers is similar to that used by adults. For this reason, it can be said that scientific inquiry is the same for all persons, young and old.

PARTS OF THE SCIENTIFIC PROCESS

Children's ways of finding out start with watching, wondering, and questioning. Their questions have more meaning if you help them use the steps or parts of the scientific process listed below:

1. *Recognize a change or problem or ask a question.* Start with observing and being curious. Young children, as they look at the dry dish on the patio that earlier in the day had water in it, may say "There is no water in this dish." They are using the first step in finding out. They are noticing that something is *different* from before.
2. *Identify the problem.* "What happened to the water?" Restate the question in the form of a problem. The problem is to find out about the disappearing water. "What do you

think happened to the water? What will happen if we put more water in the dish?"
3. *State a hypothesis.* A *hypothesis* is a tentative explanation, or an educated guess, that provides a basis for further investigation. To continue with the example mentioned above, "If we put more water in the dish, it will disappear too." This is your hypothesis or tentative explanation.
4. *Conduct an experiment.* "Let's do it and see what happens. We'll put more water in the dish and look at it before we go home. What time is it now? It's 3 o'clock. Let's write that down so we don't forget. We'll look at the dish at 5 o'clock when your mother comes to get you."
5. *Describe what happens.* "The water dried up and disappeared," or *evaporated*—a new word for a child's vocabulary.
6. *Keep a record of what is done.* "Let's write it down." It is your job to help the children observe, to make predictions, and to keep a record of what happens.
7. *Draw conclusions.* Arrive at an opinion by reasoning from the evidence. After you have made an experiment to test your hypothesis and observed what happened, draw some conclusions about the experiment. *Classify*, or group, objects or bits of information that are alike together as you form your conclusion. "When the sun shines on water, the water evaporates."
8. *Repeat the experiment* (either in the same way or in a similar way). After several experiments, the children see that water evaporates faster when the sun shines. When water is put in the dish later in the day, it does not evaporate as fast (observation). "Why?" (state the problem). "Can you guess the reason?" (hypothesis). "Let's compare the time it takes the water to evaporate when we put it in the dish in the afternoon and the time it takes the water to evaporate when we put it in the dish in the morning" (experiment). "We'll keep a record and compare how long it takes (describe and record). "What happened?" (draw conclusions). "What will happen if we do it again?" (try it again).

THE IMPORTANCE OF PERSONAL DISCOVERIES

Young children can be and usually are active investigators if they are encouraged to explore. By using the scientific process, they become discoverers in a personal, active, but *orderly* way. When children learn facts from a child caregiver, they usually take the information for granted without becoming actively involved.

Children can learn by looking at a product and having someone explain what happened. But the experience is much more rewarding if they are actively involved when the process is taking place. For example, children can see the product of evaporation—an empty dish—and an adult can explain what happened to the water. However, by involving them in experiments with the process, you are enriching their experience because they learn what happened first-hand.

Children cannot learn everything by themselves. Sometimes they must depend on others to tell them what they want to know. But remember, wherever and whenever possible, it is better for children to discover things for themselves and to participate in a process that results in information gained and understood.

PROVIDING SCIENCE EXPERIENCES FOR YOUNG CHILDREN

As a child care aide, you will provide science experiences for young children. Your assignment will include (1) using guidelines for science experiences, (2) making science experiences available throughout the day, (3) preparing materials and equipment, and (4) planning and evaluating your participation with your supervising teacher.

GUIDELINES FOR PROVIDING GOOD SCIENCE EXPERIENCES

Ways to enhance science experiences may be summarized as follows:

1. Encourage children to comment on and discuss what they see.

2. Supply accurate information at the children's level of understanding.

3. Take advantage of children's interest and curiosity.

4. Ask open-ended, divergent questions.

5. Develop a collection of information and materials that can help you and the children find answers to questions.

6. Don't give answers too readily; ask questions to stimulate children's thinking and to discover what children have on their minds.

7. Set an example of investigative behavior that shows a sense of excitement.

8. Make enough plans so that children can succeed in their process of discovery.

9. Relate science experiences to other parts of the day and other subject areas.

SCIENCE EXPERIENCES THROUGHOUT THE DAY

Science experiences fall into three major categories: teacher-planned, spontaneous, and child-initiated.

Teacher-Planned Science Experiences. These may be selected and carried out by the teacher, by the aide, or by both together. Examples of planned experiences are collecting materials and presenting activities related to magnets; making arrangements for a pet and its owner to visit the center; inviting a resource person who knows about living things.

Science Discovery Learning Center. A *discovery learning center* is any part of the room that invites children to find out for themselves. It is a place for touching, smelling, hearing, and seeing; it does not have to be limited to any one spot. However, one basic location is usually set aside for the grouping of materials that will stimulate children's discovery.

Here, children pick up shells and feel their smoothness, listen to the "ocean," and talk about shapes and sizes. They compare different kinds of stones and rocks while sorting them into groups that are alike in some way. With magnets, they explore which objects can be

Figure 19-2. A discovery learning center provides a variety of objects and materials for children to touch and feel. (Kenneth Karp)

picked up and which cannot. You can help a child think about this experience by making a simple chart to help summarize what happens.

Planting provides much discovery: what and how often to water and feed, and the effects of sunlight and temperature change. House plants, grass seeds on a sponge, beans planted around the edge of a jar, or gardening provide lessons in growing.

Tasting different kinds of fruits and vegetables and recording one's experience on a graph is truly a discovery. The feel, smell, appearance, and enjoyment are different for each food and each child. Discussion of fruits and vegetables may lead to discovery of other foods to eat, especially if the parents of a child with a different cultural background are willing to share their native foods with the children.

Here are some samples of science discovery learning centers:

Living-Nonliving Center

· Houseplants and seedlings
· Bulb garden, terrarium
· Pine cones, milkweed pods, cattails
· Leaf collection
· Stones—smooth, rough, various shapes, classified in egg cartons; compare sizes and shapes, roughness and smoothness

Mechanical Center

· Magnets: bar, horseshoe, iron filings, various metals, fishing game, nonmetal things
· Turn-a-gear toy

· Mechanical board of gears, locks, light switches
· Keys and locks

Sound Center

· Tuning forks of several sizes; have pan of water available for experimenting
· Glasses of water filled to various heights, with wooden striker
· Wooden sticks with strings stretched to eight lengths between them
· Telephones of cups and strings
· Rhythm instruments: dry gourds, rhythm sticks, jingle bells, tambourines, triangles (Don't settle for only homemade sounds. Try buying well-made and tuneful instruments each year. Your collection will grow and children will profit.)

Other Ideas. While a science discovery center provides direct experiences for children, it may also help them extend their understanding through items that *represent* direct experiences. For example:

· *Models:* Cranes, rockets, cars, human body.
· *Photographs, pictures:* Foods, different seasons of the year, different kinds of shells, trees and animals.
· *Single-concept chart* (several facts about one idea or thing, simply illustrated): Flowers, for example. Flowers grow. Flowers are different colors. Flowers are different shapes.
· *Experience chart:* On a large chart you print what children tell you about their experience of an activity. For example, it may relate to growing, picking, cooking, and eating spinach. The children will enjoy illustrating the experience chart.
· *Individual booklets the children make:* Like an experience chart but in book form.

Visitors to the Child Care Center. Pets and their owners who come to visit provide good learning experiences if the visits are planned. Your supervising teacher will advise you about whether a pet visit will meet local child care standards and whether or not it will be a good choice for the children. Pets that are not used to excitement or that must be viewed from a distance are not good visitors, while those that can be touched and watched at close range are most welcome. A follow-up activity such as reading a story about an animal like the one that visited would be a good idea. Contact an organization in your community that cares for pets, or the local zoo, and see whether they will bring some animals to the center. Arrange a field trip to see the animals in their natural habitat. (Chapter 15 gives other suggestions about visitors and field trips.)

Field Trips. Science understandings may be extended through field trips, especially in the area of nature study. Children enjoy exploring nature and benefit from gaining a respect for it. Teach your children to respect nature in the following ways:[1]

1. By example, teach your children to leave nature neat and clean. Pick up your own litter on field trips.
2. Teach respect for the life of the flower or plant; emphasize that it lives for all to see. If growing things are picked, they will quickly die.
3. Teach respect for wild animals. Since they are wild, we cannot get close to them. Therefore they should be left alone while we admire them from a distance.
4. Teach respect for snakes, insects, and other wild creatures, not fear. The way we approach wild things influences their response to our presence. Creatures that bite or sting when alarmed are best left untouched, but they can be observed and studied from a distance.
5. Teach respect for storms; not fear, but a knowing alertness about thunder, lightning, wind, and cloud formations. A storm can be frightening to a child unless he or she is helped to understand it. A child needs to learn when to find shelter and where to find it when out of doors.

[1]Emelda Kunau and Robert Moorman, *Adventures with Children Through Nature,* Iowa State University of Science and Technology, Cooperative Extension Service, Ames, Iowa, 1969, p. 11.

6. Teach respect for water, not fear of it.

Fear as a method of controlling children's behavior will not give them an understanding of *why* they should respect nature. It would only interfere with their appreciation of their world.

Spontaneous Science Experiences. These are science experiences that are not planned ahead of time. They are very informal, yet delightful for children. A child asks a question, or makes an observation and discovers something special, such as a new anthill. These incidental learnings become more accurate and relate to other concepts as you ask questions or make observations that stimulate children's interest, expand their concepts, and encourage more precise observations.

Child-Initiated Science Experiences. These science experiences start with the interests of the children. They differ from spontaneous ones in that some planning is usually needed. For example, George has a hamster he wants to bring to class. Mary's brother collects shells. Can Mary bring the collection to class and share it with the children? Parents offer to bring different animals to the child care center. These resources are important and should be enjoyed and valued. Plan with your supervising teacher so that the experience can benefit the children to the fullest.

Whether planned ahead of time or spontaneous, science experiences may present themselves to children at various times throughout the day. If you are aware of the situations in which such experiences can arise, you can help children recognize concepts they may overlook or not have words to describe.

PREPARING MATERIALS AND EQUIPMENT

Preparing yourself is a first step in making science experiences more meaningful to children. This should be followed by getting the children's materials and equipment ready for planned science activities. To do this well, you will have to clarify your goals for the planned experience with your supervising teacher. Then, collect the items you will need and see that they are in good working order. Prepare the location

Figure 19-3. Before you involve the children in a science activity, prepare all the materials and equipment necessary. (Bart Fleet)

where the experience is going to take place. If the experience is going to be messy, protect the area with some type of covering, such as plastic or newspapers.

PLANNING AND EVALUATING WITH YOUR SUPERVISING TEACHER

There are some science activities that your supervising teacher or the licensing standards of your community may not let you plan for the children. For example, you may not be able to have pets in the center; or you may not be able to take the children on certain field trips. As with all other parts of the program, the supervising teacher decides which science activities to include in the program and which ones to assign to you. Carry out your assignment as well as you can. Be aware of the many ways that you can extend the effectiveness of your supervising teacher to make science experiences—both planned and spontaneous—more meaningful for children throughout the day.

Science experiences are not complete until they have been evaluated. Each day, think back on the science experiences. Did you see something that was new to you? Did the children find something that they had not seen before? Were you asked a question that you could not answer? Where can you find the answers? Did you promise to bring something to class tomorrow? What awareness did you have of the children's interests? Discuss these questions and the science experiences related to them with your supervising teacher. Follow up your good intentions, and listen to the advice of your supervising teacher.

You have information to get; objects to collect and bring to class; resource persons and reference books to consult. Effective child caregivers do not stop with good intentions; they carry them out.

CHAPTER SUMMARY

1. Science experiences for young children have four objectives: *(a)* developing awareness, curiosity, a sense of wonder, and appreciation for themselves and their world; *(b)* en-couraging a scientific attitude; *(c)* developing the skills needed to find answers; and *(d)* evaluating information collected.

2. Awareness and curiosity are stimulated by repeating familiar sensory experiences and introducing new ones. A result of this awareness and curiosity is questions. Children who hear good questions learn to ask questions which will help them get information for themselves.

3. The first step in making science meaningful to young children is to have it become meaningful to the caregiver. Children's science questions should be answered accurately. Caregivers should constantly try to improve their knowledge of science concepts.

4. The objectives of science for young children are to become more aware, more curious, more precise, and more accurate in the process of finding things out and using these findings in various and appropriate ways.

5. The scientific process is part of a young child's experiences. The processes of scientific inquiry are the same for a young child as for an adult.

6. Science experiences are available throughout the day in a child care center. These experiences fall into three categories: teacher-planned science experiences, spontaneous science experiences, and child-initiated science experiences that require some advanced planning.

7. No matter what type of science experience takes place, careful evaluation of the event is necessary to complete the activity.

• WHAT NEW TERMS HAVE YOU LEARNED?

Several new words and ideas were presented in this chapter. To see whether you understand them, match the letter of each term below with the numbered phrases under "Definitions."

Terms

a. Single-concept chart
b. Science discovery learning center
c. Divergent question

d. Interpret
e. Experience chart
f. Convergent question
g. Hypothesis
h. Child-initiated science experiences
i. Draw conclusions

Definitions

1. Has only one correct answer
2. Location in room that invites children to find out for themselves
3. Is open-ended
4. Chart telling of children's experiences
5. To explain the meaning of findings
6. To summarize what happened
7. Chart giving facts about one concept
8. Planned science experiences stimulated by children
9. Possible explanation

• STUDENT ACTIVITIES

1. Do you agree or disagree with the following statements?
   a. The natural curiosity and awareness in children can never be turned off.
   b. Young children are active investigators if they are encouraged to explore.
   c. If science is not a meaningful part of a child care aide's life, chances are that the children will not have someone to stimulate their excitement at discovery.

d. Questions beginning with "can," "is," or "will" require either yes or no answers.
e. Questions that may be answered several ways are called divergent questions.

2. List the five senses and match a science activity with each.
3. List four objectives to be considered for presenting science experiences to children in a child care center.
4. Describe the difference between a planned science experience and a spontaneous science experience. Give an example of each.
5. The skills of observing, classifying, inferring, and drawing conclusions are parts of the
   a. Problem-solving ability
   b. Scientific process
   c. Coping skills
   d. None of the above

6. The list below is made up of spontaneous and planned science experiences. Identify each as either planned or spontaneous.
   a. A child finds a bug in the yard.
   b. A red hen is brought into the center by a parent.
   c. A teacher provides magnifying glasses to look at rocks.
   d. Johnny discovers his shadow.
   e. Mary discovers that she can lift a hollow block by pushing one end of the board up.

20 | ASSISTING WITH MATHEMATICS EXPERIENCES

After you have studied Chapter 20, you should be able to:

1. Name three meaningful mathematics experiences for young children and tell how they relate to later math experiences
2. List at least five terms you should know regarding mathematics for young children
3. Identify at least five opportunities available in the daily schedule that can be used for math experiences
4. Describe and demonstrate the main steps in providing planned mathematics experiences

EARLY MATHEMATICS EXPERIENCES

Sammy tells you that Bart and Nancy are not here today. Sally pours water from a small cup into a large bottle. Lewis helps set the table and puts one napkin in front of each chair at the table. Each of these actions can be seen as an example of a mathematics concept that children use often.

MEANINGFUL MATHEMATICS EXPERIENCES

The beginning of mathematical learning grows out of the young child's daily experiences. It is your responsibility to recognize the math concepts that children encounter—not only the vocabulary of these concepts but also the ideas and principles that they represent. Your goal for each child is to provide experiences involving meaningful concepts that the child understands. Direct experiences such as noting that two unit blocks match one double block build accurate concepts. Indirect experiences such as pencil-and-paper activities may not.

Meaningful math experiences help children understand simple math terms. They come to see that math is used every day as they discover space, number, and measurement.

You will be guided by your supervising teacher as to how formal the math experiences are going to be in your child care center. Methods of presenting numbers and other math concepts vary from spontaneous daily math experiences to planned lessons using workbooks. Keep in mind that you must take advantage of every opportunity to help children understand concepts of mathematics, whether spontaneous or planned in nature. Daily reinforcement will help children learn.

Here are some things for you to do in helping children with mathematics:

Figure 20-1. Use objects—like clocks—that can be examined and handled to help children understand math concepts. (Jane Hamilton-Merritt)

1. Become aware of the math opportunities available throughout the day.

2. Provide time for children to handle and use materials as they discover patterns, shapes, space, numbers, and so on. Repetition helps children to become comfortable with new concepts and to enjoy old ones in new situations.

3. Listen carefully to each child. Is the child using one-to-one correspondence or counting by rote—saying the numbers without thinking of the objects they represent?

4. Take time to help a child learn one concept at a time, whether it is a basic one or a new one. "Roger counts so fast, he doesn't take a breath until he finishes. I'll work with him at the flannel board."

5. Select activities that use numbers, time, space, and measurement. "Today we're going to hear a story about a little worm that crawled very slowly. He was called an inchworm because he moved inch by inch. Do you know how long an inch is? I'll show you

on this ruler. It measures things in inches. You can tell how many inches there are when you measure things with it. Use it to measure things."

6. Extend, clarify, and strengthen spontaneous references to math concepts. Example: When water overflows from a quart jar when filled with a measuring cup, "The jar is full. How many cups of water did you put in it? Do you want to empty it and fill it up again? This time count each cup of water you put in the quart jar. I'll watch you . . ." (and maybe help count).

7. Call attention to math concepts such as numerals in the room—the clock face, telephone numbers, pages of books, the calendar, prices on groceries in the housekeeping corner, ads in the newspaper, etc. Remember that time and space also involve math concepts—"today we are playing doctor and nurse; yesterday we played store." "Let's crawl through the tunnel, then over the log."

8. Use mathematics terms accurately. If you do not know or understand a concept or the meaning of a term, ask your teacher to explain it to you or to tell you of a reference that will help. Don't guess. See Table 20-2 in this chapter.

9. Encourage children to discover the answers—don't be too ready to supply them.

MATHEMATICS CONCEPTS IN THE DAILY SCHEDULE

The daily schedule is full of opportunities for math lessons. Table 20-1 gives examples of concepts that are available every day. After reading and studying this list, use the same format to list activities in the daily schedule you use with your children. There are a lot of math activities you can use to help the children learn about math concepts.

MATHEMATICS VOCABULARY FOR YOUNG CHILDREN

To provide young children with meaningful math experiences, you must speak with them

Figure 20-2. To help children grasp a difficult math concept, give them clues such as "The jars are full. How many cups of water did you pour into them". (Jane Hamilton-Merritt)

Colored cubes
Puzzles, geometric shapes
Nested toys
Balls of several sizes
Unit blocks
Hollow blocks
Large wooden beads of many colors
Containers of different sizes—cans, boxes, milk cartons, baskets
Measuring cups and spoons
Bottlecaps, aluminum washers, clothespins
Light and heavy objects, water, feathers, corks, balloons
Egg cartons, buttons, empty spools
Sponges, rocks, metal objects
Paper bags of many sizes
Scraps of cloth of many shapes and colors
Clock
Calendar
Timer
Balance scales
Pegboards
Flannel board
Toy telephones, cash register, play money
Various types of dials, radio, TV
Children's socks, shoes, mittens
Scraps of lumber (no splinters)
Nails, hammers, rulers, yardstick

in a way that they understand. Table 20-2 lists words you should use in talking with children to help them understand math concepts.

MATERIALS FOR DEVELOPING MATHEMATICS CONCEPTS

The following list gives some ideas for materials that can be used to create meaningful math experiences. As you can see, many of these items can be found around the home, yard, or child care center. You should be able to think of many other examples and use them in working with the children:

MATHEMATICS AND OTHER PARTS OF THE PROGRAM

As you can see from Table 20-1, many activities provide learning experiences in several subjects. As a child care aide, you may have a choice of emphasizing whether the activity is related to mathematics, science, music, or other subject areas. The following activities are especially flexible in regard to emphasis and labeling:

· *Blocks:* mathematics, art, language skills, motor skills
· *Cooking:* science, mathematics, language
· *Games:* motor skills, mathematics, music
· *Finger plays, songs, stories:* language, mathematics, music
· *Collections:* science, mathematics, language
· *Observations:* science, mathematics, language

270

Table 20-1 MATHEMATICS CONCEPTS IN THE DAILY SCHEDULE

Daily schedule	Concepts	Ways to strengthen math concepts
Greeting, health check	One child, one teacher—one-to-one correspondence Ordinal numbers	Relate to one child at a time "It's your turn *next*" or "You were the *first* one at school today."
Free-choice time (child-selected activities)	*Blocks* Shape: square, rectangle, cylinder, cube Awareness of height One-to-one correspondence sorting Counting, ordinal numbers	"Put two squares *alongside* the unit block. Are they the same length?" "Your tower comes up to your belt buckle." "Bring me an armload of blocks" (one boy—one armload). "We have *three* blue trucks; Joe is playing with the *first* one, John has the *second* one, and George a *third*."
	Housekeeping Cooking: capacity, part—whole, counting, space Setting table: sets Sorting groceries: classification *Science discovery area* Measuring: weight, volume, counting Number concepts Size differences Classifying: sets Measuring *Music* Counting One-to-one correspondence Measuring speed (fast, slow)	Mix 2 cups of flour and 1 cup of salt. "The egg carton holds 12 eggs—one *dozen*." "Fill the muffin cups *half full*. "As the muffin batter cooks, it expands and will take up more space." "Put a knife, fork, and spoon at each place." "The cookie boxes go on this shelf." "Will it sink or float?" "How many acorns did you find on the nature walk? Fred found four: two *big* ones, and two *little* ones." "Can the gerbil reach the water spout?" Finger plays, songs. "Clap your hands at the *same time* I beat the drum." "Let's *count how many times* . . . 1, 2, 3," etc.

(Continued next page)

Table 20-1 MATHEMATICS CONCEPTS IN THE DAILY SCHEDULE (Continued)

Daily schedule	Concepts	Ways to strengthen math concepts
Group time	Counting Time, sequence	"Five little ducks went out to play." "Let's sing 'Old MacDonald' *first*." (Use models or flannel board figures.) After song, "Did Old MacDonald have five animals? Let's *count* them."
	Likenesses, differences, sets One-to-one correspondence	"Let's look at their legs. How *many* have *two* legs? Which ones? How many have four legs? Which ones? How many have ears? tails? two eyes?" (Check to see whether each child is grasping the concepts.)
	Calendar—days of week	"*Wednesday* of *next week* is Valentine's Day. Let's count the days . . . five days. How many days are we in school before Valentine's?"
	Weather	"Did it rain *yesterday?*"
	Ritual Who's missing?	What comes *next* . . . "We didn't sing a good morning song. Any requests? Who's absent today? How many? Boys? Girls?"
Snack time	Shapes Counting, one-to-one correspondence	Identify *shape* of cookies, napkin. Boys, girls, glasses, children, napkins, cookies, etc. "Rupert took *one more* cookie *than* Hubert. Hubert had one less.
	Sets	Each child may have *two* cookies and *one* refill of juice."
	Part—whole	"Pour your glass half full." "How many more cookies do we need?"
Outdoors	One-to-one correspondence Measuring	"*One* child on the swing at a time." "The tomato plant we planted is still growing, let's measure it."
	Counting	"We found a nest with *three* eggs in it."
	Space Number concept	"Put your foot on the rung *below*." "Hold on with *two* hands."
Transition	Ordinal number	"Steve is *always* the *last* one inside."
	Pairing	"No, Steve and Chuck make a *pair* of slowpokes—they both are the

Table 20-1 MATHEMATICS CONCEPTS IN THE DAILY SCHEDULE (Continued)

Daily schedule	Concepts	Ways to strengthen math concepts
		last ones in. They come in *together.*"
Rest	Space	"Stretch out so you don't touch anyone."
	Time, sequence	"We'll rest *until* the record ends, *then* we'll see a filmstrip."
	Pattern	Run, walk. tap, tap, tap your foot, etc.
	Language arts center Counting, sorting,	Looking at books—allow children time. Look at book with a child. "*How many* do you see?"
	Naming shapes, numerals	Use shapes at flannel board, on magnetic board.
	Pattern sequence	Have children copy pattern on flannel board or magnetic board. "Tell what comes next in story." Repeat special phrase, such as "Run, run, run, catch me if you can. . . ."
	Art center One-to-one correspondence Time sequence	Each child wears a smock. "Put it on *before* painting your picture and take it off *after* you finish." "Look at the color on your brush. Put it *in* the can with the same color. The orange brush goes *in* the orange can."
	Space	"See if you can cover your paper with your fingers."
	Size Shape Counting	Clay: "Arthur made *big* flat cookies. Ray's are *round* like little balls. Let's *count* the cookies you have made."
	Manipulative table activities Space: sorting, counting, pattern, measuring	Puzzles: "Turn the piece until it fits." Pegboard: "You chose *all* the red ones."
	Number	"How many green ones do you have?"
	Classification	"You have the blue pegs on the outside and yellow pegs on the inside."

(Continued next page)

Table 20-1 MATHEMATICS CONCEPTS IN THE DAILY SCHEDULE (Continued)

Daily schedule	Concepts	Ways to strengthen math concepts
	Number	"How can you make the red rubber band stretch over three nails?"
Clean-up time	One-to-one correspondence Time sequence	"The big truck goes here." "*Tomorrow* may I ring the bell?" "*It's time* to clean up."
Bathroom	One-to-one correspondence	"*One* child uses the toilet *at a time.*"
	Ordinal number	"You're *next*; you won't have to wait long."
	Time, pattern sequence	"*After* using the bathroom, wash your hands." "*Now it's time* to sit in the circle."
Going home	One-to-one correspondence Time	"Don's mother is here, Sue's dad has come for her, Billy's mother and sister came for him."

Table 20-2 MATHEMATICS VOCABULARY FOR YOUNG CHILDREN (SLASH INDICATES OPPOSITES)

Concept	Term	Words used to describe
Space	Position	Top/bottom, center Above/below High/low On top of/underneath In front of/in back of, between Beside, next to, together Here/there Near/far
	Shape	Circle, sphere Square, cube Rectangle Triangle Curve Straight
Quantity	Amount	Zero Another Several/single Pair, both Add, substract, divide, multiply Count Same as, equal to

Table 20-2 MATHEMATICS VOCABULARY FOR YOUNG CHILDREN (SLASH INDICATES OPPOSITES) (Continued)

Concept	Term	Words used to describe
	Value	Cent, penny Nickel, 5¢; dime, 10¢; quarter, 25¢ Money Cost, worth Sell/buy, trade
Measure	Size	Equal, even Balanced/unbalanced Same/different Rule, yardstick Inch, foot, yard Long/short Small/large Length Width Distance
	Weight	Heavy/light Ounces, pounds Easy to lift/hard to lift
	Speed	Fast/slow Speedometer Faster than/slower than
	Time	Morning, afternoon, evening Day/night Early/late Minute, second, hour Old/new Yesterday, today, tomorrow Before/after Names of the months Names of the days of the week
	Temperature	Hot/cold Warm/cool Thermometer, Fahrenheit, Celsius Degree
	Capacity (volume)	Cup, pint, quart, gallon Ounce Measure Full/empty Tablespoon, teaspoon Recipe, directions Level, rounded, pinch Half a, half of

Table 20-3 EARLY AND LATER MATHEMATICS EXPERIENCES

Early math experiences	Example	Later math experiences
Discovery of space		
Exploration of space, Positional relationships, Shapes	Crawling in the box, on top of the box; building with blocks	Geometry
Number		
Number concepts	Counting one, two, three	Constant value of numbers
One-to-one correspondence	One boy, one chair	Place value represented by numbers
Parts—whole	Leaves, branches, trunk of tree	Addition, subtraction, division
Measurement		
Making comparisons	Comparing your string of wooden beads with your height	Measuring size, weight, height, etc., with standard units of measure

Source: Adapted from Marguerite Brydegaard and James E. Inskeep, Jr., *Mathematics Experiencing*, EKNE Study/ Action Publication, National Education Association, Washington, D.C., pp. 13–24.

EARLY MATH EXPERIENCE RELATED TO LATER MATH CONCEPTS

Have you ever watched or heard a young child count "1, 2, 3, 4, 5" yet not be counting the exact number of objects at hand? This child has heard numbers and can say them in sequence (one after another), but the concept of one number representing one object, or *one-to-one correspondence*, is not understood. It is not until he or she understands the concept of each number representing an object that a child really begins to learn the science of mathematics.

The mathematics experiences of a child's early life lay the foundation for later, more formal, math experiences. In Table 20-3, beginning concepts are compared with advanced concepts that children meet as they grow older.

MATHEMATICS TERMS AND CONCEPTS YOU SHOULD KNOW

Sometimes the phrase "new math" scares someone who has not been taught the old subject in this new form. The basic mathematics concepts have not changed, but the words used to describe them have. Basic terms that every aide should know are listed in Table 20-4.

RECOGNIZING METRIC MEASUREMENT

A *measuring system* refers to units of number, size, weight, and volume. In the system most familiar to us, each measurement has a different numerical label without a common base. For example, 1 foot is 12 inches, 1 cup contains 16 tablespoons, and 1 quart is made up of 2 pints. In the metric measuring system, units of 10 form the common base. Figure 20-4 shows you the relationship between metric and U.S.C.S. units of measure.

STEPS IN PROVIDING PLANNED MATHEMATICS ACTIVITIES

Planned mathematics activities may include those available in the mathematics learning center, or instruction may be individualized to strengthen a concept for a child who needs special help.

THE MATHEMATICS LEARNING CENTER

Many times you will be asked to set up the mathematics learning center. Follow the same steps that you took for setting up other learning centers. Select the activities to be included,

Figure 20-3. As a caregiver, you can bring math experiences into almost any activity. For example, the children could count the crackers they have for a snack or subtract those they've eaten. (Kenneth Karp)

Figure 20-4. Here you can see the relationship between metric and U.S.C.S. units of measure.

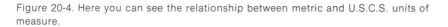

| 1 Millimeter

| 1/16 Inch

1 Centimeter

1/2 Inch

2 Centimeters

1 Inch

1 Decimeter

4 Inches

Table 20-4 MATHEMATICAL TERMS AND CONCEPTS

Terms	Concepts	Examples
Number	How many items	Ten fingers
Numeral	The symbol used to represent a number	10, ten, X
Cardinal number	Number name used in counting	One (1), two (2)
Ordinal number	A number that tells which one in a series	First, second, third first, last
Set	A collection of objects	Five objects, a table setting, items in a pocket
Elements or members of a set	Objects in a set	Four balls in a basket, musical instruments in a collection, a bat and ball
One-to-one correspondence	Each element of one set is paired precisely with an element of another set and vice versa	One hand—one mitten Two hats—two coats One numeral for each duck when counting
Subset	A set within a set. Every element is an element in another set.	Five fish in an aquarium (members of set) Three had flowing tails (subset) and Two had stiff tails (subset)
Empty set	A set with nothing in it (without members or elements)	Five meatballs for supper (one set) minus Five meatballs eaten (another set) equals zero meatballs left (an empty set)
Comparison of numbers	Comparing unit value of one number with unit value of another number. The symbol for *greater* (more) *than* is $>$. The symbol for *less* (fewer) *than* is $<$. It is easier for young children to understand the concept of *greater than* than it is for them to understand *less than*.	$8 > 3$ Eight is greater than three $2 < 5$ Two is less than five
Comparison of sets	Comparing the value of one set with another using the words *more than* and *less than*	There are more boys in the class than girls
Conservation of quantity or of volume	The rule that the quantity of materials or amount of volume remains the same no matter what shape it takes	The quantity of dough clay is the same whether it's in a ball or a long roll; or one large ball or four smaller ones. Whether you put a cup of water in one glass or two, it still measures one cup of water.

prepare the materials, identify visual areas that children can comfortably use, and make the area inviting for children to explore and discover for themselves.

HELPING A CHILD LEARN A MATHEMATICS CONCEPT

Most of the learnings regarding math for the young child come out of daily experiences—children carry heavy things (weight), they talk about what happened to them this morning (time), they push trucks *under* the block built bridge (position in space). However, there will be times when you must help an older child with a math concept in a more formal way. Your teacher may give you this assignment because a child is limited in language or has been absent and has missed the basic concepts that the other children have learned. Whatever the reason, you need to carry out the assignment in a meaningful way. Here are some guidelines to help you:

Preparing for the Experience

1. Plan an experience where the child can manipulate or handle objects to reinforce the concept being learned.
2. Choose a location that is free from noise and confusion.
3. Collect supplies and materials and arrange them in an interesting way.
4. Remove any extra items or unnecessary decorations so that the child is not distracted and the concept to be learned is seen clearly. A child who knows the concept you are teaching may be able to focus on the important things and ignore the others, but this will not be possible for children who have yet to grasp the idea.
5. Place items on a shelf where the child can reach and return them.
6. Make individual containers available for small quantities of pegs, beads, crayons, and the like.

Supervising the Experience

1. Talk with the child in a warm, friendly way. Ask about things or people that are special.

Find out in conversation what past math experiences the child has had.
2. Identify your task for the day. You may put this in the form of a game. "Today we are going to play a counting game."
3. Start with an activity at which the child can succeed: "Help me find the buttons on my shirt. Let's count them."
4. Teach one concept at a time. When the child understands one thing, then add another that extends the concept further; or combine two concepts that the child already knows.
5. Follow through on the one assigned activity. If the child does not understand a concept, use another activity relating to the same concept. Or go back to a concept that has already been learned and then return to the new one. If the child tends to get off the subject, help by saying, "Let's learn about circles now. We'll talk about your dog when we are finished with our lesson."

Following Up the Experience

1. Have the child put materials used back in their proper places.
2. Show approval for success; try to avoid failure, yet indicate items needing further work.
3. Refer to the next lesson time if one is scheduled.
4. Evaluate your experience with your supervising teacher.

CHAPTER SUMMARY

1. Meaningful early math experiences can be found in many everyday experiences in the child care center. These early math experiences help prepare children for later, more formal mathematics lessons. As a child care aide, you should know the vocabulary and recognize the materials used in developing mathematical concepts.
2. Careful planning, knowledgeable supervision, and meaningful follow-up activities are essential to carrying out a successful mathematics experience.
3. Remember, it is important that you under-

stand the concepts of mathematics before you attempt to pass this knowledge along to the children in your care.

• WHAT NEW TERMS HAVE YOU LEARNED?

Several new words and ideas were presented in this chapter. To see whether you understand them, match the letter of each term below with the numbered phrases under "Definitions."

Terms

a. One-to-one correspondence
b. Subset
c. Positional relationship
d. Conservation
e. >
f. Set
g. Numeral
h. <
i. Members of set
j. Ordinal numbers

Definitions

1. Things in collection that make up a group
2. A collection
3. It remains the same
4. Last one to finish his or her milk
5. On top of the box
6. "8"
7. Greater than
8. Less than
9. One chair for each child
10. Two girls in the class

• PROJECTS, DECISIONS, ISSUES

1. Develop a bulletin board that illustrates three different mathematics experiences for young children. Tell the class how each math experience illustrated relates to later mathematics experiences (Table 20-3).
2. Plan a scavenger hunt that can take place in the classroom or outside. Hide examples of each of five math terms. Write the directions as you would for a scavenger hunt. Have classmates work in pairs and bring back the examples.

3. Check the daily schedule in the child care laboratory and compare it to Table 20-1. Then observe in the child care laboratory, noting when and how the child care aide actually utilized the opportunity to present a math concept. Select five different times in the daily schedule.
4. Select a math experience; give a demonstration on how you would present it to a child or several children. Use the three main steps discussed in the chapter.

• WHIFS (WHAT WOULD YOU DO IF . . .)

1. Rose, who is 3½ years old, is counting 1,2,3,5,10,9,7. . . . She tells you "I know how to count." What would you do?
   a. Report to her parent her inability to count by rote
   b. Stop her and make her start over
   c. Tells her she's wrong
   d. Listen and then tell her to count her fingers
   e. Other responses

2. Stanley is looking at pictures of birds in a book. You ask him to count the birds in one of the pictures. Quickly he says "1,2,3,4,5," without actually counting each bird. What would you do?
   a. Tell him to start over
   b. Have him place his finger on each bird as he counts
   c. Listen and say nothing
   d. Tell him he's not doing it right
   e. Other responses

3. Viola tells you "I'm having a birthday party and when it comes I'll be 3 years old" as she holds up two fingers. Her birthday is 6 months away. What would you do?
   a. Tell her it's a long time before her birthday
   b. Show her three fingers
   c. Comment "That's nice," since it's so far away
   d. Look up her birthday
   e. Other responses

4. Cynthia is playing in the sandbox. She is filling the san pail and gets frustrated (begins

to throw sand) when her pail is full. What would you do?

a. Tell her, "Your pail is full . . . see if you can turn it over and make a castle"

b. Say "Here's another pail"

c. Warn "If you can't play nicely, you'll have to leave the sandbox"

d. Ignore her

e. Other responses

5. It's time to go outside, and Ben runs to the door shouting, "I'm first." What would you do?

a. Say nothing, he got there first

b. Have him go sit down

c. Agree that he is first in line

d. Tell him that he was first yesterday and must give someone else a chance today

e. Other responses

6. Marie has collected leaves in the yard. She carries them around in a basket and then sits down to rest, looking a little lost. You suggest that she sort them. She does not understand what you mean in regard to what to do with them. What would you do?

a. Put the leaves in piles yourself

b. Ask her to find two leaves that look alike

c. Point out the color of one leaf and have her find another one of the same color

d. Ask another child to help her

e. Forget it, she isn't ready to learn how to sort yet, and besides, she's tired

f. Other responses

• STUDENT ACTIVITIES

1. List five steps you would take to help a child learn a basic mathematic concept.

2. List four techniques of supervising the activity.

3. List four steps you would take to conclude the activity.

4. Make a drawing of each of the following shapes, and find examples of them in the environment: square, circle, triangle, diamond, rectangle.

PART FOUR

CHILD CARE AIDES WORK WITH SCHOOL-AGED CHILDREN

You have learned a great deal about infants, toddlers, and preschoolers—what their special needs are, what kinds of programs meet those needs, and how you, as caregiver, help to carry out a program. Now you will study school-aged children. You will find out what children aged 6, 7, and 8 are like—what their special needs are and what kinds of programs meet those needs.

The term *school-aged children* refers to all children who attend school. But children aged 6 through 8 also need supervision before and after school, during the summer months, and on holidays. Therefore they are the ones in whom you, as a caregiver, would be most interested.

How are school-aged children different from preschool youngsters? And how do these differences affect the activities included in a program designed especially for them?

In terms of physical development, preschoolers are just learning large-muscle skills—they are very active, but their movements are not completely rhythmic. They need activities that stimulate them to use their large muscles (climbing, pushing, pulling, running, balancing, and so forth). In contrast, school-aged children have well-developed large-muscle skills, and they enjoy activities that test their skills, strength, and endurance (such as bike riding and active games).

Preschoolers spend much of their time exploring and learning, using their sensorimotor skills to gain knowledge and information. At the same time, they are developing their fine motor skills and learning eye-hand coordination. As a result, activities for preschool children often involve touching, tasting, hearing, seeing, smelling, and manipulating objects. School-aged children already have small-muscle skills, and they enjoy using them to make arts and crafts items.

Socially, preschool youngsters are just beginning to be aware of adults and children outside of their families. Their social interaction with peers is in its early stages, and they need supervised activities to develop social skills. Caregivers must encourage preschoolers to interact with one another on a one-to-one rather than a group basis. School-aged children are quite different, however. They are very much aware of their peers—in fact, in many cases, their peer group influences them more than their family does. They are interested in group activities involving skills and more complicated games. Moreover, they like to initiate and plan their own activities as a group. School-aged children are also becoming aware of their community. They may enjoy the feeling of acceptance and accomplishment that comes from performing a community service.

Preschool children of both sexes play together as do younger school-aged children (6- and 7-year-olds). Older school-aged youngsters like to divide into boy and girl activities. Eight-year-olds are aware of peers of the opposite sex but often behave in a negative way toward them.

In terms of emotional development, preschoolers are involved in finding out who they are (self-concept) and in learning self-discipline and self-help skills. They need caregivers who will help make these processes positive and productive. School-aged children need a different kind of guidance, because they are testing themselves and establishing their standards. Caregivers must help them develop their own values, listen to their points of view, and provide situations in which they can "do it themselves" with a minimum of adult interference.

Emotionally, preschoolers are likely to become frustrated easily, especially when their language skills are not developed enough for them to express feelings in words. Caregivers must schedule activities that help preschoolers release tensions and avoid fatigue while also giving them enough time to become successfully involved. School-aged children, however, are fairly even-tempered. They are in a period of *equilibrium* (an even-tempered stage) up until they reach the preteen years, which are considered a period of *disequilibrium* (an uneven-tempered stage). They also need activities that allow them a feeling of accomplishment and satisfaction, but they are more interested in product than process. They need help in scheduling and using their time, but they are more readily able than preschoolers to accept limits.

The intellectual development of preschool children focuses on language skills, on concepts gained through sensorimotor skills, and on learning to make observations and draw conclusions. Preschoolers need an environment that stimulates their curiosity and provides many opportunities to make discoveries and have first-hand experiences. They must also learn and practice listening and speaking skills. School-aged youngsters, however, are able to use language to think and to communicate. They need opportunities to increase their vocabulary and their reading and writing skills. By discussing their ideas, they build more accurate concepts and positive values. They need to be challenged to use their memories and understanding of concepts in solving problems and extending their knowledge. School success is important to them. Activities that strengthen their reading, writing, and math skills will also help build a positive self-concept.

Now you have an idea of how school-aged children differ from the preschoolers you have studied. Chapter 21 describes the great need for good programs for school-aged children and the kinds of programs that are now available. In Chapter 22, you will learn about the qualities that a good program for school-aged children should have, the activities that are appropriate for each age group, and the role of the caregiver.

21 SCHOOL-AGED CHILDREN: THE INDEPENDENT ONES

After you have studied the introduction to Part IV and Chapter 21, you should be able to:

1. Describe how school-aged children (ages 6 through 8) differ from preschool children in terms of physical, social, emotional, and intellectual development as identified in the introduction to Part IV
2. Identify the need for supervised care of school-aged children when school is not in session
3. List three programs available for school-aged children
4. Name one key idea each about the setting, sponsorship, and funding of programs for school-aged children
5. List three items that parents consider important in programs for school-aged children

THE NEED FOR SUPERVISED CARE OF SCHOOL-AGED CHILDREN

Over half the mothers of children aged 6 to 17 years work outside the home.[1] Yet the child care centers and staff members supervising these children are limited in number. As a result, many school-aged children go without supervision when school is not in session. Out-of-school supervision of such children must add to—not replace or duplicate—the services available from children's families, schools, and communities.

PROGRAMS AVAILABLE

Only a limited number of programs are available for school-aged children. The main ones are described below:[2]

1. *School-based day care programs* are operated by public schools or other organizations in public school buildings. These have increased over the past several years.

[1]U.S. Department of Labor, "Monthly Labor Review; Reports on Women Who Head Families," News USDL 76-965.
[2]U.S. Department of Health, Education, and Welfare, Office of Child Development, *Report of the School Age Day Care Task Force,* June 1972.

2. *Recreational agencies and groups* such as boys' clubs, YMCA, YWCA, Scouts, and 4-H clubs offer some care for school-aged children, and many have excellent potential for developing more. Their locations and buildings vary.

3. *Churches and community centers* provide day care or make buildings available to non-profit agencies.

4. *Proprietary day care centers* accept school-aged children who have preschool brothers and/or sisters enrolled; this is an added service to parents. Usually the programs, staff, buildings, and equipment are designed for preschool children, and school-aged youngsters may feel out of place.

5. *Family day care homes* often accept school-aged children who have preschool brothers and/or sisters already enrolled. Usually, such homes are in the children's neighborhoods, and they can offer individual attention because a group usually includes approximately six youngsters.

CHARACTERISTICS OF PROGRAMS

Programs for school-aged children are classified much as preschool programs are—by setting, sponsorship, funding, and needs.

SETTING

Programs for school-aged children may be offered in many different settings—public schools (or a separate building on school grounds), apartments in a housing project, family day care homes, churches, community or recreation centers, and even mobile vans that use parks, museums, and other community resources. Unfortunately, too many programs for school-aged children are tacked onto preschool programs in child care centers or onto public school programs as an afterthought. As a result, planning, staffing, and equipment may not be adequate.

Another type of program for school-aged children is located in a recreation center, where the focus is on equipment and a place for children to go rather than on a planned program.

Figure 21-1. Many school-aged children are involved in a variety of after-school activities—sports, scouts, clubs, and so on. (Kenneth Karp)

Close supervision is seldom provided, and children come and go as they wish. Therefore, parents are not assured that their children will receive safe supervision. In such a case, close relationships with a caregiving adult are incidental rather than planned on a continuing basis.

Scouts, boys' clubs, YWCA, YMCA, and other youth organizations also provide programs—but not on a regular basis. During the period when a program is offered, supervision is provided; but when the program is over, the supervision ends.

SPONSORSHIP AND FUNDING

Programs for school-aged children are sponsored and funded much as all other child care programs are. Sponsorship and funding affect the kinds of programs offered. Table 21-1 lists the persons, agencies, and organizations that provide sponsorship or resources for child care programs. Even though there are many sources of funding for these programs, the money itself is often limited, as it must be shared with various community programs and services.

Table 21-1 SPONSORSHIP AND RESOURCES OF PROGRAMS FOR SCHOOL-AGED CHILDREN

Sponsor or resource	What they do
Persons Family child care mother Recreation leader Child care aide Teacher's aide Child care worker Vista volunteer Community resident	Interaction between child and adult as a "significant other" Listener Counselor Disciplinarian Teacher Protector Friend
Agencies Public health service Welfare agency Human resources departments Housing authority United Fund Parks and recreation department Local school districts Community school programs Colleges and universities Federal programs Private businesses, including private child care centers	Source of funds (money) Establishment and reinforcement of program guidelines (rules) Staff training Meeting special needs such as health care Provide staff Provide facilities Stimulate interagency communication and cooperation

Organizations
Boys' clubs
Scouts
4-H clubs
Church organizations
Salvation Army
Civic clubs
  Civitan
  Kiwanis
  American Legion
  Police Athletic League
  Little League
Big Brothers
	Provide leadership, staff, facilities, equipment, supplies, and programs

Source: Adapted from Elizabeth Diffendal, *Day Care for School-Age Children,* p. 31, Exhibit 1, edited and published with permission of UNCO, Inc., by the Day Care and Child Development Council of America, 1012 Fourteenth Street N.W., Washington, D.C. 20005.

NEEDS AFFECTING GOALS AND PLANNING

In Chapter 3, you learned that available resources and children's needs help to determine program goals, which is the first step in planning a program. The same principles apply to planning programs for school-aged children. Here are some of the needs that parents consider most important:

1. Parents feel that constant supervision is the most important part of a program for school-aged children. They want someone to know where their children are, whom they're with, and what they're doing.

2. Next, parents want a tutoring program to help children with their studies. This usually involves extra, individual help after the regular school day is over. If a child is having trouble with schoolwork, parents want help for that child.

3. Parents of children aged 6 to 10 years believe that a recreation program with active games is the third most important item, while an afternoon snack or evening meal is fourth on their list. Perhaps their comments reflect the fact that programs for school-aged children should not be just "some more school."

4. Finally, parents of school-aged children need full day care for sick children so that parents are not forced to miss work.

The special needs of parents and their school-aged children vary, and the program planning should reflect those different needs. Being absent from a job can mean loss of the job; therefore it is important that parents be absent from their work as little as possible. Care for sick children helps these parents maintain good attendance records.

Figure 21-2. There is a need for programs designed especially to provide supervision and care for children between the ages of six and eight years. (Kenneth Karp)

CHAPTER SUMMARY

1. The physical, emotional, social, and intellectual growth and development of school-aged children are different from those of preschoolers. School-aged children are not just "older" preschoolers.

2. There is a need for programs designed especially to provide supervision for children between 6 and 8 years of age during times when school is not in session.

3. Although a wide variety of such programs are offered in schools, family day care homes, proprietary day care centers, and community or recreation centers, not enough programs are available to school-aged children who need them.

4. Parents consider careful supervision, tutoring, recreation, nourishment, and care for sick children to be the most important aspects of a program for school-aged children.

• WHAT NEW TERMS HAVE YOU LEARNED?

Match the following terms with the descriptions below:

Terms

a. School-based
b. Family day care home
c. 6- to 8-year olds
d. School-aged children
e. Youth agencies
f. Tutoring

Definitions

1. All children who attend school
2. Children who need supervision before and after school
3. Program operated in a school facility
4. Boys' Clubs, Girls' Clubs, YMCA, YWCA, Scouts
5. Extra, individual help for children with their studies
6. A neighborhood home caring for preschool children who are related to school-aged children

• PROJECTS, DECISIONS, ISSUES

1. Select a 3-year-old child in the child care laboratory and an 8-year-old child you know. Write a paper describing how they differ physically, socially, emotionally, and intellectually.

2. Interview the school principal about the need he or she sees for supervised care of school-aged children in the district in which your school is located. Compare the principal's identification of needs with those expressed in this chapter. Share the results of the interview with class.

3. List the programs in your city or county that serve school-aged children. Who sponsors them? How are they funded?

4. You are asked to help a group of parents who are trying to get help from the community to start a program for school-aged children. You volunteer to make posters to use in the campaign. The posters must include the three items the parents consider most important in such a program.

22 PROGRAMS FOR SCHOOL-AGED CHILDREN: COMMUNITY INVOLVEMENT

After you have studied Chapter 22, you should be able to:

1. Name at least five characteristics of good child care programs for school-aged children
2. List at least four different kinds of appropriate activities for school-aged children
3. Describe two ways to get ready for, carry out, and follow up on program activities for school-aged children
4. Describe the desirable qualities of a caregiver who works with school-aged children

CHARACTERISTICS OF A GOOD PROGRAM FOR SCHOOL-AGED CHILDREN

The needs of school-aged children determine the goals and content of a program for them. A good program for school-aged children should provide the following.

SUPERVISION

In a good program for school-aged children, supervision is provided in relation to physical care and emotional protection.

Physical Care. This means a setting that provides safety, comfort, and security; nourishing food (breakfast, snack, or meal as needed); enough well-organized space; and supervision that includes health and safety measures as well as protection from overactive, aggressive peers.

Emotional Protection. School-aged children also need protection from too much anger, fear, or excitement—either from themselves or from peers. A good program provides children with a sense of emotional safety that helps them to feel confident and successful, to enjoy their peers, and to trust caregivers who supervise them.

STIMULATION OF ABILITIES

Programs for school-aged children should include activities, projects, and experiences that encourage intellectual and physical development.

Figure 22-1. A program for school-aged children could include tutoring in difficult subjects. (Kenneth Karp)

Intellectual Development. Caregivers should encourage activities that reflect the school-aged child's desire to gain new information. Collections (stamps, bugs, stones, butterflies, model cars or airplanes) and "learning how" activities (learning to cook, swim, or play the piano) stimulate mental growth. Tutoring in subjects that children are having trouble with at school is another way to stimulate their intellectual development.

Physical Development. Activities that give children opportunities to practice using their bodies, to test old skills, and to develop new ones promote physical development. Jumping rope, softball, tumbling, bicycle riding, and skate boarding all provide school-aged children with the chance to prove their value to themselves and to peers.

Development of Meaningful Relationships. In a program for school-aged children, children are part of a group. The *dynamics of the group*— that is, the interactions of individuals within a group—give children many opportunities to learn about themselves, their peers, and their

caregivers. Meaningful relationships are based on (1) the development of a positive self-concept, (2) an appreciation of ethnic or cultural heritages, and (3) an awareness of and a respect for individual differences.

Children (and adults) need to feel good about themselves. The building of a positive self-concept continues beyond the preschool period. For preschoolers, the self-concept is based on their own feelings about themselves and the feelings of the significant adults in their lives. For school-aged children, the good opinion of peers is an important part of building a positive self-concept. School-aged children who are enrolled in a child care program during hours when their parents are unable to supervise them have a special problem in regard to self-concept. Because the centers are mostly involved in caring for preschool children, school-aged children are often labeled "nursery children." This can be difficult for children to handle and may be harmful to their self-esteem, especially when most other children at the center are younger. Caregivers involved in programs for school-aged children are aware of this problem. They try to lessen it by encouraging each child to invite a friend from school to visit the center occasionally, particularly on special days. They also arrange for the children to participate in school and neighborhood activities, such as joining a school club or a neighborhood Scout group. This kind of planning will help school-aged children feel more involved in their neighborhood instead of separate from it.

Programs for school-aged children should include experiences that help children to increase their self-respect as well as their respect for others. The values and concepts that they began to build as preschoolers must be developed further. This is done when caregivers encourage one child to help another who is younger or when they plan ways to include children from different ethnic backgrounds in the group in meaningful ways.

ENCOURAGING CHILDREN TO WORK

The experiences of identifying a task and then completing it helps children to learn to accept responsibility for their words and actions and to develop coping skills. Activities that stimulate children to work are those which provide choices and encourage independence.

School-aged children do not want to be limited to decisions that adults make for them. A program must provide them with choices—the chance to participate in planning and in carrying out a plan. School-aged children want to feel that their efforts are needed and that they have something to offer.

School-aged children need the safety and love of familiar people, but they also want to experience the feeling of doing things for themselves. Caregivers must be sensitive to these somewhat *opposite needs* and must try to meet them both. By encouraging children to be independent in situations where they will be successful and by recognizing that the children are growing up, caregivers help them to manage many tasks by themselves, to improve their skills, and to try new ones. Asking children to do errands for the child care center (buying stamps at the post office, returning books to the library, purchasing small items for special projects) is an excellent way for caregivers to show children that their independence is recognized and appreciated.

SUPPLEMENTING HOME, SCHOOL, AND COMMUNITY RESOURCES

Programs for school-aged children should not repeat or take the place of things that are already available to the children. Instead, the programs should balance the children's day and try to meet needs that are not met by the family, the school, or the community. Whether children are in need of special tutoring, nourishment, adults to talk and listen to them, or exercise and the space in which to unwind, the program should include what may be missing from the children's day.

The use of community facilities should be considered part of these programs. Caregivers should help to introduce children to the resources available in the community (libraries, schools, playgrounds, parks, recreation centers, and swimming pools) and should encourage children to participate in the programs and activities offered.

INCLUDING PARENTS IN THE PROGRAM

No matter how good a program for school-aged children is, its effect is limited because it is available only for a designated period of time—perhaps a year, a summer, or a semester. In contrast, a child's family is usually available for a lifetime.

Parents Help Plan. Parents often recognize the need for these programs before the community as a whole does. They struggle with the problem of needing supervision for their school-aged children while not having the money to pay for it. They can tell you what their children's needs are—what kind of care is required, when, and how much they can afford to pay. They can identify experiences and services that the community already provides as well as the special problems of each of their children.

Parents Stimulate Participation. If parents believe that the program for their school aged children is a good one, they encourage their children to attend. Parents can help to develop the good things started by the program. They feel important when they are recognized and asked to help with part of the program. For example,

Figure 22-2. By participating in an extracurricular activity such as a group play, the parents can learn more about their children's interests and abilities. (Michael Weisbrot)

Carlotta's mother is glad to teach the children how to make pizza; Jonathan's and Russell's father builds a balance beam; and Louise's parents play their guitars and sing songs with the children.

On the other hand, parents can also discourage their children from participating in a program especially if they do not feel welcome. Such parents may require that the children do errands, may not sign permission slips for special events, or may criticize those who supervise the program.

Parents Learn from Involvement. As parents become involved in the projects of a program, they see the example of good interaction between their children and the adults who are important to them. By being involved, parents learn about children's interests and abilities. In helping to add a backstop to the ballfield, assisting with field trips, or sewing costumes for a play, they come to understand the characteristics of children in this age group. For exam-

ple, a parent who gets angry when a daughter giggles will see that other young girls also giggle as they enjoy a private joke together.

In helping with the program, parents make friends with other adults who are interested in their children. After long hours at work and with few resources for play, being involved as a volunteer in a program for school-aged children is recreation for many parents.

PROVIDING ACTIVITIES FOR SCHOOL-AGED CHILDREN

As you know, every project has three parts—preparation, participation, and follow-up. These steps are just as important in carrying out programs for school-aged children as they are in programs for preschoolers.

PREPARATION

In preparing to provide activities for school-aged children, these steps are important:

1. Caregivers get acquainted with the children, find out what their abilities and interests are, and match activities with abilities. Table 22-1 gives guidelines to help you identify the interests and abilities of children aged 5 to 8. Study it to learn which activities are most beneficial to them.

2. Caregivers plan *with* the children. School-aged children participate in choosing and planning their activities, while caregivers help them to identify their goals and choose ways to carry them out.

3. Caregivers plan for adequate supplies and supervision. School-aged children are able to use supplies and equipment by themselves, but caregivers must provide what is needed for projects that the children plan. Caregivers must also arrange schedules so that supervision will be adequate. This planning includes keeping track of which children are participating in school or community programs or using community or school facilities. When children are not present in the setting where the program is, caregivers need to know where they are.

PARTICIPATION

Your role as caregiver in a program for school-aged children will depend on the staff organization of the center where you are working. You may be assigned to work with a particular group, such as the first- and second-graders, or you may be supervising a certain activity, such as team sports or handicrafts. Your supervising teacher will discuss your participation and responsibilities with you, so that you can carry out your assignment successfully.

At times, you will be teaching children new techniques and skills. It is important for you to understand and be patient with children who are just learning to do something new. They are interested in making a finished product, and this is a slow process. You will have to deal with a certain amount of untidiness as children leave their unfinished projects set up for completion later in the day or on the following day.

At other times, you will be the significant adult who helps children to reach goals they have set for themselves. School-aged children need adults they can trust with their secrets and problems. You can encourage them to find solutions to problems by helping them decide for themselves what is important and how to accomplish it. Caregivers must give individual attention to each child over a period of time and plan ways to include all children in activities.

Table 22-1 ACTIVITIES APPROPRIATE DURING EARLY CHILDHOOD

Characteristics of 5- to 8-year-olds	Opportunities 5- to 8-year-olds need	Appropriate activities
Their large muscles (trunk, legs, and arms) are more developed than the smaller muscles (hands and feet).	To experience many kinds of vigorous activities that involve many parts of the body. To engage in many developmental activities for small muscles.	Activities such as hanging, running, jumping, climbing, dodging, or throwing at an object. Beanbag toss, jacks, bouncing balls, hopscotch, "O'Leary."
They have a short attention span.	To engage in many activities of short duration.	Choice of activity where a child can change frequently, and activities that can be started quickly, such as "Magic Carpet," "Pincho," "Hill Dill," and stunts.
They are dramatic, imaginative, and imitative.	To create and explore. To identify themselves with people and things.	Invent dance and game activities, such as cowboys, circus, Christmas toys; work activities such as pounding, sawing, raking, and hauling. Other play activities: farmers, mail deliverers, grocers, elevators, bicycles, leaves, scarecrows.
They are active, energetic, and responsive to rhythmic sounds.	To respond to rhythmic sounds such as drums, rattles, voice, nursery rhythms, songs, and music.	Running, skipping, walking, jumping, galloping, dodging, swimming. Singing and folk games such as "Oats, Peas, Beans, and Barley Grow;" "Farmer in the Dell"; "Dixie Polka."

(Continued next page)

Table 22-1 ACTIVITIES APPROPRIATE DURING EARLY CHILDHOOD (Continued)

Characteristics of 5 to 8-year-olds	Opportunities 5- to 8-year-olds need	Appropriate activities
They are curious and want to find out things.	To explore and handle materials with many types of play.	Using materials such as balls, ropes, stilts, beanbags, bars, ladders, trees, blocks. Games and activities such as hiking, "Run Sheep Run," "Huckle-Buckle," "Bean Stalk."
They want chances to act on their own and are annoyed at conformity.	To make choices, to help make rules, to share and evaluate group experiences.	Variety of activities with minimum of rules, such as "Center Base," "Exchange," "Midnight," and "Red Light." Made-up activities, dances, and games.
They are continuing to broaden social contacts or relationships.	To cooperate in play and dance, to organize many of their own groups.	Group games, such as simple forms of dodgeball, kickball. Dance and rhythmic activities, such as "Gustaf's Skoal," "Dance of Greeting," "Bow Belinda."
They are individualistic and possessive.	To play alone and with groups. To play as individuals in larger groups.	Individual activities such as throwing, catching, bouncing, kicking, climbing, stunts, running, hopping, skipping, building with blocks, jumping. Dance activities which allow for expression of self, such as clowns, aviators, firefighters, tops, airplanes. Activities which may use small numbers of children such as "Stride Ball," "Cat and Rat," "Hill Dill," "Cowboys and Indians," tag.

A Variety of Activities. Table 22-1 lists some of the many kinds of activities that are appropriate for children with various interests at different stages of development. But you probably wonder what kinds of activities school-aged children *generally* enjoy.

Art Activities. Soap carving; papier-mache puppets; embroidery (especially on denim jackets or jeans); decorating a T-shirt or a piece of fabric with initials; and making letter pictures (using a letter as the basis for a picture).

Music Activities. Folk and square dancing; tuning bottles, clay pots, or glasses; making musical instruments; playing and practicing the piano, autoharp, or some other instrument; chorus; and choral speaking (speaking as a group).

Science Activities. Making an insect net and using it to catch insects for a *collection* (group classified according to likenesses); studying animals on the playground; cooking (jelly, desserts); caring for pets; making a garden; setting up a "weather station"; learning about fire.

Math Activities. Using money, budgeting time, number games, measuring things.

Language Activities. Making television sets

and developing programs for them; telling shadow stories; making up plays with props and costumes; writing letters to pen pals; making party favors; making and sending greeting cards.

Motor Skills. Learning through creative movement; using sheets, streamers, and hoops; team sports and games (volleyball, tumbling); testing skills, strength, and endurance.

Social Activities. Parties, picnics, trips, visiting friends.

Service Projects. Collecting for needy groups, working with service organizations, working on a service project in Scouts.

A balanced program includes physical, creative, and intellectual activities as well as social and service ones.

FOLLOW-UP

It is just as important that school-aged children help with clean-up activities as it is for preschoolers. School-aged children have more fully developed skills; therefore more should be expected of them in all areas, including housekeeping.

Children need the child care aide's guidance and encouragement in evaluating their own performance in relation to their goals. Child care aides should help them to evaluate themselves fairly.

Child care aides must adjust their guidance techniques to the ages of the children with whom they are working. Guidance should be provided indirectly through scheduling and a well-organized environment and directly by consistent, well-defined rules that are enforced by caregivers who set a good example in their own behavior. Here are some important ideas about guidance for caregivers who work with school-aged children:

1. Let school-aged children work out their own differences whenever possible. If children are evenly matched in a conflict, it is better to stay out of it. The child care aide's effort to help may make matters worse, rather than solving the problem.
2. Younger school-aged children need a balance between nurturing and guidance.

3. Give help only to avoid frustration or failure; then, limit assistance to identifying the problem and suggesting possible solutions.
4. Stop dangerous activities at once and remove the children from the danger, whether it is an object or a person. After the children have calmed down, encourage them to discuss what happened and why.

CHARACTERISTICS OF THE CAREGIVER

Caregivers who work with school-aged children should have all the characteristics outlined earlier as well as the following:

1. *Enjoy children's independence.* School-aged children want to decide how to spend their own time; therefore caregivers should enjoy watching children plan and carry out their own ideas.
2. *Be a good listener who knows about many subjects.* Children of school age need caregivers who are trusting friends to talk *with* them and to help them find answers to their

Figure 22-3. Caregivers should encourage school-aged children as they try to learn new skills, like playing the piano. (Rita Freed, Nancy Palmer Photo Agency)

questions. Caregivers must respect the children's desire for privacy when they talk.

3. *Have many skills and be interested in continued learning.* Caregivers must know how to do many things. They need skills and must enjoy learning new ones so that they can help children to learn, grow, and develop the habit of continued learning.

4. *Be interested in and informed about current happenings.* Caregivers who work with school-aged children need to know what is "in" and must appreciate children's interest in styles—fashions in dress, hair, music, movies, cars, phrases, and community activities are part of school-aged children's conversation and should be part of the caregiver's too.

5. *Supply fair discipline and general planning.* Caregivers must provide children with a general structure of rules and resources within which they can do their own planning. School-aged children still need the safety and security of reasonable limits, and caregivers must be fair and consistent in enforcing rules.

EVALUATION

Are you interested in working with school-aged children? Do you have the necessary skills and characteristics? Are you afraid or unsure of yourself around school-aged youngsters, or do you look forward to working with them each day? How would you rate your performance in working with them? Did you find their behavior acceptable? You should ask yourself these questions and discuss them with your supervising teacher in order to evaluate your performance and your career goals.

CHAPTER SUMMARY

1. Programs for school-aged children should balance the children's day by adding to—not replacing or duplicating—services and programs available elsewhere.

2. Programs should include adequate supervision, activities that stimulate physical and intellectual development, opportunities for children to develop meaningful relationships, activities that encourage children to work, and the involvement of parents.

3. School-aged children are eager to make decisions for themselves, and caregivers should be aware of this when they plan and carry out program activities. Caregivers must also match the interests and abilities of children with the activities selected for them.

4. The role of the caregiver in a program for school-aged children depends on the resources and organization of the staff, the setting, and the needs of the children enrolled.

5. Caregivers must enjoy the independence of school-aged children, they must have a variety of skills and must know about many different things; they must be interested in school-aged children and the things that are important to them; and they must be able to enforce rules fairly and consistently.

• WHAT NEW TERMS HAVE YOU LEARNED?

Several new words and ideas were presented in this chapter. To see whether you understand them, match the letter of each term below with the numbered phrases under "Definitions."

Terms

a. Collections
b. Group dynamics
c. Opposite needs
d. Part of physical care
e. "Learning how" activities
f. Emotional protection

Definitions

1. Providing safety from too much anger, fear, excitement
2. Stamps, bugs, stones, butterflies
3. Cooking, swimming, playing piano
4. Ways individuals react and interact with each other
5. Ensuring safety, comfort, and security
6. Dependence and independence

• PROJECTS, DECISIONS, ISSUES

1. Visit a child care center that provides a good program for school-aged children. Report to class five characteristics that you consider an important part of the program you observed—characteristics that helped to make it a good program for school-aged children.

2. List four different kinds of activities that you see school-aged children engaged in at a child care center in your neighborhood. Identify those that you think are beneficial and those that may be harmful.

3. Volunteer in a child care center that serves school-aged children. Your teacher will tell you the minimum amount of time required. Prepare, carry out, and follow up on at least one activity that school-aged children would enjoy. Follow-up should include evaluation of your performance as well as completion of housekeeping aspects of the activity.

4. Using posters, role-playing, or puppets, prepare a class presentation regarding desirable qualities of a caregiver who works with school-aged children. This may be a committee effort of two or three students.

PART FIVE

YOU:
A CHILD CARE
PROFESSIONAL

Part V deals with you as a child care professional. The emphasis is on getting along with other people and on personal growth.

In Chapter 23, you will learn that good staff relationships are built by learning your assignment and by being willing to help others with theirs. Teamwork results when communication is effective. Use of verbal and nonverbal communication, listening attentively, and reporting appropriate information are all part of communicating effectively. Both formal (scheduled) and informal (spur-of-the-moment) communication are needed when working with and in behalf of children. At first, your role in communicating with parents will be limited to informal conversation. Later, when you have been assigned more responsibility, you will help to plan and carry out activities involving parents.

In Chapter 24, all the information is devoted to *you*, the potential child care aide. It helps you review the qualities of a good child caregiver, and it highlights key factors related to personal and professional growth. After studying the last chapter of the book and thinking about the many things you learned in other chapters, you should be able to decide whether you really want to be a child care aide.

23 | STAFF RELATIONS AND COMMUNICATION

After you have studied Chapter 23, you should be able to:

1. Identify three ways in which children know whether staff members get along or not
2. Name at least four responsibilities that a child caregiver has as an effective team member
3. List four ways in which child caregivers communicate
4. State three guidelines for effective communication with parents

As a child caregiver, you are being watched. Children are your most important audience, but not the only one. Staff members—including other child caregivers, support staff (cook and janitor), and administrative staff (director, social worker, secretary)—also see how you get along with children and adults.

It is important to children that child caregivers work together as a team. This chapter focuses on staff relations and communications—the skills that create effective caregiving teamwork.

STAFF RELATIONS AND CHILDREN

Children are easily affected by the kinds of adult relationships they see around them every day. Working with very young children is different from working with machines like a typewriter or a calculator; it is an occupation that serves people, like working in a restaurant or a hospital.

Caregivers work with children—living, thinking, feeling, *young* human beings. Since child care aides work with such young and responsive people, effective *interpersonal skills* are essential.

Children see and imitate the actions of the adults around them. They know and are affected by the way caregivers get along with each other.

WHEN STAFF MEMBERS GET ALONG

Positive interactions affect children. Children know when their caregivers like each other. They can tell by observing such things as:

· Body language—posture, a pat on the shoulder, a wave as greeting, relaxed use of the body
· Facial expression—a smile, wink, or nod of agreement; eye glances; a pleasant, peaceful facial expression

Figure 23-1. Children see and imitate the actions of adults around them. They are very sensitive to how their caregivers treat them and each other. (Michael Weisbrot)

- Cooperative planning—caregivers planning together and carrying out plans and rules with consistency
- Relaxed atmosphere—low-pitched voices, patient responses from adults, a flexible schedule, time for discovery
- Stimulating activities for children—adults putting children first, adult feelings second
- *Consistent* caregiver responses—children being able to count on similar responses for similar behavior

Positive Things Happen. When staff members get along, adults work together and children tend to do likewise. *Empathy* (seeing another person's point of view) is apparent. Adults can see the child's point of view as well as that of another staff member. A team feeling is also apparent. "We" do things, rather than "me, myself, and I."

WHEN STAFF MEMBERS DON'T GET ALONG

Negative interactions affect children. Children

know when things are not right between adults. They can tell by such things as:

- Body language—stiff, jerky, quick movements, tense, uptight posture
- Facial expression—angry looks, little *eye contact* (looking each other directly in the eye) making faces at someone, rolling eyes, sighing
- Conflicting planning—one person saying one thing, another something else
- Tense atmosphere—the desire to avoid involvement
- Limited activities—fewer activities available, staff members tending to do less when energy is spent on emotional conflict
- Inconsistent responses—usually related to inconsistent planning; may relate to competition or direct conflict

Negative Things Happen. When things are not right between staff members, children feel unsure. Gossip and negative comments lead children and adults to become defensive and to justify their own feelings and actions rather than seeing someone else's point of view.

GOOD STAFF RELATIONS

Good staff relations begin with *you* and with how you work as a team member.

YOUR PART

You are part of a team whose goal is to help children grow. Child caregivers who like themselves also like others, both adults and children. The messages that other people get about your feelings toward them (that is, your *feedback*) helps others to like themselves when it is warm and accepting.

You like yourself better when you feel that others think positively about you. For example, when you have carefully planned a flannelboard story and the presentation results in a good time for you and the children, you know that the experience was good. Your good feeling about this experience helps you to *empathize* (to feel as others do) with children who have successful experiences. Another example is when you help a child learn a new skill, such as how to button a sweater; the child gets the message of success. Children like themselves better when they accomplish something, and they like you for having helped them do it. Such happy experiences become *self-fulfilling;* that is, the child comes to expect that the next project will be successful—and it usually is because of this positive attitude.

As a child care aide, you expect success with children, work to achieve it, enjoy the experience, and get positive feedback from the children. This could be called *the success circle*, which is shown in Figure 23-2.

TEAMWORK

A child care aide works as part of a team with many other people, including other staff members and the families of children. All these people play an important role in children's development.

To participate effectively as a member of a child care team, you should:

1. Honor the objectives of the center and follow its rules while trying to achieve the objectives.
2. Know your own duties and distinguish them from those of other staff members. Understand individual roles and cooperate with other staff members.
3. Accept responsibility and be willing to follow directions. Show initiative and volunteer to help others.
4. Communicate effectively, using *verbal* and *nonverbal* communication skills (both with and without words). Empathize and be willing to accept others as they are. Have a sense of humor and be able to laugh at yourself. Learn the names of children, parents, and staff, so that you can call them by name. Listen carefully.
5. Use good work habits. Complete assigned tasks. Be on time. Show a sense of teamwork, such as being dependable, flexible, and willing to help others.
6. Demonstrate professional ethics. Do not talk about the children and other staff members away from the center. Look at situa-

Figure 23-2. The success circle plays an important role in anyone's behavior—caregiver or child. You build up feelings of confidence when you make plans, undertake an activity, do well, receive praise, and feel proud of yourself.

THE SUCCESS CIRCLE

tions without favoritism and respond in a way that is in the best interest of the children and the center.

COMMUNICATION AND STAFF RELATIONSHIPS

Child caregiving teamwork results when communication is effective. Communication may be verbal or nonverbal. It includes listening and reporting.

VERBAL COMMUNICATION

Verbal communication involves the process of using words. How you use words affects your relationships with other people. A pleasant voice that indicates friendliness builds good feelings. Using words that are understood and acceptable to others also promotes good relationships.

As a child care aide, you should speak clearly so that the children hear how words should sound when spoken correctly. Even though *you* may know what you're saying, others will not understand you if you do not speak calmly and distinctly.

It is important to speak loudly enough to be heard but without sounding as though you were giving orders or shouting. Use a low-pitched voice and speak slowly enough that children and others can hear what you are saying.

NONVERBAL COMMUNICATION

You can communicate in many ways without ever saying a word. Such nonverbal communication involves posture, gestures, facial expressions, and touch. Your general appearance also communicates how you feel. For instance, how you wear your hair, your personal grooming, and your choice of clothing all say something about your attitudes.

LISTENING SKILLS

Listening is a very important communication skill. To be an effective caregiver, you must listen to children, coworkers, parents, and your supervising teacher.

Good listening habits ensure that you get the message you were supposed to get. For example, suppose the teacher of the 4-year-old group asks you to put extra buckets and shovels in the sandbox *before* the children go outside. Did you hear the request accurately? Or did you just "get the general idea"?

To become a good listener, you should:

1. Look directly at the person who is talking.
2. Listen carefully to what is being said.
3. Be interested in the topic and in the person speaking.
4. Rephrase what has been said to see whether you understand what you have been told.

THE IMPORTANCE OF REPORTING

Reporting may involve writing (when it is called *recording*) or telling something to the appropriate person at the appropriate time. The following should be reported to your supervisor.

Accidents. Although some incidents may not seem important at the time, *all* accidents should be reported to your supervisor. If a child falls and scrapes a knee, or one child bites another, or someone has a toileting accident, report such incidents. Your supervising teacher needs to know how accidents happen so that parents can be informed.

Behavior Changes. If a child has tried often to climb the jungle gym and kept failing but finally succeeds, share this information with your supervisor in an informal way. Report the opposite case too: if a child who has a good sense of balance suddenly becomes clumsy, the behavior change must be reported and observed carefully in the future. There may be some physical cause for the change. Interactions between children should also be reported: "Billy and Mike played together this morning. It's the first time Billy has played with *anybody*."

Needs Regarding Equipment and Materials. Report equipment that needs repair, as well as dangerous circumstances. "I've noticed that the children can reach the latch on the gate.

They like to slide the bolt back and forth." And make a report when supplies are getting low and need to be replaced.

Parent-Home Information. You may be the only person who has certain information the parent gives or who sees situations that must become part of a child's permanent record. The following items are examples of this kind of information:

· A change of job, telephone number, or residence
· Evidences of child neglect or abuse (no breakfast, marks on body)
· Clothing too small, in need of repair, or unavailable
· Bits of conversation which indicate that the family needs help
· Family often late in picking up child
· Child's pick-up arrangement is dangerous.

Staff Happenings. What do you report to a supervisor about the staff members? Report positive things. Nothing promotes good staff relationships so much as positive reinforcement— seeing and commenting on good relationships and situations. "The new schedule *really works*." "Ms. Mitchell (a coworker) can get Stephen to put on his sweater when I can't." "The children like the way Mr. Green (the cook) fixes squash."

Report situations that bother you. "When I leave there is no one to look after the 4-year-olds and they need someone to supervise them." "I don't have a place to put my things after the secretary leaves." It's better to discuss these problems with your supervisor than to become upset and perhaps take out frustration on the children.

Sometimes you may want to ask your supervisor to explain problem areas that involve other staff members. Perhaps you have seen someone on the staff handle a child roughly. "I'd like you to tell me again what kinds of discipline or punishment are allowed" is a lot better as an introductory statement than saying, "Ms. Rush hits the children with a ruler." Concerns of this kind, although embarrassing and difficult to discuss, must be reported so that the supervising teacher can look into them. Such problems should not be discussed among staff members but in private, with your supervising teacher. In reporting an item of this kind, be sure that the event actually happened and that the charge is not just gossip.

Reporting Methods. Most reporting may be done in a routine way. For example, when equipment needs repair, you may have to fill out a "Request for Repair" form. There may be a special form for reporting an accident or requesting supplies.

Sometimes reporting is done informally by telling your supervisory teacher what you have observed. This is particularly true of children's behavior.

Centers use different kinds of records or forms for reports and different people may have the responsibility to record the children's progress. Child care aides may be asked to contribute to this recording procedure. The teacher might ask you, "What have you observed about how Dennis handles puzzle pieces?" or "Does Vickie know the color red?" Notice that the first question requests that you describe, while the second calls for a simple yes or no answer.

Although the method of recording will vary with the center, all recording should be accurate and should be done as soon after the event as possible. Do not wait 6 weeks to record Don's success in learning to pump on the swing or Zeke and Stacy's cooperative effort in building an upright block structure. The children will probably have "graduated" to more challenging skills by then.

In writing records, emphasize facts, including a description of the child's physical behavior, what the child said, and the setting in which the child was observed. It is very important that you write down what actually happened rather than what you think occurred. Opinions are valuable, but they must be identified as your *thoughts* about the situation.

STAFF CONFERENCES

Sometimes communication among staff members takes the form of a conference. Conferences may be scheduled or unscheduled; they

Figure 23-3. Staff conferences are important. They give aides an opportunity to discuss problems, report and receive information, and make plans on behalf of the children. (Kenneth Karp)

may involve only two people or an entire group. Decisions may be reached quickly, or they may involve much discussion and consideration.

INFORMAL, UNSCHEDULED CONFERENCES

Informal conferences are often called *pop conferences*. These are on-the-spot conferences that may take place on the way to lunch, during rest period, or in the parking lot—wherever and whenever staff members need to discuss something. This kind of conference is unscheduled, requires little or no preparation, and enables people to communicate quickly. Many teacher-parent conferences are pop conferences. A parent may want to report that his or her child had a restless night, for example. Note the similarity between pop conference and informal reporting.

SCHEDULED CONFERENCES

Scheduled conferences may serve individuals or groups. An individual conference may be requested by an aide or by the supervisor. The time of the conference will depend on the schedules of each person involved. Besides

these conferences, there may be a scheduled conference, such as the evaluation meeting that each child care aide has with the supervising teacher.

Although staff conferences may be scheduled as needed, their number and regularity vary from center to center.

Staff conferences help you in many ways. Below is a list of ways that conferences help build good staff relationships and help you perform your assignment:

· You know what's going on; conferences are times of information-gathering.
· You have a time and place to express what's bothering you.
· You and all staff members get the same information at the same time and can discuss problems together.
· You have a chance to interact and plan cooperatively on behalf of a child or family.
· You report information for other staff members to use in their assignments.
· You receive information about the center regarding enrollment, the budget, procedures for ordering supplies, and so on.
· You share in contributing to and recognizing staff roles.
· You have the time to identify and cope with problems as a group, or with someone else who can help you.

Since conferences may take place during the workday, you may be asked to take care of the children while the staff conference is being held. In that case, your supervising teacher will tell you what happened at the conference later.

PARENT-STAFF COMMUNICATION

In learning to be a child care aide, you will come to know the parents of the children. Your role in working with parents will probably be limited to informal communication rather than conferences. Your supervising teacher or a caseworker will carry out that responsibility.

Accepting parents as they are is the key to communicating with them. You should be grateful to the parents for bringing their children to the center. If their children were not enrolled, you would not have the experience of caring for them.

Since your contact with parents is most likely to be informal, the following guidelines should help:

1. Accept parents as they are; do not try to make them over.
2. Call parents by name (Mrs. Jones, Mr. Smith) and use eye contact. Only use given names if you personally know the parents and customarily call them by their given names socially.
3. Report incidents of their children's behavior that are positive. Leave negative or complicated experiences for your supervising teacher to handle in conference.
4. Keep information about the family and the child care center confidential. Report things that seem to need handling to your supervising teacher.
5. Be pleasant; have the children ready for their parents when they come to pick them up at night.
6. Assist parents in helping children leave the child care center. Sometimes children would

Figure 23-4. Parent-aide conferences are valuable for discussing the overall progress of the child. (Michael Weisbrot)

rather stay at the center than go home. Tell the children it is time to go home and that you will see them tomorrow.
7. If asked by parents for help that you are not assigned to give, refer them to someone on the staff who can help.

WAYS PARENTS AND STAFF COMMUNICATE

Even though your assignment will not include parent conferences at first, you need to know the various ways that parent-staff communication takes place. Parents and teachers communicate in the following ways:

Home Visits. Staff members visit children's homes.

School Visits. Parents visit the child care center on a scheduled or unscheduled basis.

Casual Visits. These are like pop conferences. They may take place on a parent's day off, when the parent brings the child and stays to enjoy the experience, or when the parent arrives early to pick up a child.

Planned Conferences. Scheduled conferences are valuable for discussing the overall progress of each child. They also indicate that communication is not limited to problems. When they enroll their children, all parents are informed of the practice of scheduling conferences periodically. Thus, they will not be afraid that the conference is scheduled to point out negative behavior; all parents have conferences from time to time.

Parent Meetings, Study Groups. These gatherings are for fun, for getting to know one another better, and for learning. Parents may request topics and plan the meetings or participate in them. Usually, all staff members attend or help with the meetings.

Parent Participation. Parents who volunteer to work in child care centers are valuable communicators.

Telephone Conversations. Many times a telephone call is the most effective way to get information about a child's problem. But even though such calls can be helpful for gathering information and throwing light on a problem at hand, communication should not be limited to telephone conversations.

EVALUATION OF YOUR STAFF RELATIONS

When you accept a child caregiving assignment, you accept two responsibilities: The first is to do the job to the best of your ability, and the second is to get along well with people. This is especially important in child caregiving, since working with young children is an occupation that serves people. Each and every person with whom you have contact is important and unique.

Constructive criticism is not always easy to take, yet it is an important part of growing on the job. Your supervising teacher will make suggestions and offer guidance to you from time to time. Be a good listener, accept constructive criticism, and use it to help evaluate your progress as a caregiver.

The following ''Ten Commandments for Human Relations'' are rules for good living, but they can also be used to evaluate your effectiveness as a member of the child caregiving team. Read each item carefully and decide whether you are following these rules:

TEN COMMANDMENTS FOR HUMAN RELATIONS

1. Speak first to every person you meet. There's nothing better than a cheerful word of greeting.
2. Smile as you greet people. It takes only 14 muscles to smile but 72 to frown.
3. Call people by their names. It shows that you think them important enough to remember their names.
4. Be cordial. Act as though everything you do is a pleasure.
5. Be friendly and helpful. There's no better way to build friendship than to give your own first.
6. Show a true interest in people. If you try, you'll like most people.

7. Be generous with praise and stingy with criticism.
8. Be considerate of the rights of others.
9. Be quick to give service. People will remember and tell others how you helped.
10. Take the nine suggestions above, add a sense of humor, and mix with some patience and humility.[1]

How do you rate your human relations? Child care aides should work constantly to improve their relationships with others on the child care team.

Consider the beginning of your child care assignment as the start of a great and continuous adventure in the art of human relations.

CHAPTER SUMMARY

1. Good staff relationships are built by learning your assignment and being willing to help others with theirs. Children observe and imitate the actions of the adults around them. They know and are affected by how child caregivers get along with each other.
2. A child care aide works as part of a team with many other persons, including other staff members and the families of children. All work together to help children grow and develop when a team effort is made.
3. Child caregiving teamwork rests on effective communication. Therefore a key to establishing good staff relationships and being a better child care aide is skill in communicating. Use of verbal and nonverbal communication, listening attentively, and reporting appropriate information are all part of communicating effectively.
4. Communication may be informal and shared casually at unscheduled times, or it may be formal as scheduled during conferences. Both formal and informal communication

[1]*Florida Resource Guide,* Home Economics Division of Vocational Education, Florida State Department of Education, Tallahassee, 1975, p. 226.

are needed when one is working with and in behalf of children.

5. Your role in working with parents will, at first, probably be limited to informal, cordial communication rather than formal, scheduled conferences. As you communicate with parents, accept them as they are and reflect upon and appreciate their strengths.

6. Evaluate your relations with the staff and your communication skills by using the "Ten Commandments of Human Relations." They serve as useful guidelines to the building of effective staff relations.

• WHAT NEW TERMS HAVE YOU LEARNED?

Several new words and ideas were presented in this chapter. To see whether you understand them, match the letter of each term below with the numbered phrases under "Definitions."

Terms

a. Empathy
b. Self-fulfillment
c. Interpersonal skills
d. Pop conference
e. Feedback
f. The success circle
g. Eye contact
h. Consistent

Definitions

1. On-the-spot conference
2. Messages about your actions that you get from other people
3. The ability to feel as others feel
4. Anticipating success and working to achieve it
5. Staff relations and communication
6. Repetition of cycle of good feelings which leads to positive feedback
7. Looking directly at person who is speaking
8. The same each time it occurs

• PROJECTS, DECISIONS, ISSUES

1. Pick a team sport or an organization that you are personally acquainted with and enjoy because there is good team effort involved. See if you can identify what makes this an enjoyable experience for you and a successful one for the organization. If your experiences do not include successful team effort, list the qualities that may contribute to lack of success in this endeavor. Apply the principles related to these experiences to the child care aide's role as part of a child care team.

2. Demonstrate at least three ways in which children know whether staff members get along or not. This may be done with puppets, role-playing, or a "what's my line" kind of game.

3. From a collection of written reports, select those that represent good reporting and identify your reasons for choosing them.

4. Role-play a child care aide giving the supervisor an oral report; discuss with your fellow students your effectiveness in communicating the message to your supervisor.

5. Discuss the following statements with your classmates and decide whether you agree or disagree with them. If you disagree with a statement, edit it to make it one with which you can agree.

   a. Parents like the friendliness of being called by their given names; therefore child care aides should address parents by using their given names.

   b. Child care aides should only report positive aspects of children's behavior to parents and the supervising teacher.

   c. When a child does not want to leave the center, the child care aide should engage the parent in conversation so that the child can continue playing.

   d. There is so much for children to learn that child caregivers should provide activities for children right up to the time the parents come to pick them up. The parent is responsible for getting the child ready to go home.

24 PERSONAL GROWTH

After you have studied Chapter 24, you should be able to:

1. Define personal growth
2. Identify four characteristics of personal growth and give an example of each of them
3. Evaluate your commitment to child care as a profession
4. Recognize at least three factors that aid professional growth in a child caregiver

WHAT IS PERSONAL GROWTH?

Personal growth is that part of growing that focuses on you as a person and that leads to maturity. It includes your physical, social, emotional, and intellectual development. It refers to the past, present, and future. You are the sum of all your experiences. All of them contribute to the abilities, feelings, and thoughts you have now. When you have had many good experiences, you anticipate that there will be many more to enjoy and to challenge you. If you feel that your experiences have been unpleasant or negative, you tend to be afraid and hesitant to try new ones.

EARLY EXPERIENCES WITH CHILDREN

Let's look at student experiences with young children. Some students know and enjoy many little children. They are sought after as baby-sitters. Mothers know that these students like children and provide good care for them. The children know it too, and they like to have these students come to baby-sit. Students with this kind of reputation seek new experiences with young children. Most have decided to work with young children as a career.

On the other hand, students who have had experiences with young children that are unpleasant or frightening are unsure about future experiences with young children. Their motivation for child care training is likely to be limited, and their attitude is indifferent or cautious.

Whether you think your experiences have been positive or negative, your present feelings and actions can lead to personal growth in the future. But students are seldom able to move ahead entirely on their own. It is most likely that help from someone who is trusted and admired, such as your child care teacher, will enhance your personal growth. The experience of

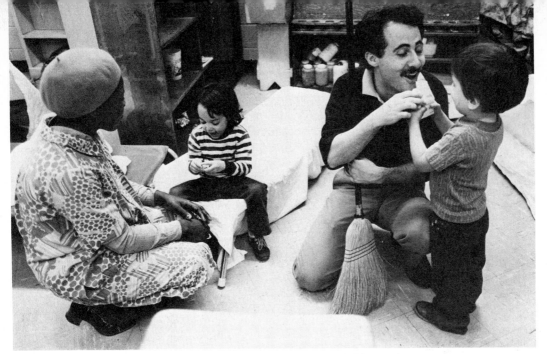

Figure 24-1. To do a good job as a caregiver, you must keep yourself in good health. Eat a balanced diet, wear comfortable clothes, and get enough rest and exercise. (Kenneth Karp)

working with young children can help, too. Child care students experience personal growth as they study the behavior of young children. They may see reasons for their own feelings. They may also identify childhood experiences that have helped to shape their own present moods and behavior. These perceptions can help you change bad habits, give you more self-confidence, or help you develop a healthier self-concept.

INTERACTION WITH ADULTS

Personal growth is more than personal experiences with young children. It includes interaction with adults—coworkers, parents, and teachers. Interaction with your peers, other students in child care training, and other friends—both male and female—is important too.

Personal growth involves your interests and the steps you are taking toward maturity and a better life. It includes the things you like and can do as well as the kind of person you want to become and the ways you may find to reach your goals.

CHARACTERISTICS OF PERSONAL GROWTH IN A CHILD CARE AIDE

As mentioned earlier, growth is a personal quality. It reflects the individuality of each person who is growing in a unique way. Let's look at some characteristics that reflect personal growth in a child care worker.

PHYSICAL DEVELOPMENT: LOOK AND FEEL GREAT

Often the professionalism of a child care aide is rated according to the appropriateness of his or her behavior and appearance.

It's easy to become careless about your appearance when you are around young children.

Your appearance reflects your physical and mental health. Posture, grooming, and choice of clothing communicate your alertness. Although you should wear washable, comfortable clothing, select styles and colors that look good on you. Get enough rest and exercise. A regular routine helps you feel and look great. It will help you maintain your proper weight. Eat nourishing food. It takes a lot of energy to work

313

with young children. These things seem simple when they are daily habits. However, when they are not, it takes a great deal of effort to make them part of your daily schedule.

EMOTIONAL DEVELOPMENT: RECOGNIZE YOUR FEELINGS AND EMOTIONS

Self-understanding is especially important to anyone who wishes to help children. The kind of person a child caregiver is affects the self-concept developed by the children receiving care. Young children are sensitive to all we do and say. They imitate us. They reflect our actions and feelings. If we feel comfortable about ourselves, children will behave in a way that indicates they feel comfortable about themselves also.

"Know Thyself." These two words were spoken by wise people thousands of years ago, and they still apply. They ask you to recognize your abilities, your feelings, and your thoughts about yourself. Self-knowledge leads to success on any job, including working with children. It leads to acceptance of and respect for yourself.

Dr. Elizabeth Sheerer, Head of the Child and Family Development Department, University of Georgia, has identified four categories that describe people who accept and respect themselves.[1] Such people:

1. Have developed certain values and principles upon which they rely as a general guide for behavior
2. Take responsibility for their feelings, reactions, behavior, and for creating and solving their own problems
3. Are able to accept themselves as they are and consider themselves as valuable as other people
4. Have confidence in their abilities to meet the problems of everyday life

Which of these qualities do you recognize in yourself? Which ones do you need to work on?

[1]Elizabeth Sheerer, *Four Categories under Acceptance of and Respect for Yourself,* paper presented at Family Counseling Workshop at the University of Georgia, Athens

Develop a Good Self-Concept. Your self-concept is important to young children because you will behave as you think others see you. For example, if you think that other people see you as being kind to young children, you *will* be kind to young children in order to fulfill these expectations.

How do you rate your *self-concept*? A good self-concept indicates a feeling of self-worth and acceptance. A poor self-concept includes insecurity, self-consciousness, and feelings of inferiority. To change from a poor self-concept to a good one, begin by identifying and giving yourself credit for your positive thoughts and actions. Your self-concept affects the children with whom you work. They too are developing concepts about themselves. Your feelings of confidence and achievement enable you to reinforce the kind of behavior in children that helps them to develop self-respect and self-control.

Accept and Respect Others. Child care aides should accept and respect not only themselves but also other adults and children. The person who accepts and respects others must also demonstrate empathy.

Be Emotionally Independent of Children. A child care worker shows warmth to children yet is not emotionally dependent on them. When you work with children day in and day out, it is easy to become attached to them. You may even feel *possessive* about them, feel that they belong to you. Talking about the children with your co-workers helps you broaden your reference from "my child and my program" to "our children and our program."

SOCIAL DEVELOPMENT: HAVE FUN WITH YOUR PEERS

Your social growth is important to the children you take care of and is therefore an important part of this book. Being a mature person is a child care skill. You are a more interesting and sensitive person if you are involved in other concerns in addition to child care.

Select Friends Who Are Not Child Caregivers. Do you have some friends who do not work with children? Spending your leisure time only with coworkers limits your personal growth. When coworkers get together for fun, they often end up talking about the children, the job, and each other. In effect, they eat, sleep, and drink the work. This is not good. Too much attention to any one thing can make you uninteresting.

Have fun doing adult things. Bowling, bike riding, dancing, and hiking are just a few. People need both male and female companionship at any age, but especially if they are young adults. Don't overlook the stimulation of getting to know people with different cultural backgrounds. Different foods, clothing, and family customs add interest to friendships.

Whether you live with your parents or are on your own regarding housing, take the responsibility for your recreation time. Join some group activities at which you can meet your peers. Volunteer to help at church or in community service clubs. Get interested in local politics. Know the candidates and support those who support child care programs and other services that benefit the community.

INTELLECTUAL DEVELOPMENT: THINK ADULT THOUGHTS

"Living" a child care assignment can make you a dull person. You will note the emphasis on the word "living." As child caregivers, we often find ourselves in a rut because we have limited our interest to the children in our care. We have spent all our time thinking or working with children and have not tended to our own personal development. We like what we are doing, and the children do too. What's wrong with this comfortable routine?

We may become so involved in helping chil-

Figure 24-2. Caregivers should not limit their interests and experiences to child care. Developing friendships with other adults and taking part in adult activities will make you a well-rounded person. (Michael Weisbrot)

dren to grow that we forget about our own continuing need to grow. After working all day with children, using simple language, and simplifying thoughts, caregivers need the stimulation of adult reading and conversation during their off-duty hours.

Read a book for fun, one that is geared to *your* intellectual level instead of a child's. Being a well-rounded adult includes thinking adult thoughts, having new experiences, and bringing them to your job.

EVALUATE YOUR COMMITMENT TO CHILD CAREGIVING

Identifying goals is part of personal growth. As child caregivers broaden their interest in young children to include the professional goal of working with them, they make a commitment to their work. This means that they take responsibility for serving young children to the best of their ability.

Child caregivers usually love their work. Seeing a child move from failure to success is a priceless reward. No amount of money can equal the feeling of achievement and personal pleasure that one senses when a child learns to skip or walk a balance beam for the first time after many unsuccessful tries.

What about the child care student who does not share this commitment? If you find that you do not like child caregiving, recognizing this is also growth. In fact, it's good to find out early in your career that you would rather do something else. Unfortunately, there have been child caregivers who did not identify their unhappiness early; therefore they struggled for years attempting to perform tasks that were unpleasant to them, the children, and other staff members. When this happens, everyone suffers.

PROFESSIONAL GROWTH

When you choose child care as a career, at the same time challenge yourself to keep growing professionally, to learn more and do more to serve children and their families. There are

many ways that child caregivers keep learning about their assignments and about young children. Let's look at some of them.

GROW ON THE JOB

Children deserve your best performance. You can provide it when you keep yourself up to date on new techniques and understandings that are related to young children's programs and behavior.

Below are some of the ways you can grow professionally:

Observe Your Coworkers. Watch how they handle children in different situations. Ask for advice when you have a problem that you can't seem to solve by yourself.

Figure 24-3. Make an effort to grow professionally. Read magazines and journals about child care and education; join child care organizations; and watch for advancement opportunities. (Kenneth Karp)

Be Attentive at Staff Meetings. Probably at first you will just listen, unless you are asked to speak. Notice how both good and bad news is presented. Learn what is important to discuss at such meetings and what should be held for informal communication.

Read Professional Books and Journals. Some centers will have this material on hand. If not, ask some of your supervisors whether they have such publications. Or obtain them from your local library. Local, state, and federal government agencies also provide some of this information free. Check it out. The names of some well-known journals are *Childhood Education, Today's Education, Young Children, Early Education, Instructor,* and *Teacher.*

Join Professional Organizations. The National Association for the Education of Young Children (NAEYC), The Association for Childhood Education International (ACEI), Elementary, Kindergarten, and Nursery Education Section of National Education Association (EKNE-NEA), and The Day Care Council of America (DCCA) are a few of the national organizations focusing on young children. Regional groups such as the Southern Association for Children Under Six (SACUS) and state-affiliate groups of the regional and national associations provide opportunities to attend professional conferences and read stimulating literature.

Usually a newsletter and journal are included in the membership costs. Such dues are lower when you join as a student. After you graduate from a child care educational program, these associations can become a source of on-the-job or continuing education. Your connection with a professional association also increases your ability to persuade lawmakers to enact legislation that is favorable to your profession. Through conferences and journals, you will be kept informed about laws that affect child care programs.

CHAPTER SUMMARY

1. *Personal growth* focuses on your social, physical, emotional, and intellectual devel-

Figure 24-4. Child care offers you a lively and satisfying career. (Kenneth Karp)

opment—that is, on how you grow as a person and a professional. In short, personal growth refers to the process of growing up (maturing).

2. Three things help you to mature: a good self-concept, an aliveness that comes from living a full life, and coping with personal problems in an adult manner. This kind of outlook helps you assess your strengths and weaknesses realistically so that you know which areas to maintain and which to improve.

3. Appearance reflects your personal growth; so does attempting to learn more about your job and the whole field of child development. You should also seek activities and friendships away from the center, so that you are not always living in a child's world or discussing the problems of children and the center.

4. Good child caregivers are well-rounded in-

dividuals who are confident of their abilities, willing to learn about child caregiving, and interested in a variety of topics.

5. Child caregivers who grow personally are more interesting to children and to adults, and they help others grow. As they continue to grow, they become more interesting people and more effective and stimulating child caregivers.

• WHAT NEW TERMS HAVE YOU LEARNED?

Several new words and ideas were presented in this chapter. To see whether you understand them, match the letter of each term below, with the numbered phrases under "Definitions."

Terms
a. Personal growth
b. Self-concept
c. "Living" a child care assignment
d. Accepting commitment
e. Professional growth
f. Possessiveness

Definitions
1. Steps toward maturity
2. Way one thinks of oneself
3. Taking responsibility for an assignment
4. Thinking in terms of "my children" and "my program"
5. Spending all your time involved with child care
6. Learning and doing more in your profession

• PROJECTS, DECISIONS, ISSUES

1. Complete this sentence. "To me, personal growth is . . . ; personal growth is not. . . ."

2. Develop a collage that represents at least four characteristics of personal growth. This can be done by using magazine pictures and personal artwork, or it can be a musical or poetic presentation. You may wish to work with someone else on this project. If so, discuss your committee plans with your teacher.

3. Select a person you consider mature and identify the qualities that influenced your choice. Does this person have characteristics that would make him or her a good child caregiver?

4. List characteristics that you consider essential in a child care aide. Check your personal characteristics against this list. Do you feel good about the comparison? What does this tell you about your personal commitment to child care as a profession?

5. Interview at least three child care workers, preferably one who has completed professional training within the last 2 years, one 5 years ago, and one with 10 or more years of experience. Ask them how they provide for their professional growth.

• STUDENT ACTIVITIES

1. List some characteristics that indicate personal maturity.
2. List five different social activities a child care worker should become interested in in order to become a more well-rounded and interesting person.
3. List five activities that a child care worker should pursue to grow professionally.
4. List five activities that would help a child care worker to improve physically.
5. List five activities that would help a child care worker to grow emotionally.

GLOSSARY

Accident-proof Environment: A safe environment.

Activity Areas: Locations within a room that are identified for different activities—learning centers, play areas, centers of interest.

Activity Songs: Songs that tell children what to do.

Adult-Child Interaction: Feelings and communication between children and adults.

Anecdotal Record: Report of an important incident which does not necessarily include every detail.

Aspects of Growth and Development: General characteristics of various age groups and stages of development.

Assistant Level of Employment: Level-II child care worker.

Attachment: Close relationship with another person; an emotional bridge.

Attention Span: Time spent with an activity.

Basic Movement Pattern: Basic pattens in motor development (that young children can achieve).

Basic Personal Needs: Things that people need in order to survive: water, food, air, protection, and love.

"Beautiful Junk": Discarded materials and equipment used in teaching.

Board-sponsored Center: Non-profit center with governing board.

Booster: Shot that is part of immunization schedule and strengthens previous shots.

Center-based Enrichment Programs: Programs focusing on children's learning in group settings.

Checklist: List of predetermined items to be used for evaluating activities, behaviors, equipment, or setting.

Child Care: To provide care for a child or children.

Child Care Aide: Child care worker who helps someone else provide care; title referring to the role of aiding or helping someone else.

Child Care Center: Place where group of children receives care.

Child Care Center for Children with Special Needs: Child care programs for children who are handicapped emotionally, physically, or intellectually.

Child Caregiver: Person who puts child's needs before his or her own while warmly encouraging the child to try new experiences.

Child Caregiving: Giving of oneself while caring for a child.

Child Care Licensing: Government regulations for child care.

Child Care Occupations: All jobs that relate to children and to child care services.

Child Care Services: Kinds of services provided in various child care settings and programs.

Child Care Staff: Everyone who is employed to carry out a child care service.

Child Care Team: People on a child care staff working together as a team to provide child care service.

Child Care Worker: Person who has a job that relates to children; title or label referring to anyone who works with or cares for children as part of employment.

Child Centered Programs: Programs that focus on letting children use resources available.

Child Development Program: Term used in most home economics classes to identify the program about young children.

Childhood Diseases: Contagious diseases of childhood such as measles, mumps, chickenpox.

Child-initiated Activities: Activities children can begin by themselves, without direction from adults.

Children's Home: Institutional child care facility that offers service on 24 hour basis.

Commitment: Accepting responsibility for something.

Communicable Diseases: Diseases that can be spread from one person to another.

Communication: Sending a message and having it understood.

Competencies: Abilities to perform tasks at a predetermined standard.

Compensate: To make up for experiences missed in previous years.

Compensatory Education Programs: Programs whose purpose is to supplement or add to children's experiences with information and activities that will help their learning in school.

Competence: The knowledge and skills necessary to accomplish tasks under specified conditions and with specified accuracy.

Comprehensive Child Care Center: Center that provides a safe environment and enriched child care program, with health and social services for children and their families.

Concept: Idea.

Conservation of Quantity: No matter what the shape of the container, its volume or possible contents remains the same.

Consistent Care: Same kind of care all the time.

Consistent Guidance: Guiding children in the same way, with the same rules, all the time.

Constipation: Lack of bowel movement.

Consumable Materials: Supplies, items that are used up.

Contagion Period: Period during which the sick child can infect other people.

Controlling Activities: Activities which restrict children's movement and response.

Convergent Questions: Questions that have only one right answer.

Cooperative Play: Playing together, often with friends.

Copes: Handles. Manages to solve problem.

Coping Skills: Problem-solving skills.

Creative Movement: Movement which expresses children's learnings.

Cue: Signal.

Curriculum: Program, experiences available for children.

Curriculum-centered Programs: Programs which center curriculum in behalf of children and are often based on a specific set of educational methods.

Custodial Child Care Center: Center that meets minimum requirements of child care licensing; i.e., providing for health and safety of children and also stimulating intellectual, social, and emotional growth of children.

Day Camp: Social enrichment program for children of kindergarten age and older, scheduled in the summer.

Day Care Center: Child care center; any place operated by a person, society, agency, corporation, institution, or any other group wherein are received for pay children under 18 years of age for group care, for less than 24 hours per day, and without transfer of custody from the parents.

Day Care Licensing Standards: Government regulations regarding licensing standards for day care centers.

Day Care Operator: Owner of a child care center.

Dependence-Independence: Describes children's wanting to be cared for at times and wanting to care for themselves at other times.

Desirable Standards: Enriched program provided for children, beyond the meeting of minimum standards.

Developmental Child Care Center: Center that provides programs to help children develop socially, emotionally, physically, and intellectually.

Diaper Gait: Way a toddler walks, with legs far apart for comfort and balance.

Diaper Rash: Chafing in the diapered area.

Diarrhea: Frequent loose bowel movement.

Direct Child Care Tasks: Jobs in which child care aides work directly with children.

Direct Experiences: Firsthand experiences in which children handle, see, smell, taste, and hear objects or experiences.

Direct Guidance: Techniques used to guide children's behavior.

Discipline: Guidance, way in which adults help children learn to control their actions and make decisions.

Discovery Learning Center: Any location in the room that invites children to find out for themselves.

Disequilibrium: In relation to childhood behavior, even-tempered period.

Evacuating: Getting people out of a room or building.

Evacuation Plan: Procedure for getting children and staff out of the building; applied during fire drill.

Experiment: To try out.

Expressive Language Skills: Using words to express oneself.

Eye Contact: Looking directly into another person's eyes.

Eye-Hand Coordination: Coordinating and using the eyes and hands together.

Facilities: Buildings and equipment.

Family Day Care: Child care that is provided in a private home for a few children unrelated to the caregiver, for fewer than 24 hours.

Family Day Care Mother: Caregiver who provides family day care.

Family-Style Food Service: Style of food service in which serving dishes are placed on the table.

Feedback: Messages received regarding what is said or done.

Fine Motor Skills: Control of small muscles.

Finger Play: Activity in which fingers represent an idea, concept, story, poem, or song.

First-Aid Kit: Box containing items needed to give treatment for an injury.

Firsthand Experience: Direct experience.

Follow-through Program: Compensatory program for children in kindergarten and primary grades.

Food "Jag": Wanting only certain foods for a period of time.

Food Service in Child Care Centers: Usually consists of midmorning snack, lunch, and afternoon snack.

Franchise Child Care Center: Chain of centers in different locations having the same name, housing facilities, equipment, and staffing pattern.

Freeing Activities: Activities that help children to be free and relax and to enjoy them while they are doing them.

Free Play: Period during which children are free to choose what they want to play with.

Genitals: External sex organs.

Governing Board: Professional business and community leaders who spell out policy and guidelines for the operation of nonprofit child care centers.

Gross Motor Skills: Control of large muscles.

Group Time: Group language activity; story time.

Guidance: Discipline; the way in which adults help children learn to make their own decisions.

Head Start Program: Compensatory program in education providing social services for prekindergarten children from low-income families.

Health Check: Checking for signs of illness upon arrival at child care center.

Home-based Child Care: Child care service in child's own home or someone else's home.

Home-based Enrichment Programs: Programs focusing on children's learning activities within the home and family.

Home Visitor: Child caregiver who visits homes often to show parents how they can teach their children.

Hourly Care: Child care service by the hour.

Hyperactive: Extremely active.

Hypothesis: Prediction or educated guess.

Immunization: Using a vaccine to make the body build up defense against a disease.

Improvise: To make something up or devise a makeshift arrangement.

Inappropriate Behavior: Behavior that needs improvement or change.

Indirect Experience: Symbol representing a first-hand experience, such as drawing picture, taking a photograph, or reading about something.

Indirect Guidance: Environmental factors that provide guidance for children.

Individual Activities: Activity involving one child.

Infancy: First year of a child's life.

Infant: Baby child between birth and 12 months of age.

Infant Cues: Signals or signs given by an infant.

Inquiring Attitude: Wanting to find out, to get answers.

Intellectual Development: Mental growth and how children use their minds.

Interacting: Getting along with others; relating with others.

Isolate: Keep away from, as isolating sick children from the group.

Jargon: Nonunderstandable speech with full inflection.

Kindergarten: Program that focuses mainly on education enrichment for four- and five-year-olds.

Kinesthetic Sense: Awareness of position of body in space and the way muscles are used to control and balance the body.

Laboratory School: School to teach students how to work with young children, usually connected with child care training programs.

Language: A structure of words used in communicating with others.

Language Arts: Ability to use language to communicate.

Language Arts Programs: Experiences and activities related to language development in a child care center.

Language Skills: Listening, speaking, writing, reading.

Large Muscles: Muscles in arms, legs, neck, and trunk.

Learning Centers: Locations within a room that are identified for different activities; activity areas.

Learning Style: Way that a child learns best.

Learning Tools: Ways of learning through experiences and activities.

Level-I Child Care Worker: Entry-level person who carries out someone else's plan under the guidance of a teacher or assistant.

Level-II Child Care Worker: Person who plans and carries out a program for young children under the guidance of a supervisor.

Levels of Employment: Relationships among staff positions.

License: Document provided by the state government that gives a child care center legal permission to operate.

Limits: Rules.

Long-Term Goals: Program's purpose over a long period of time, perhaps months or years.

Lowercase Letters: Small letters of the alphabet.

Manipulative Activities: Activities in which children handle objects.

Manipulative Materials: Items that are handled, such as pegs, puzzles, blocks, paintbrushes, and crayons.

Manners: Thoughtfulness toward others.

Manuscript Lettering: Uppercase and lowercase letters of the alphabet, capital and small letters.

Match: Balance between the environment and a child's development; comparison of two things.

Materials: Supplies.

Melody: In music, theme or tune.

Minimum Standards: Minimum requirements, very least requirements to assure safety and well-being of children.

Model: To set a good example.

Motor Development: Muscle and body development and control.

Motor Skills: Ability to use muscles to control movement.

Movement: The child's use of muscles and body to change position and location.

Music Listening Center: Area where items enabling children to explore sound are placed.

Nonproprietary Child Care Center: Nonprofit child care center sponsored by community organizations.

Nonverbal: Communication without words—with facial expression, gestures, and posture.

Nursery School: Half-day program focusing on educational enrichment for two- to four-year-olds.

Nurturing: Providing close contact and emotional warmth while caring for children.

Objective Recording: Written description of what and how a child does something.

Objectives: Short-term goals (daily or weekly).

One-to-One Correspondence: Equality between one unit and another, one-to-one relationship.

One-to-One Relationship: One person (adult) interacting with one child; one-to-one correspondence.

Open-ended Questions: Questions having more than one answer; divergent questions.

Orderly: Neatly arranged.

Paraphrase: Rephrase or say another way.

Parent Cooperative: A group of parents who participate in a program for their children.

Parent-Child Center Program: A parent-education, child-stimulation program for infants, toddlers, and parents of low-income families.

Parent Fees: Money paid by parents for child services.

Parenting Skills: Ability to guide children's growth and development.

Peers: Persons of the same age.

Perception: Understanding of what one sees.

Personal Growth: That part of growing which focuses on you as a person and that leads to maturity.

Physical Development: Children's use and development of their bodies.

Physical Fatigue: The feeling of tiredness from using one's body.

Planned Language Activities: Activities planned to encourage children's language development.

Planning Periods: Special times when staff members plan activities and program objectives and discuss children's growth and development.

Play: The way children learn, a tool of learning.

Play Equipment: Toys.

Playschool: Social enrichment program scheduled at various times during the week.

Pop Conferences: Short, unscheduled conferences.

Positive Reinforcement: Recognizing good efforts; i.e., giving praise.

Possessive (regarding children): Treating children in your group as though they belong to you.

Precautions: Measures taken in advance to ensure the safety of children and staff.

Primary Caregiver: Main person who gives care to a child.

Process: The "doing" part of an activity.

Product: Picture or object that results from an experience.

Professional Management Level of Employment: Personnel who administer a program.

Profit Child Care Center: Child care center in business to earn money, to make a profit from fees collected from parents.

Program: Activities and experiences that are planned for children.

Program Goals: Purpose of the program and what is to be achieved.

Program Planning: Establishing goals, outlining a routine, planning activities, preparing for them, deciding teaching strategies, making staff assignments, and coordinating efforts between home and the child care center.

Proprietary Child Care Center: Child care center that is a business and makes a profit from fees collected from parents.

Props: Accessories—for example, hats or tools— that identify an occupation or a trade.

Pulling Up: Infants pull themselves up by holding to object such as cribs; infants who do this are called "pull-ups."

Punishment: A penalty for doing something wrong.

Reading Readiness: Children's readiness for reading; being interested in sounds and meaning of words.

Receptive Language Skills: Ability of children to understand what is being said to them.

Recording: Writing a report.

Rectal Temperature: Temperature taken in the rectum rather than the mouth.

Resources: Equipment, space, staff, and time available in child care services.

Responsive Environment: Environment in which stimulation is suited to the child, environment that child is able to change.

Rhythm: Beat of music.

Ripple Effect: Being affected by the actions, feelings, or words of someone else, as a pebble affects the ripples in a pond.

Routine: Doing the same thing over and over each day; for example, eating, resting, toileting.

Safety Hazards: Things in the child's environment that can be identified as dangerous to safety.

School-based Day Care Program: Program operated by a school or by another organization in school buildings.

Scientific Process: Orderly way of discovering how things are put together or changed.

Self-Concept: Mental picture of oneself.

Self-Discipline: Self-control.

Self-Esteem: Self-value.

Self-fulfilling: Describes process in which expectations lead one toward achieving anticipated results.

Self-Help Skills: Skills by which children perform tasks related to their own care, making them self-sufficient or able to do for themselves.

Self-Image: Self-concept; mental picture of oneself.

Self-Respect: Self-appreciation.

Sensorimotor Learning: Using the muscles and senses to gain information.

Separation Anxiety: The fear and insecurity that results from separation from a significant other, especially a mother.

Sequence: The order in which events occur.

Sequence of Cues: Steps taken in getting ready for rest.

Settings: Places, environments.

Short-Term Goals: Program's purpose for a short period of time (sometimes called *objectives*), such as a day or a week.

Significant: Important.

"Significant Other": Important person in one's life.

Signs of Fatigue: Signs that tell you a child is tired: drooping eyelids, slumped posture, overactivity.

Sliding-Scale Fee: Fee charged on basis of ability to pay.

Small Muscles: Muscles in the hands, fingers, toes, and eyes.

Smock: Loose-fitting shirt or overblouse worn to protect clothing.

Social Development: Ability to get along with others; interaction with others.

Social Enrichment Program: Program designed to help children learn how to get along with other children.

Social Learnings: Social experiences; called *social studies* in school curriculum.

Society: Social groups or units.

Solitary Play: To play alone.

Spatial Awareness: Awareness of body in relation to other people and objects.

Sponsor: Person or organization that takes responsibility for, and in many cases provides the money for, a child care center.

Sponsorship: Person or organization responsible for the child care service.

Spontaneous Activities: Unplanned activities that happen on the spur of the moment.

Staffing Pattern: Type of organization used by a child care center to group staff members and their responsibilities.

Staff Role: Duties assigned to a child care worker and the relationship of one staff member to another.

Stimulating Experiences: Experiences that help children become aware of, curious about, and responsive to learning.

Structured Activities: Teacher-directed activities.

Subjective Report: Personal view—an opinion or judgment as opposed to simply "giving the facts."

"Supervision": The competency necessary to see what is and what is not going on during an activity.

Supervisory Level of Employment: Personnel responsible for the work of other people.

Supplies: Consumable materials used for children's activities.

Supportive Child Care Tasks: Jobs that help produce a safe and stimulating environment.

Symbols: Pictures, designs, shapes.

Task: Job.

Teaching Moments: Moments when young children want to know (to learn) and do.

Teaching Strategies: Methods used or ways in which teaching is done.

Temper Tantrum: Kicking and screaming behavior indicating anger and frustration.

Tempera Paint: Watercolor paint pigment used in powdered or liquid form.

Toddle: To walk with uneven and unsure steps, resulting in frequent falls.

Toddlers: Children able to walk without support, with uneven movement; these are usually 2-year-olds.

Toileting: Process of helping toddler and young children develop control of urinating and bowel movement.

"Total Child" Concept: Concept that stresses all aspects of child's growth—physical, mental, social, and emotional.

Transition: Change from one routine or activity to another.

Transition Procedures: Ways that change takes place from one activity to another.

Trial-and-Error Method: Trying various solutions until one is found that works.

Unstructured Activities: Activities in which children are not organized or directed by teachers; child-directed activities.

Uppercase Letters: Capital letters of alphabet.

Verbal: Using words to communicate.

Visual Barrier: Objects that block vision.

Visual Discrimination: Ability to see likenesses and differences.

Visual Memory: Remembering what has been seen.

Wet Clay: Natural clay used with water.

INDEX